BOWL

GOLD

SUPER BOWL I
Chiefs vs. Packers
Photograph by Neil Leifer

Sports Illustrated

SUPER
BOWL
GOLD

50 YEARS OF THE BIG GAME

SUPER

CONTENTS

KOSTYA KENNEDY
Editor

STEVEN HOFFMAN
Creative Director
HOFFMANNOLI DESIGN

CRISTINA SCALET
Photo Editor

KEVIN KERR
Copy Editor

JOSH DENKIN
Designer

GARY GRAMLING
DAN GREENE
EMILY KAPLAN
ELIZABETH
McGARR McCUE
Writer-Reporters

STEFANIE KAUFMAN
Project Manager

DISPATCHES FROM THE FRONT

BY PETER KING

I'VE COVERED 31 OF THE 49 SUPER BOWLS. Lord willing, I'll make it to a 32nd in a back-to-the-future Super Bowl (for me) this season. My first was in 1985 in Palo Alto (Niners over Dolphins). My 32nd will be at the second Bay Area Bowl, this time in Santa Clara. Memories abound. Thirty-one of them, for my 31 games:

XIX San Francisco 38, Miami 16 Postgame, press box at Stanford Stadium. Writers scrambling to meet deadlines. Most from South Florida writing some version of: Dan Marino, 23, will be back. Often. When Miami gets a good defense and running game around him, the Dolphins will be a fixture in this game. Marino played another decade and a half and never got back.

XX Chicago 46, New England 10 This was going to be a dynasty, a steamroller of a team. But these Bears never got back to the Super Bowl. My recollection from Chicago's postgame locker room: Walter Payton looked really ticked off. He didn't score that day. William (Refrigerator) Perry did.

XXI New York Giants 39, Denver 20 I covered the Giants for *Newsday*. The morning after the game, I rode in the car with Bill Parcells to the postmortem press conference, with league security czar Charlie Jackson driving. A beaming Parcells leaned forward in the backseat and asked Jackson, "Hey Charlie, was Ditka this happy last year?"

XXII Washington 42, Denver 10 Zzzzzz. Best memory of the week: Sitting next to Joe DiMaggio on the L.A.-to-San Diego puddle jumper the Monday before the game. Asked him about Marilyn Monroe. "She was a fine girl, a fine person," Joe said.

XXIII San Francisco 20, Cincinnati 16 Joe Montana's late drive killed the Bengals and then Cris Collinsworth talked about Montana as if he were a deity. "How are you supposed to beat those guys with a quarterback like that?" he said.

XXIV San Francisco 55, Denver 10 My first year covering football for SPORTS ILLUSTRATED. The drumbeat of free agency was loud, and in the 49ers locker room I thought, This might be the last great team I cover. Free agency will make it impossible for teams to keep their players. I was wrong—but I put this Niners team, on this day, at the top of the great Super Bowl performances I've ever witnessed.

XXV New York Giants 20, Buffalo 19 Most improbable result of my 31 Super Bowls. Parcells told offensive coordinator Ron Erhardt the week before the game, "Play clockball." And New York played keepaway from the great Bills offense. I never blamed Scott Norwood. A 47-yard field goal was hardly a gimme for an average kicker, which he was.

XXVI Washington 37, Buffalo 24 The skywalk Super Bowl, held in the Metrodome. Hardly went outside all week. Players not pleased to be in Minnesota in late January. The Bills laid another egg. Early third quarter, Washington went up 24–0. Man, I've seen some lousy Super Bowls.

XXVII Dallas 52, Buffalo 17 I did the day-after car thing two years in a row with Jimmy Johnson. Year 1: A rollicking great time with Johnson and his sons, partying from the long night before. Quotes I don't recall, but the overriding feeling from Johnson was, I'm on top of the world and no one can push me off it.

XXVIII Dallas 30, Atlanta 13 Year 2, with Jimmy: 180-degree turn. He's exhausted, and not happy. I tell him what one more Super Bowl might do for his legacy. "I don't give a [expletive] about my legacy," he says. Strange attitude for a Super Bowl champ. Two months later, Johnson and owner Jerry Jones get an ugly divorce.

XXIX San Francisco 49, San Diego 26 Steve Young, who'd thrown six touchdown passes, hugs the Vince Lombardi Trophy so tight in the winning locker room I thought he might bend it. "They can never—NEVER—take this away from us!" he yells. That night, I'm with Young in his hotel suite for a family party, and someone yells out an anti-Montana, "Joe Who?" Young immediately shushes the guy. "No, no, no, this is no time for that," he said. Classy.

XXX Dallas 27, Pittsburgh 17 Losing coach Bill Cowher comforts one of his crying daughters after the game. He tells her there's no shame in losing if you've tried your best, and Daddy's going to be O.K. She stopped crying. I wrote Cowher a letter that week, telling him how impressed I was.

XXXI Green Bay 35, New England 21 Brett Favre tells me he'd give me time after the game, but I can't find him. I go to his hotel, the Fairmount in New Orleans, and look for him. When we spot each other, he motions to an exit door. We go into a stairwell, sit on a luggage cart, and spend 45 minutes dissecting the game. Now there's a Super Bowl memory.

XXXII Denver 31, Green Bay 24 John Elway got his Super Bowl ring. In the tunnel underneath the stadium after the game, Elway's smile could be seen for half a mile.

XXXIII Denver 34, Atlanta 19 A surreal game, made so by the arrest of Falcons safety Eugene Robinson for soliciting a prostitute the night before, and made even more so after the Denver win, when Elway didn't seem nearly as joyful as the previous year. I'm sure he knew he'd played his last NFL game.

XXXIV St. Louis 23, Tennessee 16 After so many suspense-less Super Bowls, this one went to the last play, and the last tear. Rams coach Dick Vermeil, who could cry over his car getting tuned up, cried twice after the game in my presence. "You coach so long," he choked out, "and you always wonder if a day like this would ever come . . . and it came."

XXXV Baltimore 34, New York Giants 7 Mismatch. I'll never forget the Giants' Tiki Barber running a sweep around left end, and Ray Lewis coming from 15 yards away to catch him from behind and smother him. Long, long day for New York.

XXXVI New England 20, St. Louis 17 On the in-stadium TV feed, John Madden felt strongly that the Patriots, in the last 90 seconds of a 17–17 game, would play for OT. But here came Tom Brady, dinking-and-dunking the Pats downfield, and starting his career of postseason greatness.

XXXVII Tampa Bay 48, Oakland 21 Raiders center Barret Robbins went AWOL the Friday night before the game after having a manic episode, too nervous to play. Part of a strange, strange weekend, with Jon Gruden getting revenge on his former team.

XXXVIII New England 32, Carolina 29 Until Super Bowl XLIX, this was the best fourth quarter ever: Carolina 19, New England 18. Six scores, the last a 41-yard field goal by Adam Vinatieri with four ticks left. Panthers QB Jake Delhomme was great in that fourth quarter. Two big TD throws in the last seven minutes.

XXXIX New England 24, Philadelphia 21 "What are the Eagles DOING?" I said as Donovan McNabb lollygagged through a four-minute TD drive late in the game. The Eagles were down 10 and needed two scores, and the drive started with 5:40 left. At one point, it took McNabb 67 seconds to run two pass plays. Nonsensical.

XL Pittsburgh 21, Seattle 10 Rolling with Jerome Bettis after his last game as an NFL player, partying in his hometown of Detroit. At one bar we go through metal detectors to get in. At another, I see Mike Tyson. All the while, Bettis is beaming.

XLI Indianapolis 29, Chicago 17 Can't forget the scene on Friday with 15 Colts employees (plus a local cop) helping Peyton Manning get his game footballs in condition, throwing them at the ground and rubbing them on the turf at the Dolphins' practice facility where Indy was. Well, something worked.

XLII New York Giants 17, New England 14 After the game, I'm told David Tyree had missed five catchable balls in Friday's practice, and Eli Manning went to

Tyree and said, "Don't worry, I'm still coming to you Sunday." Did you know The Velcro Catch was David Tyree's last NFL catch? True fact.

XLIII Pittsburgh 27, Arizona 23 The 100-yard James Harrison pick-six. Until Malcolm Butler's interception in XLIX, this was the greatest defensive play in Super Bowl history.

XLIV New Orleans 31, Indianapolis 17 How gleeful Sean Payton was after this game, knowing his unconventional onside kick call at the start of the second half turned the tide. "There's the man who won the game," defensive coordinator Gregg Williams said, nodding at Payton afterward. That would be the last happy moment between Payton and Williams, whose testimony helped get the Saints whacked hard by the NFL in its bounty investigation of the team.

XLV Green Bay 31, Pittsburgh 25 Aaron Rodgers Greatness Day. Big throws under pressure—that's the memory. Plus the fact that it felt like Antarctica all week in the Dallas–Fort Worth area.

XLVI New York Giants 21, New England 17 Watching the unassuming, expression-less Eli Manning get hauled from one postgame interview to the next, teammate Justin Tuck says, "That's the same way he would have looked if we'd lost."

XLVII Baltimore 34, San Francisco 31 The Harbowl. The winner, John Harbaugh, was drained when I found him 70 minutes after the game. Drained over beating his brother Jim. "I am totally devastated for my brother," John said. "I don't really feel emotion right now. No tears. I never thought you could feel 100 percent elation and 100 percent devastation at the same time. But I learned tonight you can."

XLVIII Seattle 43, Denver 8 Loud crowd, yes, but I'm still trying to figure out how a center snaps the ball over his quarterback's head when the quarterback's not looking—on the game's first play. Disaster day for Peyton Manning. But Seattle, which I saw practice all week, was going to win anyway. The Seahawks went after the Broncos the way the Cowboys crushed the Bills.

In the thick of it: King, postgame, at XLIX.

XLIX New England 28, Seattle 24 The strangest ending to the best Super Bowl I've seen. So strange, in fact, that a guy who might not have dressed for the game, marginal defensive back Malcolm Butler, kept the owner of the team, Robert Kraft, waiting afterward to take a photo together—that's how thick the crowd was around America's newest hero. Butler won the game with a pick and the kid was so overwhelmed it looked as if he'd pass out from the fame.

You've got quite a bit to live up to, Super Bowl 50. ∎

SUPER BOWL XXX
Cowboys vs. Steelers
Photograph by Robert Beck

SUPER BOWL III
Joe Namath's Media Day

Photograph by Walter Iooss Jr.

SUPER BOWL XLIX
Media Day
Photograph by Rob Carr/Getty Images

SUPER BOWL XLV
Packers vs. Steelers
Photograph by Juan Ocampo/UPI/Landov

THE FANTASTIC VOYAGE

Chiefs coach Hank Stram (left), commissioner Rozelle and Hunt—who coined the name "Super Bowl"—on the field before the first big game.

IN A GREAT COLISEUM half a century ago, two champions (the NFL's and the AFL's) played a football game. That annual title game, the Super Bowl, has grown to ever greater excess, taking on the nation's spirit. A few brave travelers have been there all along

BY AUSTIN MURPHY

ITH APOLOGIES TO LAO TZU, the journey of a thousand miles began, in Larry Jacobson's case, with the desire to impress an attractive lady friend. The year was 1967 and her name was Ann, recalls Jacobson. When he asked her to join him for a day trip from San Francisco to Los Angeles for the first AFL-NFL World Championship Game—the first Super Bowl wasn't even *called* the *Super Bowl*—Ann told him she'd get back to him.

After consulting a few of her girlfriends in the office, in part to determine whether there even was a football game in L.A., she came back with a hesitant yes. Off they went to Memorial Coliseum. In those days, you could get a round trip on Pacific Southwest Airlines for $27. The rental car was eight bucks, tickets were $12 a piece. Parking was five. After "an inexpensive dinner," recalls Jacobson, who turned 76 in 2015, "I brought it in under $100."

Thus was born a hard-earned streak: Jacobson has been to every Super Bowl since. If his name and mug seem familiar, you may have seen him in a 2010 Visa commercial celebrating the select fraternity of fans who'd attended every Super Bowl. Membership in the Never-Miss-A-Super-Bowl Club—the "Four Hoarse Men of the Apocalypse," as SI once coined them—has since shrunk by one: Bob Cook, of Brown Deer, Wis., died a few days after Super Bowl XLV, a game he saw from his hospital bed as his beloved Pack beat the Steelers, 31–25.

That left Jacobson, Tom Henschel of Pittsburgh, and Don Crisman of Kennebunk, Maine, as the remaining members of

this exclusive club. It used to happen every so often that a pretender would claim membership in the group, perhaps to bask in their reflected glory, and, more plausibly, to score Super Bowl tickets. But the imposters were easily smoked out.

Newcomers might be asked, ever so casually, about their recollections of the balloon race preceding Super Bowl IV, at Tulane Stadium. The balloon representing the NFL lifted off prematurely, failed to gain altitude—this proved an augury of how the game would go: the Chiefs quickly deflated the favored Vikings 23–7—then crashed into stands.

"If they have no recollection of that," says Jacobson, "they weren't there."

"We asked one guy, 'What did you think of No. 8, in Houston? How about that stadium?'" Crisman recalls. "And he started talking about how great the Astrodome was. That gave him away. That game was played at Rice Stadium."

When Cook found his fellow NMASBers he was the last to join the club, and faced a rigorous, if informal, entrance exam. Trying to sound innocuous, Jacobson asked Cook how he'd returned to Wisconsin following Super Bowl I. "LAX was fogged in for two days after the game," recalls Jacobson, who flew out of Burbank instead. Cook informed them that he'd taken a bus to Las Vegas and caught a flight from there. "I've been to every Super Bowl," he exclaimed. "Now stop testing me!"

They are drawn, these liver-spotted and arthritic pilgrims, to the flame of what former NFL chief marketing officer Mark Waller calls America's "last, great campfire." That's right, a salesman-type came up with that poetic evocation, just as the NFL, despite its periodic tone deafness to social issues, and the avarice baked into its DNA, has created a cultural colossus that transcends sport and bestrides the globe. The plot points of any Super Bowl production—national anthem, halftime extravaganza, best and worst commercials, and *oh, yeah* the plays on which the game swings—become a kind of coast-to-coast currency. They enter what Joseph Campbell might have described as our national mythos, which is another way of saying they spend time trending on Twitter. They make great gifs.

FOR REAL FOOTBALL FANS, THERE'S A KIND OF AMERICAN connection to the game," Joe Price was expounding. "In a deep, mythic sense, it's about the conquest of territory." Price is a professor of religious studies at Whittier College in Southern California—alma mater, incidentally, of Richard M. Nixon, who once upon a time suited up for the Poets' football team. While Tricky Dick failed to distinguish himself on the gridiron (Price describes him as a "benchwarmer" and "human tackling dummy" in college) his passion for the game led Nixon to become the first President to place a phone call to the coach of the winning Super Bowl team. That phone call from the POTUS, now ingrained in the pageant, "confers a kind of benediction on the event—almost a patriotic and government endorsement," says Price.

While he speaks with authority on football, and has attended a half dozen Super Bowls, Price is a baseball guy at heart ... and in his larynx. The 66-year-old has sung oratorio, studied voice and belted out "The Star-Spangled Banner" in 21 major league stadia and 100 minor league ballparks. One evening, as he walked off the field after singing the national anthem for the Class A Salem-Keizer Volcanoes, he was motioned to the home dugout by skipper Tom Treblehorn, who showed Price his stopwatch. "One minute, six seconds," said Treblehorn, approvingly. "That's the fastest time of the year."

This calls to mind former SPORTS ILLUSTRATED football writer Paul

Deflategate, 1970: A pregame balloon crash into the stands at Tulane Stadium augured a day of less than buoyant play in Super Bowl IV.

Zimmerman, the legendary Dr. Z, who could be as caustic and curmudgeonly as he was entertaining and insightful. At every game he covered Zim used a stopwatch to time the duration of the national anthem. Brisk was good; brisk was encouraged. Singers who took too long, who made a meal of "Rockets' red glare" and otherwise delayed the opening kickoff, met with the good doctor's displeasure.

Surely he forgave Whitney Houston, who took just under two minutes to deliver an orchestra-backed anthem before Super Bowl XXV in 1991—when the U.S. was engaged in Operation Desert Storm. "Houston's performance now stands as one of the classic renditions," judges Price, who ticks off the various ways the Super Bowl celebrates, and mirrors, American culture.

The salute to patriotism and the military blends seamlessly with the homage paid to capitalism, embodied by the compound of corporate tents that spring up around every Super Bowl. The parties therein are sprinkled with celebrities, many delivered by private jet, in the days before the game. To behold the halftime show, and the keenly anticipated,

Houston had no problem, warbling a long and soulful national anthem amid the Gulf War-inspired patriotism that surrounded Super Bowl XXV.

really reached critical mass, with Green Bay systematically dismantling the Chiefs, 35–10.

For a while there, the Super Bowl got a rep for being a Super Bore. Between 1983 and '93, only two games were decided by less than 10 points; the average margin of the other nine was 26.7 points. But the pendulum swung back. New England's Houdini-like escape in Super Bowl XLIX—made possible by Malcolm Butler's sensational goal line pick—was merely the latest cardiac-arresting conclusion in a series of tight games, dating back to the Giants' 17–14 nail-biter over New England in 2008, an outcome highlighted by David Tyree's "helmet catch." And the outlier in that batch, Seattle's 43–8 evisceration of the favored Broncos in Supe XLVIII, held its own grim fascination. It was riveting, in a morbid, rubbernecking way, to see Peyton Manning, the season's MVP, neutralized and humbled by the Seahawks' Legion of Boom defense.

"I'd say 25 percent of the games are very good, 50 percent are O.K., and 25 percent aren't very good," says Jacobson, a San Francisco native. "But even the bad ones are really *good* for some people. When the 49ers routed the Broncos in [Super Bowl] XXIV—I mean, I loved that."

"The game wasn't exciting," Dr. Z allowed in his game story following the Bears' 46–10 beatdown of the Patriots in 1986. "So what? Go down to Bourbon Street if you want excitement. It wasn't competitive. Don't feel cheated. Louis-Schmeling II wasn't very competitive, either. Nor was the British cavalry charge at Balaklava, but Tennyson wrote a poem about it. This game transcended the ordinary standards we use in judging football. It was historic."

By this time, the Super Bowl had achieved escape velocity, morphing from just another huge football game to an international, cultural extravaganza. The pregame hype had swollen accordingly, which suited Jacobson just fine. "I like the hype!" he insists. When news broke in early 1998 of a possible sex scandal between President Bill Clinton and a White House intern, "that was all over the front pages, instead of the Super Bowl hype," recalls Jacobson. "And I missed the hype!"

Asked to expound on the how the big game has changed over the decades, Crisman mentions the halftimes, which were "far more bare bones" back in the day. There was also more commingling of fans and players. For the first dozen or so Super Bowls, "even as high as XIII

in-game TV commercials—a de facto film festival unto itself—is to understand how fully this hypertrophied unofficial holiday has pulled the planets of media and entertainment into its gravitational field.

The Super Bowl blends all these elements "in a way that no other sports league, or championship, has been successful in doing," concludes professor Price, who then puts his finger on still another trait increasing the game's appeal to Americans: gratification need not be deferred. Where other sports determine their champion with a best-of-seven series, "the Super Bowl happens on a single date, at a particular site," allowing for an intensity of focus "which builds to a crescendo that is unique to this game."

THAT CLIMAX, OF COURSE, IS NOT ALWAYS . . . CLIMACTIC. Larry Jacobson never did seal the deal with Ann, his date to the inaugural "AFL-NFL World Championship Game." In the end, he remembers, "we decided to be friends." And that game, played before a stadium less than two-thirds full, never and XIV," he recalls, it was far more common to encounter players in taverns the night after the game—and, if the Raiders happened to be contesting the Super Bowl, the six nights preceding it, as well.

These were simpler, pre-Instagram times. Although the host cities and bars have become jumbled in his mind through the decades— Pat O'Brien's in the French Quarter? The Fontainebleau on Miami Beach?—Crisman has "distinct memories" of making small talk, and perhaps hoisting a stein, with "name players" such as Ray Nitschke, Johnny Unitas, Len Dawson and, years later, Doug Williams.

He *can* pinpoint, with certainty, where and when he met Lamar Hunt. Thirty-three years into their respective streaks, Jacobson and Crisman were oblivious of one another's existences until Jacobson spied a story on Crisman in the Super Bowl XXXIII game program. He tracked down Crisman's phone number and the two agreed to meet the following January in Atlanta. Sitting at the Buckhead Diner, subtly testing one another, they saw Hunt come in, and engaged him in small talk. Here was a serendipitous confluence: the fans who'd made the Super Bowl their grail chatting up the man credited with coining the expression: "I have kiddingly called [the game] the 'Super Bowl,'" Hunt wrote to then-commish Pete Rozelle in 1966, the year the AFL-NFL merger was announced, "which obviously can be improved upon." It never was.

Hunt also introduced Crisman and Jacobson to his wife Norma, whom he believed to be the only woman who had been to every Super Bowl. After their meal, Crisman and Jacobson (each satisfied that the other was not an imposter) stopped by Hunt's table to thank him for making time to speak with them. "Don't be silly," replied Hunt, who died in 2006. "Anyone would've done it."

"Even Al Davis?" Jacobson rejoined, and they all had a good laugh.

This was early in the year 2000. It had been 16 years since Rozelle forced a smile and handed Davis the Lombardi Trophy for the third time. Each such exchange was galling, no doubt, for the commissioner whose primary bête noir and antagonist, pre- and postmerger, was this irascible and litigious maverick in silver and black.

Still, Davis and the Raiders, a supremely talented congeries of outcasts, reprobates and party animals, made the staid NFL—and the Super Bowl itself—an infinitely more interesting place.

There was Ted (the Mad Stork) Hendricks, whose elevator, his coach John Madden once observed, "doesn't go all the way to the

The hands-on Davis roiled the NFL establishment, but his raucous Raiders won three Lombardi Trophies—including this one at Super Bowl XV.

top," and who once arrived at Raiders practice riding a horse and wearing a black German army helmet embellished with the Raiders logo. Hendricks, a four-time Super Bowl winner, was tame compared to 6' 8", 300-pound Raiders defensive end John Matuszak (two Super Bowls), who was once jailed for shooting at freeway signs while driving intoxicated. When teammate Ken Stabler arrived to bail him out, he was greeted with the sight of Matuszak wearing only handcuffs, a pair of elephant skin cowboy boots—and his Super Bowl ring.

But the Tooz mellowed . . . at least according to the Tooz. Before the Raiders traveled to New Orleans to face the Eagles in Super Bowl XV, he assured jittery NFL officials that he'd turned over a new leaf. "I've grown up," he assured reporters. "I'll keep our young fellows out of trouble. If any players want to stray, they gotta go through Ol' Tooz.'"

Ol' Tooz was subsequently spotted shirtless and hammered drunk in a French Quarter blues club at 3 a.m., a violation of curfew that

Crisman, Henschel and Jacobson, gleeful together at Super Bowl XLIX, are soon to celebrate a golden anniversary of their own.

coach Tom Flores took in stride but which his Eagles counterpart, Dick Vermeil, found egregious. "If he was an Eagle," scolded Vermeil, "he'd be on a flight back to Philadelphia, right now."

But he was a Raider, which meant that Matuszak was soon celebrating his team's 27–10 win over presumably better-rested Philadelphia.

Super Bowl annals, it turns out, are full of (anti-) heroes who disdained critics and curfews alike. On the eve of that first-ever AFL-NFL championship in LA, reserve Green Bay receiver Max McGee hit the town *hard*, then confided to starting wideout Boyd Dowler the next morning, "I hope you don't get hurt."

Dowler separated a shoulder when the game was just minutes old. After borrowing a helmet—he'd left his in the locker room—McGee trotted onto the field. A short time later, he made a one-handed snag of a Bart Starr pass, then ran 23 more yards to score the first touchdown in Super Bowl history.

The days of encountering players in the host city's public houses on the evenings—and early mornings—preceding the game are at an end,

Crisman believes. But it's possible he was going to the wrong bars. He must have missed places like Empire and Jetz & Stixx, in and around Phoenix on the nights leading up to Super Bowl XXX between the Steelers and the Cowboys, a team of vastly talented players with correspondingly large appetites.

"The police came in and gave us a list of places not to go," Dallas guard Nate Newton is quoted as saying in Jeff Pearlman's book, *Boys Will Be Boys*. "I wrote 'em all down and went there."

IT'S A LONG ROAD, FROM THE UNSMILING RECTITUDE OF Dallas coach Tom Landry to the unapologetic intemperance of Dallas coach Barry Switzer, who partied as hard, or harder, than any of his players at that 30th Super Bowl (which, incidentally, they won.) Crisman, Henschel and Jacobson have traveled that road. But how much further can they go?

"Larry says he's not quitting until he's in a box," says Crisman, who intends to cross the country for Super Bowl 50, to be played at Levi's Stadium in Santa Clara, then bring down the curtain on his streak. "I'll be 80 years old, my hip is going to give out. It's really exhausting, but I've made a pact with myself and with the guys. I'm going to make it to 50. That a nice round number to stop at."

And if his Patriots make to the 51st Super Bowl? "Then I may have to rethink that."

Yes, Crisman has spent plenty of time reflecting on the meaning of the streak, and has had some misgivings, of course. "My wife is very active in a local church, with food drives and a soup kitchen," says Crisman. "Meanwhile I'm flying out to go to parties and watch adults play a kid's game. Some days I do get a little disgusted with myself."

His introspection is admirable; his disgust, however, misplaced. Yes, this game has become a bloated monument to decadence and wretched excess. No, the league didn't do itself any favors a few years back, when it threatened to bring legal action against churches who advertised Super Bowl "viewing parties," citing copyright infringement laws.

But as the philosopher Marshall McLuhan told *The New York Times* around the time of Super Bowl III, "the games of every culture hold up a mirror to the culture." For all its warts, this contest reflects something beautiful back at us. It's a vast, unifying force. A campfire. ■

1st QUARTER

Packers, Dolphins, Steelers: The game grew up on the shoulders of giants

January 15, 1967: At Los Angeles Memorial Coliseum some 62,000 people saw the NFL's Packers play the AFL's Chiefs, and were witnesses to history.

Photograph by Neil Leifer

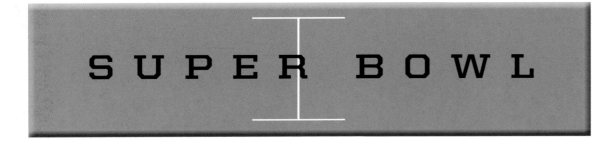

SUPER BOWL I

GREEN BAY
PACKERS | 35

KANSAS CITY
CHIEFS | 10

THAT THE vaunted NFL would allow a team from the seven-year-old AFL to face its champion was a concession in itself. True, the favored Packers won easily in what some called the Supergame, but this football showcase was here to stay.

WEATHER
72°, fair

POINT SPREAD
Packers by 14

TIME OF GAME
2:37

TV AUDIENCE
51 million

First shake: The Packers' Davis (87) and Skoronski; the Chiefs' Gilliam (65) and Mays.

Photograph by Neil Leifer

Under these blue skies, before grandstands less than full, an American tradition was born.

Photograph by Walter Iooss Jr.

NFL MVP Starr stayed calm even while foes flailed all around him.

Photograph by Neil Leifer

Statistical Leaders

Rushing JIM TAYLOR (GB) 17 carries, 56 yds, 1 TD

Passing BART STARR (GB) 16 of 23, 250 yds, 2 TDs

Receiving MAX MCGEE (GB) 7 catches, 138 yds, 2 TDs

MVP BART STARR Packers Quarterback

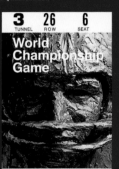

The Ring
Lombardi helped design; HARMONY, COURAGE, VALOR inscribed on side

Anthem Performers
University of Arizona and Grambling College Marching Bands with the Super Bowl Chorus

Halftime Performers
University of Arizona and Grambling College Marching Bands with Al Hirt

Attendance 61,946

Ticket Price $6-$12

Behind the Scenes

Vince Lombardi was not pleased with the practice site in Santa Barbara, saying, "This place is like a resort.... I don't want these guys looking at mountains all day." So the offense ran plays away from the hills, so as not to be distracted by the idyllic view.

They Said It

"The Packers beat us in the first half. The Packers and the Packer mystique beat us in the second half."
—Chiefs defensive end JERRY MAYS

Double Vision

The game aired on NBC (the AFL's network) and CBS (the NFL's broadcast partner)—the only Super Bowl shown on two networks. Each paid $1 million for the rights.

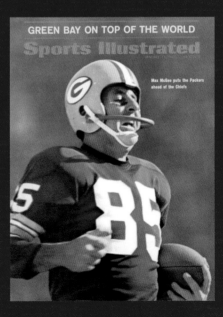

PUT IT IN THE BOOKS

With little to gain and plenty to lose, Green Bay made history | BY TEX MAULE

FOR TWO QUARTERS IT SEEMED THE Chiefs might turn the Super Bowl into a Super Upset. The AFL champions, seven-year-old babes in the jungle of pro football, had played the merciless machine that is Vince Lombardi's NFL champion Packers to a standstill, blunting the famed running attack, harassing the game's best passer, moving the ball down the field to trail only 14–10. Then the superdream came to a nightmarish end. The Packers stormed out of the weeds, where they had been lurking for a half, and suddenly the first game between the two long-feuding leagues became a rout.

Green Bay struck savagely and often at the Chiefs' weak spots, and when it was all over the Packers had demonstrated to their own satisfaction—and to the AFL—that they are indeed the finest football team in creation. The score was 35–10, and even Lombardi, the game ball clutched to his breast like a No. 1 draft choice, permitted himself a smile.

The game began slowly as Green Bay quarterback Bart Starr probed cautiously until producing the game's first touchdown eight minutes and 56 seconds in. Packers receiver Max McGee ran an inside move on cornerback Willie Mitchell, then reached back with one hand to catch Starr's pass, snapped the ball to his chest and went in for a 37-yard touchdown.

That did not create noticeable consternation among the Chiefs. Scrambling constantly, Kansas City quarterback Len Dawson threw very well. When he completed a tying touchdown pass to Curtis McClinton, the surprisingly small crowd, most of whom seemed to be pulling for the Chiefs, cheered the seven-yard play with slightly unbelieving exuberance.

But in the second quarter Starr led a Packers' touchdown drive of 73 yards on 13 plays and Kansas City's hopes must have begun to die. Though a field goal narrowed the score to 14–10 at the half, the Packers made a few adjustments during the intermission and after an interception by safety Willie Wood led to a Green Bay touchdown early in the third quarter, the Chiefs never again got beyond the Packers' 44-yard line. Green Bay, under the cool, intelligent marshaling of Starr, moved the ball almost at will.

Although some NFL coaches had expressed doubt that the Packers could get excited about this game after heroically beating the Cowboys in the NFL championship game, the Green Bay players seemed intent on doing a job on the Chiefs. "Look," said safety Tom Brown, "we have had a great season. We won 12 games, and we only lost two, and we beat Dallas for our second straight championship. You know something? If we lose this game, the season won't mean anything. No one will remember that. You know what they will remember? That the Green Bay Packers were the NFL team that lost to Kansas City in the first game played between the leagues."

Although the Chiefs felt keenly the responsibility of representing the AFL, they did not seem as aware of their potential place in history as did the Packers. They appeared more relaxed, despite a healthy respect for their opponents. "We are just going to have to hang tough in there," said defensive back Johnny Robinson. "I don't see how we can stop them from getting maybe four, five yards at a crack, so we'll have to wait and hope for the breaks and take advantage of them."

McClinton, Kansas City's 227-pound fullback, went to bed each night with a Green Bay roster and studied his opponents until he fell asleep. After all this rumination, he arrived at an opinion at some variance with the consensus. "This idea of making them a two-touchdown favorite is ridiculous," he said. "That is way out of line. The way I see it, they shouldn't be more than a three-point favorite. They get one point for the winning habit, one point because I think they are at the height of their maturity and one point because they have a strong big-game history."

The feeling in the Chiefs camp seemed to be that if they lost, at least they would not disgrace themselves. The Packers, on the other hand, never thought of losing. "We have to show how big a difference there is between the teams," defensive end Lionel Aldridge announced. "How bad should we beat them? I don't know, but one touchdown won't be enough."

The eventual 25-point margin should have been sufficient even for Aldridge. The only people in the stadium who needed more convincing were the Chiefs, who licked their wounds and felt they weren't really that bad. They did allow, though, that the Packers were pretty good. "The thing is, they never block the wrong man—they're always in your way," Kansas City linebacker Sherrill Headrick said of Lombardi's bunch. "And their backs always hit the hole. On their sweeps I was getting blocked by a different guy each time—the tight end, the pulling guard, the back. I don't know where they all came from." ∎

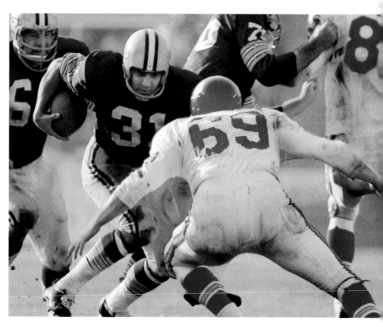

Jim Taylor scored in his final game as a Packer.

Photograph by Walter Iooss Jr.

BY Jim Taylor

Packers Fullback

All of our championship games had plenty of hype, but it kind of got to be old hat. We had been pretty consistent through a number of years with our tradition and our winning ways, and we'd gotten accustomed to playing in those games with Lombardi. We were a seasoned and veteran team, and we had just been named the NFL champions. We knew that the AFL had good players and played a good caliber of ball, though maybe not quite against the competition that the NFL had. We didn't necessarily feel like the Chiefs were inferior, but we felt confident we could perform and be victorious.

My touchdown in the second quarter was an off-tackle play. The pursuit was flowing to the outside, and I cut back and got it in the end zone because of the good blocking of our linemen. And Bart Starr had an outstanding game. He was very cool, very exceptional under pressure. He didn't get excited in big games; he just continued to play at a very high level. He was very, very deserving of the MVP award.

Chiefs safety Johnny Robinson and I had been on the same team at LSU. Once you're on the field in a different color jersey, that's your opponent, but we were old friends, and I talked to him after the game. We're still friends today.

I felt good about beating the Chiefs and winding down my nine seasons in Green Bay. My first year with the Packers, in 1958, we won one game. Lombardi got there the next year. His leadership made us successful, and his teams produced a dozen players who are in the Hall of Fame. That's a testament right there.

BY Willie Mitchell

Chiefs Cornerback

None of us knew the impact that this game would have. It wasn't the turning point of our lives, but it was a history-making event that has allowed the Kansas City Chiefs and me to be in the limelight of the Super Bowl forever. The press was saying how great the NFL was as opposed to the AFL and that Vince Lombardi was the greatest coach in football. They didn't give us credit for being as good football players as we were. As a team we were feeling great. In our practice sessions it wasn't a bother to us or a worry if we didn't win. Having the opportunity to play in the game was the greatest thing.

I thought we had the wrong defense in place. Instead of playing man-to-man, we played a combination defense. My responsibility was to cover the outside of the field, but the Packers kept throwing that ball to the inside. I wasn't getting help from the middle linebacker or from the free safety. I just thought we should have changed things up and gone with man-to-man, but the coaches never did change the coverage. When you lose like that, you remember a lot of things that didn't work and you think, What if some of those things had been corrected?

Somebody had to take the blame for the loss, and it came down to two people: the defensive coach and Willie Mitchell. My family was waiting for me when we came out of the dressing room. My mother inspired me more than any coach. She always talked to me in a positive way, and she just grabbed me and said, "Willie, I know you think you lost the game, but you didn't lose the game. The team lost the game. Don't look at it any other way than that."

Down again: Green Bay sacked Dawson four times. | *Photograph by Walter Iooss Jr.*

"We have to show how big a difference there is between the teams," Green Bay's Lionel Aldridge said beforehand. "How bad should we beat them? One touchdown won't be enough."

McGee beat Mitchell here, and also got past him for the first Super Bowl touchdown.

Photography by Walter Iooss Jr.

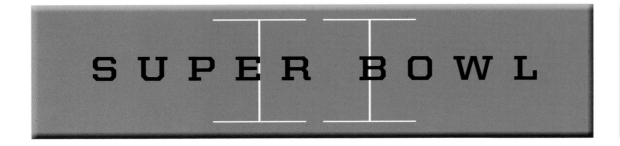

SUPER BOWL II

January 14, 1968
Orange Bowl, Miami

HEAD COACHES
VINCE LOMBARDI Packers | JOHN RAUCH Raiders

GREEN BAY PACKERS | 33

OAKLAND RAIDERS | 14

Anderson (14 carries, two catches) and Ben Wilson (17 carries) got a mid-game breather.

Photograph by Walter Iooss Jr.

THE STORY LINES were clear as the second World Championship Game neared: The Pack was far superior (even though Oakland had gone 14–1) and Green Bay's coach, Vince Lombardi, could soon step down. Clear, yes, and exactly right.

WEATHER
68°, sunny

POINT SPREAD
Packers by 13½

TIME OF GAME
2:34

TV AUDIENCE
39.1 million

Guiding the offense in his businesslike way, Starr handed off 40 times. He also threw for 202 yards and a touchdown.

Photograph by Walter Iooss Jr.

Anderson, also the team's punter, went through
a huge hole for his third-quarter score.

Photograph by Herb Scharfman

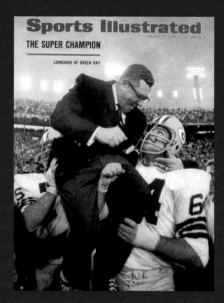

PACKERS, NO DOUBT

The players called it an off day, but Green Bay was always in control | BY TEX MAULE

PLAYING METHODICALLY AND almost without verve, the Packers won the championship of professional football under the warm Miami sun. They beat the Raiders 33–14 on what can only be described as an off day. To be sure, an off day for Green Bay is equivalent, roughly, to a superhuman effort by most mortal teams. Against the young, eager and at times impressive Raiders, the off day certainly was enough.

Even making unaccustomed mistakes—"We did not play as well as we have," said linebacker Lee Roy Caffey, "but I guess it turned out all right"—Green Bay was clearly superior to a Raiders team that had won 14 games and lost only one in the AFL. "The [AFL is] getting better," Packers defensive tackle Henry Jordan said after the game. "If they improve as much each year, they'll be on a par with us soon. This was a tougher team than Kansas City, especially on defense. "

The Packers, no team for frippery, did the things they have done so well for so long. The first time they got the ball, Starr directed them in his businesslike way from the Green Bay 34 to the Oakland 32, and Don Chandler kicked a 39-yard field goal. At the end of the first quarter, Starr marched them from the three to the Oakland 13 and Chandler kicked another field goal. The longest gains on the two drives were a 17-yard pass to Carroll Dale and a 14-yard run by Starr himself.

The Oakland cornerbacks, as expected, played much tighter on the Green Bay wide receivers than is customary in the NFL. This cost them a touchdown in the second quarter when Starr, on first down from his own 38, found Boyd Dowler deep down the middle for a 62-yard touchdown.

In the second half the Packers seemed sharper and more determined and guard Jerry Kramer explained why. "Some of us old heads got together," he said. "We decided we'd play the last 30 minutes for the old man. I wouldn't be surprised if Lombardi retires before too

long and all of us love him." Unlike Oakland, Green Bay is not an openly emotional team. But implied in Lombardi's hints at retirement was the possibility that this would be his last game. There was also the possibility that this would be the last game for some other longtime Green Bay heroes. The veterans needed no greater incentive: If they were going to retire, it would not be after a loss to an AFL team.

Starr put together the game clincher early in the third quarter. It was third-and-one on the Green Bay 40. Starr faked to the fullback, dropped back and lofted the ball to elderly Max McGee. Starr has used this ploy successfully many times in the NFL, but it seemed to come as a complete surprise to the Raiders. "One of the safeties woke up late," McGee said. "He started over and Bart saw him and adjusted to throw away from him. That's why I had to turn around to catch the ball. It was a great throw by Bart."

McGee caught the ball behind Rodger Bird for a 35-yard gain to the Oakland 25. Donny Anderson and Dale caught two shorter passes down to the Oakland one, and then Anderson cantered through a wide gap in the Raiders line for the touchdown. In the fourth period Herb Adderley ran 60 yards with an intercepted pass to put the game far out of reach.

The Packers prepared for the Super Bowl with the emotion of a surgeon scrubbing for a routine operation. They were stationed at the Galt Ocean Mile Motel, a sunny, comfortable hostelry on the ocean and they worked out on a baseball field. Lombardi, who for two years has been hinting that he may retire, seemed a bit drawn at the end of what has been a particularly demanding season, and so did the team. Over the first two days in the Florida sun the players were a bit sluggish, but tongue-lashings by Lombardi got them out of that.

Paul Hornung, driving a multicolored jalopy, visited his old teammates and revealed how strong Lombardi's hold is, even after a player has retired. "I had a dream

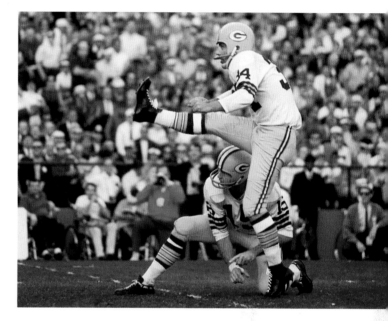

Chandler didn't miss: four field goals, three points after.

Photograph by Walter Iooss Jr.

that I came by and snuck Max McGee out after hours," Hornung said. "Vinnie found out about it and darned if he didn't fine me five thousand bucks, even if I wasn't with the team any longer. The thing that woke me up was that I dreamed I paid the fine."

The Raiders were careful to say nothing that might incite Green Bay and spoke of the Packers with exaggerated respect. Many of Oakland's young players recall watching current Packers stars on television during their junior high school days. "It's a little like playing against your father," one of them said. "These guys were my childhood heroes."

After the game, Lombardi smiled happily. "It wasn't our best effort," he said. "All year it seems like when we get a couple of touchdowns ahead, we let up. Maybe that's the sign of a veteran team."

Then someone asked if he planned to retire. Lombardi smiled again but did not answer. ∎

"We wanted to make them put the ball in the air," said Adderley, who ran back this interception 60 yards for a TD.

Photograph by Neil Leifer

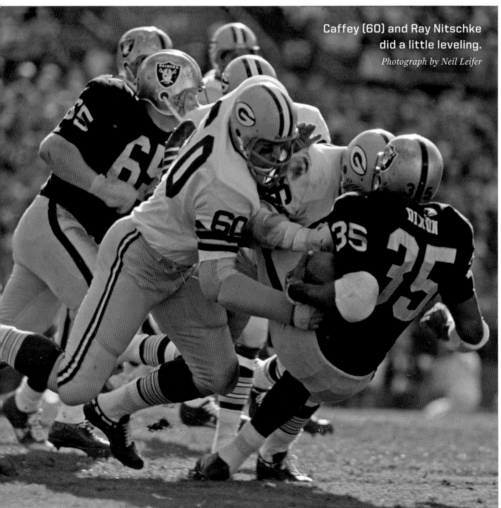

Caffey (60) and Ray Nitschke did a little leveling.

Photograph by Neil Leifer

BY Jerry Kramer

Green Bay Guard

The Thursday before the game, Coach Lombardi finished giving us our schedule for the day, and he turned and walked off. He got about 15 or 20 steps away, and he comes back and says, "This may be our last time together." At the time, I was writing *Instant Replay*, a diary of the season, with Dick Schaap. I decided to take my tape recorder into the locker room. I figured if it was Lombardi's last game, he couldn't fine me, and it would maybe help Dick and make it a better book. So I put the recorder in my locker and turned it on.

Before we went onto the field, the coaches left. We went around the room. Max McGee said, "Well, we've been going a long time now, and we sure as hell don't want to let these guys beat us. Let's take care of business." Ray Nitschke said, "Just play with your hearts, man." Herb Adderley said, "Hit, man. Just hit." We were a wonderful team. We loved one another. It was like a brotherhood. To wear that ring with three diamonds on it and to tell everybody that's for three titles in a row? That's something I'm still proud of.

As far as the famous photo *[right]* I had said that if this was Lombardi's last game, I didn't want him walking off the field, I wanted him carried off, and it should be our captains who do it. Coach Lombardi was standing on the sideline, and when the gun sounded, he walked three or four paces onto the field. Forrest Gregg was close by and said, "Jerry, let's pick him up." We hoisted him on our shoulders. It was the right way for him to leave the Green Bay Packers.

BY Bill Miller

Raiders Wide Receiver

I went to college at Miami, so a lot of people I knew were at the Super Bowl, local people who got tickets. Two big football players were rolled out before the game and at halftime. They must have been 30-feet high or so. One had the colors of the Raiders, and the other had Green Bay colors. It was something to see. They introduced each player on the starting lineup, and you thought you were the big man on the block, especially when you ran out on the field.

This was our big opportunity. Green Bay was a big team, and Lombardi was a big coach. I don't know if I had much confidence before the game. We weren't sure if we could move the football. By halftime we had shown we could move up and down the field, but we only scored two touchdowns that day, both of them on passes to me. I caught five balls, but I thought I could have caught a lot more if Daryle Lamonica had thrown to me more.

They keep my name big here in St. Augustine, Florida, where I live. I caught two touchdowns in the Super Bowl. When I go out to eat or go to a bar around here, all the owners know I did that. There's a lot of tourists who come down to Florida and they don't know my name or even know I played, really. The owners I know down here say, "Oh, that guy over there, Bill Miller, caught two touchdowns in the second Super Bowl." That stands out to people.

Implied in Vince Lombardi's hints at retirement was the possibility that this would be his last game. Said guard Jerry Kramer, "We decided we'd play the last 30 minutes for the old man."

Kramer saw Lombardi, and raised him.
Photograph by Neil Leifer

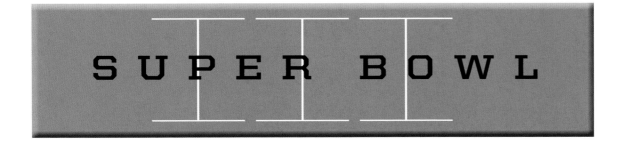

SUPER BOWL III

NEW YORK
JETS | 16

BALTIMORE
COLTS | 7

Some 1,200 miles south of Broadway, Joe was in his element.

Photograph by Walter Iooss Jr.

"WE'RE GONNA win the game. I guarantee it," Broadway Joe Namath declared. It was a preposterous pregame boast. The Colts were so heavily favored, the AFL still an afterthought. Of course, Namath was right—he made sure of that.

WEATHER

73°, partly cloudy

POINT SPREAD

Colts by 18

TIME OF GAME

2:44

TV AUDIENCE

41.7 million

With one splendidly executed touchdown drive and a game full of precision and poise, Namath turned himself into a lasting legend.

Photograph by Walter Iooss Jr.

A GUARANTEED SHOCKER

The underdog Jets won their lone Super Bowl, lifting the AFL to new heights | BY TEX MAULE

BROADWAY JOE NAMATH IS THE folk hero of the new generation. He is long hair, a Fu Manchu mustache worth $10,000 to shave off, swinging nights in the live spots of the big city, the dream lover of the stewardi—all that spells insouciant youth in the Jet Age.

Besides all that, Namath is a superb quarterback who in the Super Bowl last week proved that his talent is as big as his mouth—which makes it a very big talent, indeed. He went from Broadway Joe to Super Joe on a cloud-covered afternoon in Miami, whipping the Colts, champions of the National Football League, 16–7 in the process.

Almost no one thought the Jets could penetrate the fine Baltimore defense, but Namath was sure of it and said so. "We're a better team than Baltimore," he said before the game. He was lying by the pool at the

Even when up against it the Jets were unfazed.

Photograph by Neil Leifer

Galt Ocean Mile Hotel, where the Jets stayed, tanned and oiled against the sun. Namath reminds you a bit of Dean Martin in his relaxed confidence and in the droop of his heavy-lidded eyes. He is a man of immense self-assurance and, as he showed early in the week, a man of startling honesty.

"Earl Morrall would be third-string quarterback on the Jets," he said of the Colts QB. "There are maybe five or six better quarterbacks than Morrall in the AFL."

It was called loudmouthing, bragging, but as it turned out, Super Joe told it the way it was. In a surpassing display of passing accuracy and mental agility, he picked apart the Colts defense. Then, with a comfortable 16-0 lead, he prudently relied upon a surprisingly strong running game through most of the fourth quarter to protect that lead. He read the puzzling Colts defenses as easily as if they had been printed in comic books, and the Colts blitz, a fearsome thing during the regular NFL season, only provided Namath with the opportunity to complete key passes.

"We want them to blitz," Jets coach Weeb Ewbank had said before the game. "Joe reads the blitz real well." When it was over, Namath said, "I'll tell you one thing. No champagne in the dressing room of the world champions is a ridiculous thing. Of course, I've never been here before."

Having embellished his image a bit, he went on to more serious things. "Do I regret what I said before the game?" he asked rhetorically. "No, I meant every word of it. I never thought there was any question about our moving against their 'great' defense. I'm sorry that Don Shula took what I said about Morrall as a rap. I only meant it as a statement of fact."

Aside from the virtuoso performance by Namath, the Jets victory was built on an exceptionally strong performance from an offensive line that had protected its quarterback like the palace guard all year, dogged, insistent running by fullback Matt Snell and an inspired performance by the supposedly weak Jets secondary.

On a brilliantly executed 12-play, 80-yard touchdown drive Namath accepted all the variations, stunts and devices of the Colts defense with equanimity. He began by using Snell four times in a row for 26 yards. Snell is a 219-pound fullback in his fifth year with the Jets and he reserved his best performance of the season for this game. Early in the week Snell had a damaged knee drained of fluid, but now he ran as friskily as if he had 18-year-old, undamaged legs.

"Their defensive line likes to hit and slide off the block," he said later. "They have great pursuit, so we didn't want to try to run anything that would delay hitting the hole."

After Snell's four runs Namath hit Bill Mathis on an outlet pass for six yards, went to George Sauer in the cracks of the zone twice (for 14 and 11 yards) and then hit Snell for 12 yards, down to the Baltimore nine.

From there, Namath calmly went back to the run and Snell carried twice, scoring from four yards out, over the vulnerable right side of the Colts line.

On the first play of the second half, the Jets recovered a Tom Matte fumble and Jim Turner kicked a field goal to make it 10–0. When the Jets stopped Baltimore again, Namath took his team back down the field, where Turner kicked another field goal.

At this point, with three minutes left in the third quarter, Baltimore coach Shula turned to John Unitas, the master quarterback who spent most of the season on the bench nursing a tennis elbow. Johnny U. got the Colts their touchdown and showed flickers of his old mastery as he led them 80 yards for the score. Yet, in a way, it was sad. Unitas hit four passes, but he missed six, and when Baltimore tried an onside kick and recovered the ball on the Jets' 44 with 3:14 left, Unitas couldn't pull it off. He hit three passes in a row, but then he missed three to lose the ball.

Namath won this one—a historic game for the AFL—and so the era of John Unitas ended and the day of Broadway Joe and the mod quarterback began. ■

JUST THE FACTS

Statistical Leaders

Rushing **MATT SNELL** (NYJ) 30 carries, 121 yds, 1 TD

Passing **JOE NAMATH** (NYJ) 17 of 28, 206 yds

Receiving **GEORGE SAUER** (NYJ) 8 catches, 133 yds

MVP JOE NAMATH Jets Quarterback

The Ring
14-karat gold with a 75-point
diamond surrounded by six
20-pointers

Anthem Performer
Lloyd Geisler

Halftime Performer
Florida A&M University
Marching Band

Attendance 75,389

Ticket Price $12

Behind the Scenes

When Jets assistant Clive Rush knocked on Joe Namath's door at curfew (11 p.m.) on Super Bowl eve, Namath answered in his underwear and said he'd be up watching film on the Colts. "Fine," Rush said. "If you detect anything new let me know right away."

They Said It

"Hey, you guys hear the latest? We've just been made 14-point underdogs to the College All-Stars."

—Jets linebacker **RALPH BAKER** to reporters after the game, referring to the annual summer event

You Snooze, You Win

Jets Emerson Boozer, Matt Snell and Joe Namath overslept and missed the team's only public workout for the week. They were each fined $50.

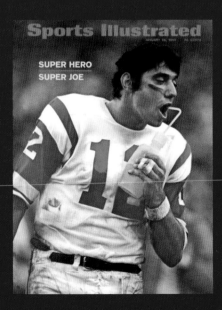

In the balanced offense, Bill Mathis carried
the ball three times and caught three passes.
Photograph by Herb Scharfman

Snell rushed for just four scores all season before plunging
in with the only TD the Jets needed on Super Sunday.
Photograph by Walter Iooss Jr.

"All week you read about Joe Namath against the great Baltimore defense. Nobody wrote anything about our defense," said Jets linebacker Larry Grantham. "We felt we had a chance to shut them out."

In as a backup, Unitas led the Colts to a touchdown but no more.

Photograph by Neil Leifer

BY Randy Beverly

Jets Cornerback

As far as the media and the fans and everyone, we had already lost the game before it started. We looked at it as if, What do we have to lose? All we had to do was show up and play. We watched film for two weeks. We saw some things we felt we could overcome. The coaches put together a game plan for us that really worked. Everything we saw on film we saw on the field. There were no surprises.

They tried to get us away from all the activity ahead of the game. They didn't let our wives come down until three days before. We were kept alone. Being in Florida was nothing new to us. It was like going to Miami to play the Dolphins. The weather was great. The guys were in the ocean, having a pretty good time.

The first interception I got was great because it was on their third drive, and they were about to score. It was like, O.K., now who's in charge? We were a little angry because people thought we were going to get beaten so badly. We resented that. We held our heads high after the game. We were just having a great time in the locker room. We were a bunch of loose guys anyway.

My wife and I went out to dinner after the game. There were other players in the restaurant. There were a lot of fans who came up to me and congratulated me on the game—people who weren't from New York, and that felt good. We knew our fans loved us, but when the out-of-towners congratulated you, that meant something.

BY Tom Matte

Colts Halfback

Everybody said we had no respect for the Jets. That's B.S. Weeb Ewbank did a great job of coaching against us. Matt Snell, a fellow Ohio State Buckeye, had a real good game. I was the first guy in Super Bowl history to reach 100 yards rushing, though—Snell got past 100 yards after me.

If anyone deserves to be in the Hall of Fame as the backup quarterback, Earl Morrall deserves it. Earl just didn't have it that day, that's all. I thought Don Shula should have put Johnny Unitas in earlier once he saw that Earl didn't have it. That might have given us that adrenaline shot we needed to get going.

To me, the failed flea-flicker in the second quarter cost us the game. Jimmy Orr was in the end zone waving his arms, and Earl didn't see him. We had done that play a number of times during the season, and you threw the ball to the deepest guy. It was just before halftime, and Orr supposedly blended in with the band.

Namath played O.K. He didn't set the world on fire, and as far as being the MVP, I thought Snell deserved it. But the guy who really deserved it was Weeb Ewbank. He outcoached Shula. That game made football what it is today. Everyone thought the NFL would dominate; this game proved we couldn't. It really helped football, and it gave everybody credibility in the AFL. We had a pretty damn good football team. We just made some mistakes, and that was the problem.

With the deed done, Namath exited to a locker room bereft of champagne.

Photograph by Walter Iooss Jr.

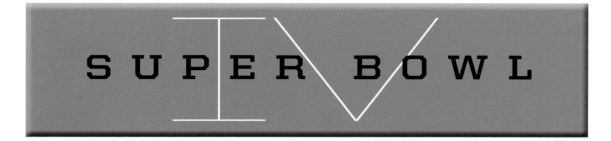

SUPER BOWL IV

January 11, 1970
Tulane Stadium, New Orleans

HEAD COACHES
HANK STRAM Chiefs | BUD GRANT Vikings

KANSAS CITY CHIEFS | 23

MINNESOTA VIKINGS | 7

Stenerud was the man with the golden and record-setting leg.

Photograph by Walter Iooss Jr.

THEY MAY have been heavy underdogs, they may have had a precedent of Super Bowl failure, but the Chiefs knew things that the Vikings did not. With this win, Kansas City and coach Hank Stram helped usher in a new era of the sport.

WEATHER
61°, tornado threat

POINT SPREAD
Vikings by 12

TIME OF GAME
2:40

TV AUDIENCE
44.3 million

Dawson was the deliverer and executioner of many of Stram's innovative strategies.

Photograph by Neil Leifer

Dawson's passing accuracy took him to the Hall of Fame.

Photograph by Neil Leifer

JUST THE FACTS

Statistical Leaders

Rushing MIKE GARRETT (KC) 11 carries, 39 yds, 1 TD

Passing LEN DAWSON (KC) 12 of 17, 142 yds, 1 TD

Receiving JOHN HENDERSON (MIN) 7 catches, 111 yds

MVP LEN DAWSON Chiefs Quarterback

The Ring
One side: AFL seal, crown
Other: Super Bowl score, trophy

Anthem Performers
Doc Severinsen and
Pat O'Brien

Halftime Performers
Southern University Marching
Band with Al Hirt, Lionel
Hampton, Marguerite Piazza
and Doc Severinsen

Attendance 80,562

Ticket Price $15

Behind the Scenes

It was so cold the week leading up to the game that the fountain in front of the Fontainebleau Hotel, where the Chiefs stayed, was frozen solid. The temperature fell to 22", the lowest in New Orleans in more than 90 years.

They Said It

"I hope Joe Namath and the Jets are as proud of us as we were of them last year."

–Chiefs center E.J. HOLUB of his AFL brethren

Fowl Play

Three thousand pigeons were released in the stadium as actor Pat O'Brien (*Knute Rockne, All-American*) read the anthem before the game.

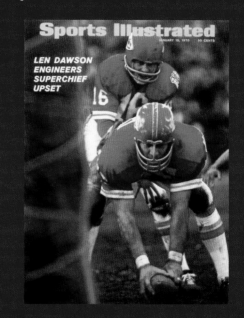

WHAM! BAM! STRAM!

In this Big Game the Chiefs and their coach ruled with ingenuity and intent | BY TEX MAULE

AN UNLIKELY LOOKING LITTLE man who favors red vests, checked trousers and infinite variety has put the art of invention back into football. Hank Stram, coach of the Chiefs, threw some of his fanciest formations at the Vikings in the Super Bowl and beat them for the championship of the football world by a humbling margin, 23–7.

Of course Stram did not do this all by himself. The Chiefs' lines—on both offense and defense—gave the Purple People Eaters a world-champion case of indigestion. Len Dawson, who before this game was considered a rather namby-pamby type of quarterback, given to collapsing in a heap before any kind of rush, faced the famous charge of Minnesota's Four Norsemen coolly and threw with marvelous aim. He sorted through the multiple options of the vastly complicated Stram offense as deftly as a computer and came up with the right call on almost every occasion.

"The decade of the '60s was the decade of simplicity," Stram said. "During the '60s the good teams—the Packers, for example—came out almost all the time in the same set and ran the play. In effect, what they said was here we come, see if you can stop us.

"Well, the '70s will be the decade of difference—different offensive sets, different defensive formations. What we try to do is to create a moment of hesitation, a moment of doubt in the defense . . . football teams reflect the personality of coaches, and I like to think my personality is reflected in the variety of the Chiefs' attack and defense. I like to see Hank Stram in the stacked defense and the 18 different offensive sets we use and the 300 and something plays we can run off those sets."

There are only so many places you can run on a football field against any pro defense, and only so many ways you can run there, but Stram strives mightily to mask where his team will go and how it will arrive at the point of attack. "Let's put it this way," he said. "It's always the same face, but with different makeup."

As much of the country saw, the Vikings were never in the game. Kansas City began the scoring, ominously enough for Minnesota, with a record 48-yard field goal by Jan Stenerud. When he added another, from 32 yards out, and yet another, from the 25, the Vikings resembled anything but two-touchdown favorites.

Minnesota fumbled Stenerud's kickoff after that third field goal, and the Chiefs struck quickly for a touchdown, with Mike Garrett carrying for the last five yards on a pretty piece of deceit by the K.C. line. Vikings defenders were looking for a sweep as Garrett knifed through the left side of the line.

As the third quarter began, the Vikings woke up briefly and managed a 69-yard drive, Dave Osborn lunging acrobatically for four yards and a touchdown in typical Osborn fashion. With the score 16–7 Minnesota needed a touchdown and a field goal to go ahead—and had time to get them. But time ran out on the Vikings when Kansas City scored its second TD. With the ball on the Vikings' 46, Dawson dropped back and fired short to Otis Taylor, who ran long—all the way in for the score. Taylor went into the end zone standing up, and the Chiefs were Superchiefs.

Jack Patera, who coaches the Vikings defense, said after the game, "We were aware of all their sets. All we could do was try to help the defense recognize them and hope for the best." He had a sheaf of play cards underneath his arm and he held them up. "Against the teams we play in the NFL we have a file that tells us their preferences and what they do best," Patera said. "Here's the Kansas City file. I can't tell you what they do best, because they do so many things and do all of them well."

On defense the Chiefs may not have been as esoteric, but they were equally effective. To keep Minnesota quarterback Joe Kapp confined, they played in what the pros call an odd line—a formation with a tackle nose to nose with the center. The odd line not only contained Kapp, it shut off much of the violent Vikings running game.

And so, in agony for the Vikings and delirium for the Chiefs, the old order changes. Next season both leagues will be realigned under the NFL umbrella and the Super Bowl will be a less emotional confrontation. You will recall that in the first Super Bowl the Packers beat the Chiefs 35–10. Stram used almost the same game plan for that game as he did this year.

"I was criticized then," said Stram. "Our defense wasn't that good then. But I don't have time to gloat now. I will just hold to my philosophy, and that includes winning with grace and style.

The Packers had laughed at what they saw in some of the 1966 AFL game films—not at the Chiefs, but at some of the opposition. This time Stram and the Chiefs may have had a few chuckles themselves. ■

Forward-thinking Stram initiated the "moving pocket."

Photograph by Neil Leifer

IV

CHIEFS | VIKINGS

And so, in agony for the Vikings and delirium for the Chiefs, the old order changes. Next season both leagues will be realigned under the NFL umbrella.

Curley Culp kept Osborn (seven rushes, 15 yards) under wraps.

Photograph by James Drake

THE WAY IT WAS

BY Len Dawson

Chiefs Quarterback

Safety Johnny Robinson and I were roommates on the road. Before the Super Bowl, he said, "Can you score against these guys?" I said, "I'm telling you something, John, we've got a game plan, and there's no question I can put points on the board." I said, "Tell me about Joe Kapp and the offense. Can you handle them?" He said, "We might shut them out." That was the confidence he had. Look who was playing defense for us: Junious (Buck) Buchanan, Curley Culp, Bobby Bell, Willie Lanier and Emmitt Thomas—all in the Hall of Fame.

Toward the end of the first half, we were on about the five-yard line. I called most of the plays, but here comes Gloster Richardson into the huddle with a play from Hank Stram. He said, "The coach wants 65 Toss Power Trap." I said, "Are you sure? We haven't worked that play, even in practice, for weeks." Richardson said, "He said 65 Toss Power Trap." I said, "You better be right." I called it, and it was a perfect play. Our tight end, Fred Arbanas, made not one, but two blocks: on the linebacker and the safety. I don't think Mike Garrett was touched going into the end zone. With that 16–0 lead, it was virtually over. We had 'em.

Later in the locker room someone said the President wants to talk to you. I said, "The President of what?" He said, "The United States." I said, "Are you kidding?" President Nixon had called and talked to Stram and wanted to talk to me. I got on the phone, and I was flabbergasted. He congratulated me. It was very special.

BY Carl Eller

Vikings Defensive End

People didn't attempt many 50-yard field goals in those days and we didn't expect that anyone would attempt a field goal from more than 40 yards out against us in the Super Bowl. Then Jan Stenerud kicked one from 48 yards to start the scoring. The Chiefs didn't progress very well against our defense, but they came away with three scores through Stenerud's leg. That was very disappointing. We thought, *Wow, what have we got to do to stop these guys?*

We were kind of parochial in the way we approached the game. We tried to stay away from the hoopla. We respected the Chiefs because they were the AFL champions, but we were going to come back and redeem the National Football League. We had never played the Chiefs. The AFL and the [wide-open] style of play—the emphasis was a little different, particularly with us coming from the NFL's Central Division, which was running and ball control. I don't think we underestimated that they would be a challenge, but I thought we were certainly capable of meeting it. I felt like we were a better team.

We learned that this was a really big deal. It was not just another game. It was not just a championship. It was, like, everything. Getting to the Super Bowl was one thing, but losing? It was a hollow feeling in your belly. I think that not winning the Super Bowl created a strong desire to go back and redeem ourselves.

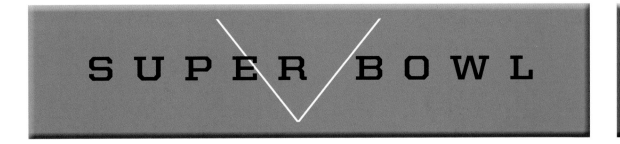
January 17, 1971
Orange Bowl, Miami

HEAD COACHES
DON MCCAFFERTY Colts | TOM LANDRY Cowboys

BALTIMORE COLTS | 16

DALLAS COWBOYS | 13

THE AFL-NFL merger was now complete and the steady old Colts were back in the big game, against the debuting Cowboys. History was made for ineptitude—11 total turnovers—but in the end, someone did have to come out on top.

WEATHER
70°, partly cloudy

POINT SPREAD
Colts by 2½

TIME OF GAME
2:39

TV AUDIENCE
46 million

Renfro had his fingers in on a freak touchdown play that went the Colts' way.

Photograph by Walter Iooss Jr.

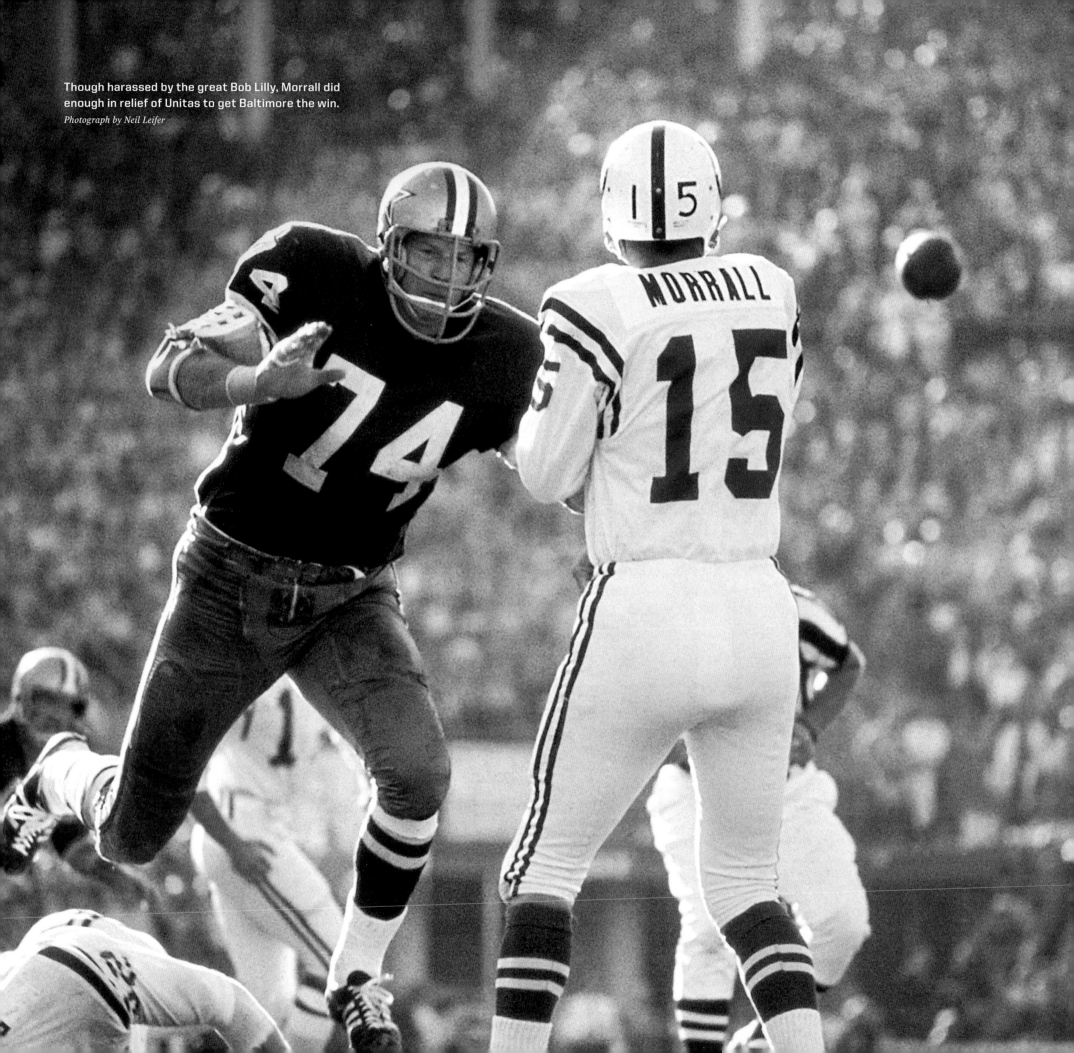

Morton was cowed by the Colts defense, including Curtis (32) whose pick set up the winning kick.

Photograph by Walter Iooss Jr.

JUST THE FACTS

Statistical Leaders

Rushing **WALT GARRISON** (DAL) 12 carries, 65 yds

Passing **EARL MORRALL** (BAL) 7 of 15, 147 yds

Receiving **JOHN MACKEY** (BAL) 2 catches, 80 yds, 1 TD

MVP **CHUCK HOWLEY** Cowboys Linebacker

The Ring
Seven blue sapphires in a horseshoe; a one-karat diamond

Anthem Performer
Tommy Loy

Halftime Performers
Southeast Missouri State University Band and Anita Bryant

Attendance 79,204

Ticket Price $15

Behind the Scenes

The Colts took a different airline, stayed at a different hotel and practiced at a different location than they had when they came to Miami in 1969 and were beaten by the Jets in Super Bowl III.

They Said It

"I don't want to win one for the old AFC. I want to win one for old B.R. and the Colts."

—Colts defensive tackle BILLY RAY SMITH, who retired after the game

Flight Delays

The Air Force sent four jets to fly over the stadium during the playing of the national anthem. The planes got there, but arrived two minutes after the anthem was completed.

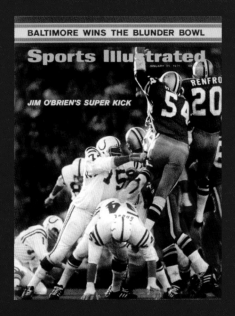

BOO-BOOS AND A BOOT

A Super Bowl of shoddy play got salvaged by a dramatic kick | BY TEX MAULE

PERHAPS THE GAME SHOULD be called the Blunder Bowl from now on. The Colts are the new world champions, but they won by default, not design. They defeated the Cowboys 16–13 on a field goal by rookie placekicker Jim O'Brien with five seconds left, one of the few plays of the day that worked as it was supposed to.

Before this flicker of excellence, the Colts had entertained the Miami fans and a TV audience from the reaches of West Germany to Japan with five fumbles, (four recovered by Dallas), three interceptions and a blocked extra point. That ought to be enough to present almost any opponent with a ball game, but Dallas proved it was not just any opponent. Indeed, the Cowboys demonstrated that they had an even greater talent for making the big boo-boo. And to think TV folks were worried that situation comedy was dead.

No one has ever accused Dallas's Craig Morton of being a great quarterback, and after this game it is unlikely that anyone ever will. He completed 12 of 26 passes—most of them short ones—but he also threw three interceptions and missed open receivers repeatedly. "It was a great challenge," he said sadly after the game. "I just didn't do it." But there is no need for Morton to take more than his share of the blame. Cowboys, Colts, officials and fate all ganged up to give pro football fans a hilarious—and thrilling—afternoon.

To chronicle events is to catalog catastrophe. Colts quarterback Johnny Unitas set the tone by throwing an interception to Dallas linebacker Chuck Howley, who made a diving catch and returned it to the Baltimore 46, where Unitas, of all people, tackled him.

The Cowboys moved quickly backward to their 31 and had to punt, giving Ron Gardin his first serious chance on the return. Gardin darted nimbly to his left, leaving the ball behind on the nine-yard line, where Dallas recovered. The Cowboys were able to score, but naturally not a touchdown. Morton missed Reggie Rucker in the end zone and Dallas settled for a field goal.

Dallas's led 6–0 when there came a Colts play that, as Baltimore receiver John Mackey said, was not part of the plan. Unitas had been having trouble against the Cowboys' meticuous defense. The rush of the front four was hurrying him, the linebackers were dropping off into his passing lanes and the defensive backs clung tenaciously to his receivers. But now he tried a pass to Eddie Hinton that was far over his head. Hinton jumped and touched the ball with his fingertips, deflecting it toward Mel Renfro, a Cowboys defensive back, who also seemed to touch it with his fingertips. The ball finally came to rest in the sure hands of a surprised Mackey, who scored to complete a 75-yard play.

So, despite its errors, Baltimore was even at 6–6. (The extra point was blocked.) Not for long. Unitas, running when his receivers were covered, fumbled as he was hit, with Dallas recovering on the Colts' 28. Morton threw a short pass to Duane Thomas, who ran it in. The Cowboys had a 13–6 lead.

Nor did Baltimore's chances seem to improve when on the next series Unitas, back to pass, was smashed by George Andrie, the ball fluttering into the hands of Renfro for yet another interception. Unitas suffered a hairline fracture of his rib cage and left the game. This set the stage for Earl Morrall, the goat of the Colts' Super Bowl debacle against the Jets two years ago.

In the second half Morrall moved the Colts to the Dallas 15, primarily on a 45-yard pass to Tom Nowatzke. But under a vicious rush by Andrie, Morrall was intercepted by Howley in the end zone as the last period began. That was the sixth Baltimore turnover, but with about nine minutes left to play, Dallas answered with another of its own. Morton was intercepted by safety Rick Volk who carried the ball to the Dallas three-yard line. Two Nowatzke plunges, plus the extra point, tied the game.

Everyone knew that whoever made the last mistake would lose, and with less than two minutes to go, Morton tried another pass. The ball bounced off the fingers of receiver Dan Reeves and was intercepted by linebacker Mike Curtis who brought it to the Dallas 28.

Blunder Bowl it may have been, but Baltimore was now through with the silly business. Twice Morrall handed off to Norm Bulaich, who ground out three yards to the 25. With nine seconds left, O'Brien came on. He caught the kick firmly and it stayed inside the right post by six feet. That was it, 16–13 Baltimore.

Esthetically, it wasn't good football, but it was not boring. Colts defensive tackle Billy Ray Smith summed it up well. "We figured we could win if our offense didn't put us into many holes," he said and, as the reporters around him laughed, he added, "Let me put it this way. They didn't put us into any holes we couldn't get out of." ∎

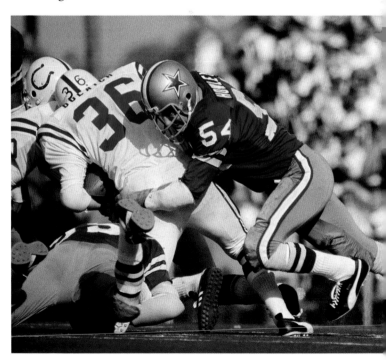

Howley, here stopping Bulaich, left with hardware.
Photograph by Walter Iooss Jr.

BY Bill Curry

Colts Center

There really was a sense of mission and purpose because we had been so embarrassed by Super Bowl III. Don Shula, who had been our coach in that game, lived in Miami Lakes. We called him and invited ourselves over. We all loved Shula, so during the week before Super Bowl V four or five of us went over there for coffee. It was a very affable time, hanging out with him.

I felt confident about the field goal at the end of the game because I thought Jim O'Brien was a very poised player for a rookie. I had been the long-snapper for most of the year so I had worked with him every day. We all thought he was a space cadet because he had that hippie hair, and he acted like a hippie. But we liked him; we thought he was a good kicker. Before the kick there were guys on our sideline holding hands and praying.

And when he made the field goal? It was pandemonium. The guys went crazy. Everybody was jumping around like a bunch of kids. I was so tired, I don't think I ran out there. I just rejoiced.

Honestly, one of the biggest disappointments of my career is what we, the offense, *didn't* do in Super Bowl V. We had been so resolute coming off that Jets game two years before when we turned the ball over so badly, and then this was worse. Yes, we had the ring and we were champions, but it didn't feel like we had won the game. It felt like our defense had won it. Some people called it the Blooper Bowl. That's embarrassing.

BY Walt Garrison

Cowboys Fullback

Our goal at the start of this season was to go to the Super Bowl, and we did. But I think we wasted all our energy on the playoffs and then relaxed and forgot what we were doing there. The next year, our goal in training camp was to *win* the Super Bowl, which we did. We knew better.

There was a news conference every day leading up to Super Bowl V. You went in, and they had your name on a table. You sat down at the table. If anybody came over and talked to you, you stayed there and talked to 'em. If nobody showed up after 30 minutes, you could go back to your room. I had some interviews but not the way Roger Staubach or Craig Morton or Bob Lilly did.

My wife and in-laws came to town, although I never saw them until after the game. There was a party and there was a lot of bitchin' going on about what we should have done. When you get your butt kicked, there ain't nothing to be happy about. The next year, when we won, it was a great party, but that first year, it was low-key. We had a couple of beers and sandwiches.

This was a pretty sloppy Super Bowl. Chuck Howley played a great game. I still think the MVP should have come from the winning team and not the losing team, but I was glad to see Hog Meat get it because he did play a hell of a game. I just remember Jim O'Brien kicking that field goal. I was pulling against him, but it didn't work.

Just getting to the Super Bowl is kind of like winning the lottery, I guess. The first time, you're really excited. If you win it again, you handle it better.

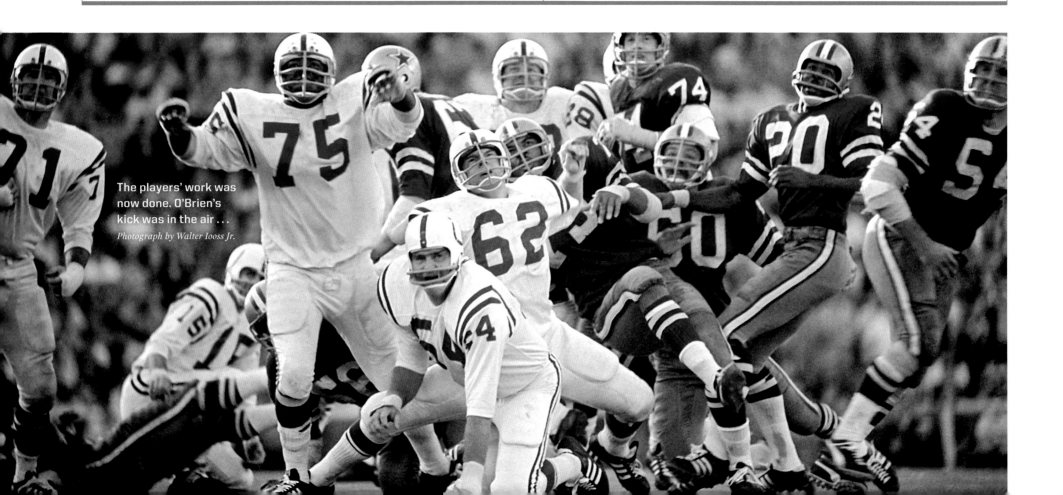

The players' work was now done. O'Brien's kick was in the air . . .

Photograph by Walter Iooss Jr.

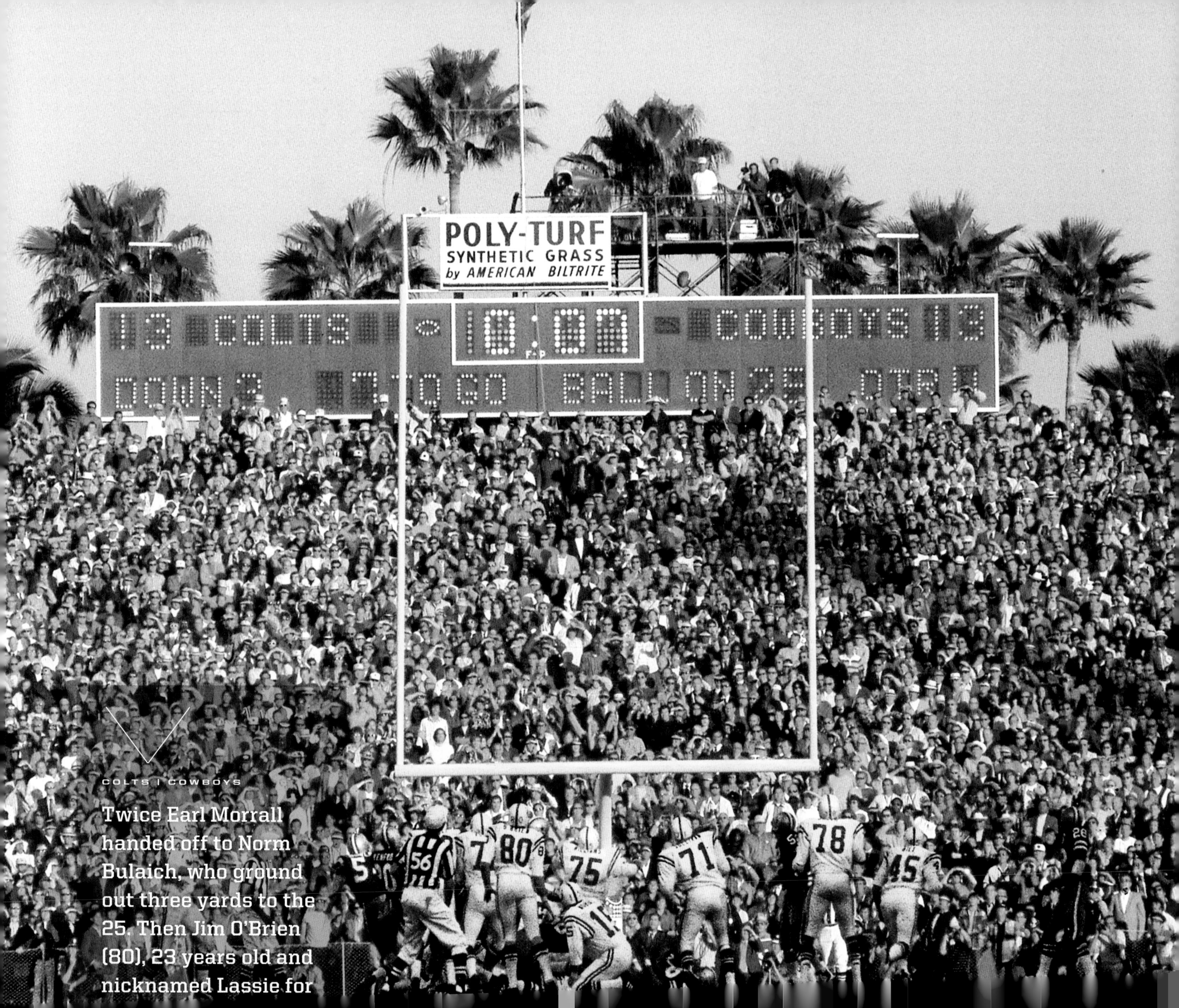

POLY-TURF
SYNTHETIC GRASS
by AMERICAN BILTRITE
COLTS
COWBOYS
DOWN
TO GO
BALL ON
QTR

COLTS | COWBOYS

Twice Earl Morrall handed off to Norm Bulaich, who ground out three yards to the 25. Then Jim O'Brien (80), 23 years old and nicknamed Lassie for

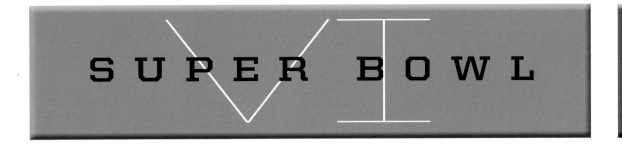

SUPER BOWL VI

January 16, 1972
Tulane Stadium, New Orleans

HEAD COACHES
TOM LANDRY Cowboys | DON SHULA Dolphins

DALLAS
COWBOYS | 24

MIAMI
DOLPHINS | 3

THIS WAS the season of the Cowboys' emergence and of Roger Staubach's. After taking over at QB, he became the NFL's top-rated passer. Dallas's D, the first to hold a Super Bowl foe without a TD, may have also had a hand in the success.

WEATHER	POINT SPREAD	TIME OF GAME	TV AUDIENCE

39°, windy	Cowboys by 6	2:45	56.6 million

Skirting the issue: The Kilgore (Texas) Junior College Rangerettes spread pregame cheer.

Photograph by NFL Photos/AP

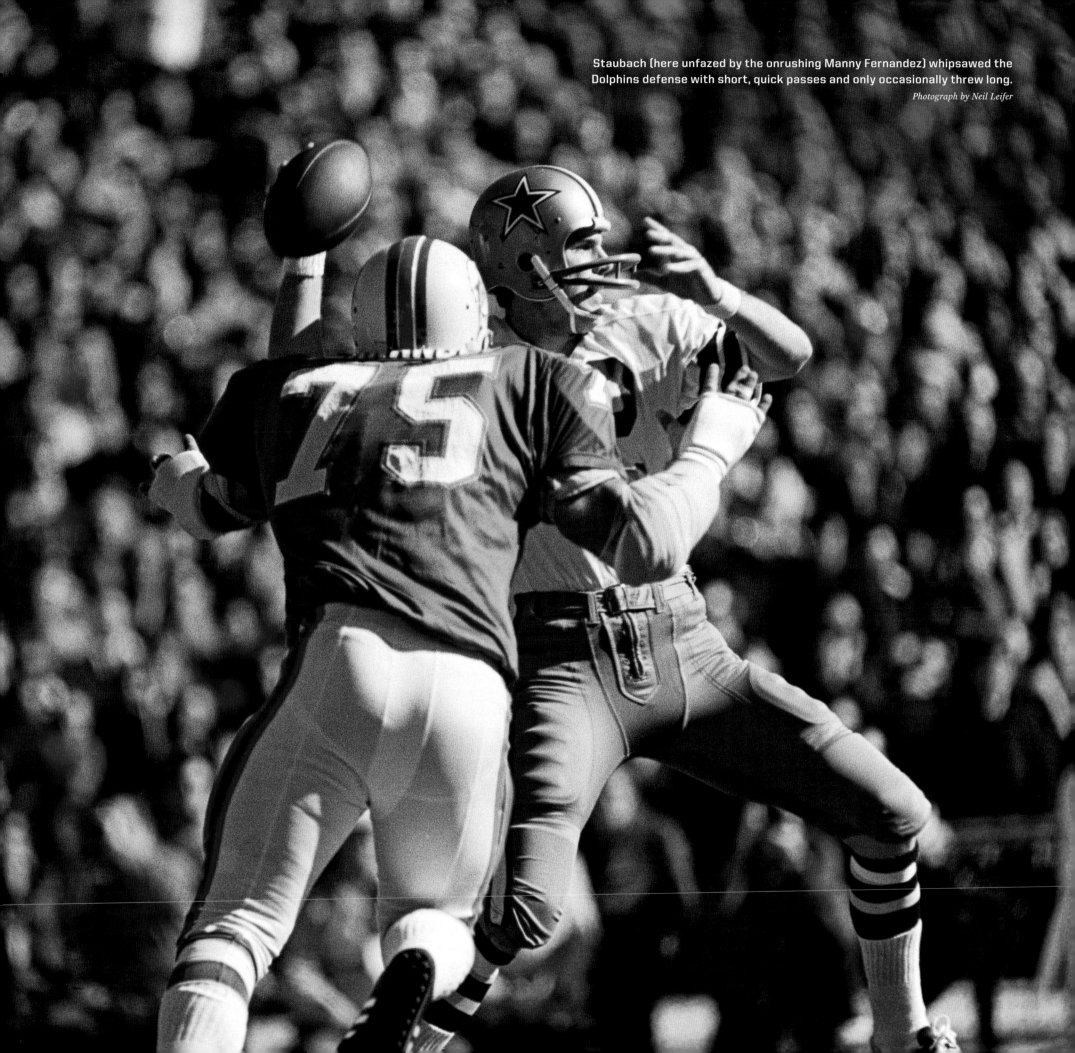

Staubach (here unfazed by the onrushing Manny Fernandez) whipsawed the Dolphins defense with short, quick passes and only occasionally threw long.

Photograph by Neil Leifer

Alworth had two catches, this one for the touchdown that put Dallas ahead by 10.

Photograph by Herb Scharfman

JUST THE FACTS

Statistical Leaders

Rushing **DUANE THOMAS** (DAL) 19 carries, 95 yds, 1 TD

Passing **ROGER STAUBACH** (DAL) 12 of 19, 119 yds, 2 TD

Receiving **PAUL WARFIELD** (MIA) 4 catches, 39 yds

MVP **ROGER STAUBACH** Cowboys Quarterback

The Ring
Star-shaped sapphire centered on an 80-point diamond

Anthem Performer
U.S. Air Force Academy Cadet Chorale

Halftime Performers
Ella Fitzgerald, Carol Channing, Al Hirt and the U.S. Marine Corps Drill Team

Attendance **81,023**

Ticket Price **$15**

Behind the Scenes

President Richard Nixon, a Dolphins fan, called Don Shula before the game to suggest that Miami run one of the plays in its arsenal—a quick slant to Paul Warfield—in the Super Bowl. Miami did, but the pass fell incomplete.

They Said It

"Don't mess with Dallas!"
–Cowboys general manager **TEX SCHRAMM** to the Dolphins bus as it pulled up beside the Cowboys bus leaving the stadium

Most Volatile?

Irascible Cowboys running back Duane Thomas cut off communication with the media before the Super Bowl. The writers nearly voted Thomas as MVP, but, reportedly wary of Thomas's standoffishness, gave the award to Roger Staubach.

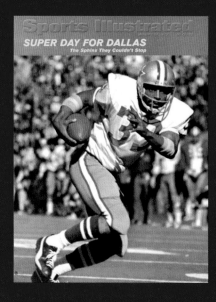

THE LAWS OF LANDRY

Behind its coach's precise planning, Dallas was brilliant in its execution | BY TEX MAULE

IT CAN TAKE A SPELL TO GET ALL THE bugs out of a computer, but head programmer Tom Landry finally has his Cowboys printing out to perfection. At least there wasn't any evidence of a breakdown in New Orleans, where the Cowboys demolished the Dolphins 24–3. They were all but unstoppable on the ground, with celebrated nonstop nontalker Duane Thomas, Walt Garrison and Calvin Hill amassing most of a Super Bowl–record 252 yards rushing and, once Roger Staubach got his receivers sorted out, overwhelming through the air as well.

And Miami, to its enduring sorrow, made mistakes. In the first period Larry Csonka, the burly running back who had not fumbled all season, lost the ball on the Dallas 46, and linebacker Chuck Howley recovered. Twelve plays later Mike Clark kicked a field goal that gave Dallas a lead it never relinquished.

The Cowboys got their first touchdown on a seven-yard Staubach-to-Lance Alworth pass completing a 76-yard second-period drive. With the score 10–0 and less than two minutes before halftime, Miami finally made a threatening gesture, driving to the Dallas 24, but had to settle for a 31-yard Garo Yepremian field goal after Paul Warfield failed to hang on to a tipped Bob Griese pass on the Dallas two. Still, there was the appearance of a contest at halftime. Not for long. The Cowboys wrapped it all up early in the third quarter, driving 71 yards in eight plays, with Thomas going in from three yards out to make it 17–3.

In truth the outcome had been signed, sealed and delivered long before. Landry—and the computers he uses to analyze opposing offenses and defenses—had dissected the Dolphins in the days before the Super Bowl. Going into the game, Dallas had expected to run up the middle, throw to their backs and seal off the most sharklike Dolphin, middle linebacker Nick Buoniconti. They did all of those things just about as the computer and Landry had predicted they could.

Miami, naturally, realigned its defenses at halftime to stop the Cowboys ground attack up the middle, and Landry, just as naturally, guessed they would do that and struck elsewhere. Said Dave Manders, the Cowboys center: "We figured at the half they would adjust to stop the inside stuff, so we swept in the second half with quick pitchouts wide."

While the Cowboys prepared for this game with precision, the Dolphins were in their first Super Bowl and someone asked coach Don Shula if his club was relaxed. Shula smiled. "They are individuals," he said. "The ones who are always relaxed before a game are relaxed and the ones who are always tense and serious are tense and serious. . . . I think our players have been themselves this week."

"The Dolphins are a well-coached young football team," Dallas's Dan Reeves said before the game. "That makes it fairly easy to prepare for them. Because they are disciplined and well-coached, you know exactly what they are going to do."

In the Cowboys' third-quarter drive, Landry's meticulous preparation and his halftime adjustment worked to perfection: Their slip-wedge blocking sealed off Buoniconti, and Thomas sliced back off the right side for 23 yards to the Miami 22. "Landry is the quietest guy in the world when he's losing, but if he beats you he gigs you a little bit," Reeves said. And now Landry, winning, gigged the Dolphins with a flanker reverse by Bob Hayes good for 16 yards to the Miami six. Thomas scored his touchdown two plays later.

In the fourth period the Cowboys' intimate knowledge of Miami's attack again paid off. The Dolphins had reached their own 49, with third-and-four coming up. Twice before, on third down and comparable yardage, Griese had thrown to Kiick, completing both. Sure enough, Griese called the same play and Howley was lying in wait. He picked off the pass in front of the flabbergasted Jim Kiick and ran 41 yards to the Miami

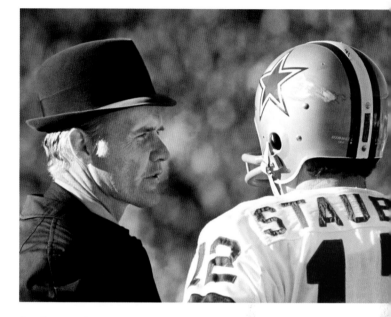

Cowboys colloquy: the coach and the QB, engaged.

Photograph by Jerry Cooke

nine. "We'd been faking at cutting off that pattern all day," Howley said. "This time it was no fake."

Staubach's pass to tight end Mike Ditka made the score 24–3 and the Miami fans, who wave white handkerchiefs when their heroes score, used the cloths to wipe away tears. They had the opportunity to shed a few more on the last Miami march, which came to a dolorous end on the Dallas 16, Griese fumbling the snap and Cowboys end Larry Cole recovering.

Later, in the dispirited Dolphins dressing room, Griese was asked if he had felt frustrated during the game. He sighed and said, "A number of times, my man, a number of times."

"The way I see it," Staubach was saying at about the same time in the Dallas dressing room, "was that in today's game my people were doing a lot of things right and maybe Griese's were doing a lot of things wrong." ∎

BY **Bob Lilly**

Cowboys Defensive Tackle

We had been labeled as "can't win the big one" through the years. We could have gone to the first two Super Bowls, but we couldn't get by Green Bay. Then we lost to Cleveland a couple years in the playoffs. Then we lost Super Bowl V to the Baltimore Colts. We were bound and determined to redeem ourselves.

We watched probably 10 films of the Dolphins from that year and they were outstanding. They had a great running attack. Fortunately for us, coach Landry's flex defense put our players in position to stop the run. When you stop the run and make it second- or third-and-long, you can beat up on the quarterback a bit. On my 29-yard sack, we stunted on both sides. On my side George Andrie went first and I went around him; they picked up George but no one got me. From our other side Larry Cole came around and we got back there quick. We had Bob Griese like bulldoggers in the rodeo where one guy's in on the horse and the other guy's trying to rope him or bulldog him. Griese made a turn to my side and I caught him before he could throw. I got the sack, but Larry helped me.

About the middle of the fourth quarter, we started having that feeling that rises up, that exuberance. The last minute or so, we were hollering and jumping up and down on the bench. After the game ended, it was like everyone had lifted a 100-pound sack off of everyone's backs. What a feeling. It had nothing to do with rings or money. It was just being world champions.

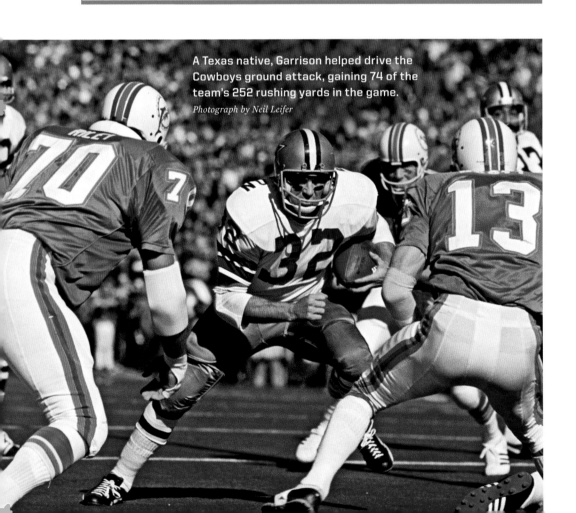

A Texas native, Garrison helped drive the Cowboys ground attack, gaining 74 of the team's 252 rushing yards in the game.

Photograph by Neil Leifer

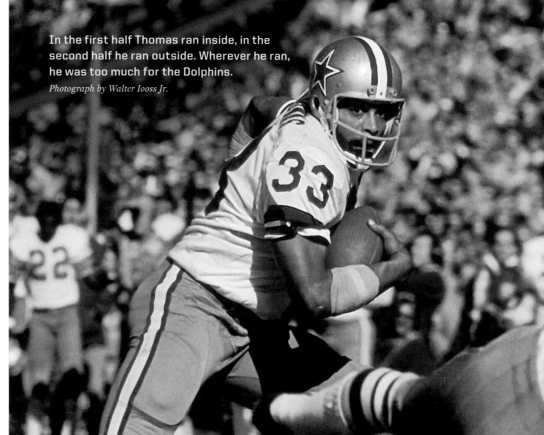

In the first half Thomas ran inside, in the second half he ran outside. Wherever he ran, he was too much for the Dolphins.
Photograph by Walter Iooss Jr.

VI

COWBOYS | DOLPHINS

"The Dolphins are a well-coached young football team," Dallas player/assistant coach Dan Reeves said before the game. "That makes it easy to prepare for them."

Howley foiled the expectant Kiick.
Photograph by Walter Iooss Jr.

BY Paul Warfield

Dolphins Wide Receiver

The Cowboys were prepared to stop me at all costs. Anytime I lined up as the flanker on the strong side, Mel Renfro, their outstanding cornerback, would play on my outside shoulder and he would receive inside help from Cornell Green. And on the weak side Renfro would get help from Cliff Harris. They had that alignment on me throughout the game, especially in any passing situation.

That strategy worked for them very well. But toward the end of the first half, there was one exception when I went into the middle of the field and Green was a little late getting to me. It looked like we were going to have a touchdown. I was watching the ball come into my hands and all of a sudden Cornell reached and barely ticked the ball. It was like a foul tip in baseball: It kept going at the same speed and I couldn't adjust. Had I been able to, we may have gotten a touchdown to help inspire us. Who knows?

But I can't take anything away from the Cowboys. We were beaten by a better football team that day—a veteran football team. For our club, it was a maturing experience that we had to go through. We hadn't been thoroughly battle-tested and we were just happy to be there. A lot of those young players thought, Hey, we've accomplished a lot. We were so thoroughly beaten in that game that we decided to take responsibility for it, to become the champions that we could become the next two years.

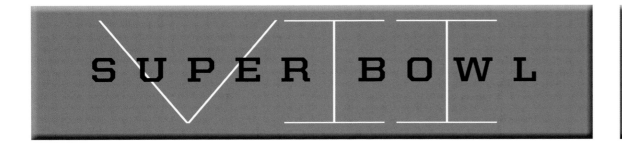

SUPER BOWL VII

January 14, 1973
Memorial Coliseum, Los Angeles

HEAD COACHES
DON SHULA Dolphins | GEORGE ALLEN Redskins

MIAMI
DOLPHINS | 14

WASHINGTON
REDSKINS | 7

Mountains of Miami men: Buoniconti (85), Doug Swift (59) and Fernandez.

Photograph by Walter Iooss Jr.

MIAMI HAD nearly stalled in the AFC title game, edging the Steelers 21–17, and found itself in a quarterback quandary. So although the Dolphins came in as winners of 16 straight, they seemed anything but perfect. Until, of course, they were.

WEATHER

84°, sunny

POINT SPREAD

Dolphins by 1

TIME OF GAME

2:40

TV AUDIENCE

53.3 million

Csonka, it was said, rumbled in the game like a rhino.

Photograph by Neil Leifer

Vern Den Herder (83) and Bill Stanfill put the crunch on Kilmer.

Photograph by Neil Leifer

JUST THE FACTS

Statistical Leaders

Rushing **LARRY CSONKA** (MIA) 15 carries, 112 yds

Passing **BILLY KILMER** (WAS) 14 of 28, 104 yds, 3 INTs

Receiving **ROY JEFFERSON** (WAS) 5 catches, 50 yds

MVP **JAKE SCOTT** Miami Safety

The Ring
The 17 small diamonds around the center stone represent 17 wins

Anthem Performers
Little Angels Choir of
Holy Angels Church

Halftime Performers
Andy Williams, Woody
Herman and the University
of Michigan Marching Band

Attendance 90,182

Ticket Price $15

Behind the Scenes

Washington coach George Allen sent an assistant to the Coliseum days before the game to chart how the sun set. Allen aimed to use this information if granted the choice of which goal to defend. After Miami won the toss and elected to receive, the Redskins chose to begin and end the game defending the eastern end zone.

They Said It

"To win this game, I'd let you stick a knife in me and draw all my blood." —Redskins coach **GEORGE ALLEN**

Stealing Time

As Dolphins coach Don Shula was being carried off the field in celebration, a fan pulled the watch from Shula's left wrist. The coach jumped down, cornered the man and got the timepiece back.

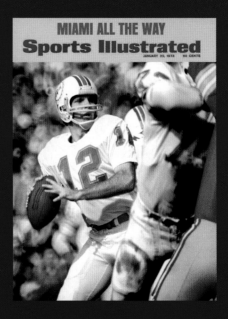

COMPLETE PERFECTION

If not for a late Miami miscue, the Redskins would not have scored at all | BY TEX MAULE

IT WAS NOT ALWAYS EASY, AND FAR LESS dramatic than it might have been, but the Dolphins finally demonstrated rather conclusively that they are the biggest fish in the pro football pond. They defeated the Redskins before the sweltering and smog-beset crowd in the Los Angeles Memorial Coliseum. This meant that the Dolphins went an entire season without a loss, 17 straight. No other NFL team has gone undefeated for a season, and no club is likely to do it again soon, either. On the record, then, Miami is the best team in pro football history.

The Dolphins won the game with a nearly impeccable first half; with an extraordinarily accurate passer in quarterback Bob Griese; with a rhino of a runner, Larry Csonka; and, above all, with a defense that may have been No Names, but was plenty of adjectives as well. Try tough, tight, dashing and daring for starters. The special stars were tackle Manny Fernandez, who keyed the line; middle linebacker Nick Buoniconti, who intercepted one pass; and free safety Jake Scott, who intercepted two. As an extra fillip, the Dolphins produced the most valuable Redskin when a field-goal attempt by their kicker, Garo Yepremian, turned into the most hilarious play seen in a Super Bowl and gave Washington its touchdown.

With 2:07 left in the game and Miami leading 14–0, Yepremian, the tiny placekicker from Cyprus, was attempting a 42-yard field goal as a kind of icing on the Dolphins' cake. The kick was blocked and the ball bounced back toward Yepremian who made the mistake of picking it up. The ball slipped from his hand as he drew back to throw and bobbled about his shoulders until he batted it into the air where Washington cornerback Mike Bass snatched it and took off. Running almost unhampered, he went 49 yards for the score.

When the Redskins got the ball back, on their own 30 after a Dolphins punt, there were 74 seconds left to try for a tying touchdown. They could not advance so much as a yard. The end came, symbolically, with the Dolphin defense swarming over quarterback Billy Kilmer. For its last fling, Washington did not even get off a desperation pass.

Griese, on the other hand, threw very well, and an 18-yard pass to Paul Warfield pass got Miami within range for its first touchdown. The score came on third-and-four from the Washington 28. The Redskins knocked down Warfield coming off the line of scrimmage but Howard Twilley, on the other side, came off free. He ran a quick three-step turn in, then cut back to the outside. Griese's pass hit him at about the five-yard line and Twilley fought his way into the end zone.

Washington, a fine second-half team, had a shot to come out of the first half down only 7–0, or better. But with the Redskins facing a third-and-three on the Miami 48, linebacker Doug Swift crashed on a blitz, zeroing in on Kilmer at about the same instant as would-be pass catcher Larry Brown reached Buoniconti. "It was either get sacked or get the ball right out to Larry," Kilmer explained, "and I forced it."

The ball flew directly into Buoniconti's hands at the Miami 41, and he hustled it all the way back to the Redskins 27. Griese, starting his first game since he went out with a broken ankle on Oct. 15, came on the field and, cool and sharp, marshaled his attack. There were only two minutes left in the half, but Griese calmly called for running plays by Jim Kiick and Csonka. Then, on third-and-four from the 21, he threw to tight end Jim Mandich who made a lovely diving catch at the two-yard line. Two plays later Kiick rode Csonka's coattails over right guard for the touchdown.

Neither team voiced any doubt as to which was the better team this day. "They're like swarming bees," said John Wilbur, the Redskins guard. "You think you've blocked them well, and you only get two, three, four yards before they're all over you."

Leading up to a game like the Super Bowl, it is probably best to take it easy. At least it now seems so. Miami coach Don Shula was relaxed and amiable throughout, and was almost elfin in the interminable interviews that are a requirement for Super Bowl coaches.

Redskins coach George Allen, though, grew more querulous as the week wore on. In his last press session he snapped: "This is the first time in 23 years as a head coach I have missed a meeting with my team. I hope you fellows don't ask me the same questions today that you've been asking me all week." When Allen was not bemoaning the fourth estate he took

Shula's third season in Miami ended in his first title.

Photograph by Neil Leifer

after his players' wives. "If we could arrange for the wives to be in Chicago, I'd be happy," he announced, only half in jest.

As Super Bowl VII sank slowly in the West, the only sad Dolphin was little Yepremian, whose faux pas could have cost more than embarrassment. "That championship ring will hang heavy on my hand," he said, shaking his mournful face.

The empty fingers of the Redskins will hang heavier still. ∎

"They're like swarming bees," said John Wilbur, the Redskins guard. "You only get two, three, four yards before they're all over you."

Swift (59) buzzed into Brown's grill.
Photograph by Walter Iooss Jr.

Mandich's sweet grab at the two-yard line set up Miami's second TD.
Photograph by Long Photography

THE WAY IT WAS

BY Manny Fernandez
Dolphins Defensive Tackle

It might surprise you to hear that there wasn't a lot of hype about going undefeated. I knew we had not lost a game, but I didn't realize it had never been done before. And I think most of the guys didn't realize that. We were just trying to win a Super Bowl. We were pretty embarrassed the year before and we wanted to get beyond that. That was our motivation all year: redemption.

The whole game plan on defense was to stop the run. Larry Brown was the leading rusher in the NFL that year [by his 101.3 yards per game]. He was pretty impressive, but not that day. They started off trying to single block me, but they ended up doing double and triple teams. I felt I was having a good game, but it's like Kenny Rogers says, "You never count your money when you're sittin' at the table." It was a fight to the end.

And we didn't let them score—Garo [Yepremian] did. Just for the record, we pitched a shutout defensively. It would have been the only shutout in Super Bowl history. I had some very choice words for Garo when he got to the sideline. All of a sudden it was a ball game. Then the offense kind of let us down. They did not hang onto the ball and run out the clock, so it was up to us to go out and stop them [one more time]. And we did.

The team party was two-fisted drinking all night long. This was a team that was close and still is close. It's about as close to being family as you can get. It just shows that if a group of men get together and dedicate themselves totally to a mission, there's not much that can stop them.

BY Larry Brown
Redskins Running Back

If we had played the Sunday after we beat Dallas in the NFC title game, we could have beaten anyone. However, two things occurred in that two-week period before the Super Bowl. One was based on the fact that we had never been to the Super Bowl and did not know what to expect. In those two weeks, there were many, many distractions—family members, friends wanting to get tickets. And with the media frenzy and the other distractions, by the time the game came around we were mentally exhausted. George Allen was antsy and nervous. We could tell. The day we arrived in Los Angeles, he said there would be a curfew beginning that night. We had thought everything would be the same as if we were playing a regular game at home. Curfews would be implemented later in the week, not upon arrival. So that didn't sit well. It was the first thing that made things kind of ugly. The organization got the jitters, being in that environment. We burned so much nervous energy prior to the game.

That's not to say the Dolphins didn't deserve to win. They played very, very well. That defensive line, that front four, was really tough—especially Manny Fernandez. Everywhere I went, I saw him. We had a great opportunity early in the fourth quarter. Billy Kilmer threw a pass to Jerry Smith. He was wide-open, and the football hit the goalpost, because back then the goalpost was on the goal line. That would have been a touchdown. But that's "what if." The late touchdown we scored off their field goal attempt was a lift we needed, but we still had to go out there and win the battles on the front line. We didn't.

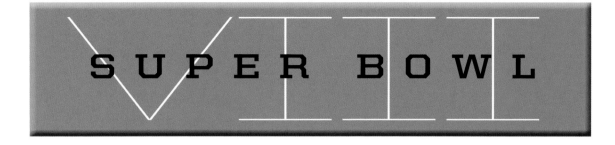

SUPER BOWL VIII

January 13, 1974
Rice Stadium, Houston

HEAD COACHES
DON SHULA Dolphins | BUD GRANT Vikings

MIAMI
DOLPHINS | 24

MINNESOTA
VIKINGS | 7

WITH TWO losses, Miami did not flaunt the pristine record of the year before. And yet its defense was even stingier this time, its rushing attack more efficient. Some say this was the best of those 1970s Dolphins teams. The Vikings might agree.

WEATHER
50°, overcast

POINT SPREAD
Dolphins by 6½

TIME OF GAME
2:29

TV AUDIENCE
51.7 million

Csonka's profile was clear: He was the heart of Miami's offense.

Photograph by Neil Leifer

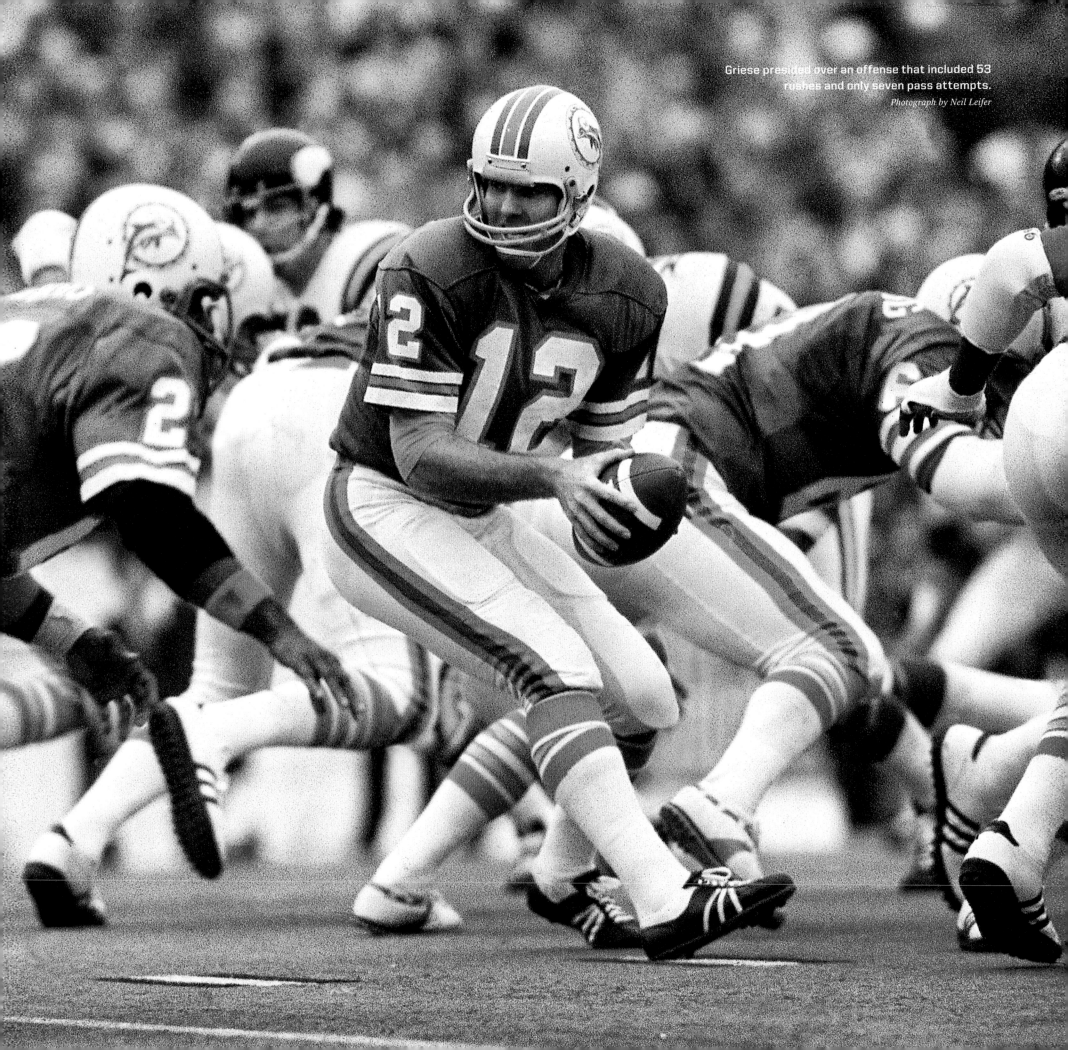

Excerpted from **SPORTS ILLUSTRATED** *January 21, 1974*

DOLPHIN DOMINANCE

Starting with a methodical opening drive, Miami manhandled Minnesota | BY TEX MAULE

SUPER BOWL VIII HAD ALL THE excitement and suspense of a master butcher quartering a steer. The slaughterhouse was Houston's Rice Stadium and the butcher was Miami quarterback Bob Griese, whose deft dismemberment of the Vikings may have had a certain esthetic appeal for serious students of the science of football, but did away with drama. The suspense in the game, which Miami won 24–7, lasted for five minutes and 27 seconds, the time it took Griese to march his Dolphins 62 yards in 10 plays after the opening kickoff. Most of the drive was predicated on the Miami offensive line shunting aside Minnesota defenders, especially middle linebacker Jeff Siemon, who was attacked by a bewildering variety of blockers.

Griese wound up this opening salvo by turning a Minnesota ploy against the Vikings. With a first-and-goal on the Minnesota five-yard line, he forsook power for finesse. The two excellent Dolphins guards—Bob Kuechenberg and Larry Little—pulled and took off in tandem to their right. The Vikings line, keying on the guards and reading sweep, went with them and Griese handed the ball to Larry Csonka, who ambled through the hole created by the absence of Minnesota's left tackle, Gary Larsen. It was a clever call and a cleanly performed play and it was typical of the way the Dolphins executed their appointed tasks—and their opponent—throughout the chill, foggy afternoon.

When the Vikings took over after the Miami touchdown, they ran three ineffectual plays and had to punt. Then the Dolphins sliced them up again, using 10 plays to go 56 yards at an expenditure of five minutes and 46 seconds. This time Jim Kiick thrust over from the one.

The Miami game plan was not based on throwing the ball; it was founded primarily on clearing out the middle of the Minnesota defensive line and handing the ball to Csonka. It made a lot of sense. Griese threw only seven passes, completing six, all but one in the first half. With the Dolphins holding a 17–0 halftime lead—Garo Yepremian kicked a 28-yard field goal, to boot—they didn't need to pass. But the one time Griese put the ball in the air in the second half doomed any chance the Vikings had of winning. This came early in the third period, on third-and-five from the Vikings 38, when Minnesota seemed to be stiffening a bit. The pass went to Dolphins All-Pro wide receiver Paul Warfield who fled down the left sideline, kicking past Bobby Bryant to make a diving fingertip catch. The play covered 27 yards, put Miami on the Vikings 11 and set up the touchdown that took the game out of reach. Csonka—who else?—scored it by running over some Minnesota people from the two.

Before the game a panel of spiritualists and mediums had unanimously predicted the Vikings would win because all the planets in coach Bud Grant's birth line were in a favorable position. The mediums certainly did not get the message. Each time Minnesota showed signs of making a game of it, the planets evidently careened out of alignment. Late in the first half, with a yard to go for a first down and six for a touchdown, Oscar Reed was stopped for no gain, fumbled and the Dolphins recovered. Viking John Gilliam returned the second-half kickoff 65 yards to the Miami 34, but a clipping penalty on tight end Stu Voigt brought the ball back to the Minnesota 11-yard line. And so on.

After the game, Grant said quietly, "I knew we were in trouble after their first drive. They didn't do anything we didn't expect; they ran the plays we saw in the movies.... There's no secrecy about this thing. They blocked well and they tackled well."

Csonka, who got a game ball, emerged from the Super Bowl tired and battered. After his 33rd carry, with 1:18 left, he slowly rose to his feet and staggered to the huddle. Shula took him out, to a great ovation.

During the game Griese often turned to Csonka and asked what he would like him to call. The first touchdown play was such a request. "I said X block to the left and the Roll Right, Trap Left," Csonka related. "But it wasn't the plays. I can't say enough about my offensive line. You hear about second effort, but second effort doesn't count unless you get that first shot through the line and that's what they give me."

Csonka agreed with Grant that Miami's opening touchdown drive established the tone and tempo of the game. "Scoring first means a lot," he said. "What it does is establish the supremacy of your offensive line. In the old days offensive linemen were regarded as the animals of pro football. Now they are getting to be the intellectuals. And ours are the best."

Even the most fanatic adherent of the old NFL must admit that this Dolphins team rates as pro football's best in recent years. It has magnificent young personnel and its coaching is impeccable. Miami also has an unnatural resource common to all championship teams—a charismatic player who has the ability, under pressure, to produce up to and beyond his normal capability. For the Dolphins he is Larry Csonka. ■

Shula coached until '95, but this was his last title.

Photograph by Neil Leifer

Vern Den Herder put pressure on Tarkenton, who said, "I've never seen the Dolphins play as well as they did today."
Photograph by Walter Iooss Jr.

JUST THE FACTS

Statistical Leaders

Rushing **LARRY CSONKA** (MIA) 33 carries, 145 yds, 2 TDs

Passing **FRAN TARKENTON** (MIN) 18 of 28, 182 yds

Receiving **STU VOIGT** (MIN) 3 catches, 46 yds

MVP **LARRY CSONKA** Dolphins Running Back

The Ring
Two 60-point diamonds with the inscription BACK TO BACK

Anthem Performer
Charley Pride

Halftime Performer
University of Texas Marching Band

Attendance 71,882

Ticket Price $15

Behind the Scenes

In the third quarter, with the ball at Minnesota's two-yard line, Bob Griese forgot the snap count. Larry Csonka told him it was on two. Jim Kiick said it was one. The ball was snapped on one; a surprised Griese bobbled it, then got it to Csonka who scored a TD.

They Said It

"I don't think our players have seen anything like this since junior high." —Vikings coach **BUD GRANT** on his team's bare-bones practice facility at Delmar Stadium

The White Stripes

This is the only Super Bowl played using striped footballs, which in the 1970s were sometimes used for visibility (the Houston sky was darkened by clouds) and on special occasions.

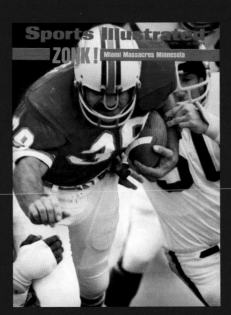

BY Bob Kuechenberg

Dolphins Guard

I have fond memories of the Super Bowl and of my preparation. I'd sneak into the coaches' locker room, open the refrigerator, steal two or three beers, and wrap them in a towel. Then I'd go watch film in solitude. Alan Page was lefthanded and for a right defensive tackle, the inside is where the quarterback is. Alan had the fastest inside move of anybody. I'm thinking, There's got to be something.

I said, You know what? Look at that: When he's going inside, his inside foot is four or six inches further back than it is normally. I called my offensive line coach, Monte Clark, and said, "I think I've got something on Page. If you block him by the book, there's no stopping him. He eats the book for breakfast." I asked to change our blocking. Monte said, "Let me talk to the boss." Tomorrow comes and Monte says, "Kooch, I've got bad news: Not only does the boss say no, he says hell no."

On the game's first third down, I saw Alan's foot go back. The pass protection was supposed to be Jim Langer, the center, and me buddy-blocking the middle linebacker and Page. Well, Page just about took the handoff from Bob Griese. There was no way Langer could snap the ball and block him at the same time. No one could. I lost it at that point. I turned to the sideline and said, "I'm doing it my way." I did, and Alan Page never made a tackle after that.

As the clock ticked down at the end of the game, Larry Csonka got called off the field to get a big hug and I did too. That was the only hug I got from coach Shula in my career. That was his way of saying thank you.

BY Bobby Bryant

Vikings Cornerback

We just didn't play well. Right from the start, Miami ran right over us. We couldn't stop them and the feeling very quickly was, "This is going to be a long day." It was the way they were running the ball. It was mostly Larry Csonka, and Mercury Morris got some of the yardage too. They were just running the ball at will on us.

One play that stands out was that 27-yard pass that Paul Warfield got on me. That brought them into the red zone. We had heard for the whole week that Warfield had a pulled hamstring. They wanted us to believe that he couldn't run. He was running pretty well when the game came around and on that play he had me beat. Bob Griese threw the pass well. I was right behind Warfield and I was able to tackle him shortly after he caught it, but that put them down there. He only caught a couple of passes that game.

I don't think Warfield liked me. The first time we played one another, when he was with Cleveland in 1969, I intercepted three passes against him. And after he caught his first pass, in this Super Bowl—it was an out pattern for a six-yard gain—I pushed him out-of-bounds. He just said: "That all you got, Bryant? Because if it is, I'm gonna wear you out all day."

As it turned out, he didn't really have to. They had a game plan that worked very well. It started on the line. Everybody knows that a game is won or lost right there on the line of scrimmage, and it was obvious that Miami controlled the line of scrimmage that day.

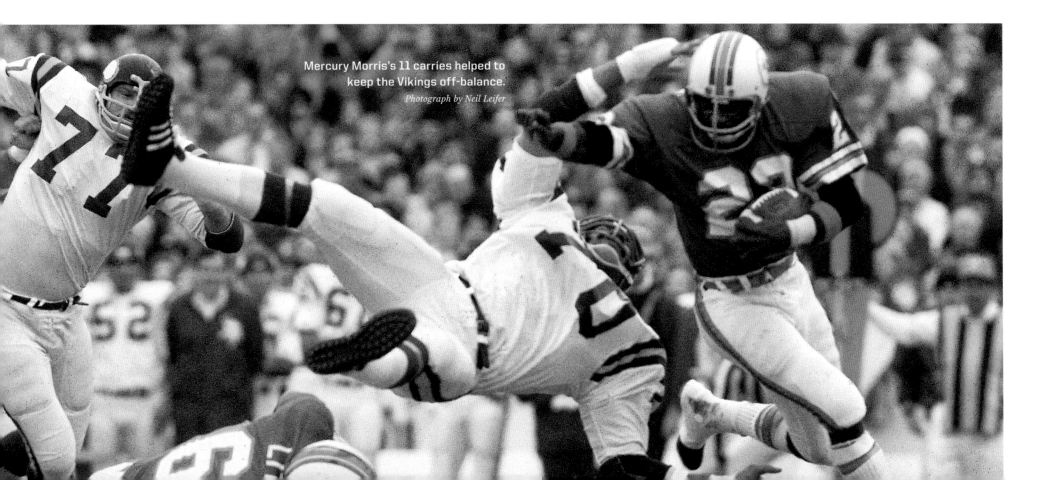

Mercury Morris's 11 carries helped to keep the Vikings off-balance.
Photograph by Neil Leifer

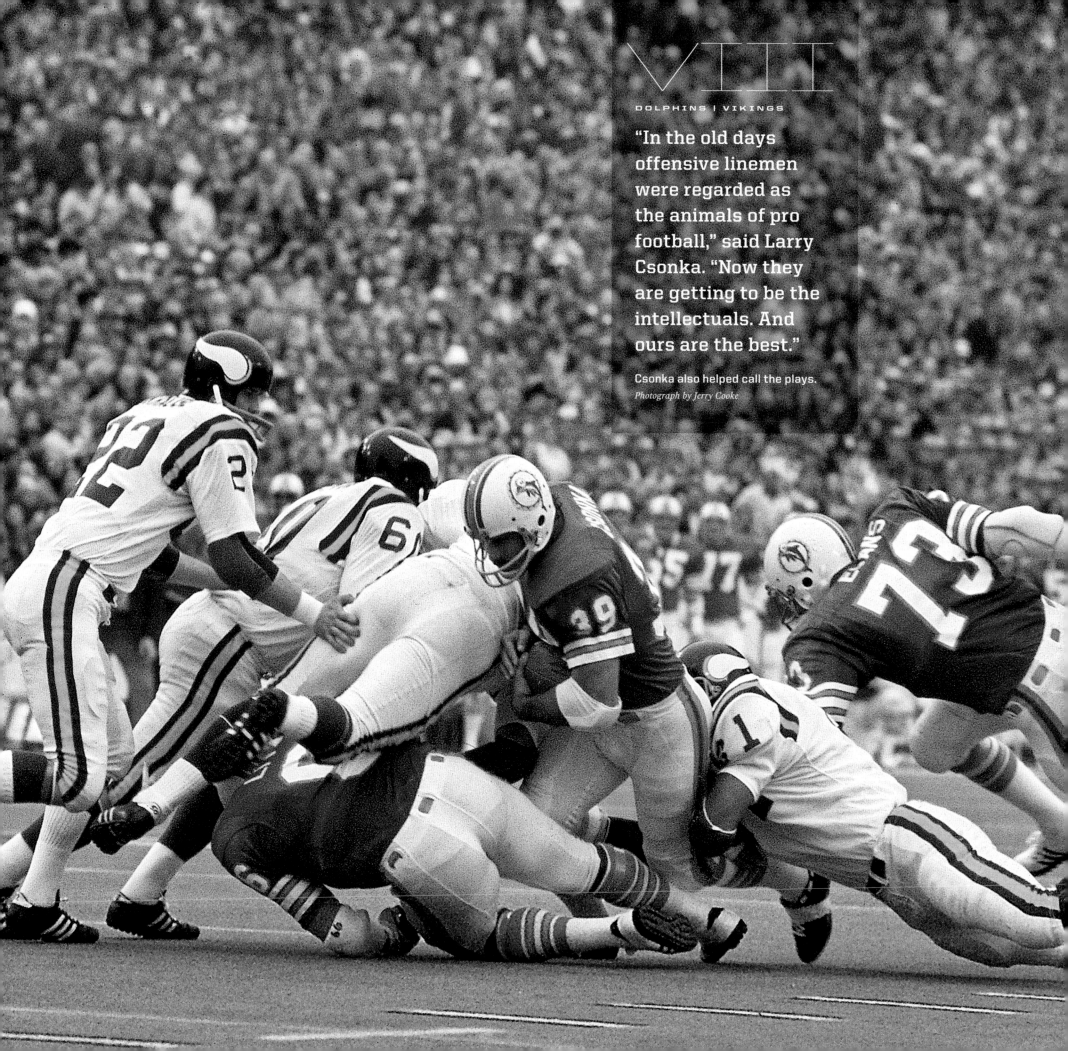

"In the old days offensive linemen were regarded as the animals of pro football," said Larry Csonka. "Now they are getting to be the intellectuals. And ours are the best."

Csonka also helped call the plays.
Photograph by Jerry Cooke

SUPER BOWL IX

PITTSBURGH
STEELERS | 16

MINNESOTA
VIKINGS | 6

THE VIKINGS had been to big games to no avail, while the Steelers, in their fifth decade, were playing for their first title. This Super Bowl didn't just crown a champion. It gave the NFL a look (and a shudder) at what Pittsburgh had in store.

WEATHER	POINT SPREAD	TIME OF GAME	TV AUDIENCE

46°, high winds	Steelers by 3	2:56	56 million

Noll had lifted once lowly Pittsburgh to the NFL elite, so he in turn was carried off.

Photograph by James Drake

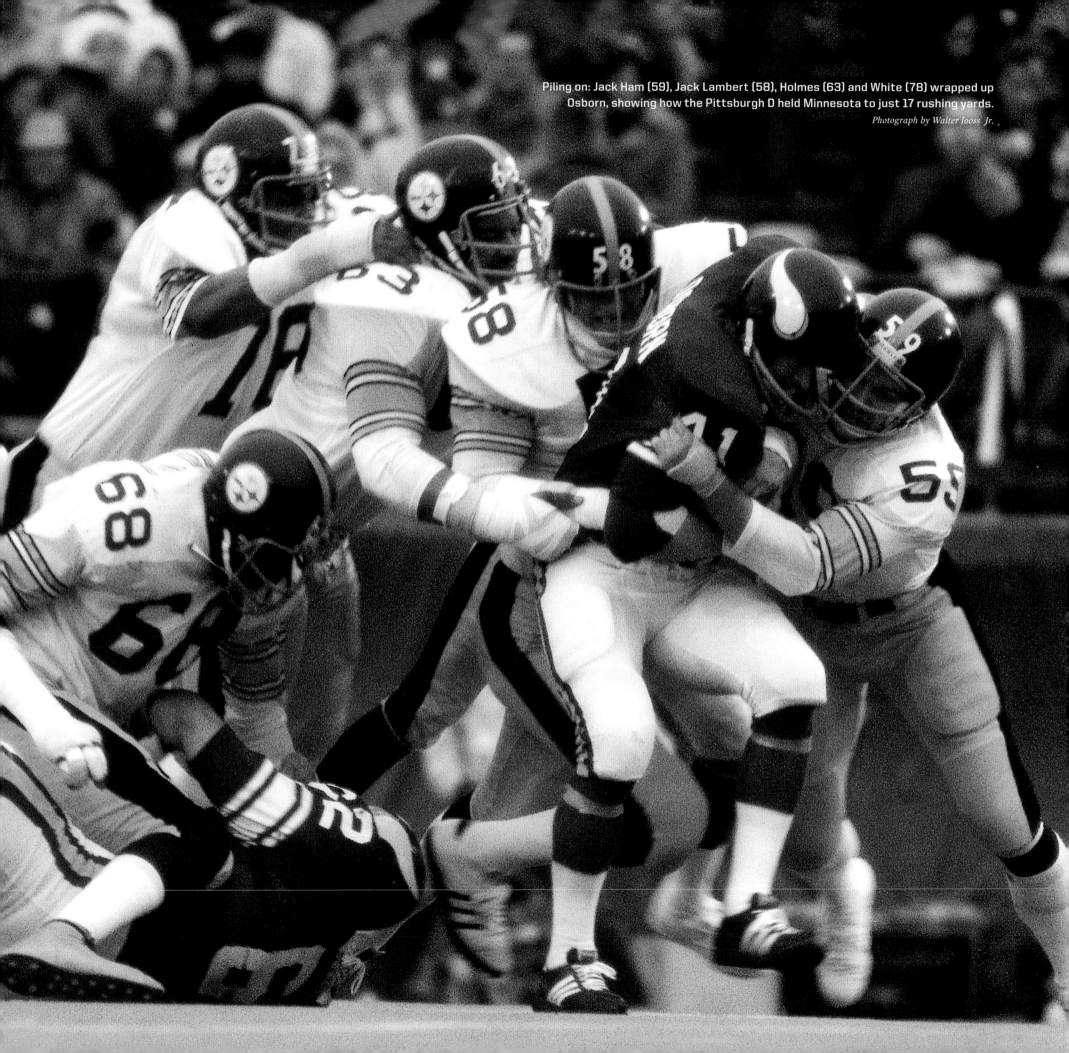

Piling on: Jack Ham (59), Jack Lambert (58), Holmes (63) and White (78) wrapped up Osborn, showing how the Pittsburgh D held Minnesota to just 17 rushing yards.

Photograph by Walter Iooss Jr.

Harris broke Larry Csonka's Super Bowl records for rushing attempts and yards in a game.

Photograph by Walter Iooss Jr.

JUST THE FACTS

Statistical Leaders

Rushing **FRANCO HARRIS** (PIT) 34 carries, 158 yds, 1 TD

Passing **FRAN TARKENTON** (MIN) 11 of 26, 102 yds, 3 INTs

Receiving **CHUCK FOREMAN** (MIN) 5 catches, 50 yds

MVP FRANCO HARRIS Steelers Running Back

The Ring
The engraved score of a play-off win vs Buffalo is wrong. It says 32-6. Actual score: 32-14.

Anthem Performer
Grambling State University Marching Band

Halftime Performers
Mercer Ellington and the Grambling State Band

Attendance 80,997

Ticket Price $20

Behind the Scenes

Slippery spots on Tulane Stadium's artificial turf led Steelers QB Terry Bradshaw to change into longer cleats at halftime. He completed five of nine passes for 48 yards (two sacks) in the first half and four of five for 48 yards (no sacks) in the second.

They Said It

"This team has been loose and casual all year. But just before we went out on the field there was a period of quiet. Somebody said, 'Hey, what the hell's all this?' And we started yucking it up again." —Steelers linebacker **ANDY RUSSELL**

Dome Deferred

This was the last pro game at Tulane Stadium; it was supposed to have been played at the Superdome, but that wasn't ready in time.

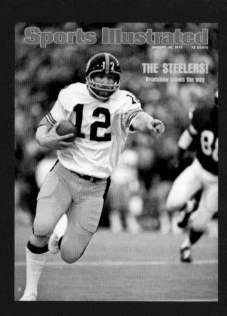

Excerpted from **SPORTS ILLUSTRATED** *January 20, 1975*

HELLO, PITTSBURGH

By manhandling Minnesota, the Steelers shucked off a tradition of losing | BY DAN JENKINS

AND NOW, FOR AN ENCORE, the Steelers defense will pick up Tulane Stadium and throw it into the middle of Bourbon Street. L.C. Greenwood, or perhaps Mean Joe Greene, will swallow what is left of Fran Tarkenton in a crawfish bisque. Why not? Along with Ernie Holmes and Dwight White, they have already enjoyed dining on the Minnesota running game—has anyone tasted Chuck Foreman's jersey lately?—and making Vikings fly this way and that through the frozen gray sky over New Orleans.

In the 16–6 Super Bowl win that Pittsburgh richly deserved, the Steelers defense was so magnificent that the Vikings offense never scored a point, except two for Pittsburgh. The Steel Curtain was physical and unyielding; at one point, with a yard to go for a first down, Tarkenton decided his best play was a long count that might lure the Steelers offside, evidently because he felt he had no hope of making the yard any other way.

The Steelers defense shut down the Vikings running game just as it had done to Oakland's in the AFC championship. Tarkenton must have known. He went to the air early and stayed there, not that it did him much good. Rolling to his right to evade swarming Pittsburgh defenders, he threw 26 times and completed just 11 for only 102 yards. Three of his passes were intercepted, four were deflected, many were hurried.

With defense like this, it was inevitable that the game would have a lot of insane turnaround plays, and it did. How about a safety, which made the score 2–0 Pittsburgh at halftime? Tarkenton, on his own 10-yard line, faked a quick pitchout and tried to hand the ball to Dave Osborn on a dive. But the ball either hit Chuck Foreman's hip or Foreman's hip hit the ball, and the next thing anybody knew Tarkenton was scrambling—after the ball, which was scooting toward the end zone—and being pursued by every Steeler but Art Rooney. Tarkenton prevented a touchdown by recovering the ball and sliding across the goal line with it for the safety.

The final embarrassment for the Minnesota offense came after it got the biggest break of the game early in the fourth quarter with Pittsburgh leading 9–0. The Steelers' Mike Wagner drew an interference call for shoving John Gilliam on a deep pattern, which gave Minnesota a first down at the Pittsburgh five. Suddenly it was a game again, but on the next play, Greene pinched so fast on a Foreman stab at the middle that Foreman fumbled, and after poking around for a while Greene came up with the ball. As he trotted off the field, Greene, who earlier had intercepted a pass, gestured triumphantly, shaking his fist at the Vikings, a Steeler way of saying who was the boss.

For those who enjoy the mystique of pro football technique, let it now be recorded that the violent Pittsburgh defense was a basic 4–3 with a singular stunt; Greene and Holmes played over the Minnesota center and crushed him, pinching first one way, then another. The result was that Minnesota's guards could not pull, and thus the Vikings had no blocking for their ground game. Minnesota coach Bud Grant, having now lost a third Super Bowl, was more bitter than after the other two. He said, in fact, that it was not a good football game: "There were three bad teams out there. Us, Pittsburgh and the officials."

That was not accurate. Pittsburgh did what it had to do on defense, and in the meantime a couple of guys on the Steelers' offense—Terry Bradshaw, the "dumb quarterback," and Franco Harris—did not have a bad day at all. Harris continually tore away at the Vikings. For example, a fumble on the second-half kickoff gave Pittsburgh the ball at Minnesota's 30, and in four plays the Steelers had a touchdown, largely because of Harris. He rumbled for 24 yards, lost three and then scored from the nine.

And it was Bradshaw who saved the day for the Steelers. With the score 9–6 following the blocked punt and more than 10 minutes remaining, Bradshaw took Pittsburgh 66 yards in an 11-play scoring drive that consumed more than seven minutes. Three times he completed third-down passes, the last a four-yard bullet to tight end Larry Brown for a touchdown.

Poor Bradshaw had to devote most of the week to defending himself. "If we lose it's because I'm dumb," he said. "If we win it's because everyone played well and I got caught up in the action. The only thing that can change my image is the press. People are funny. If you talk slow, you're dumb. If you talk fast, you're a sharpie. If you dress one way, you're a hippie. Another way, you're a conservative. I'm sick of it. Even when I play well I'm a dumbbell. I go to the trouble to have lunch with a reporter this week and the first thing she asks is, 'Terry, are you really that dumb?' I just walked away."

He also said, "I think it's O.K. for kids to idolize football players. You need idols so you can daydream." ∎

From left: Ron Shanklin, Mel Blount, White and Holmes.
Photograph by James Drake

BY **Jack Ham**

Steelers Linebacker

The drama was that it was the first time for us going to the Super Bowl, so everybody was saying you're first-timers and it's the Vikings' third time, so that should be a negative. But there was a mismatch for us. We had L.C. Greenwood and Dwight White on the outside and Joe Greene and Ernie Holmes on the inside. That was just a dominant front in our stunt 4–3 defense.

We didn't feel, as a team, that their offense could methodically move down the field against us. It pretty much unfolded like that. For some reason, the Vikings were trying to run into that stunt with Joe and Ernie. If you're gonna try to run against us, you don't want to run in there. You're running into the teeth of our defense. That's not how you attack us.

There are certain things you forget from a game but not that last minute and a half when you run the clock out. Donnie Shell, who wasn't a starter back then but was a demon on special teams, was on the sideline just jumping up and down. White was going crazy. You almost pinch yourself.

It really is about the journey. When you get over the hump of being a good team and break through, it's very special. The Chief, Art Rooney, had a reputation of being a nice guy in the NFL and his teams would play hard but not win big games. When Pete Rozelle gave him the Lombardi Trophy in the locker room, Art Rooney just said, "Thank you." Typical. If you knew the Chief, that was him. But to quiet all that noise was pretty special for him in his own very unassuming way.

BY **Fran Tarkenton**

Vikings Quarterback

I had a chronically bad shoulder made worse by doctors giving me cortisone when I was with the Giants. Then the Vikings doctors shot me up with butazolidin [an anti-inflammatory pain-killer often given to horses] to allow me to play. My right shoulder continued to deteriorate and it flared up early in the '74 season against Dallas. That whole year, I couldn't throw a ball more than 40 yards.

Just before the half in the Super Bowl, John Gilliam was running across the five-yard line and I was at about the 30, and he was open. It would have been a great touchdown in a tight game. I threw and the ball hung because I didn't have anything on it. Mel Blount hit Gilliam about the time the pass got there and dislodged the ball. If I'd have had my arm, we would have had a touchdown.

In the three Super Bowls I played in, we always had an extra week between the games. You know what we did? We went home. I came to Atlanta. We didn't practice that whole week. Now I look back and think, What were we thinking? Before every game I played in Minnesota, I worked with our offensive coordinator and my great friend, Jerry Burns, and put in our offensive game plan together. In the three Super Bowls, they put the game plan in while I was in Atlanta. I never had any input. We broke our routine and our preparation. We took seven days off. Our whole rhythm stopped. I don't think we gave ourselves a chance.

Tarkenton's attempt at a pitchout went awry and he wound up sliding into the end zone to cover the ball . . .
Photographs by Heinz Kluetmeier (top) and James Drake

IX
STEELERS | VIKINGS

The Steelers defense
was so magnificent
that the Vikings
offense never
scored a point, except
two for Pittsburgh.
The Steel Curtain
was physical
and unyielding.

...giving Pittsburgh a second-quarter
safety for the game's first points.
Photograph by James Drake

SUPER BOWL X

PITTSBURGH **STEELERS** | 21

DALLAS **COWBOYS** | 17

Bradshaw was left dazed and disoriented after a fourth-quarter hit.

Photograph by John Iacono

AS AMERICA turned 200 its favorite teams met again. Dallas had the ring of destiny—a wildcard team that had conjured a playoff win with a Hail Mary—but on this day the magic, a trick of pulling footballs out of thin air, belonged to a Steeler.

WEATHER

57°, sunny

POINT SPREAD

Steelers by 7

TIME OF GAME

2:58

TV AUDIENCE

57.7 million

The last of Swann's four receptions
came with 3:02 left, and decided the game.

Photograph by John Iacono

Himself a maestro, Stallworth played
second fiddle to Swann's virtuoso performance.

Photograph by NFL Photos/AP

Statistical Leaders

Rushing FRANCO HARRIS (PIT) 27 carries, 82 yds

Passing TERRY BRADSHAW (PIT) 9 of 19, 209 yds, 2 TDs

Receiving LYNN SWANN (PIT) 4 catches, 161 yds, 1 TD

MVP LYNN SWANN Steelers Wide Receiver

The Ring
14-karat gold; palladium
trophy at center, flanked by
50-point diamonds

Anthem Performer
Tom Sullivan

Halftime Performer
Up With People

Attendance 80,187

Ticket Price $20

Behind the Scenes

Lynn Swann wasn't sure he would play, having suffered a
concussion during the AFC title game. He spent two days in
the hospital and was partly motivated to return after Dallas
safety Cliff Harris told reporters, "I'm not going to hurt anyone
intentionally. But getting hit again while he's on a pass route
must be in the back of Swann's mind."

They Said It

"I hope the sharks eat Staubach."

—Steelers linebacker JACK LAMBERT upon
hearing the location of the Cowboys' beachfront hotel

Sunday at the Movies

Scenes for *Black Sunday*, a film about a fictional terrorist attack on
the Super Bowl via the Goodyear blimp, were shot during the game.

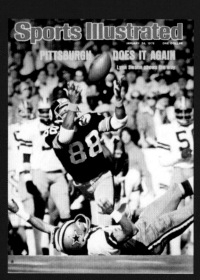

SWANN'S SWEET SONG

Pittsburgh's soaring receiver, helped by his brave QB, took over the game | BY DAN JENKINS

FOR ALL THE GAUDY THINGS that happened, memories of the 1976 Super Bowl will keep going back to the Steelers' Lynn Swann climbing into the air like the boy in the Indian rope trick, and coming down with the football. He didn't come down with many passes, only four, but he caught the ones that mattered. That is why it will seem that he spent the day up there in the crisp sky, a thousand feet above the Orange Bowl.

The thinking beforehand was that Pittsburgh could win this game only if Franco Harris trampled through a thing called the flex defense of the intellectual Cowboys who, in the meantime, on offense, would do enough weird things to the hard-hat Steelers to capture the day and write a perfect finish to their storybook season. Essentially Dallas stopped Harris, however, and the winning of Super Bowl X was left to Swann and the indomitable Terry Bradshaw, who seems to collect concussions and championship rings with equal facility. Just for good measure there was also a Steelers defense that could probably take apart an attacking tank battalion if it had to.

But mainly it was Swann, keeping Pittsburgh in a game that looked to be swaying, early on, toward the underdog Cowboys. It was Swann, soaring above Dallas's Mark Washington at the sideline, who fielded a Bradshaw pass of 32 yards and made the drive that put Pittsburgh back in the game late in the first quarter. And in the fourth quarter it was Swann who made the biggest catch of the day, a 64-yard touchdown heave from Bradshaw, who didn't realize until much later, after his head stopped rattling, that he had passed for a score. This was the play that put the Steelers ahead 21–10. Only a few impossible last-minute deeds by the Cowboys could have changed the outcome of Super Bowl X, and though they scored one more touchdown they just were not quite good enough to pull it off.

That last catch of Swann's has to be dwelled on, for

it had Super Bowl trophy and $15,000 to each Steeler written all over it. There was so much to the play—so much that happened. It ended with Swann catching a rocket from Bradshaw that traveled at least 70 yards in the air, Swann jumping and taking it on the Dallas five-yard line and gliding in for the touchdown, and Bradshaw barely conscious on the ground.

The play began with the Steelers trying to protect that 15–10 lead and just over three minutes left. It was third-and-four at the Steeler 36, and there was still plenty of time for Dallas's Roger Staubach and Drew Pearson to conjure up some of their witchcraft.

Perhaps we'll never know what possessed Bradshaw to call 69 Maximum Flanker Post when the world had a right to expect Pittsburgh to try only for the first down. It may be that Bradshaw is not as dumb as it has become numbingly popular for critics to suggest. He faded back to throw the long one—a wild gamble, it appeared. Alas, Dallas had figured it properly; the blitz was on, and D.D. Lewis came storming at Bradshaw from his blind side, with Cliff Harris behind him.

Bradshaw took a step to his right and Lewis missed by a hair. That gave Bradshaw time to unload the pass.

In the next instant Harris destroyed Bradshaw with a whack the 80,197 in the crowd might have heard if their attention had not been turned to the flight of the ball and the blur of Swann's footrace with the Cowboys' Washington—who covered Swann as well as anyone could, but could not leap as high or as deftly at the right time. It was a beautiful throw, a perfectly run pass route and a marvelous catch, all at the most splendid moment—for Pittsburgh—of a rather important game.

Bradshaw did not know what he had wrought. People bent over him as he lay there, but he wasn't hearing them. They told him when they led him to the sideline. They told him when they sat him down, and a few minutes later they were telling him again that he had done this terrific thing, as they walked him toward the dressing room. "I was in the locker room and the game was just about over when I understood it," said Bradshaw.

There were enough bizarre events throughout the game to daze the most ardent fan. Dallas took a 7–0 lead, the TD coming after Steelers' punter Bobby Walden dropped the snap. The Cowboys, with enough hard hitting, led 10–7 through three quarters until the Steelers, with a safety and two field goals went ahead. Next came Swann's dramatic touchdown catch to make it 21–10. A thrilling Staubach-to-Percy-Howard pass of 34 yards ended the scoring.

The Cowboys reacted to the loss with a humor and graciousness that reflects Landry's control of the squad. Staubach said, "We had our chances. Overall, Pittsburgh is the best, but it was a good season."

Yes, and for football fans it was a great Super Bowl, with Swann rising to the occasion—up, up and away—and making the game something for everyone to take home to think about until next year. ∎

Bradshaw, with his poise and his big plays, prevailed.

Photograph by Neil Leifer

Pittsburgh's emotional leader, Jack Lambert, looked as though he hated everyone in white. The Steelers didn't draw a penalty all game, but it was not because Lambert didn't try.

Linebacker Lambert (58) was a handful for back Preston Pearson.
Photograph by Heinz Kluetmeier

THE WAY IT WAS

BY Rocky Bleier

Steelers Fullback

The pressure was on because we were the defending champions. And we were playing the Cowboys, who were obviously a dominant team in the NFC. In the second quarter Roy Gerela missed a field goal for us and one of their safeties, Cliff Harris went over to "congratulate" him. Seconds later—*boom!*—Cliff's on the ground and Jack Lambert's over him, saying, "You don't intimidate us. We intimidate you." Today, Lambert would have been kicked out of the game. But nothing happened, except that for us it was a spark. It got us on track. Our eyes were wide-open.

Lynn Swann's catches were big. Those are moments that lift a team. But the crux of the game, for me, came with less than two minutes left. It was fourth-and-nine and we had the ball on their 41-yard line and we led 21–17. Bradshaw had gotten knocked out of the game; Terry Hanratty was in. I'm thinking we have to kick. Maybe you pass and if it's intercepted, it's like a punt. If you run it, you have to give it to Franco. Hanratty comes back from the sideline and I say, "What's the play?" He gets in the huddle and calls it. It turns out I'm carrying the ball.

We break the huddle and he says, "Run as much time off the clock as you can." I'm not that guy. I'm an A-to-B guy. The ball is snapped and I get two yards. It took six seconds. The clock stops to change possession and the Cowboys drove into our territory. But then, after two incompletions, Glen Edwards saves my ass and intercepts the ball. When you win, there are no sins. It was a general absolution.

BY Drew Pearson

Cowboys Wide Receiver

We were the wild-card team, and three weeks earlier we had beaten the Vikings on a Hail Mary. The path we took gave us a feeling like we might be a team of destiny. When we got to the Super Bowl we said, O.K., it's the Pittsburgh Steelers. We knew how good they were with the Steel Curtain defense. And most of the talk leading up to the game was about the Steelers. The only talk we were getting was because of Thomas (Hollywood) Henderson. There was a lot of back-and-forth. By game time, both teams were ready to back up what they were saying.

We wanted to set up the pass with the run and we did it very effectively on our second series. Roger Staubach faked the handoff and I ran what we called a "spurt" route; you take it upfield and kind of spurt across the field. Golden Richards ran a great post route to clear it out. When I came across, I was wide-open and Roger hit me in stride for a 29-yard touchdown. We were leading. We were excited. And we thought: We've got a chance to beat these Steelers.

Things settled down throughout the game. We were stopping them. It took great plays by Lynn Swann to keep their drives moving and watching that was painful. I wanted those kind of catches. Coach Landry used to tell us that if you're going to create a name for yourself, a legacy, do it in the biggest games. And here Swann was doing it. Those plays Lynn made were pretty much the ball game.

Swann outleaped Washington time and again.
Photograph by Heinz Kluetmeier

SUPER BOWL XI

OAKLAND RAIDERS | 32

MINNESOTA VIKINGS | 14

THE ORNERY Raiders had won 75% of their games in eight years under John Madden, but only now had they reached the big game. The foe? Seasoned Minnesota, another big-winning team, but one that seemed to save its worst for last.

WEATHER
58°, sunny

POINT SPREAD
Raiders by 4

TIME OF GAME
3:03

TV AUDIENCE
62.1 million

Snake-smitten: A jovial Madden (right) celebrated with Stabler after the win.

Photograph by Heinz Kluetmeier

Davis punished the Vikings' right side all game, and got loose for a 35-yard gain.

Photograph by Tony Triolo

SUNDAY SMACKDOWN

When the Vikings stumbled yet again, Oakland overpowered them | BY DAN JENKINS

FOR YOUR FINAL HALFTIME stunt, ladies and gentlemen in the stands for Super Bowl XI, write down on your cards what you think of the Vikings so far. Now hold the cards up.

Nah, it would never clear the censors. The football game was essentially over by then, as so many Super Bowls have been concluded prematurely by the Vikings. The only fascinating part was how ingeniously easy Minnesota made it for the Raiders this time. It was perfectly evident that Oakland came to play a superb game; it was just that no one realized they wouldn't have to.

Before the final score becomes a question for trivia experts, let it be stated that the bearded, brawling Raiders won the "World Championship Game" 32–14. The Vikings had gotten two big breaks in the early proceedings—a missed Oakland field goal and a blocked Oakland punt—and still wound up trailing the Raiders 16–0 at halftime. After that it was perfectly clear to the 100,421 Pasadena witnesses that the Vikings were going to do for the Raiders what they had done for the Chiefs in the 1970 Super Bowl (they lost 23–7), what they had done for the Dolphins in the '74 Super Bowl (they lost 24–7), and what they had done for the Steelers in the '75 Super Bowl (they lost 16–6).

When it was over, poor Fran Tarkenton repeated what he had said after two of those wonderful exhibitions: "They played extremely well. We played lousy."

Before the Vikings started making a 137-yard runner out of Oakland's Clarence Davis, and letting Ken Stabler find Fred Biletnikoff and Dave Casper open all over the field, there was this bizarre turnaround in the first quarter which may have had something to do with the destiny of both teams. What it did was so discourage the Vikings that they looked forever after as if they would rather have been somewhere else—like ice fishing, perhaps.

When Vikings linebacker Fred McNeill flew in from the left side to block a punt by Ray Guy—something no sane person thought could happen—and then covered the football on Oakland's three-yard line, doing this 10 minutes into the first period with the score still 0–0, there was reason to suspect that these old men of the North were finally going to overcome their bad Super Bowl habits. That feeling didn't last long.

After Chuck Foreman gained one yard, Tarkenton decided to give the ball to Brent McClanahan for another stab into the middle of Oakland's line. Somewhere in there McClanahan lost the ball—either because Otis Sistrunk growled at him or Phil Villapiano bit him. McClanahan later explained the fumble by saying, "No comment, no comment, no comment, no comment." Eight of those, in fact. In any case, Willie Hall came up with the ball for the Raiders. And after that it was just a question of whether Stabler wanted to pass for more yardage than Davis ran for.

As Stabler drove the Raiders down for their first flicker on the scoreboard—a 24-yard Errol Mann field goal—a pattern began to emerge. Casper was going to be open, so was Biletnikoff, and Davis was going to burst through openings, most often to his left against the overaged and undernourished right side of Minnesota's defense. That Oakland intended to direct its

ground game to Minnesota's right side was hardly a secret, for the Raiders have always had great success running in that direction behind the massive bodies of guard Gene Upshaw (255 pounds) and tackle Art Shell (290)—not to mention tight end Casper (230) when he sets up left. "When we put Casper over there with Shell and Upshaw," says coach John Madden, "we've got some tough bunch."

They sure had. It was like tanks against Jeeps, battleships against Corvettes. "We knew it had to be won in the pit," Upshaw said afterward. "The game plan was to run at 'em. We knew if we could run at 'em, Snake [Stabler] would get 'em on the passing." Or as Davis said, "All the glory should go to the guys up front."

Halfway through the third quarter, Davis, who played after O. J. Simpson and before Anthony Davis at USC, had already gained more than 100 yards, reeling off dashes of 20 yards and 35 yards and 13 yards and 18 yards. Oakland wound up establishing a team record for total offense with 429 yards, as Stabler pierced the Vikings by completing 12 of 19 passes for 180 yards. This included a nifty pass to Biletnikoff at the Minnesota one, followed by a lob to Casper for Oakland's first touchdown.

The Raiders scored their second touchdown when Biletnikoff made a sliding catch of a 17-yard pass at the goal line and then Pete Banaszak took it across, giving Oakland that 16–0 halftime lead. A 40-yard Mann field goal made it 19–0 in the third quarter.

One thing Minnesota's latest Super Bowl caper does, quite naturally, is bring up all those questions about Tarkenton again. He is now 0 for 3 in the spectacle, and he has also thrown only two touchdown passes—and one of those was to Oakland's Willie Brown, the one that Brown returned 75 yards for the Raiders' grand final touchdown in the fourth quarter. ■

Biletnikoff: 4 catches, 79 yards, 1 Monte Johnson hug.

Photograph by Walter Iooss Jr.

JUST THE FACTS

Statistical Leaders

Rushing CLARENCE DAVIS (OAK) 16 carries, 137 yds

Passing FRAN TARKENTON (MIN) 17 of 25, 205 yds, 1 TD

Receiving SAMMY WHITE (MIN) 5 catches, 77 yds, 1 TD

MVP FRED BILETNIKOFF Raiders Wide Receiver

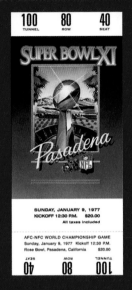

The Ring
27 diamonds set in black onyx

Anthem Performer
Vikki Carr (who sang
"America the Beautiful")

Halftime Performers
Los Angeles Unified
All-City Band in Disney's
"It's a Small World"

Attendance 103,438

Ticket Price $20

Behind the Scenes

On the morning of the Super Bowl, Oakland cornerback Willie Brown told Gene Upshaw, "I'm going to intercept a pass and run it back for a touchdown." In the fourth quarter, he did just that, returning a Fran Tarkenton pass a Super Bowl-record 75 yards.

They Said It

"We're ready. We're going to kill these guys."
—Raiders coach JOHN MADDEN to owner Al Davis on the eve of the game

Canton Crew

Nine of these Raiders made the Hall of Fame: Fred Biletnikoff, Willie Brown, Dave Casper, Ray Guy, Ted Hendricks, Art Shell, and Gene Upshaw, plus coach John Madden and owner Al Davis.

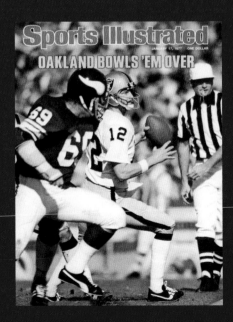

Stabler's day in the sun included a touchdown pass and no turnovers.
Photograph by Walter Iooss Jr.

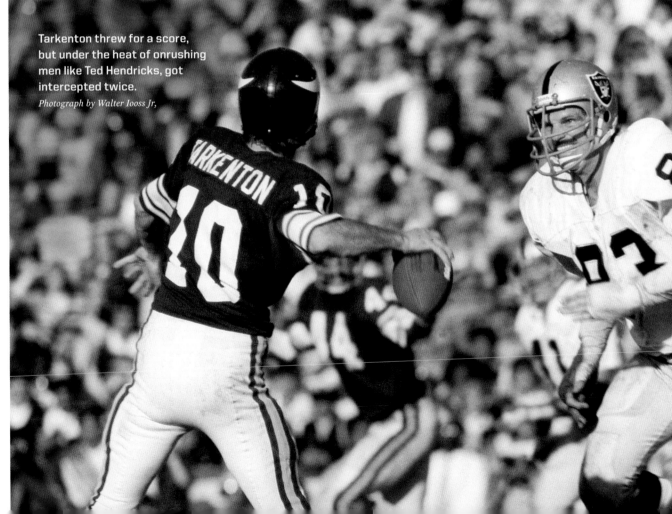

Tarkenton threw for a score, but under the heat of onrushing men like Ted Hendricks, got intercepted twice.
Photograph by Walter Iooss Jr.

A true warrior at left guard, Upshaw got the better of Vikings Hall-of-Famer-to-be Alan Page all game long.

Photograph by Walter Iooss Jr.

BY Art Shell

Raiders Tackle

During the week of practices before the game, shoot, I think only one ball that Snake [Ken Stabler] threw hit the ground, and the receiver just kind of fumbled it. We were loose. The day before the game was a light day and some guys took a roll of tape and made a big ball out of it and started playing softball with the helmets. I remember looking at the sideline and Mr. Davis kept looking over as if to say, 'What are we doing? Are we crazy?'

On game day, though, we were all business. Before the game, we went on the field and warmed up with our pads on. The Vikings, like some teams, didn't have theirs on. Gene Upshaw and I always warmed up next to each other and we saw some of the Vikings flipping a ball around. Gene said to me, "These guys don't know what they're in for today."

Clarence Davis had one of the best days in Super Bowl history. The system that we had was a fullback system and the guy that usually had to do a lot of blocking was our halfback, Clarence. Throughout the year, he was blocking defensive ends, blocking linebackers, because he was blocking for our fullback, Mark van Eeghen. I guess the coaches saw on film that if we ran our halfback with our fullback blocking against the Vikings, we could have success. And it couldn't have happened to a nicer guy. We used to call Clarence Mighty Mouse. He would take on anybody; I was happy for him. It was a day where we would not be denied.

BY Chuck Foreman

Vikings Running Back

I went to our pregame meal with [teammate] Ahmad Rashad. We were in the elevator and we were confident in the talent we had. I didn't think Oakland was that dominant of a team. You know how you look in your teammates' eyes to see if they're ready? I thought most of them were ready to play. And I thought Oakland was a team that we could beat.

In every Super Bowl I played in with the Vikings, we changed up what we did from what we had done to get us there. I was uncomfortable with the changes in our offense. We were trying to give them different looks and formations. It just didn't work. They physically took over the game.

We came out and made some mistakes—fumbled early, turned the ball over in the fourth quarter. You can't make mistakes and expect to win against a team like that. And they did things we weren't expecting. I certainly wasn't expecting Clarence Davis to run for more than 130 yards. We just got beat.

I know I left everything on the field and I know most of my teammates did too. It was disheartening because, wow, to be there three times, as I was, and lose all three—it was emotionally draining. Once you've lost, it's as if you never played the game. Now everybody forgets that we had great football teams. People forget how hard it is to get to a Super Bowl. They just know that we were the losers.

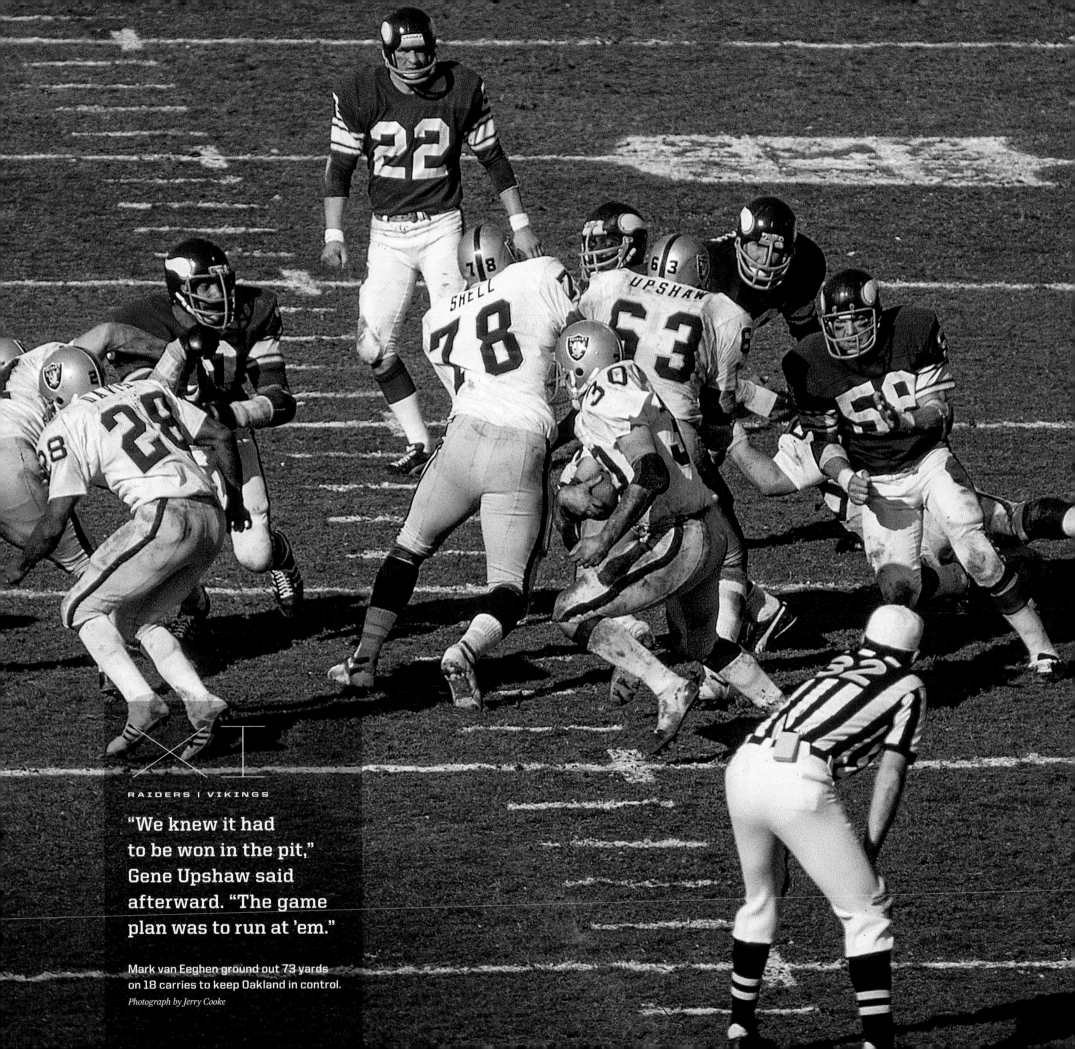

XI

RAIDERS | VIKINGS

"We knew it had to be won in the pit," Gene Upshaw said afterward. "The game plan was to run at 'em."

Mark van Eeghen ground out 73 yards on 18 carries to keep Oakland in control.

Photograph by Jerry Cooke

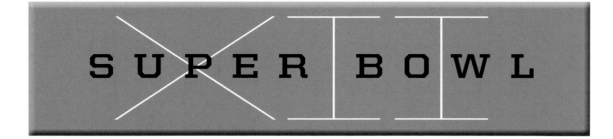

SUPER BOWL XII

DALLAS
COWBOYS | 27

DENVER
BRONCOS | 10

HERE IT was, Denver QB Craig Morton against his old team and the man who'd supplanted him, Roger Staubach. Dallas had its Doomsday Defense, the Broncos their Orange Crush. No foreshadowing, though, saw this: eight Denver turnovers.

DOME
First indoor SB

POINT SPREAD
Cowboys by 6

TIME OF GAME
3:32

TV AUDIENCE
78.9 million

After Dallas, not Denver, did the crushing, Henderson (also at right) gloated gleefully.

Photograph by Heinz Kluetmeier

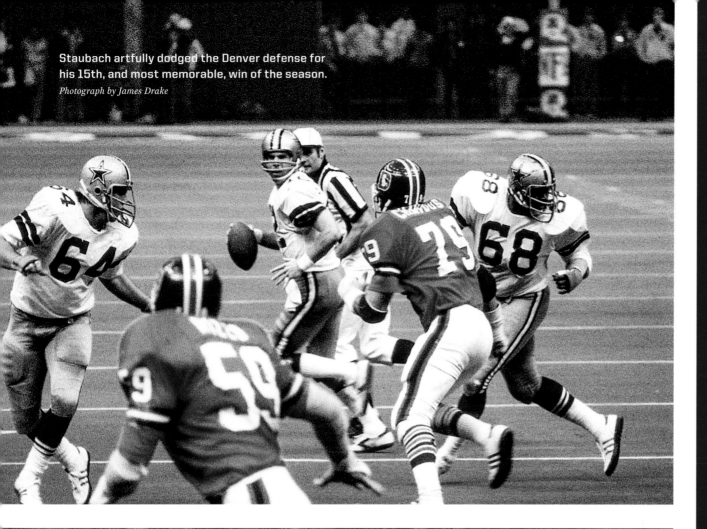

Staubach artfully dodged the Denver defense for his 15th, and most memorable, win of the season.

Photograph by James Drake

After going long, Johnson pulled in a catch for the eternal highlight reels.

Photograph by Walter Iooss Jr.

JUST THE FACTS

Statistical Leaders

Rushing TONY DORSETT (DAL) 15 carries, 66 yds, 1 TD

Passing ROGER STAUBACH (DAL) 17 of 25, 183 yds, 1 TD

Receiving BILLY JOE DUPREE (DAL) 4 catches, 66 yds

MVPs HARVEY MARTIN and RANDY WHITE
Cowboys Defensive Linemen

The Ring
A stone-in-star for each title

Anthem Performer
Phyllis Kelly

Halftime Performers
Tyler Apache Belles Drill Team, Al Hirt and Pete Fountain

Attendance 76,400

Ticket Price $30

Behind the Scenes

On Butch Johnson's 45-yard TD catch, Roger Staubach, keen to Denver safety Bernard Jackson's coverage tendencies, modified Johnson's route from an in-pattern to a post. Good move.

They Said It

"Hell, we have more fun than this in Denver."
—Broncos tackle ANDY MAURER on the lack of game-week hoopla and the midnight curfew imposed by coach Red Miller

Do Like Mike?

After drawing an unnecessary roughness penalty for a hit on Denver punt returner Rick Upchurch, Hollywood Henderson was confronted by Tom Landry. Said Henderson, shifting blame to the special teams coach, "Mike Ditka told me to do that."

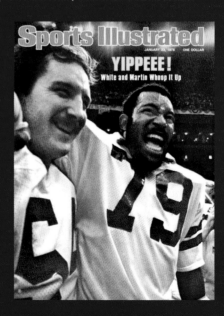

THE COWBOYS HAD IT ALL

Led by a daunting and dominating defense, Dallas dismantled Denver | BY DAN JENKINS

AS SUPER BOWLS GO, THIS ONE was way up there for mosts—it had the most fumbles, the most hitting, the most noise, the most penalties, the most tricky plays, and no doubt the most Xs and Os stamped on a coach's forehead, as Dallas's Tom Landry nailed Denver's Red Miller to a blackboard and left him there. And when last seen, the Cowboys' two biggest heroes, Randy White and Harvey Martin, were still lecturing the State of Colorado on the mysteries of the flex defense. As a final gesture of victory, another Cowboys star, linebacker Thomas Henderson, went prancing down the field as the last seconds flashed off and jumped up and stuffed a football over the crossbar.

The score was Dallas 27, Denver 10, and it seemed that close only if you were sitting on the Denver side of the Superdome. Actually, Dallas jumped to a 10–0 lead in the first quarter and after that the margin never shrunk. It was a case of the Cowboys doing just about whatever they wished on offense, and so thoroughly confusing the Broncos with their defensive manpower and quickness that Denver's assistants upstairs on the headphones must have sounded as if they were under a kamikaze attack as they screamed down to the field with their guesses and remedies.

The Broncos had the same flaming emotion that had carried them so stunningly into Super Bowl XII in the first place, but the Cowboys had everything else—the more gifted athletes, certainly the superior quarterback in Roger Staubach, and all of the smarts.

Denver never did come close to figuring out the flex defense and all the stunts and blitzes that go with it. Led by Martin and White, Dallas's front four put so much pressure on Craig Morton that he set a Super Bowl record for interceptions (four) before the first half was over. This was the quarterback who had been intercepted only eight times in 14 regular-season games. By the middle of the third quarter, Morton

had been replaced by obscure backup Norris Weese.

One had to feel sorrow for Morton, who was also a Super Bowl loser as the Cowboys QB in 1971. For one thing, he had done so much to make the Broncos a miracle story during the season and playoffs. For another, he was a good friend of many of his Super Bowl enemies; he and Roger Staubach had even hugged after the opening flip of the coin. (Dallas won that too.)

Staubach had a fine day—he was constantly motioning, screening, zoning, shotgunning, trapping and keeping the hitters off-balance. And Tony Dorsett, until a knee injury put him out late in the third quarter, was among the things Denver did not have, a runner who could scare you to death. He gained 66 yards in the first half, 22 more than the entire Denver team. Also Butch Johnson made a diving catch of a Staubach bomb for a third-quarter touchdown that will go into the scrapbooks alongside Super Bowl catches by Max McGee, Lynn Swann and Fred Biletnikoff. Johnson dropped the ball as he tumbled into the end zone, but as the reruns showed—happily for the zebras—he had retained possession just long enough.

The Dallas defense, however, had more reason to talk than anyone else and Martin, who devoured Denver tackle Andy Maurer like so much barbecued shrimp, said, "Orange Crush is soda water, baby. You drink it. It don't win football games."

White, who dined on so many platters of Denver guard Tom Glassic on the half shell, said, "We knew pressuring Craig was the key and it was all on our shoulders. We wanted it."

And then there was the gesturing Henderson, who added, "I'm sorry they took Morton out. I wanted him to throw me a couple."

The Cowboys organization had learned from past experience—a Super Bowl win over Miami in 1972, losses to Baltimore in '71 and Pittsburgh in '76—that game-preparation time can be squandered unless someone is there to take care of every detail. Things

Landry led Dallas to five Super Bowls, winning two.
Photograph by Peter Read Miller

like getting a car for a player or a plane reservation for his wife, or a dinner reservation for a distant cousin. Thus, Dallas had a special squad of people assigned to do nothing but conquer the French Quarter. The organization set up an elaborate office with seven secretaries who were there simply to handle player requests. If Martin wanted to go to the King Tut exhibition to see what a real mummy looked like, a special secretary handled it.

By reputation, Denver was supposed to be the looser team, but the Cowboys seemed less formal. At their press conferences, which are covered by all sorts of representatives of things like the *Passaic Herald-News* and the Grosse Point Crisis Club, men with the Dallas team would shout, "Who wants Charlie Waters?" Off to the side, Doug Todd, the Cowboys' PR director, held his head from the previous night's experiences in the Quarter and recited his favorite country and western lyric: "If the phone don't ring, you'll know it's me."

All of this was before Harvey and Randy and the Flex, and the words that were spoken by Morton at his own last rites: "They just took away everything we had." ∎

Until a knee injury in the third quarter sidelined him, Tony Dorsett was among the things Denver did not have: a runner who could scare you. He gained 66 yards in the first half.

A rookie, Dorsett became the first player to win a Super Bowl a year after winning the NCAA title (at Pitt).

Photograph by Walter Iooss Jr.

BY **Billy Joe DuPree**

Cowboys Tight End

Being born and raised in northeast Louisiana and with the game in New Orleans, I had a bit of a following. There was family, a couple of coaches from high school, friends from college. Before the game, I decided to go out and take care of some of them. I had to leave and go into the corridor of the building. I asked the security guy, "Is it O.K. if I go out and come back in?" He says, "Oh, no problem." So after three minutes I get back and he's not there. The new guy doesn't want to let me back in. I didn't have my pass. I can't recall how I managed to get back in. I conned him or threatened him or something.

We knew their Orange Crush defense was aggressive. With coach Landry being defensive-minded, we knew that if he understood their defense, we would have an offensive game plan to counter it. The most memorable play was probably Robert Newhouse's touchdown pass to Golden Richards. You never would have thought Robert could make that throw. It was perfect.

We knew that from our defensive side, Harvey Martin and Randy White would control Craig Morton. Craig wasn't a scrambler. He was a pocket quarterback. Harvey and Randy knew that. That's why they ended up playing so well that they won co-MVP. In the third quarter, the Broncos took Craig out and brought Norris Weese in. If Weese would have been in earlier, we might have had a much more difficult time. He was a Fran Tarkenton type who could abandon the pocket if necessary. Craig was a good quarterback but he was kind of stationary.

BY **Tom Jackson**

Broncos Linebacker

On Thursday night, Billy Thompson and I were watching TV, which was our routine. All we cared about was our opportunity to win this championship. Irv Cross was live from Pat O'Brien's, a fairly famous establishment in New Orleans. And he ended the segment with, "We'll be right back with a few of the Denver Broncos who happen to be here." It was about 10:15, 10:30 or so. And we're like, *O.K., why are guys out?* He came back from break and he had three of our offensive linemen sitting there drinking. One of them had on the hard hat where you put a beverage on top and then there's that tube that comes down and around and into your mouth. We were horrified. We said, *The Cowboys are watching this! The Cowboys are seeing this!* Two Cowboys defensive linemen ended up splitting the MVP.

The game was the worst performance, at the time, ever. There was an artist who had come to the hotel. He was painting a commemorative edition that would be delivered long after the game. He said, "I'll do something appropriate for you as the Broncos and an entirely different one for the Cowboys. It depends how the game goes." About a month later, this painting arrives—of Tony Dorsett running us over. We all have one. I put mine up in the basement. It's one of the funnier things I've ever seen. After the game I thought, 'I wonder what this guy's gonna send us.' Here it is: Tony Dorsett running over you guys going into the end zone.

Shhh—don't tell her he was only the backup. Dallas QB (and punter) Danny White celebrated with a friend on the sideline.

Photograph by Walter Iooss Jr.

2ND QUARTER

Offensive beauty: No team dazzled on the big stage quite like this era's 49ers

Jerry Rice knew how to take over a Super Bowl. The receiver holds career records of 33 receptions and eight touchdowns—including three in Super Bowl XXIV, the game pictured here.

Photograph by Walter Iooss Jr.

SUPER BOWL XIII

January 21, 1979
Orange Bowl, Miami

HEAD COACHES
CHUCK NOLL Steelers | TOM LANDRY Cowboys

PITTSBURGH
STEELERS | 35

DALLAS
COWBOYS | 31

A PAIR of grand franchises (each vying for a third title) and a pair of grand quarterbacks (each a Hall of Famer to be) met again for the championship. The game seemed up for grabs until a 19-second span in the fourth quarter changed everything.

WEATHER
71°, cloudy

POINT SPREAD
Steelers by 3½

TIME OF GAME
3:31

TV AUDIENCE
74.7 million

A touchdown and 68 rushing yards behind him, Harris went giddily into the night.

Photograph by Ross Lewis

Bradshaw didn't gain much as a scrambler, but what he could do with his arm! The Steelers QB threw for 253 yards and three touchdowns in the first half alone.

Photograph by Walter Iooss Jr.

Excerpted from **SPORTS ILLUSTRATED** *January 29, 1979*

BIG MAN, BIG PLAYS

Leading the brilliant Steelers, Terry Bradshaw had the game of his life | BY DAN JENKINS

FOR THREE QUARTERS AND almost six minutes of the fourth last Sunday, Super Bowl XIII, which Pittsburgh wound up winning 35–31, was everything pro football's championship game should be, but rarely is. It had the NFL's two best teams, the Steelers and the Cowboys, doing amazing things in heroic—and sometimes haphazard, even peculiar—fashion on the damp Orange Bowl turf.

It had Dallas's Tony Dorsett scuttling around and through the Steelers on the game's first drive only to have the Cowboys fumble away the ball on an ill-conceived, triple handoff gadget play.

It had Terry Bradshaw passing the Steelers to a quick 7–0 lead on a 28-yard lob to John Stallworth in the end zone at the end of a bang-bang 53-yard drive. It had Bradshaw losing the ball on a fumble, and then three plays later Roger Staubach combining with Tony Hill on a 39-yard touchdown pass play that tied the score at 7–7 on the last play of the first quarter. It had Bradshaw, after recovering his own fumble in the backfield, being sandwiched by linebackers Thomas (Hollywood) Henderson and Mike Hegman, with Henderson pinning Bradshaw's arms while Hegman pickpocketed the ball and ran 37 yards for a touchdown and a 14–7 Dallas lead. It had Bradshaw complaining that his left shoulder was sore and being told by a team doctor that it might be separated.

It had Bradshaw immediately returning to the game and throwing a short first-down pass to the ubiquitous Stallworth, who turned it into a 75-yard touchdown play. It had Bradshaw sending Pittsburgh to the locker room with a 21–14 halftime lead by lofting a seven-yard pass to a leaping Rocky Bleier in the end zone.

Then, in the third quarter, the game had Dallas, suddenly starting to look like the better team, all set to tie the score at 21–21, only to have tight end Jackie Smith, with nary a Steeler in sight, flat-out drop Staubach's eminently catchable pass in the end zone. The costly misplay meant the Cowboys had to settle for Rafael Septien's 27-yard field goal.

So later, after Franco Harris crashed up the middle to score on a 22-yard trap play the Steelers led 28–17 lead with only seven minutes to go. If that touchdown demoralized the Cowboys, what happened on the ensuing kickoff shattered them.

Dallas inexplicably stationed defensive tackle Randy White, who was playing with a cast on his fractured left thumb, in the middle of the field near the 25-yard line as Roy Gerela prepared to kick off. When Gerela slipped, his kick squibbed and bounced directly to the 250-pound White, who had no clear idea what to do with it. He half fumbled and half lateraled the ball, only to have it wind up in the hands of Pittsburgh's Dennis (Dirt) Winston at the Dallas 18.

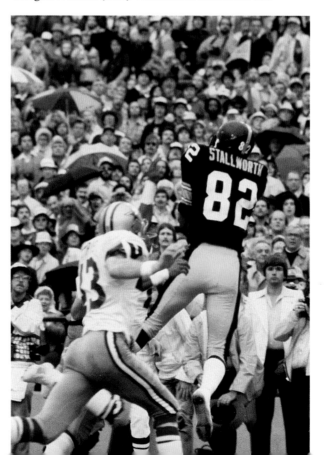

Before Dallas coach Tom Landry could even grimace, Bradshaw fired a pass into the end zone that Lynn Swann leaped up for and plucked from out of the night, as only he can. And the riskiest Super Bowl of them all was a rout, with the Steelers leading 35–17. The elapsed time between the touchdowns was 19 seconds.

Staubach rallied the Cowboys against Pittsburgh's obviously relaxed defense. He threw a seven-yard touchdown pass to Billy Joe DuPree at the end of an 89-yard drive, and—after Dallas recovered an on-side kick—passed four yards for a touchdown to Butch Johnson. With the score now 35–31 and 22 seconds to play, Dallas would have one last chance if it recovered another onside kick. But Septien kicked the ball squarely to Bleier, who fell on it on the Dallas 45.

"Our guys started celebrating when it was 35–17," Bradshaw said later. "It made me mad. They were slapping hands [and] saying how great it was. But it wasn't so great, because the game wasn't over."

All game long Bradshaw was the dominant presence, responsible for turning XIII into the best Super Bowl game of all as well as the highest-scoring. It was Bradshaw who took ferocious licks from a Dallas defense that sacked him four times. It was Bradshaw who kept playing with that injured shoulder. It was Bradshaw who kept finding Swann and Stallworth and tight end Randy Grossman just when he needed them.

"Today I relaxed, felt good and had fun," said Bradshaw. "I had a little bit of a lackadaisical attitude. I didn't want to get uptight. I don't need anyone telling me how great or how smart I am, or how smart I'm not, I just tried to go out there and help win a football game."

Which he did—and how. ∎

Stallworth had three catches, two for touchdowns.

Photograph by Heinz Kluetmeier

Statistical Leaders

Rushing TONY DORSETT (DAL) 15 carries, 96 yds

Passing TERRY BRADSHAW (PIT) 17 of 30, 318 yds, 4 TDs

Receiving LYNN SWANN (PIT) 7 catches, 124 yds, 1 TD

MVP TERRY BRADSHAW Steelers Quarterback

The Ring
Half-carat diamonds in each
star; 30 small ones surround

Anthem Performer
The Colgate Thirteen

Halftime Performer
Salute to the Caribbean
with Ken Hamilton

Attendance 79,484

Ticket Price $30

Behind the Scenes

For the first time the NFL gave the designated home team the
choice of wearing white or colored jerseys. (Previously the home
team had to wear its colors.) The Cowboys, who had lost Super
Bowl V when forced to don blue, lobbied for the change.

They Said It

"It was the closest I'll ever come to punching an official."
—Dallas cornerback BENNY BARNES after his controversial
pass interference penalty in the fourth quarter.

A Simple Plan

Bradshaw was asked his secret for reading the Cowboys
defense: "I'd look for Swann, and if he was covered I'd look for
Stallworth, and if he was covered I'd look for Franco."

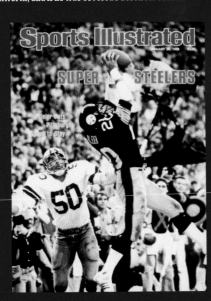

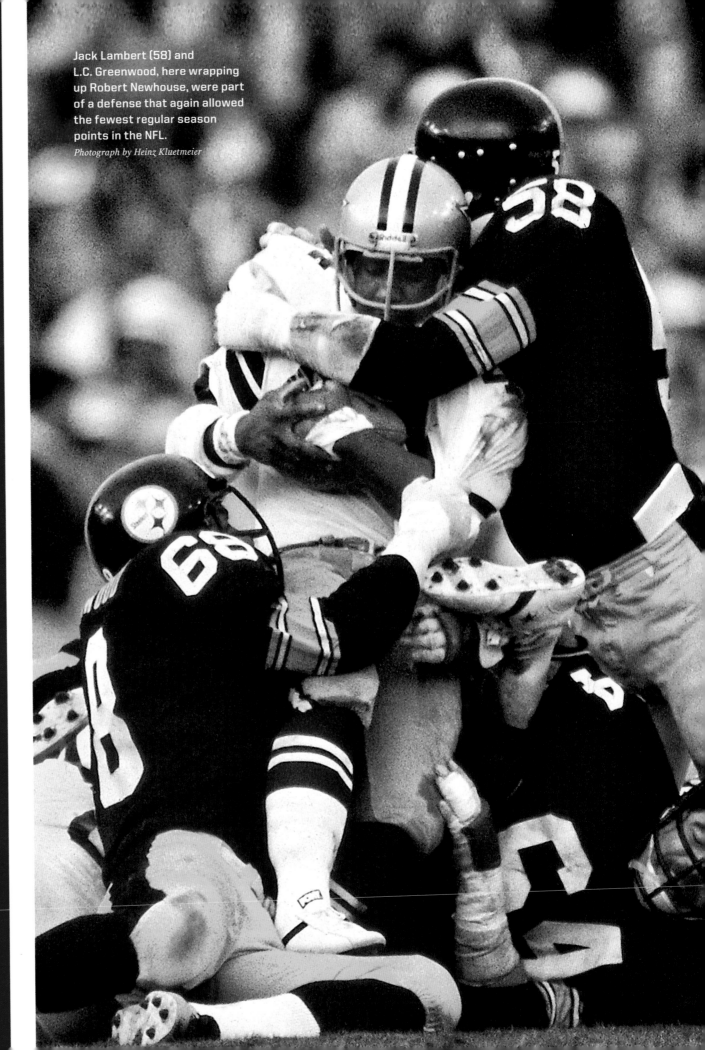

Jack Lambert (58) and
L.C. Greenwood, here wrapping
up Robert Newhouse, were part
of a defense that again allowed
the fewest regular season
points in the NFL.

Photograph by Heinz Kluetmeier

"It was a beautiful play that coach Landry conceived," said Jackie Smith. "When I slipped, I guess I was trying to be overcautious and that's why I dropped it."

Smith, a former St. Louis Cardinal whom the Cowboys had lured out of retirement, played only the one season with Dallas.

Photograph by Tony Triolo

BY Joe Greene

Steelers Defensive Tackle

We were known for our defense. People didn't score a lot on us. But the Cowboys were famous for putting points on the board—not just that year, but any time Roger Staubach was their quarterback. And they had the Doomsday Defense, which was capable of matching our defense from the standpoint of rushing the passer, stopping the run. The Cowboys were scary.

I remember chasing Roger quite a bit. He taxed the defensive line. If he wasn't scrambling around to throw the football, then he was running it. I think I missed two tackles on him; I had him by the leg and he got away from me. And sometime before the half, in the second quarter, as I was coming across the line of scrimmage, I was trapped by Herb Scott, their left guard. I saw him out of the corner of my eye, late. I tried to duck him and he caught me right under my chin. I think I was out for a good portion of that first half—I didn't come out of the game, but I was kind of woozy.

The last couple of minutes were very hectic, with the Cowboys closing the space on us. We had an 18-point lead and they scored two touchdowns and tried a last onside kick. We didn't want to go out there and have to play defense again. Even with the best defense, anything can happen. We were just rooting for the hands team to get the ball. When they did, it was total jubilation. I don't think a lot of words were said. It was just a lot of screams.

BY Roger Staubach

Cowboys Quarterback

It drives me crazy that anyone would blame the game on Jackie Smith. That's just not right. That play was actually set up for the goal line but coach Landry called it on a short-yardage situation from the 10-yard line. He really had only worked on it going to the back of the end zone as a safety valve. We'd put it in on Friday before the game and we only practiced it a few times. The way it turned out, Jack Lambert blitzed and I saw Jackie wide-open [in the end zone]. I released the ball and I think it surprised him. It was a little low, behind him [and he dropped it]. People try to point to that, but there are a lot of other plays—the interception I threw before the half, two fumbles. It wasn't just that play.

That interception before the half, that was a shame. Steelers cornerback Mel Blount really did a hell of a job. He read our play-action pass. I was doing the right read and everything, but he came off the tight end to pick it off and then the Steelers went on to score. That was a turn of events.

The Steelers were a great team and took advantage of our mistakes. But we never gave up. We were arguably playing the best team that's ever played in the NFL. I don't know a weakness that they had. For a time they controlled the league. We were the only NFC team that they knew could maybe upset them. We just didn't pull it off. We were a great team that lost to a team that was a little greater.

Bleier's touchdown catch before the half put Pittsburgh up to stay.
Photograph by Peter Read Miller

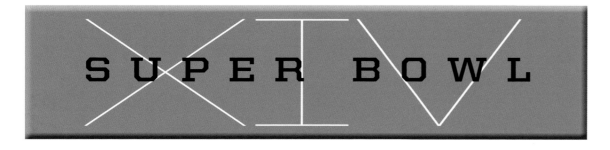

SUPER BOWL XIV

PITTSBURGH STEELERS | 31

LOS ANGELES RAMS | 19

A Steelers fan did his best to capture what Greene called "immortality."

Photograph by Richard Mackson

THE STEELERS were old hands at this, angling for their fourth title in six years. So when the plucky Rams, playing close to home, put up a spirited fight, Pittsburgh knew what to do. With a big play here, another there, greatness was sealed.

WEATHER
67°, windy

POINT SPREAD
Steelers by 10½

TIME OF GAME
2:57

TV AUDIENCE
76.2 million

Harris traveled a long way for the first of his two one-yard touchdown runs.

Photograph by Tony Triolo

Swann had five catches for 79 yards and a third-quarter touchdown before getting walloped and knocked out of the game by Pat Thomas (27).

Photograph by Walter Iooss Jr.

Excerpted from **SPORTS ILLUSTRATED** *January 28, 1980*

RISING TO THE TOP

The Rams had heart, but Pittsburgh had the difference-makers | BY PAUL ZIMMERMAN

IT WAS AN EMOTIONAL SUPER BOWL and easily the best of the 14 played so far. It was the way Super Bowls are supposed to be played, but haven't been. The score changed hands six times before it ended Pittsburgh 31, Los Angeles 19, but only the guys who laid the 11 points with the bookies read it as a 12-point Steelers win. The Rams made it that close. They stayed in it because of a sustained intensity that brought them great honor, because of an unexpectedly brilliant performance by young quarterback Vince Ferragamo, and because of a tackle-to-tackle ferocity that had the Pittsburgh defense on its heels much of the afternoon.

But the Steelers aren't exactly virgins in this type of warfare, and when they needed great plays they got them—two Terry Bradshaw-to-John Stallworth passes worth 118 yards in the fourth quarter and an interception by Jack Lambert on his own 14 that cut off the Rams with 5:24 left and Pittsburgh ahead 24–19. The Steelers routinely make great plays, and when you get all excited about those feats, they'll look at you and say things like: "I've made better catches in Super Bowls . . . a couple of one-handers one time" (Stallworth); or "It's part of our basic coverage . . . it's on the films" (Lambert); or "I really didn't think it would work . . . I hadn't been completing it in practice" (Bradshaw).

Which is why the Steelers have won four Super Bowl rings in the last six years, and why Joe Greene can say, "This game was an invitation engraved in gold."

"An invitation to what?" someone asked, on cue.

"To immortality."

As the Steelers discovered, however, it's getting tougher and tougher to stay on top. The Rams were supposed to lie down under Ferragamo, who was making only his eighth start but who led a very spirited team. Los Angeles was ahead 19–17 late in the third quarter, when a significant thing happened. The Rams had intercepted Bradshaw—for the third time—at the L.A. four-yard line, and Wendell Tyler had broken one

for 13 yards, out to the 17. Then the whistle blew to end the quarter, and the next thing you knew, the Rams were sprinting for the other end of the field.

"We talked about doing it," said left tackle Doug France. "It was to let them know we were ready to go. We had 83 yards to cover, and we had to show them we had the strength to do it. We were saying, 'Hey, we're not that tired.' "

If Hollywood, not Pasadena, had hosted XIV, the Rams would have driven those 83 yards and put the game away, and the losingest team—9–7 in the regular season—to reach a Super Bowl would have tasted the bubbly. But what happened was that the Rams ran three plays, gained six yards and punted. The Steelers got the ball on their 25. First-and-10: Jack Reynolds stuffs Franco Harris after a couple of yards. Second-and-eight: Sidney Thornton drops a screen pass. Third-and-eight at the Pittsburgh 27 and what to do? Coach

Chuck Noll sent in the play: 60 Prevent Slot Hook and Go. A pass to Stallworth, the slot receiver, who would make a little hitch inside and then take off.

There are not many ways a human can throw a football better than Bradshaw did to Stallworth on that play. Stallworth got inside Rod Perry, the cornerback, and behind Dave Elmendorf, the strong safety, and took it 73 yards for a 24–19 Pittsburgh lead. Two series later Stallworth did it again—45 yards on the same play. It set up Harris's one-yard touchdown run.

Emotions were running high in the Rams' dressing room after the game. In a corner Ferragamo attempted to describe what it had been like to face 103,985 fans and 11 Steelers in his first Super Bowl. "I tried audibling one time at the noisy end of the field," he said. "No one heard me. I was a little leery about audibling after that. There was a 30-second clock, but it was kind of concealed. It was tough to see. . . . It just hurts to know you're that good and you can't win it. It's a hurting feeling inside."

"We gave it everything we had, we went out there with everything in our hearts," Dennis Harrah, the L.A. right guard, was saying. "We picked up all their stunts, all their defensive-line games. I think we surprised them with our guts and determination." He was looking at the floor. When he looked up, you could see he was crying. "I'm sorry, but I just can't talk about it anymore," he said.

The final chapter is that the Steelers' big-play people—Bradshaw, Lambert, Lynn Swann, Stallworth, the guys who had done it so many times before—rose up one more time. "The real fact," Greene said, "was that we just had too many good football players. It had to show today because the Rams were so high emotionally and they were executing so well.

"You can't beat talent," Greene said. ∎

Swaggerin' Stallworth averaged 40.3 yards a catch.

Photograph by John Iacono

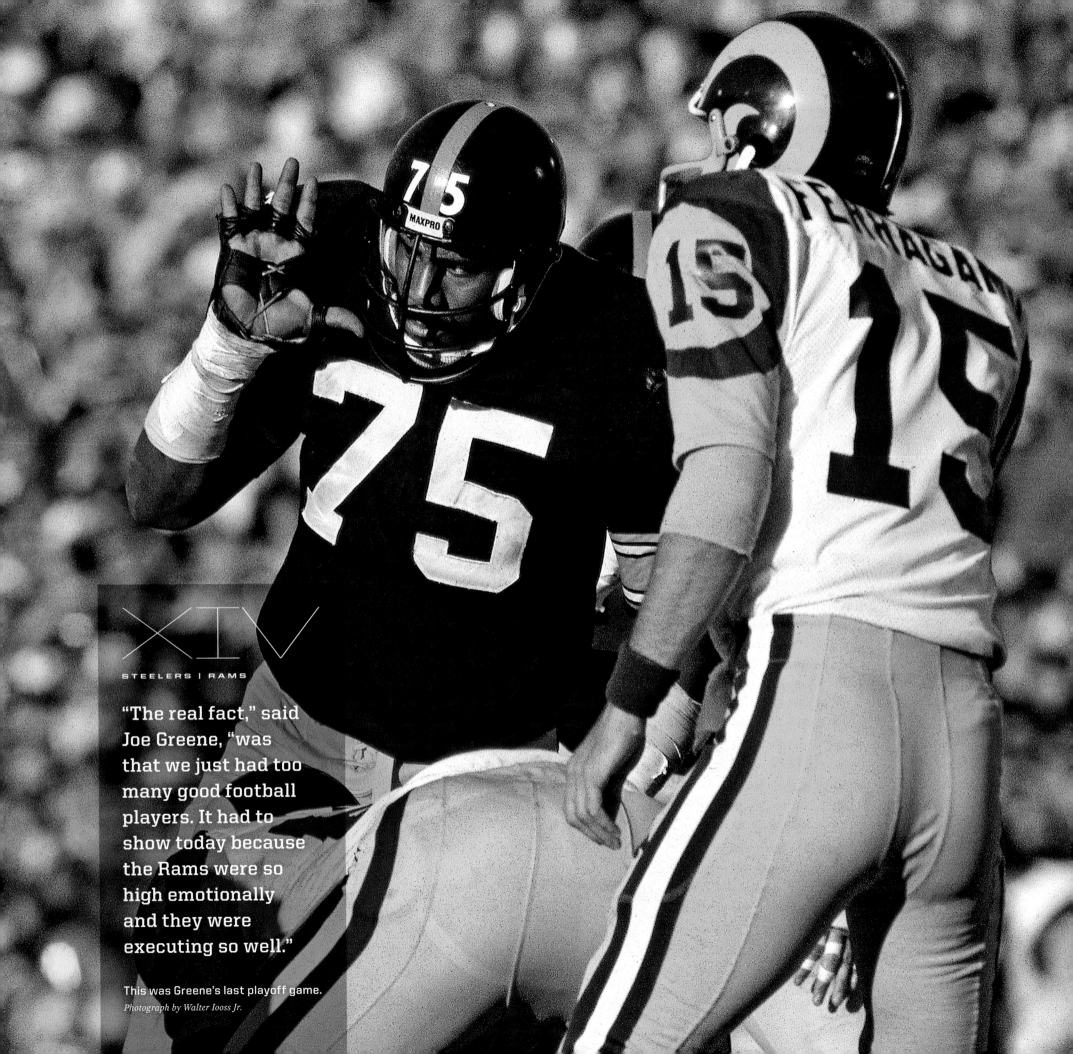

XIV

STEELERS | RAMS

"The real fact," said Joe Greene, "was that we just had too many good football players. It had to show today because the Rams were so high emotionally and they were executing so well."

This was Greene's last playoff game.
Photograph by Walter Iooss Jr.

BY Donnie Shell

Steelers Safety

You never feel like favorites. Everybody said we were such a great team, but you have to really go out and prove yourself. None of us was surprised by the close score in the Super Bowl because we had seen the Rams hit their stride during the playoffs and they were playing well.

Like the rest of the season, this game came down to making plays. John Stallworth had that long touchdown catch when he was double covered. I later worked with the Panthers and Rod Perry, the Rams' corner on that play, was the secondary coach there, so I asked him about the play. He said, "Man, that was the worst play ever. I was on the cover of SPORTS ILLUSTRATED for the wrong reasons." But for me that play was great to watch—Terry Bradshaw threw an outstanding pass. Then Jack Lambert sealed it with an interception a little later on. There wasn't ever a whole lot of celebration in the Steelers' locker room, but there was a sense of satisfaction because we had accomplished what we had set out to do.

You look back on it and you see how difficult it was to accomplish what we did. When you're playing and going through it, you don't see it. But now you see four out of six years and it's *Wow!* Before the game, the media was saying you guys are this, you guys are that, you guys are the greatest team ever. We weren't drinking the Kool-Aid during the week. But after the game, I said, "You guys can write that now."

BY Jack Youngblood

Rams Defensive End

This was one of the most trying times of my entire 14-year career. Getting up to speed to play and be captain of your football team in the NFC championship game and the Super Bowl is hard when you're gimping around with a broken leg. I had been injured a little bit here and there over the years, but nothing to that extent. Preparing was difficult, but I was determined to go.

The doctors looked at me [after I fractured my fibula in the first playoff game] and went, "You're crazy." I said, "Tell me something I don't know." They just shook their heads. We had a piece of plastic that we covered it with. We taped it up. I had the trust of the coaches that if I was a detriment to the defense I'd take myself out.

I look back and know there were moments where I was just that half a step off that could have been the difference. One play was the long ball Terry Bradshaw threw to John Stallworth. I was right there—but not there. That haunts you.

We didn't accomplish all we wanted to, but we got very, very close. And that was rewarding in itself because we had been so close to the Super Bowl so many other times. We realized we were a pretty good little football team and we could play with anybody.

For the fourth time the Steelers' No. 12 was No. 1.
Photograph by Walter Iooss Jr.

SUPER BOWL XV

January 25, 1981
Superdome, New Orleans

HEAD COACHES
TOM FLORES Raiders | DICK VERMEIL Eagles

OAKLAND
RAIDERS | 27

PHILADELPHIA
EAGLES | 10

Five days before the game U.S. hostages were released from Iran after 444 days.

Photograph by John Iacono

THE ROWDY Raiders, who put the wild in Wild Card, made history as the first non-division-winner to lift the Lombardi Trophy. Oakland didn't dominate, but it did deliver on team owner Al Davis's famous mandate: They just won, baby.

DOME

Outside: balmy 73°

POINT SPREAD

Eagles by 3

TIME OF GAME

3:13

TV AUDIENCE

68.3 million

Branch opened the scoring with this first-quarter touchdown catch.

Photograph by Tony Triolo

Rod Martin's interception and 17-yard return blunted the Eagles' opening drive, but he was just getting started.

Photograph by Tony Triolo

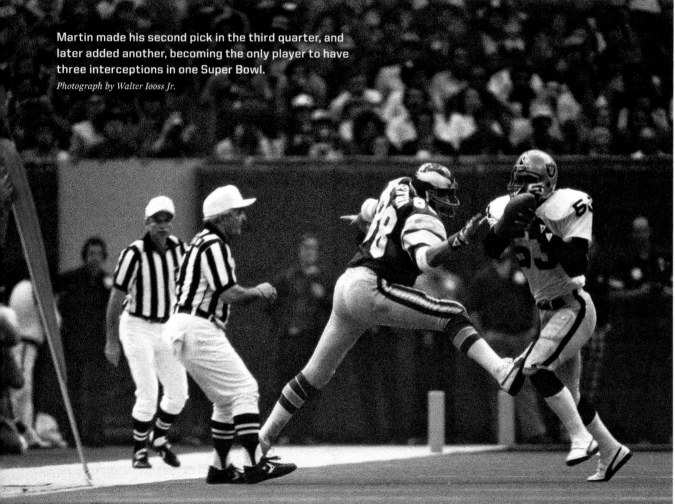

Martin made his second pick in the third quarter, and later added another, becoming the only player to have three interceptions in one Super Bowl.

Photograph by Walter Iooss Jr.

JUST THE FACTS

Statistical Leaders

Rushing MARK VAN EEGHEN (OAK) 19 carries, 80 yds

Passing JIM PLUNKETT (OAK) 13 of 21, 261 yds, 3 TDs

Receiving KENNY KING (OAK) 2 catches, 93 yds, 1 TD

MVP JIM PLUNKETT Raiders Quarterback

The Ring
The 19 small diamonds in the football crest represent the 19 games Oakland played to make it to Super Bowl XV

Anthem Performer
Helen O'Connell

Halftime Performers
Southern University Marching Band with Helen O'Connell

Attendance 76,135

Ticket Price $40

Behind the Scenes

The Raiders left their mark with the sheer number of peanuts they consumed on the sideline during the game. As one league official marveled, "The place was littered with shells."

They Said It

"If Tom Flores sent home every guy on his football team who screwed up, he'd be the only guy on the sideline."
— Raiders guard GENE UPSHAW on Eagles coach Dick Vermeil's disciplining of his team

You Hockey Puck

Seeking to loosen up the team, Eagles owner Leonard Tose brought insult comic Don Rickles into the locker room two hours before kickoff. Said QB Ron Jaworski: "I don't remember one damn joke."

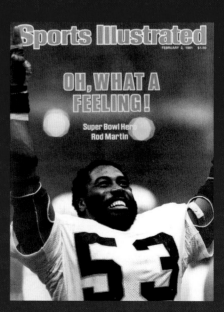

Excerpted from **SPORTS ILLUSTRATED** *February 2, 1981*

LOOSE AND DANGEROUS

Oakland's fierce band of misfits swaggered in and took control | BY PAUL ZIMMERMAN

THEIR FANS LOVE THEM BUT hate their owner. Their emblem is a guy with a patch over one eye and two swords sticking out of his head. During the week before the Raiders beat the Eagles 27–10 in Super Bowl XV, their coach collected $15,000 in fines. "Actually, that's a conservative figure," said their captain, Gene Upshaw, the left guard. "We're not a bunch of choirboys and Boy Scouts. They say we're the Halfway House of the NFL. Well, we live up to that image." Here Upshaw paused in his postgame oration for dramatic emphasis, and a smile split his face. "Every chance we get."

The Raiders are different all right. When Eagles coach Dick Vermeil sits down with his projector and cans of film in the still hours of some future night, there will come a time when he'll rub his tired eyes and ask himself, "How did they do it? We covered all the angles. We worked on everything—man, did we work. We attacked that soft zone they used, threw underneath it and moved the ball on them. We used the same pass-rush scheme that got us eight sacks when we beat them 10–7 in Philly in November. How did it happen? We're a team of character, of dedication, and we lost big in our biggest game ever. To a bunch of loose hangers like that. How?"

It starts with the offensive line, the heart and soul of the Raiders, though it doesn't really fit the Oakland image. No refugees there. Every one of the front five was a high draft choice: two No. 1s, a No. 3, two No. 4s. Proud people, solid citizens, three with Pro Bowl credentials. They smile and shake their heads when the wilder guys do a number, but they're basically serious people—guards Mickey Marvin and Upshaw, tackles Art Shell and Henry Lawrence, center Dave Dalby—and in November the Eagles had embarrassed them and dusted their quarterback eight times.

"Watch this game carefully," Lawrence had said when the Raiders arrived in New Orleans. "Last time they did things to us that they won't do this time. They stopped our running, but they won't do it Sunday. They won't get to Plunkett."

In the Super Bowl, the Raiders running game wasn't overpowering—117 yards on 34 carries—but it was solid enough, particularly on first down, to set up enough short-yardage and medium-yardage situations to keep the Eagles guessing, to keep their nickel defense off the field. The Raiders picked up 68 yards on 15 first-down rushing plays, a 4.5 average.

Then there was the pass protection. It kept the Oakland QB comfortable, gave him the assurance he could throw deep. Plunkett had to scramble a few times and his scrambles bought time, screwed up the defense and got him out of trouble. When Plunkett hit Cliff Branch for the first touchdown of the game, a two-yarder, he set it up by stepping up into the pocket, freezing Herman Edwards, the cornerback, and John Bunting, the linebacker, and allowing Branch to bend his pattern back toward Plunkett and get open. Plunkett set up his next TD, an 80-yarder to Kenny King, with a scramble to his left, and a quick decision—should he go to his primary receiver, Bob Chandler, on a deep crossing pattern, or should he hit King, who was 19 yards down the left sideline, covered by Edwards? He chose King. Edwards leaped for the interception and missed, and it was a footrace. Now the Raiders were up 14–0 in the first quarter; they were in command.

Upshaw had been the star of the midweek practices, especially the Wednesday workout which, free safety Burgess Owens said, "was so intense and vicious that I thought [coach] Tom [Flores] would have to call it off." Wednesday was defense day, and Upshaw got into a brief punch-up with defensive end Dave Browning. "It always involves punches," Upshaw said. "These are the Raiders, remember?"

Thursday was offense day, and this time Upshaw's sparring partner was Phil Livingston, a jayvee de-

Vermeil wasn't happy, yet he honored Plunkett's play.

Photograph by Manny Millan

fensive tackle. "Go hard," Raiders owner Al Davis told the rookie. "Make him work."

"I tried to kick him," Upshaw said. "I don't want to say where, but all the regulars got mad at me because the kid had just gotten married. I apologized."

The solid part of the Raiders' operation was the pass-catch game, and Plunkett completed his comeback season. Branch, who'd been socked with a $1,000 fine for missing practice eight days before the Super Bowl, wound up with five catches, two for touchdowns. "My horoscope always reads: Miss practice and have a good game," Branch said afterward, enjoying the moment immensely.

Said Upshaw: "I asked Flores, 'Hey, where does all that [fine] money go?' He said, 'To me.' By the end of the week he had enough for a new BMW. . . . Yeah, we had guys break curfew this week, but when that door opened today we were ready to play." ∎

BY **Jim Plunkett**

Raiders Quarterback

I had struggled the prior 10 years, so getting to the Super Bowl was a bit of redemption. I was not going to do anything to hurt our chances. I had that planted in my mind: no mistakes, follow the game plan, don't put us in a bad position.

After going to Bourbon Street on Monday, the first night we arrived, I literally locked myself in my room. I tacked a big sheet to my wall and using my projector I went over every piece of film the Raiders staff had put together, making sure that on every situation that came up, I knew exactly where to go with the football. I looked for every advantage, from a safety cheating over or a cornerback taking an inside position, knowing that if he does it's probably a blitz. By the time the second half rolled around, we were just in complete control. At that point it pretty much didn't matter what I called. Everything was working.

When it was over, Tom [Flores] gave his speech, Mr. Davis came in and gave his speech. The hostages had been freed from Iran a few days earlier and there was a big yellow bow tied around the Superdome. It was euphoric. A friend of mine from Stanford [where Plunkett went to school] rented out a two-story restaurant and lounge to celebrate. I had friends and family from California.

It was a hell of a trip for me. You get reenergized, thinking, Maybe I can do this again. You start thinking all these positive things after having been down for a long time. Then as you get older, you reflect and you realize, Son of a gun, I did it.

Mark van Eeghen ground out 4.2 yards a carry and won his second Raiders ring.

Photograph by Walter Iooss Jr.

The Raiders pass protection kept Plunkett comfortable in the pocket, gave him the assurance he could throw deep when he wanted to.

Plunkett was sacked only once all game—on a scramble, when he dived just short of the line of scrimmage.

Photograph by Tony Triolo

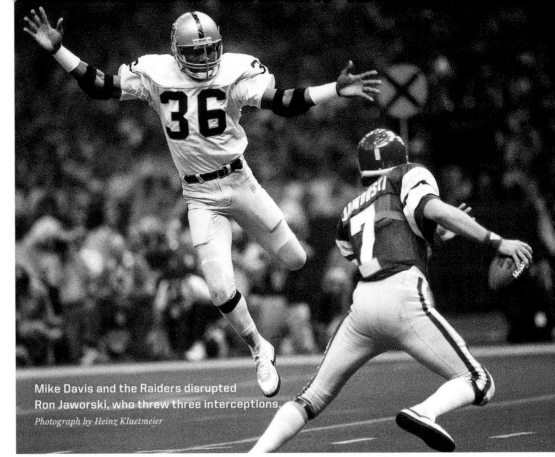

Mike Davis and the Raiders disrupted Ron Jaworski, who threw three interceptions.
Photograph by Heinz Kluetmeier

THE WAY IT WAS

BY Claude Humphrey

Eagles Defensive End

We knew we needed to get pressure on Jim Plunkett. I was a designated pass rusher. During the first quarter of the game, the defense never got him in an obvious passing situation, so I spent a lot of time standing on the sidelines. I didn't get into the game until late in the first quarter. Then later in the final quarter, I got a roughing the passer penalty. I disagreed. Now, don't get me wrong: I wouldn't hesitate to rough the passer. I just didn't think I did it that time. Then the official threw the flag right at me. I picked it up and threw it back at him. I just kind of lost it. All the other frustrations that I was feeling, to get that call on me—it was just all those things exploding inside me. Of course, I later apologized to the officials.

Their defense played fantastic against our offense. It was no contest. Rod Martin had a hell of a day. It was like he was in [quarterback Ron] Jaworski's pocket or he was lining up in our huddle. They kept scoring on us and Martin kept intercepting the ball and our defense kept running out on the field. It became a cycle. It seemed like there was nothing we could do. I never felt so helpless.

Afterward, I went straight to the locker room. I didn't even get my jersey from the game, which is bad. I should have kept it. But I packed all that stuff up and just got out of the locker room as quickly as possible and went home. I went two years before I looked at the game film. I didn't want to see it. It killed me.

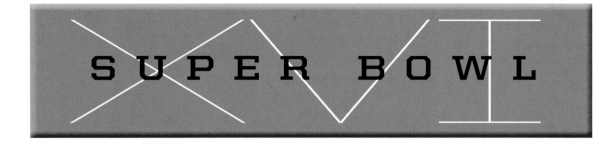

SUPER BOWL XVI

January 24, 1982
Silverdome, Pontiac, Mich.

HEAD COACHES
BILL WALSH 49ers | FORREST GREGG Bengals

SAN FRANCISCO
49ERS | 26

CINCINNATI
BENGALS | 21

THEY WERE both Big Game newbies, each team just a year removed from having posted a losing record. The Bengals had experience and talent, but for the young 49ers, and their coach and quarterback, a football revolution was afoot.

DOME	POINT SPREAD	TIME OF GAME	TV AUDIENCE

Outside: 5°, snow	49ers by 1	3:21	85.2 million

After arriving late due to bus trouble, Montana produced two TDs with no turnovers.

Photograph by Walter Iooss Jr.

114

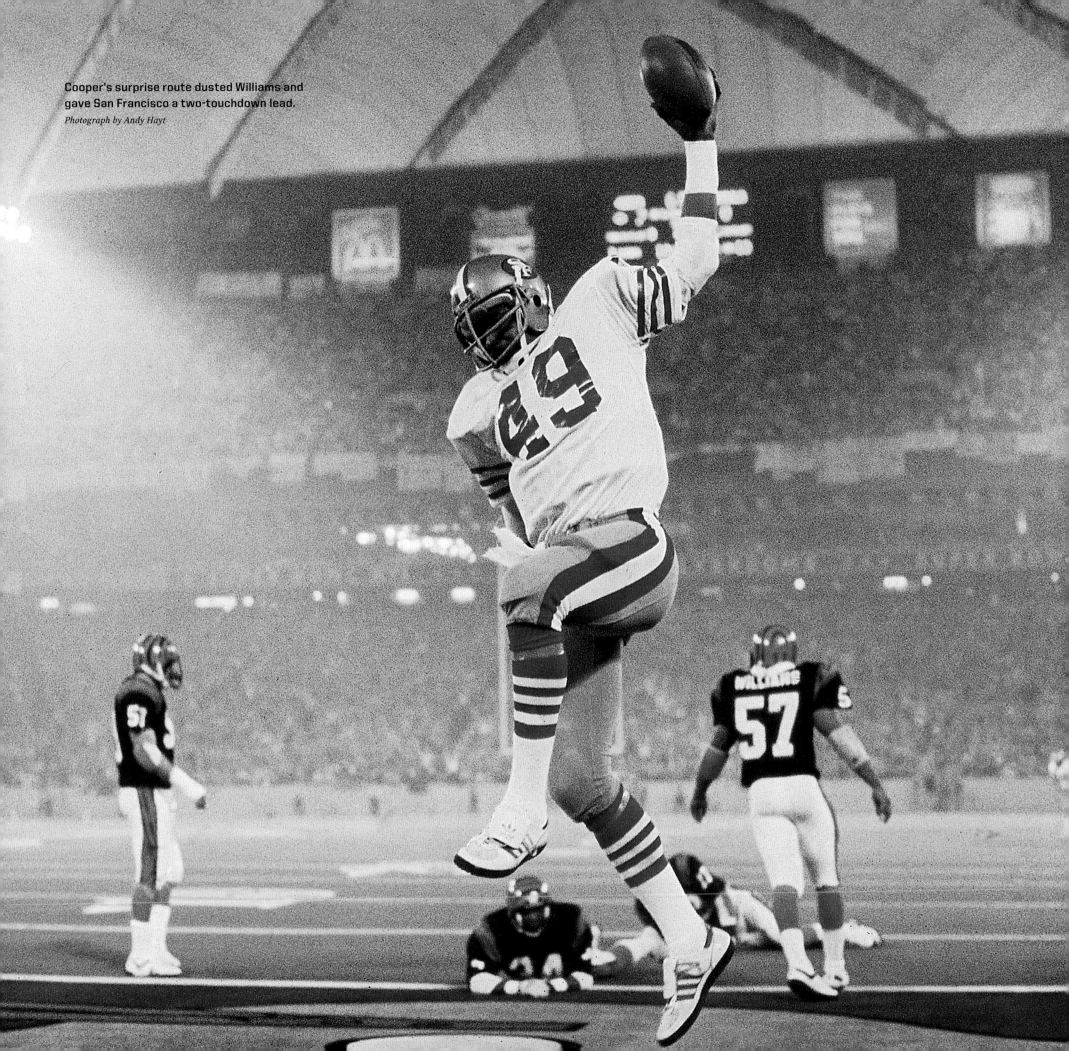

Cooper's surprise route dusted Williams and gave San Francisco a two-touchdown lead.

Photograph by Andy Hayt

Excerpted from **SPORTS ILLUSTRATED** *February 1, 1982*

BIG BAG OF TRICKS

With their innovative ways, the 49ers confounded Cincinnati | BY PAUL ZIMMERMAN

THESE ARE SOME OF THE NEW plays the 49ers put in but did *not* use in Super Bowl XVI: They had an end-around pass, Dwight Clark throwing to Freddie Solomon. They had different option passes for every running back. They had a play in which Solomon throws a pass off a reverse, and they had a pitch-and-lateral, Joe Montana to Ricky Patton to Earl Cooper. They had something called a Nickel Blizzard, a safety blitz out of the nickel-back formation. What else? Oh yeah, they also had what they call a Short Yardage Triple Pass, which means sweep, reverse, pitch back and pass. . . no, wait a minute, they *did* use that, yes they did. They used it in the first half, in which they built a 20–0 lead on the way to their 26–21 win over the Bengals.

Why didn't they use that other stuff? Well, they had enough, quite enough, more than enough. How many new toys can you fit in the attic? How many newfangled things can you throw at a team without having the Competition Committee come up with another Parity Edict in the off-season. . . *O.K., Walsh, the other guys get two weeks to prepare for Super Bowl XVII, but we're giving you three days, see.*

Brother, did 49ers coach Bill Walsh throw some stuff at the Bengals. The Triple Pass, in which Montana hands to Patton who hands to Solomon who pitches back to Montana who throws downfield to tight end Charle Young, was designed for third-and-one. It made its entry on the Niners' first third-and-one of the game—in the middle of their long, exotic touchdown drive in the first quarter—picked up 14 yards and then bowed out for the day amid polite applause.

The 49ers' most significant pass, in fact the last pass they threw, was a 22-yarder to reserve flanker Mike Wilson. It got them out of a second-and-15 in the fourth quarter, when the Bengals had closed to within six points. It launched them on their way to the field goal that made the score 23–14. It was called

Sweep Pass Right, Z-Comeback and it was put in on Wednesday, four days before the game.

"I run 25 yards downfield, then I come back to about 20," Wilson said. "All year long when we showed anything 20 yards deep, it was a takeoff, a go, so the cornerback [Louis Breeden] figured I'd keep on going."

Simple, see. Just do something you never did before, or maybe once, a long time ago, and then forgot. Like the play in the second quarter that got San Francisco its second touchdown and ended a 92-yard drive, longest in Super Bowl history. This was an 11-yard pass to Cooper, the fullback, a particular bit of nastiness designed to burn Reggie Williams, the Bengals' right outside linebacker.

Cooper had already run for two significant gains—11 and 14 yards—and this time he started up the middle, but Montana faked the handoff and Cooper took a left at the stop sign and headed for the expressway. Solomon and Mike Shuman, the wide receivers out to the left, had swooped inside, and Cooper dipped out behind them, getting an extra step on poor Williams, who'd bitten for the fake up the middle. Six points.

And when had this play, named Fox-Two Special, been seen? Only once before, in 1980, against the Patriots. It had gone for a touchdown then, too. It was used only once on Sunday. Why repeat? Got a million of 'em, fellas.

"We didn't know what to expect, given the mentality of their coach," Williams said afterward. "Plus, he had that extra week to prepare."

Walsh and Ray Wersching, the 49ers kicker, also concocted a new style of kickoff, a hard squibber designed for the Silverdome's AstroTurf, which is seven years old and rock-hard. The squibber was bobbled twice by the Bengals, both times inside their five-yard line. The 49ers recovered the second one, setting up a field goal with five seconds left in the first half. The hard squib was put in on Tuesday.

"It was," said the Bengals' Archie Griffin, who fumbled the last one, "something we didn't expect."

During the week, Montana was asked if he ever worried about Walsh's running out of new things to come up with, new tricks, new gimmicks. "I was thinking about that the other day," Montana said. "But then I figured Bill would probably just start all over again and find things that worked in high school or junior high. [On Sunday], we were afraid we were going to get a new play on our way to the game while our bus was stopped at the bottom of the hill."

On Monday the 49ers were to enjoy a motorcade through San Francisco, even the six Pro Bowl players who were supposed to be in Hawaii for NFC coach John McKay's Monday-night meeting. Sorry, league, we've got a better thing going here in San Francisco.

"It's only McKay's offense, anyway," said guard Randy Cross, a UCLA grad. "If guys from USC can learn it, how complicated can it be? We're used to something a little more interesting." ∎

Rookie Eric Wright took on Cris Collinsworth.

Photograph by Richard Mackson

JUST THE FACTS

Statistical Leaders

Rushing RICKY PATTON (SF) 17 carries, 55 yds

Passing KEN ANDERSON (CIN) 25 of 34, 302 yds, 2 TDs

Receiving DAN ROSS (CIN) 11 catches, 104 yds, 2 TDs

MVP JOE MONTANA 49ers Quarterback

The Ring
90-point center diamond and modeled after Jets' SB III ring

Anthem Performer
Diana Ross

Halftime Performer
Up With People

Attendance 81,260

Ticket Price $40

Behind the Scenes

Bill Walsh pleaded with San Francisco officials not to hold a victory parade, figuring the Bay Area populace was too sophisticated for such revelry. Walsh was shocked (happily so) to see tens of thousands of fans packed along the parade route, in the city's largest public rally since the end of World War II.

They Said It

"I snapped my chin strap, knocked the screws loose from my face bar. My nose was bleeding. It was the highlight of my life."

—49ers linebacker DAN BUNZ on the team's goal-line stand

Been There, Done That

The day after the game, Joe Montana appeared on *Good Morning America*. His interviewer? Jim Plunkett, MVP of Super Bowl XV.

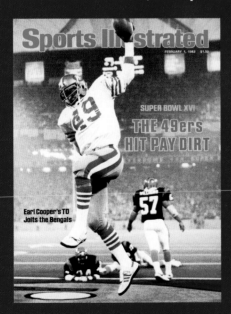

Patton (32) to Solomon (88) to Montana, and then a pass downfield to Young. The Triple Pass made one, successful, appearance.

Photographs by Tony Triolo

BY Fred Dean

49ers Defensive End

When I was with the Chargers and we would get in the playoffs, it was intense. The coaches really tensed up. But with the 49ers, Bill Walsh was different. When we first got to Detroit, it was cold and icy. Coach Walsh was standing outside the hotel in one of the bellman's uniforms and he was taking people's luggage. In doing that, he made it an enjoyable moment. If he was tense about the game, he wasn't showing it. He seemed to be relaxed. And it was reflected in how the players played. We were loose. Our feeling was, let's go out and have fun.

We jumped on them with a 20–0 lead in the first half. I know my attitude—and it was probably the same for a lot of other players—was to get kind of relaxed in that position. You feel like you're being so dominant. After halftime, they went to throwing the short passes and moved the ball more. On our goal line stand in the third quarter, they didn't run to my side, but it was a pleasure to watch the guys work. All the holes were filled and the center couldn't get on Jack Reynolds, so he was able to shoot that gap. Danny Bunz, he really made a play—both times. When it came to the bottom line, we had the people needed to execute.

When Cincinnati scored its second touchdown, things got tough for a minute. But we moved the ball for a field goal, and then Eric Wright's interception put us in position to kick another one. There were always big plays being made. When Dwight Clark recovered the onside kick, I could honestly say, "This is over." It was just a matter of the clock ticking down. It was about time to celebrate.

BY Ken Anderson

Bengals Quarterback

The coaches didn't say a whole lot to us at halftime. And as I remember—though when you get to be my age, you tend to forget a lot of things—security came through the locker room at halftime with bomb-sniffing dogs. Maybe it was the scent of the spare jerseys we had in our trunk. After getting shut out the first half, the dogs just weren't a big deal to us. The coaches kind of let us stew on our own. Then we went out and made a few plays in the second half.

That was the first Super Bowl where the losing team had more touchdowns and more total yards than the winner. We moved the ball. You just can't turn it over four times and expect to win. When we cut their lead to five points with 16 seconds left, it was too little too late. We had moved it down the field, but unfortunately it took some time to do it.

Once they recovered the onside kick, you knew it was over. Done. You realize it's the biggest game of your life and it's the most disappointing. My six-year-old son, Matt, was behind the bench. He was holding my hand as we were walking and there were so many people that he got scared and I ended up carrying him off. We got into the locker room and it was real quiet. I'm undressing. Finally I turn to my son—he was the only kid in there—and I said, "Well, Matt, that was a tough day. What'd you think?" And his eyes got real bright and he said, "Dad, it was the best halftime show I've ever seen." At least that brought a smile to my face.

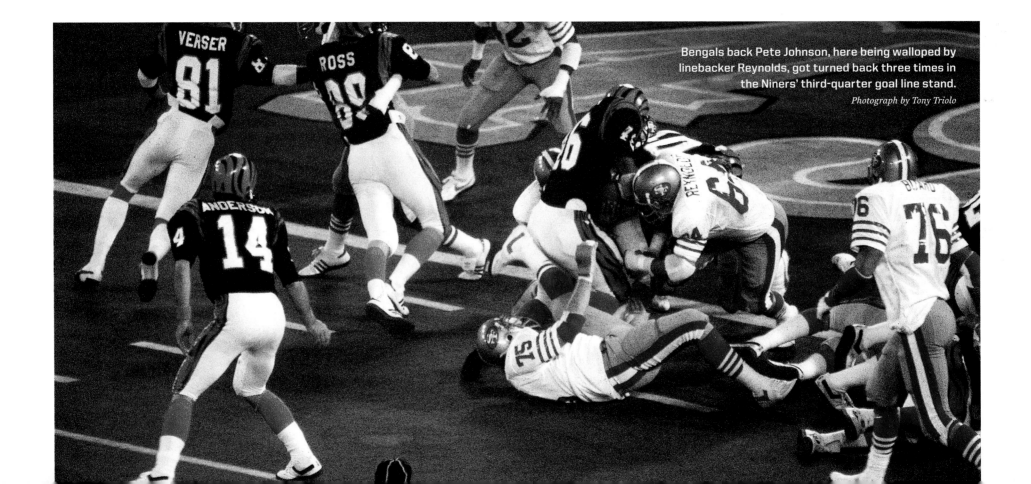

Bengals back Pete Johnson, here being walloped by linebacker Reynolds, got turned back three times in the Niners' third-quarter goal line stand.
Photograph by Tony Triolo

"We're a team of character," said 49ers coach Bill Walsh. "You could see it in our goal line stand."

After stopping the Bengals on fourth down at the one, the Niners exulted.
Photograph by Walter Iooss Jr.

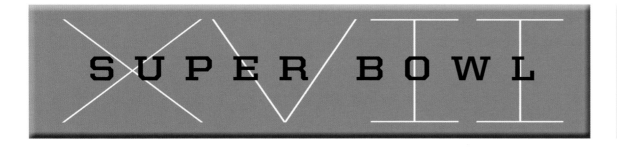

SUPER BOWL XVII

January 30, 1983
Rose Bowl, Pasadena

HEAD COACHES
JOE GIBBS Redskins | DON SHULA Dolphins

WASHINGTON REDSKINS | 27

MIAMI DOLPHINS | 17

At the Rose Bowl, loyalties were quite apparent—as well as clearly divided.

Photograph by George Tiedemann/GT Images

IN A strike-shortened year the Redskins went 8–1, then to a big-game rematch: same teams, same state as Supe VII. Back then, Miami closed a perfect season. This time Washington's second-half surge led to its first Super Bowl title.

WEATHER	POINT SPREAD	TIME OF GAME	TV AUDIENCE

61°, sunny	Dolphins by 3	3:13	81.8 million

He's a good man: Charlie Brown had six catches for Washington, including this fourth-quarter touchdown that sealed the scoring.

Photograph by Jerry Wachter

Theismann ran the game plan splendidly
and threw well enough to keep the
Dolphins' defense a few steps behind.

Photograph by Ronald C. Modra

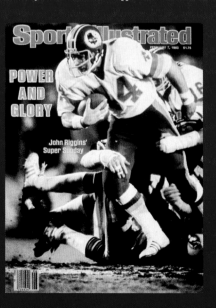

Excerpted from **SPORTS ILLUSTRATED** *January 31, 1983*

READY TO RUMBLE

Big John Riggins carried the Redskins in the game of his life | BY PAUL ZIMMERMAN

SUPER BOWL XVII—THE game, the week preceding it and its aftermath—was molded in the image of John Riggins. It bore his stamp from Tuesday Picture Day, when the Redskins fullback implacably stared out over his sea of questioners, his eyes fixed on a distant point somewhere between Anaheim and the California coast, and it carried his signature after the game when he stood on a platform in the press tent and acknowledged his selection as MVP after Washington had knocked off Miami 27–17.

What he had done on that long day's journey into night was grab modern NFL football by the scruff of the neck and toss it a few decades back into a simpler era—big guy running behind bigger guys blocking.

His numbers: 38 carries for 166 yards, one catch for 15. The entire Miami offense consisted of 47 plays for 176 yards. Both of the Riggins rushing figures were Super Bowl records; the carries set a personal mark.

He broke the 43-yard touchdown run that gave the Redskins the lead, at 20–17, in the fourth quarter, and he carried on the first five plays on their next drive and on eight of the 12 snaps overall as they put the game away. And he did all this against a Dolphins defense that was supposedly set up to stop him.

Riggins had already made sure folks knew he was around during the pre-Super Bowl week: wearing camouflage pants with an elephant gun belt buckle, he wowed a packed ballroom at the Wednesday media session. He stopped the show again on Thursday, resplendent in white tie, top hat and tails. On Friday night at Redskins owner Jack Kent Cooke's party, Riggins drew a standing ovation.

The game's crucial drive started on the Skins' 46 with 11:43 left and Miami up 17–13. Riggins hit the left side for seven yards, over the blocks of 295-pound tackle Joe Jacoby and 242-pound tight end Don Warren. Then Dolphins end Kim Bokamper stopped Riggins

Riggins sat down for air during his record-setting day.

Photograph by John Iacono

after a yard gain, and Clarence Harmon carried for a yard. Facing a fourth-and-one, Miami called timeout.

"I could tell the Dolphins were tired," Jacoby said of the Miami defense. "I could see by their breathing how tired they were, the way their chests were heaving and the steam was coming off them."

The Skins called 70-Chip, Riggins off the left side, behind the short-yardage blocking back, a chunky, little 214-pounder named Otis Wonsley, and the 240-pound extra tight end, Clint Didier. It broke cleanly. The only Dolphin who had a shot at Riggins, cornerback Don McNeal, slipped and could only attempt an arm tackle. At the end of the 43-yard run Riggins was pulling away from safety Glenn Blackwood, an astounding show of speed by a 230-pounder on his 30th carry of the day.

There was a story making the rounds about how Riggins approached Washington coach Joe Gibbs before the playoffs. "I need the ball," he told Gibbs. "You've

got it," Gibbs said. The result was 136 carries for 610 yards, ending in his iron-man stint in Supe XVII.

If you'd looked carefully, you could've seen it coming. In Riggins's eight regular-season games—he missed one with a thigh bruise—he averaged 22 carries, including two in which he had more than 30. Never in his 10 previous NFL seasons had he run so much.

There were other things different about him too. He'd come into the league as a loose kid. He laughed a lot. Once he painted his toenails green before a game. On draft day, when a writer asked him to recount his No. 1 sports thrill, he said, "Watching my neighbor's pigs being born." In 1973 he held out during the preseason, then got a Mohawk and finally shaved his head completely. His explanations were imaginative and never disappointing. The best? "In the off-season I got to observe quite a number of freaks, firsthand. I always wondered what it would be like to be treated like one of them. Well, this is the way I found out."

The sense of humor is still there and during his postgame press conference, when someone asked him, "Are you doing it any better now?" Riggins said, "I don't know; you'll have to ask my wife."

He smiled when asked if it had worried him to go into a game with so much expected of him. "I was camping one night with a fella named Glenn Jenkins in Centralia, Kansas," he said. "I could hear the coyotes howling, and they sounded like they were getting mighty close. I asked Glenn if he felt nervous, and he said, 'I've probably killed 200 of them. It doesn't exactly raise the hair on the back of my neck.' It's like NFL games. I've probably gone through 130 of them, and they don't exactly raise the hair on the back of my neck."

In the press room there was talk of how Gibbs had in a three-week series beaten coaching legends Bud Grant, Tom Landry and Don Shula. Then someone asked: "What about Riggins, Coach?" There was no hesitation. "What sets John Riggins apart," Gibbs said, "is a champion's heart." ■

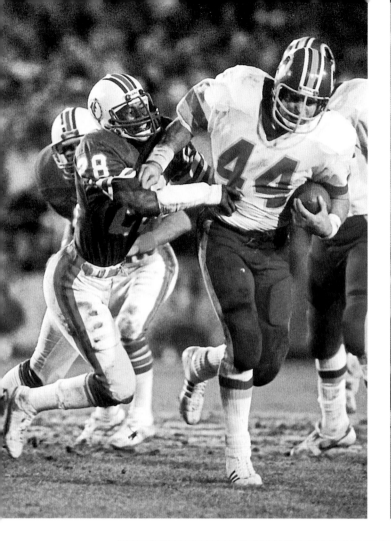

Riggins broke to the left, pushed aside McNeal and was gone.

Photographs by Ronald C. Modra (top, 2) and Tony Tomsic

BY Joe Theismann

Redskins Quarterback

During introductions I kept thinking to myself: 'Don't embarrass yourself. You can't trip. You can't fall.' So when I got to the goal line, I sort of hopped over—because I didn't want the goal line to trip me.

Joe Gibbs told us we had to run the football. He said if we were within three or seven into the fourth quarter, we would be able to win the game. They were relatively small upfront; they had a quicker defense rather than a big defense. We felt if we could get them into the fourth quarter, we could wear them down.

On John Riggins's big run, I had the perfect seat. I'll never forget the hole opening. I'm thinking, *Yeah, John's got the first down.* Then Don McNeal comes to tackle him and it looked like hot butter on a skillet. McNeal just slid down off of him. That's the power John ran with.

At the end of the game, I knelt in the huddle and looked at the guys and said, "Super Bowl–winning formation on two." I had to fight back the emotions, I was getting choked up. Two weeks after the game, I got hold of my dad and said, "You and I are going to watch this game together. I'm going to tell you what I was thinking on every play." I put the film on and I had no clue. Then we ran a reverse and I tried to throw a block and got kicked in the head and suddenly everything came back to me. I guess I didn't realize how emotionally involved I was. I always laugh at anyone saying the Super Bowl is just another game. It really isn't.

BY Bob Baumhower

Dolphins Nosetackle

Their philosophy was a lot like ours. They liked to run the ball and had a strong defense. We felt like we had to put Theismann into long-yardage situations and make him throw. Actually, we did a pretty darn good job of that for a period of time. Our defensive coordinator, Bill Arnsparger, was an absolute genius. But I've got to hand it to the Redskins. They came out with some formations that made us have to think a little bit.

Going into the fourth quarter, the game was still in hand. I remember that fourth-and-one where John Riggins bounced outside and ran for a touchdown. I think we played it pretty darn well at the point of attack. And Riggins, who's a big dude, he bounced it outside and was able to get it into the end zone. You can do a good job at the point of attack, but if you don't keep it contained, you're going to get burned. That was the turning point.

You don't forget those feelings of coming up short. It doesn't leave you. I don't know whether you call them dreams or nightmares, but you have thoughts all over the place about what you could have done. I used to wear my AFC Championship ring. It said SUPER BOWL on the side, a really nice ring. Then I was in the elevator with Lester Hayes from the Raiders at the Pro Bowl. He looked at it and said, "Oh, you got one of those losers' rings, huh?" I've never worn that ring since.

After a second-quarter touchdown catch by Alvin Garrett (89)—one of three Washington TDs on the day—a fun bunch of Redskins had something to celebrate.

Photograph by Walter Iooss Jr.

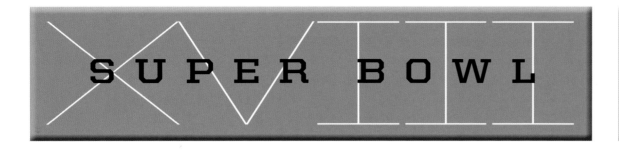

SUPER BOWL XVIII

January 22, 1984
Tampa Stadium, Tampa

HEAD COACHES
TOM FLORES Raiders | JOE GIBBS Redskins

LOS ANGELES
RAIDERS | 38

WASHINGTON
REDSKINS | 9

A hands-on owner, Davis believed he had assembled the best Raiders team ever.

Photograph by Richard Mackson

THE REDSKINS were the defending champs: 16-2 on the year, with a staunch run defense and a razzling, dazzling offense. No wonder they seemed poised to repeat. The no-nonsense Raiders, though, were having none of it.

WEATHER

68°, partly cloudy

POINT SPREAD

Redskins by 2

TIME OF GAME

3:31

TV AUDIENCE

77.6 million

The dynamic Allen, here breaking off a 74-yard scoring run, had the Redskins in vain pursuit throughout his record-setting day.

Photograph by Manny Millan

Theismann got an eyeful from linebacker Jeff Barnes, one of six Raiders with a sack.

Photograph by Tony Tomsic

BY Matt Millen

Raiders Linebacker

We knew we were the best team out there. We were on a roll. And we knew we could probably challenge any of the teams that had played before us. We thought we were for the ages.

Washington's formula was a counter-OT and a counter-OT pass off that play action. Our main focus going in was John Riggins. Although Joe Theismann could certainly have won a game by himself, we had great confidence in Mike Haynes and Lester Hayes on the outside. We were fortunate because that's the way it worked. When they tried to run, we were all over Riggo, who, for the record, was an absolute monster. You better bring extra helmets because you're going to go through at least two of them going against that big ol' crankhead that he had. There's no one comparable to him right now in the league.

The weird thing about the game is that it was kind of a matter-of-fact win. We had our party and our families were all there and it was satisfying and all that, but the look that we gave each other was, *This is what we wanted to do from the start, and we did it.* You could just look at each other and give a nod.

That may have been the most satisfying Super Bowl I was in. My rookie year, I didn't have any idea what that was about. After four years, you realize how difficult it is to get on that stage and perform at that level. Yet intrinsically we knew it would happen. There are teams that have those years. We happened to be one.

BY Joe Jacoby

Redskins Tackle

I've tried to wipe this game out of my memory. My hat is off to the Raiders. We played them earlier in the year and it was a thriller—we came back in the fourth quarter to win. We tried to use things that were successful in that game, but you also try not to repeat too much because they're going to watch the film. We were going to try to establish the run. But their front seven was shutting us down. And their corners, Mike Haynes and Lester Hayes—they were just shutting down our receiving corps. Really, nothing was operating in the way it typically would.

Everybody brings up the interception before halftime that Jack Squirek returned for a touchdown. But I think of two other big plays. One, we had a blocked punt that they scored off. The other is the broken-field run by Marcus Allen in the third quarter. From the sidelines, that wasn't very pretty. You're seeing your defense and their pursuit. He had nowhere to run on that left sideline. He reverses field, comes back and takes it straight up the middle, basically untouched. The great runner he is, he saw the opening and picked up a couple good blocks. The rest was him, just outracing the last guy.

We had a great year. In the regular season, we lost only two games and by one point apiece. Then it comes to a crashing halt in the biggest game. They were the better team that day. We made mistakes. The reason? Who knows.

XVIII
RAIDERS | REDSKINS

"They were butchering us at the line of scrimmage," Redskins running back Joe Washington said. "They just put an old-fashioned can of whup-ass on us."

A blocked punt and recovery yielded L.A.'s first touchdown of the day.

Photograph by John Iacono

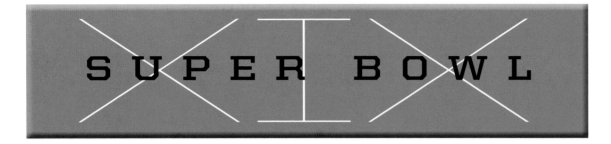

SUPER BOWL XIX

January 20, 1985
Stanford Stadium, Palo Alto, Calif.

HEAD COACHES
BILL WALSH 49ers | DON SHULA Dolphins

SAN FRANCISCO
49ERS | 38

MIAMI
DOLPHINS | 16

Bigfoot sightings: NFL mascots toed the sideline before the game.

Photograph by Peter Read Miller

NEVER HAD teams entered the big game with such fine records (a combined 33-3) and rarely had such elite and peaking quarterbacks met. This was Miami's Dan Marino versus the 49ers' Joe Montana, who continued his run to greatness.

WEATHER
53°, foggy

POINT SPREAD
49ers by 3

TIME OF GAME
3:13

TV AUDIENCE
85.5 million

There were holes in the Dolphins' defense, and Montana found them.

Photograph by Andy Hayt

JOE COOL AND COMPLETE

The 49ers' QB thrived in every way, and his teammates followed | BY PAUL ZIMMERMAN

I N THE MASS INTERVIEWS THAT GO WITH the turmoil and hype of a Super Bowl, a superathlete like the 49ers' quarterback, Joe Montana, might appear bland, even dull. But this isn't the superathlete's arena. That would be the game itself, and in Super Bowl XIX Montana transcended the hype that had relegated him to something less than a spear-carrier to Miami's dazzling Dan Marino and cut loose with his alltime performance. As a result a game that figured to go down to the final heartbeat turned into a blowout, 38–16.

Montana's sweep was so clean that after he was through, Miami coach Don Shula admitted, "It's going to be tough to live with this one.... Montana kept us off-balance the entire game. He's a great, great athlete."

Briefly this is what Montana did: He completed 24 of 35 passes for 331 yards, a Super Bowl record, and three touchdowns. He scrambled for 59 yards and

Catching and running: Tyler had 135 total yards.

Photograph by Ronald C. Modra

one TD on five carries, and he blew the game apart in its middle stages, a stretch in which the 49ers turned a three-point deficit into a 22-point lead. Montana dodged the occasional rusher who had a shot at him, threw on the run, and found holes in the Dolphins' defense—there were plenty of those—always seeming to pick the right receiver. And when he ran out of passing options he tucked the ball away and galloped.

Montana put together a complete game, in contrast to that of Marino, who was all arm and no leg, to win the battle between the NFL's best quarterbacks. When it was over, when the crowd had thinned and only Joe and his father, Joe Sr., were left in the 49ers' locker room, the younger Montana tried to put the day in perspective. "I wasn't worried about having that much to prove," he said. "I knew Marino was better, coming in, based on what he'd done this season. From a team standpoint the hype bothered me ... we all felt it. All we heard was 'Miami, Miami, how are you going to stop Miami?' Yeah, yeah, we were overlooked a little.

"As far as my own game, well, I'd have to admit it was pretty close to the best I've ever played. I didn't throw anything I didn't have confidence in."

As a team, the 49ers broke new ground. Their 537 yards of total offense, and 211 rushing yards also set Super Bowl records, so it was Marino, not Montana, who found himself trying to keep pace with an offensive adding machine. Marino's statistics look impressive, thanks to a flurry of gimme completions at the end—all told he was 29 for 50 (both records) for 318 yards—but his interceptions outnumbered his touchdowns, two to one. And he was sacked four times.

At halftime it was 28–16 San Francisco, but one of the Niners' TDs had been a gift. In the second quarter, with the score 21–10, Montana hit Freddie Solomon at the Dolphins' 13. Solomon took a step and free safety Lyle Blackwood knocked the ball loose, scooped it up and was headed for the Niners' goal line when field judge Bob Lewis ruled the pass incomplete. Bill Quinby, the

side judge, who was nearest to the play, froze and made no call. Lewis, who was behind it, did make the call, but it was the wrong one. The 49ers scored five plays later.

After the game, Shula shrugged it off. "We were dominated to the point where one play didn't make much of a difference," he said.

That was a fair and uncomplicated evaluation from a man who had grown larger than life in the hype-heavy atmosphere. The Genius Angle had gotten a lot of mileage—Shula's genius against that of Walsh—and it bothered both coaches. Another thing that had bothered Walsh was the picture being drawn of the contrasting offenses: Marino and the quick strike against the more methodical pass and run of San Francisco. "They talk about Marino's lightning-quick release, how swiftly he can complete his passes," Walsh said. "Well, we can do some of that too, you know."

Which they did. In the first quarter Montana connected with 166-pound halfback Carl Monroe for a 33-yard touchdown on a deep in-and-out over the middle. The second TD was to fullback Roger Craig, an eight-yard slant. Two passes to tight end Russ Francis set up the third score, a six-yard scramble by Montana.

The backs did the work on Niners TD No. 4, which came on Craig's two-yard burst and their last touchdown, the cruncher, was built around a 40-yard crossing pattern to Wendell Tyler. The score came on another cross, 16 yards to Craig.

Afterward the Dolphins' dressing room was overflowing with despair—and bewilderment. "It was like chasing a rabbit out there," guard Bob Baumhower said of pursuing Montana.

"If somebody had told me two weeks ago that we'd be held to 16 points," said tight end Joe Rose, "I would have laughed."

There's a segment out there that might laugh at a 38–16 game. It makes more sense to look at something like this and find greatness. In Super Bowl XIX it belonged to Montana. ∎

JUST THE FACTS

Statistical Leaders

Rushing WENDELL TYLER (SF) 13 carries, 65 yds, 0 TD

Passing JOE MONTANA (SF) 24 of 35, 331 yds, 3 TDs

Receiving TONY NATHAN (MIA) 10 catches, 83 yds

MVP JOE MONTANA 49ers Quarterback

The Ring
An image of the Golden Gate
Bridge is inscribed on one side

Anthem Performer
San Francisco Boys Chorus
and San Francisco Girls Chorus

Halftime Performer
U.S. Air Force Band

Attendance 84,059

Ticket Price $60

Behind the Scenes

While watching tape, 49ers coach Bill Walsh noticed the Dolphins linebackers turning their backs to the quarterback when covering running backs on passing routes. Just before the game, Walsh told Joe Montana to run whenever he saw the opportunity. Montana ended up rushing for 59 yards, the second-highest total of his career, including a six-yard touchdown.

They Said It

"Our objective was to contain Montana, and we did a terrible job of it." —Dolphins defensive coordinator CHUCK STUDLEY

Ticket Plan

As host of the game, Stanford received 1,500 tickets. The university's football coach Jack Elway (John's dad) wanted to give some of them to high school recruits, but the NCAA nixed the idea.

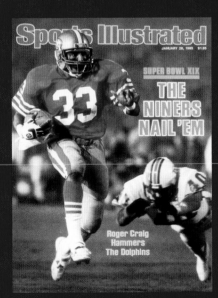

On a Niners defense that rattled Marino all day, Gary (Big Hands) Johnson was the unofficial MVP, sacking the Miami QB once and flushing him time and again.

Photograph by John Iacono

Over the second and third quarters, Montana, with plenty of help from Craig, led San Francisco on five straight scoring drives.

Photograph by Heinz Kluetmeier

BY Roger Craig

49ers Running Back

There I was, in my second year, playing in the Super Bowl. I was living the dream. It was kind of an out-of-body experience. At Nebraska we had sellouts every home game, so the crowd wasn't going to freak me out, but I was still a little nervous. The guy who saw that and came up to me was Jack (Hacksaw) Reynolds, one of those old, dusty veterans. He was always grumpy, but he liked me for some reason. So he came over to me in the locker room and said, "You have no reason to be nervous. Play every play like it's gonna be your last because you never know if you're gonna get this opportunity again." That calmed me down. I couldn't wait to get on the field. I couldn't wait to hit the Dolphins. Every play, I played my butt off. Every run I had was with bad intentions. I was so focused, I made two one-handed catches. I was the first player to score three touchdowns in a single Super Bowl, but I didn't even know I did that. What Hacksaw said was the only thing going through my mind. Hacksaw said it, and I had to do it.

I was so happy we won that I wanted to share it with my wife. We went up to San Francisco and went out to dinner. The place was screaming and hollering and crazy. People were all over me. Here I was in a limo with my wife celebrating, and meanwhile the team was down in Palo Alto having a party and a good time. No one had told me there would be a party afterward! That's how naive I was as a young guy. That was my most memorable Super Bowl.

BY Mark Clayton

Dolphins Wide Receiver

We felt they were getting a lot of pressure on Dan Marino, so we were prepared to go to a no-huddle, which we did. It resulted in our only touchdown of that game, and we kept their nickel package on the sidelines. Bill Walsh said, 'O.K., I'm going to one-up you guys. If you're going no-huddle, I'm going to leave them out there for the whole game.' They never subbed out their nickel package after we scored. We tried to go no-huddle again, but they had their pass rushing specialists in the game. It was hard to throw downfield when Dan hadn't been feeling that kind of heat all season. It threw our timing off.

Over the years, I've talked to Ronnie Lott and Eric Wright and Carlton Williamson, all of whom played in that 49ers secondary. They told me that their plan going into the game was to not let us do what we had been doing all season, which was to make big plays, throwing bombs down the field. Their plan was to keep everything in front of them and make the tackles. And that's what they did.

That was Mark Duper's third year and Dan's and my second. I felt I was going to play in at least four or five Super Bowls and win two or three. That just shows that there's nothing wrong with dreaming big, but you have to go out and play the game.

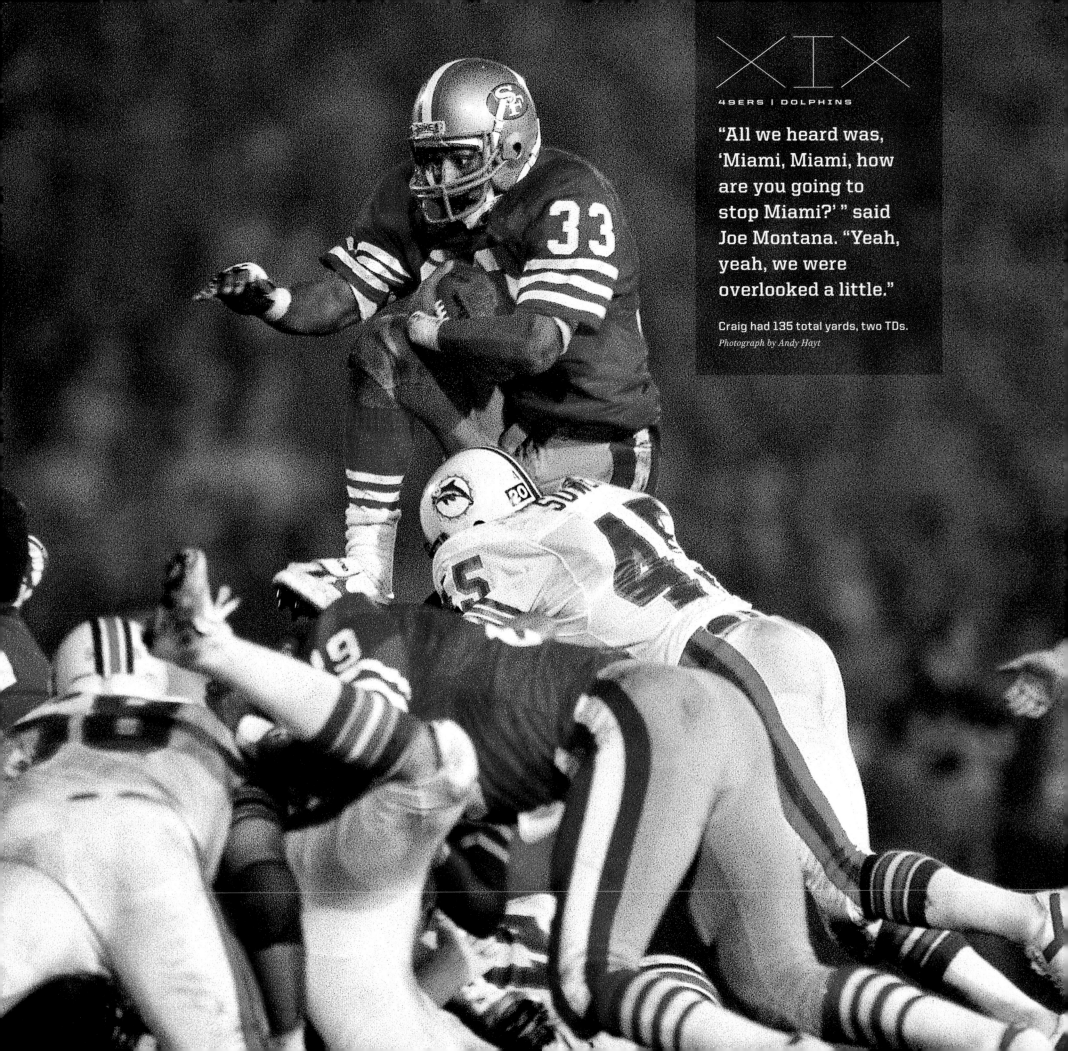

XIX

49ERS | DOLPHINS

"All we heard was, 'Miami, Miami, how are you going to stop Miami?'" said Joe Montana. "Yeah, yeah, we were overlooked a little."

Craig had 135 total yards, two TDs.

Photograph by Andy Hayt

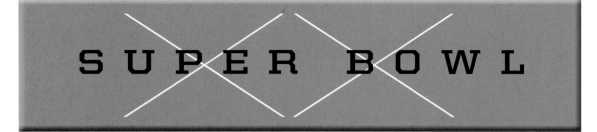

SUPER BOWL XX

January 26, 1986
Superdome, New Orleans

HEAD COACHES
MIKE DITKA Bears | RAYMOND BERRY Patriots

CHICAGO **BEARS** | **46**

NEW ENGLAND **PATRIOTS** | **10**

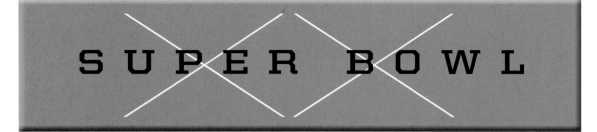

NEVER HAS a defense so dominated a Super Bowl, and rarely has a team been more colorful. These Bears became instant classics—McMahon, Singletary, Fridge, Ryan—both for what they achieved and the way in which they achieved it.

DOME	POINT SPREAD	TIME OF GAME	TV AUDIENCE

Indoors: 70°	Bears by 10	3:42	92.6 million

It was Ryan's last game running the Bears D; he left to be the Eagles' head coach.

Photograph by Tony Tomsic

138

By the time Reggie Phillips returned an interception for this third-quarter touchdown, the Bears' rout was long under way.

Photograph by Walter Iooss Jr.

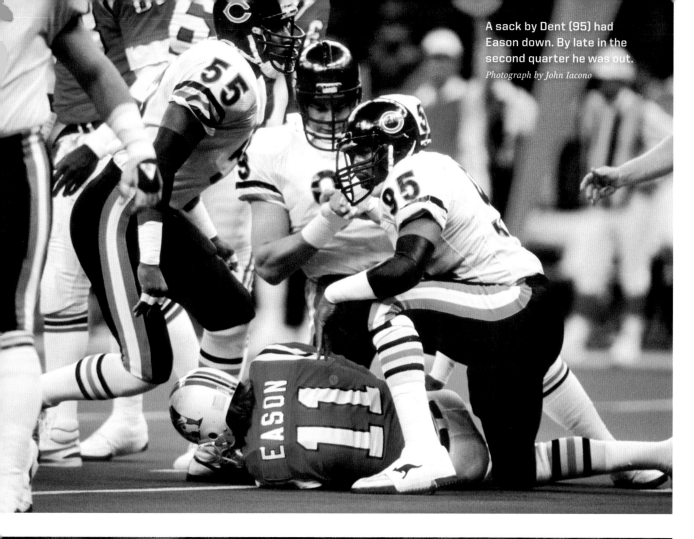

A sack by Dent (95) had Eason down. By late in the second quarter he was out.

Photograph by John Iacono

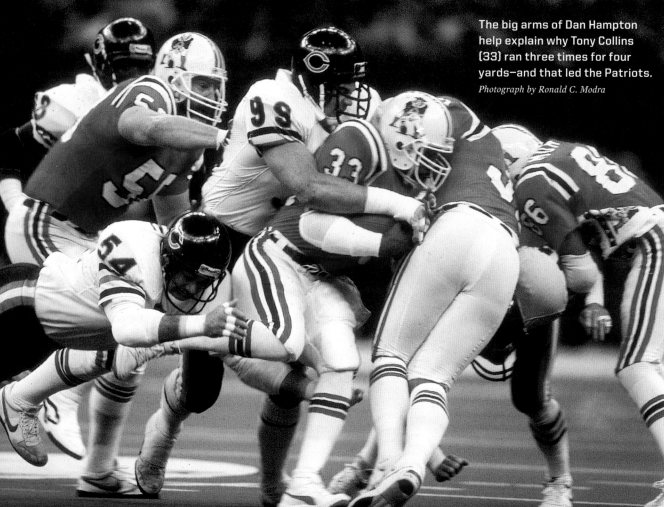

The big arms of Dan Hampton help explain why Tony Collins (33) ran three times for four yards—and that led the Patriots.

Photograph by Ronald C. Modra

JUST THE FACTS

Statistical Leaders

Rushing WALTER PAYTON (CHI) 22 carries, 61 yds

Passing JIM MCMAHON (CHI) 12 of 20, 256 yds

Receiving WILLIE GAULT (CHI) 4 catches, 129 yds

MVP RICHARD DENT Bears Defensive End

The Ring
Inscription: ATTITUDE and the initials of George S. Halas

Anthem Performer
Wynton Marsalis

Halftime Performer
Up With People

Attendance 73,818

Ticket Price $75

Behind the Scenes

At Wednesday's practice, Bears QB Jim McMahon mooned a helicopter flying overhead, the highlight of a week that included fines for wearing illegal headbands, untrue rumors he had denounced the men and women of host city New Orleans, and a successful appeal to have the team fly in an acupuncturist...partly to work on McMahon's bruised gluteus maximus.

They Said It

"Typical Bears week. The crazies are all in place."
—Bears safety GARY FENCIK

Second Wave

The Bears pulled all but one of their defensive starters with 9:43 left in the game, at which point the Patriots had gained only 81 yards. The backup D then outscored New England's offense, 2–0.

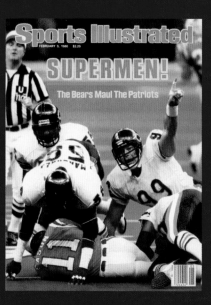

SPECTACULAR DAY FOR D

Wherever the Patriots tried to go, ferocious Bears were there | BY PAUL ZIMMERMAN

IT WILL BE MANY YEARS BEFORE WE SEE anything approaching the vision of hell that Chicago inflicted on the Patriots in Super Bowl XX. It was near perfect, an exquisite mesh of talent and system, defensive football carried to its highest degree. It was a great roaring wave that swept through the playoffs, gathering force and momentum, until it finally crashed home in pro football's showcase game.

The game wasn't exciting. So what? Go to Bourbon Street if you want excitement. The verdict on Chicago's 46–10 victory was in after two Patriots series. Don't feel cheated. Louis-Schmeling II wasn't very competitive either. Nor was the British cavalry charge at Balaklava, but Tennyson wrote a poem about it. This game transcended the ordinary standards we use in judging football. It was historic.

Mike Ditka's Bears have given Chicago its first title in any major professional sport since 1963, when Ditka himself played tight end for the champion Bears. And Buddy Ryan's defense, which virtually eliminates traditional positions, put together a string of conquests, a three-game playoff series that has never been duplicated: Bears 21–Giants 0. Bears 24–Rams 0. Bears 46–Patriots 10. Average yards given up per game: 144.7. Average gain by opponent per play: 2.6. Third downs converted: three for 36. The Bears set a Super Bowl record by allowing the Patriots only seven rushing yards. Such is the hold that Ryan, with his driving spirit, has on his players that he causes hard-eyed veterans like middle linebacker Mike Singletary to say, "Without him we don't have much. I feel honored to have been coached by him."

The Patriots had one moment of elation. On the game's second play, Walter Payton fumbled and New England recovered on the Chicago 19. "My fault," quarterback Jim McMahon said. "I called the wrong play." New England quarterback Tony Eason threw three incomplete passes, and suddenly the Bears

defenders were feeling very good about things. "We knew that if we got them in a passing situation we'd have things wrapped up," Singletary said.

Tony Franklin kicked a 36-yard field goal and New England led 3–0 with 1:19 gone, the earliest score in Super Bowl history. "I looked up at the message board," Singletary said, "and it said that 15 of the 19 teams that scored first won the game. I thought, yeah, but none of those 15 had ever played the Bears."

Chicago started the next drive on its 31, and seven plays, including a 43-yard pass to Willie Gault, got the Bears to the Patriots' 10, where Kevin Butler kicked the tying 28-yard field goal. Fullback Matt Suhey, not Payton, got the yardage on the ground. "I was a decoy, a rabbit," said Payton, who carried 22 times for 61 yards. "They were putting two guys on me."

Eason began the next Patriots series with two incompletions, followed by a 10-yard sack. End Richard Dent and right linebacker Wilber Marshall shared it, and left linebacker Otis Wilson was closing hard.

Eason's pocket had collapsed. New England had called six straight pass plays. Net result: five incompletions and a 10-yard loss. The Bears were slapping high fives because they had taken New England out of its offense before the first quarter was half over.

In the first six plays Chicago had given Eason six different defensive fronts. The second pass he threw was a crossing pattern to wide receiver Stanley Morgan underneath. Singletary bothered Morgan enough to force a dropped pass. Middle linebackers aren't supposed to cover wideouts. Next play the Bears showed Eason their 59 blitz. It was their most effective weapon of the day, an all-out rush by the three linebackers. Two of them generally were blocked, but Wilson usually came free, and on that play he hurried Eason into an incomplete. On Eason's fifth incomplete Marshall had coverage on Morgan; next play Marshall shared the sack with Dent.

New England finally tried a run on its third series. Singletary smacked Craig James for no gain. Eason tried to pass. The middle of his line caved in, and Dent and defensive tackle Steve McMichael caught him in a sandwich. The ball came loose. Chicago recovered on the Pats' 13, setting up another field goal. On the next possession James tried a sweep left. Dent stripped the ball, and Singletary recovered on the Patriots' 13. Suhey scored a touchdown on an 11-yard carry. The quarter ended 13–3 Bears, and it was all over.

"Our problem was getting manhandled," said Eason. "I tried to scramble but there was no place to go."

Right guard Ron Wooten said the major problem was the seven-man Bears rush. "The pressure just got to us," he said. "When we couldn't move the ball on our first run I thought, 'Where do we go from here? We can't pass, we can't run.' It was like trying to beat back the tide with a broom." ◼

Payton (with McMahon) played in just one Super Bowl.

Photograph by John Iacono

William (Refrigerator) Perry, a mammoth rookie defensive lineman turned folk hero, couldn't complete his first NFL pass (he got sacked), but he did score on a one-yard run.

Photographs by Andy Hayt (top) and Richard Mackson

BY Mike Singletary

Bears Linebacker

The night before the Super Bowl, coach Ditka asked a few guys to talk about what they felt and what they were going to do in the game. The first person he asked was Walter Payton. Walter talked about just leaving it on the field and how proud he was to be a part of that team. Ditka asked a couple of others—Dan Hampton, Jim McMahon. It was a really special moment. Then we broke off into offense/defense and I guess everybody knew Buddy Ryan was going to be leaving to coach the Eagles. I didn't know and I was not prepared to hear that. Buddy had told the guys not to tell me. So when Buddy gets up, he was emotional about what he was feeling and he said, "You know, you guys will always be my heroes." At that point, Hampton got up and threw a chair that got stuck in the wall. Steve McMichael knocked the projector over. Everybody was fired up and screaming. I knew walking out of that room that the game was over.

Before the game the next day, we were standing behind these huge doors at the Superdome. You could hear the fans, the noise. From where we were, it was quite a contrast. It was very quiet and very heavy, very emotional. We're holding hands and nobody's really saying anything and tears are coming out of our eyes and rolling down our face. And when they open the door, it was like opening the floodgates. Our spirits poured through the doors and we ran on the field and we were screaming. Finally, it's here. Let's just finish what we came here to do. And that's what we did.

BY Andre Tippett

Patriots Linebacker

There wasn't really a lot of trash talk leading up to the game. There was a lot during the game, though, especially at halftime. I was hot. We were all walking off the field and I must have had six of the offensive linemen from the Bears around me. They were all looking at me like, This guy has lost his mind. I did everything but foam at the mouth.

In the second half our mind-set became, Let's not embarrass ourselves any more than we already have. We've got to put some points on the board. But everything we did, they were ready for. We tried to fight to the end, although it kept getting uglier and uglier.

After the game was probably even uglier. [Linebacker] Don Blackmon and I were so upset—not at our team, but just at the outcome. It wasn't what we envisioned. We didn't take the bus back to the hotel. We found another way out and walked back with our bags on our shoulders. The hotel wasn't too far, I think we were probably two or three blocks away. We were just commiserating with each other.

To this day, I cringe when I go through Chicago. I cringe when I see the highlights too. But you have to honor and take your hat off to the better team. You could have put an all-star team together and it wouldn't have been competitive against that defense. I don't think anybody could have beaten them.

The 6' 2", 335-pound Perry, who made it 44–3 in the third quarter, also sang on the Bears' Super Bowl Shuffle album.

Photograph by Walter Iooss Jr.

SUPER BOWL XXI

January 25, 1987
Rose Bowl, Pasadena

HEAD COACHES
BILL PARCELLS Giants | DAN REEVES Broncos

NEW YORK
GIANTS | 39

DENVER
BRONCOS | 20

As the season's NFL defensive MVP, linebacker Taylor was just super, man.

Photograph by Peter Read Miller

DENVER CAME in after a pair of narrow John Elway-led playoff wins, while the Giants, with their Big Blue Wrecking Crew defense, had rolled through the postseason. And then, behind a certain quarterback of their own, they kept right on rolling.

WEATHER	POINT SPREAD	TIME OF GAME	TV AUDIENCE

76°, sunny	Giants by 9	3:25	87.2 million

Giants offensive coordinator Ron Erhardt said Simms had "as close to a perfect game as I've seen a quarterback have."

Photograph by Richard Mackson

Elway started strong, but George Martin and the Giants' fierce rush wore him down.

Photograph by Walter Iooss Jr.

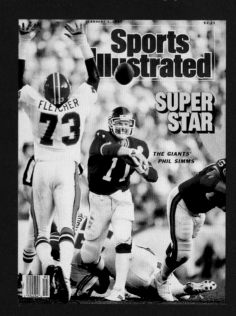

COMPLETELY MARVELOUS

A quarterback's can't-miss day won the Giants their first Super Bowl | BY PAUL ZIMMERMAN

SOMEWHERE INSIDE THE MIND of every quarterback there's a 22-for-25 day, a day when every pass has eyes and every decision is correct. For a showcase there's a bright, sunlit stadium with more than a half century of tradition, a place like, well, the Rose Bowl. There are 101,063 people in the stands, and about 2,000 writers and broadcasters to tell people about it, and nearly 90 million Americans gathered around their TV sets.

That's where the fantasy usually stays, inside, because nobody goes 22 for 25 in the Super Bowl, not in this high-powered era with sophisticated defenses featuring shifting zones and blitzes and mixed coverages. But let's say there's a quarterback who deserves this mythical kind of day, a quarterback who has spent eight years in the NFL being hammered by adversity and injury, who has heard the boos of the New York fans for as long as he can remember, a quarterback like the Giants' Phil Simms.

On Sunday, Simms got even. The Giants crushed the Broncos 39–20 in Super Bowl XXI, and Simms carved up Denver with the best percentage passing day in any NFL championship game ever.

You say someone must have gotten the name wrong, that Simms is a downfield passer, usually with a low percentage of completions. You have a point. He was below 50% for the two postseason wins, (not easy when you win by 49–3 and 17–0). Fifteen of the qualifying NFL passers had higher percentages than Simms this season. A day like 22 for 25 is for the dinkers, the dump-off artists, not the serious gunners like Simms. But there it was. The guy was simply amazing.

"He quarterbacked as good a game as ever has been played," said Giants coach Bill Parcells.

The guys on the same assembly line as Simms, the ones who work with him every day, said they had a hunch he might have a surprise like this cooked up for the Broncos. They said it started back at Giants Stadium more than a week before the Super Bowl. In a Friday practice, said center Bart Oates, "He hit everything he threw. Parcells said, 'Hey, this is too much. Save something for the game.' Phil had this strange sort of a glow. It was like he was in a perfect biorhythm stage or something."

Five hours before kickoff in Pasadena, Simms, tackle Brad Benson and guard Chris Godfrey took a cab to the stadium, a road-game ritual. "I was nervous," Benson said. "I had been nervous all week, even though I had done a good job trying to hide it. I asked Phil if he was nervous too. 'Not nervous,' he said. 'Excited.' Then he said, 'I'm telling you, I feel great. I'm gonna be throwing some fastballs today. Give me time and I'll rip 'em.'"

Simms's instructions were to throw play-action passes in the first half to temper the rush and hold in those very active, swarming Denver linebackers who were, as Parcells said, "all gassed up to get [running back] Joe Morris." And in the second half, when Denver people were starting to sag, the Giants would come back and pound them on the ground.

"They changed their whole offensive attack," Broncos linebacker Karl Mecklenburg said. "Pass first, run second. It surprised us. We thought they would try to establish the running game, but they went against their tendencies, and they did a good job of it."

The keynote series, though, came with the Giants on defense. Early in the second quarter Denver led 10–7 and had a first down at the Giants' one. They brought in their goal line offense. Quarterback John Elway tried a run-pass option, but Lawrence Taylor and nosetackle Erik Howard threw him for a yard loss. The Broncos tried a quick trap, but Harry Carson stuffed Gerald Willhite for no gain. "In New York they had scored on a pitchout from four yards out," said left linebacker Carl Banks, recalling a previous matchup between the teams. "I expected that play again [on third down], and that's what they called."

The pitch went to Sammy Winder. Banks read it from the go and got in front of Winder, along with Carson and cornerback Perry Williams. The play lost four yards. Then kicker Rich Karlis missed a 23-yard field-goal attempt. First-and-goal on the one and the Broncos came away with nothing. Later the Giants sacked Elway for a safety and although Denver closed the half leading 10–9 they seemed in shaky position.

After halftime the Giants set off the biggest single-half offensive explosion in Super Bowl history, scoring four touchdowns and a field goal on its first five possessions. Simms was 10 for 10, finding all his receivers: short, long, primary, secondary, it didn't matter.

First—soon after QB Jeff Rutledge had shifted out of punt formation to sneak two yards for a first down at the Giants' 46—Simms hit tight end Mark Bavaro for a 13-yard TD. Simms got his longest completion of the day, 44 yards to Phil McConkey, off a flea-flicker that set up the Giants' second touchdown of the half; on the way to the third TD he found Stacy Robinson for 36 yards, laying the ball in perfectly through a double zone; and to set up the last one Simms bootlegged 22 yards. The Broncos had put up a hell of a fight for two periods, but in the end they were simply overcome. ∎

Bavaro's third-quarter TD put New York ahead to stay.

Photograph by Walter Iooss Jr.

THE WAY IT WAS

BY Harry Carson

Giants Linebacker

Throughout the season, the Gatorade shower became a big thing. Our team began a tradition of pouring the big bucket of ice-cold Gatorade over coach Parcells's head when we won. Fans loved it, and we did too. It became especially big in the playoffs, and somehow, I was always right at the center of it.

Well, as the seconds started ticking away in the Super Bowl and we had the game clearly in our control, Coach probably expected that the bath was coming his way. So knowing that, I had to be extra stealthy. I took off my jersey and my pads and I somehow got my hands on a Rose Bowl security guard's jacket, which I put on as a disguise. I snuck around on the sideline and came up right behind Coach to surprise him. Little did I know that on the television broadcast, John Madden was diagramming the whole thing like it was a play with X's and O's.

And here is something most people don't know: I actually got Coach twice with the Gatorade in this Super Bowl. In most clips of the game, you see Coach standing there on the sideline as I dunk him from behind. But if you look closely, you can see that he is already shivering a bit and his sweater is already wet. I had actually gotten him about two minutes earlier, then I just lingered for the second bath. Some people saw the first dunk, but I know that everybody saw the second one.

Morris's running was supplemented by four catches out of the backfield.

Photograph by Jerry Wachter

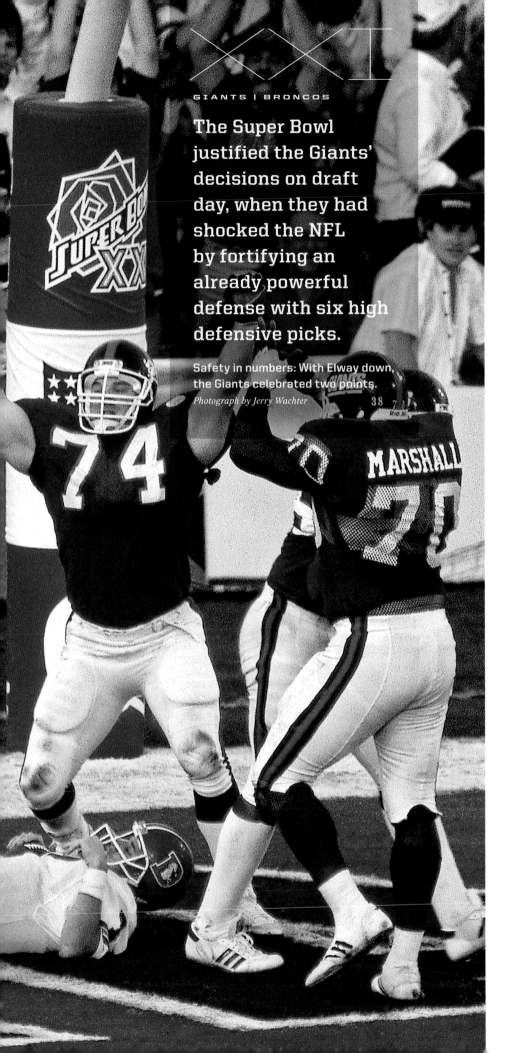

XXI

GIANTS | BRONCOS

The Super Bowl justified the Giants' decisions on draft day, when they had shocked the NFL by fortifying an already powerful defense with six high defensive picks.

Safety in numbers: With Elway down, the Giants celebrated two points.

Photograph by Jerry Wachter

Carson, in disguise, made sure Parcells would bathe in the glory.

Photograph by Peter Read Miller

THE WAY IT WAS

BY Louis Wright

Broncos Cornerback

I had played in Super Bowl XII in New Orleans, and what shocked me was how much the event had changed, even in those nine years. In my first Super Bowl, there wasn't as much fanfare. During the week, you could have walked wherever you wanted and nobody would have bothered you. But Super Bowl XXI? Coming out of the hotel, all the camera crews were waiting. There were bright lights and fans begging for autographs. Though even that was nothing like it is today. On Media Day back then me, Dennis Smith and some other defensive backs were just hanging around waiting. Nobody wanted to talk to us. So we started throwing a football around because we were bored. Nowadays there's a line to talk to the third-string tight end!

The key play came with three minutes left in the first half. We were deep in our end, and John Elway threw a 16-yard pass to Clarence Kay. The refs ruled it incomplete. But the NFL had just instituted instant replay, so as we went to a time-out, we thought they'd overturn it. But then the refs came back and confirmed it incomplete. That changed everything. The next play, Elway was sacked for a safety.

We usually got 15 minutes in the locker room, but in the Super Bowl we got 30. Only no one told us. We did our routine—met with position coaches, got a talk from Coach, then charged out toward the tunnel. But the security guards held us back saying: "You have another 15 minutes." That killed our vibe. We sat in the locker room and waited, and waited. . . . It was the longest 15 minutes of my life.

149

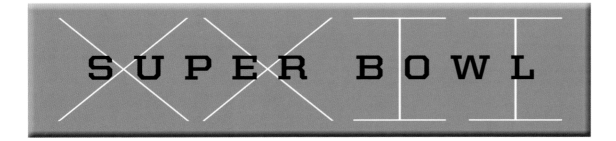

SUPER BOWL XXII

January 31, 1988
Jack Murphy Stadium, San Diego

HEAD COACHES
JOE GIBBS Redskins | DAN REEVES Broncos

WASHINGTON
REDSKINS | 42

DENVER
BRONCOS | 10

Butz on the Redskins bench: defensive tackle Dave and his son David.

Photograph by Walter Iooss Jr.

THE FAVORED BRONCOS, led again by the dashingly athletic John Elway, jumped well ahead in this game. Then Washington and its own big-play QB, Doug Williams, changed the narrative completely. Five possessions. Thirty-five points. Just like that.

WEATHER	POINT SPREAD	TIME OF GAME	TV AUDIENCE

61°, mostly cloudy	Broncos by 3½	3:40	80.1 million

BY Doug Williams

Redskins Quarterback

The first quarter was not kind to us at all. As soon as they got the ball they went in their full razzle-dazzle mode. The first play from scrimmage they scored and before we knew it, we were down 10–0. Toward the end of the first quarter, I hyperextended my knee. I didn't know if I was done or not. I remember being on the sideline and a bunch of teammates and trainers huddled around me. I told them, "Don't touch me. Don't touch me. Because if the good Lord gets me up, you bet I am going to go finish this game." And sure enough, I got back in there, and that second quarter was something special. We ran 18 plays to score 35 points. Sometimes I just have to think about that and let it settle. I mean, in today's game, you might go 11, 12 or 13 plays on one drive to score. For us to run 18 plays and score 35? It didn't hit me until many years later how special that really was.

To get to the Super Bowl, I took the road less traveled. Of course, in the week leading up to the game, and probably even the day of the game, so much attention centered on the fact I could be the first black quarterback to win a title. The day of the game, though, that was not my No. 1 focus. There was so much else I had to think about on the field to help our team win. But after the game, I did let the historic moment sink in a little bit. As we walked off the field, tackle Joe Jacoby came up next to me and patted me on the back. He said, "Red, green, black or yellow, you're our quarterback."

BY Tyrone Braxton

Broncos Defensive Back

We started the game with a bang. Everything was going our way. And when we kicked off after the field goal that made it 10–0, Washington's Ricky Sanders fumbled the return. There was a huge scrum, a pileup like I had never seen. I remember looking in and thinking one of my teammates had it. I thought, *Oh, we have it! We're going to get the ball back again!* But when everyone peeled away, I realized the Redskins had recovered. That moment was the beginning of the end for us.

What Washington was able to do—score 42 unanswered points—is something unlike anything I'd ever seen. And that fumble recovery was the turning point.

I was a rookie that year, mainly playing on special teams. Yet I did get some action in the secondary, mainly as a third-down guy. There was one play I'll never forget. The Redskins were up 28–10 in the second quarter, and I was called in. I jogged in with some swagger—I was all hyped-up, like, Here I am, a rookie playing in the Super Bowl! I looked at the Washington huddle, and Doug Williams peeked up and looked at me. The look in his eye was, "Ah, good. A rookie is in." I told myself, *If they come after me, I'll be ready.* Something happened with our coverage, and Clint Didier, their tight end, was open in the end zone. *Oh shoot.* I ran over to him, but it was too late. Touchdown. I was the closest one there, but Clint wasn't actually my guy. To this day, nobody believes me.

Gracious through the pregame hype, Williams was equally so in victory.
Photograph by Andy Hayt

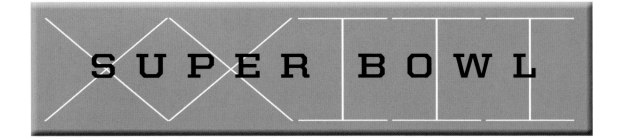

SUPER BOWL XXIII

January 22, 1989
Joe Robbie Stadium, Miami

HEAD COACHES
BILL WALSH 49ers | SAM WYCHE Bengals

SAN FRANCISCO
49ERS | 20

CINCINNATI
BENGALS | 16

The Bengals and Niners agreed on one thing: The sod near midfield was in lousy shape.

Photograph by Richard Mackson

JOE MONTANA was slipping, wasn't he? Benched in the playoffs the year before, then consigned to sharing QB duties with Steve Young for much of the regular season. Joe was 32. Had we seen the best of him? No, folks. Not by a long shot.

WEATHER

76°, high winds

POINT SPREAD

49ers by 6

TIME OF GAME

3:24

TV AUDIENCE

81.6 million

Rice's fourth-quarter snare resulted in the
Niners' first touchdown and tied the game.

Photograph by John W. McDonough

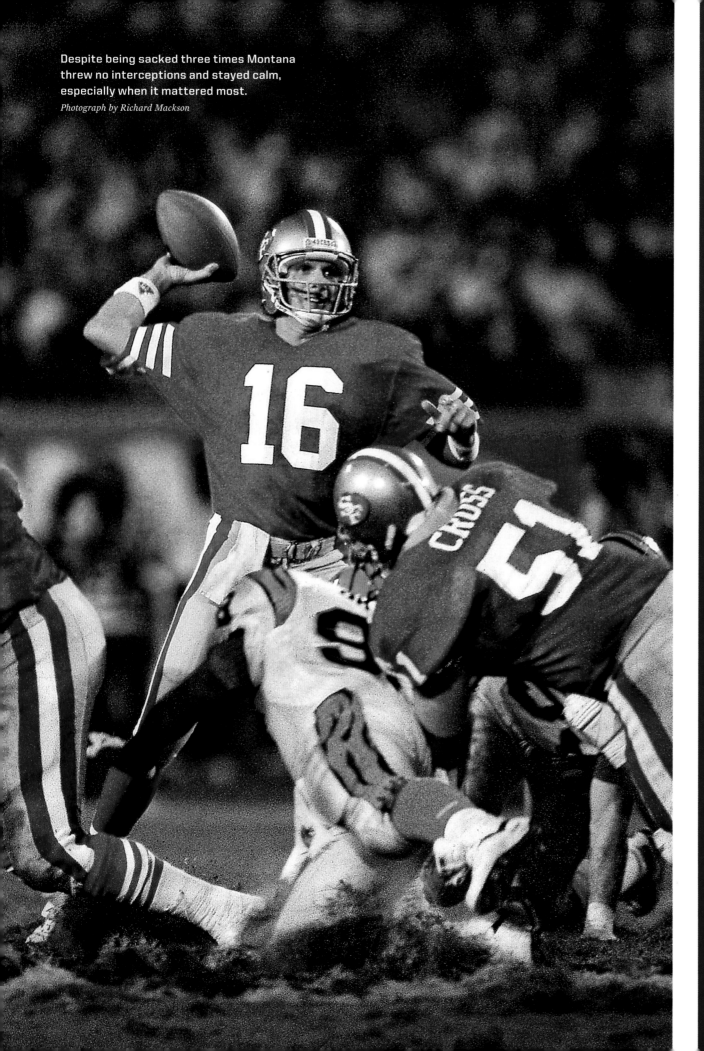

Despite being sacked three times Montana threw no interceptions and stayed calm, especially when it mattered most.

Photograph by Richard Mackson

Statistical Leaders

Rushing **ICKEY WOODS** (CIN) 20 carries, 79 yds

Passing **JOE MONTANA** (SF) 23 of 36, 357 yds, 2 TDs

Receiving **JERRY RICE** (SF) 11 catches, 215 yds, 1 TD

MVP **JERRY RICE** 49ers Wide Receiver

The Ring
Shank inscription reads
TEAM OF THE 80S

Anthem Performer
Billy Joel

Halftime Performer
Elvis Presto

Attendance 75,597

Ticket Price $100

Behind the Scenes

At the start of the 49ers last drive, Joe Montana said to his teammates, "Hey, check it out," recalled tackle Harris Burton. "In the stands, there's John Candy." Sure enough it was the comic actor, and Joe's cool set the tone for the Niners' winning march.

They Said It

"Holding, bad snap, downfield penalty. I did it all today, didn't I? But you'll be amazed at what a great game I had 10 years from now when we're looking back on it."

—49ers center RANDY CROSS

Way to Go, Daddy-O

Cincinnati's Stanford Jennings, whose wife Kathy had a baby girl the afternoon before the game, scored on a 93-yard kickoff return in the third quarter, a gift to tiny Kelsey.

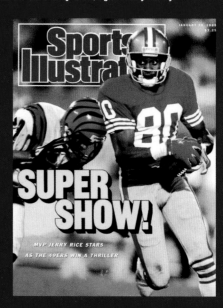

Excerpted from **SPORTS ILLUSTRATED** *January 30, 1989*

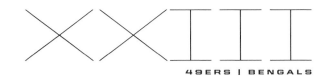

NOBODY FINISHES BETTER

A thrilling final drive, led by you know who, saved the Super Bowl | BY PAUL ZIMMERMAN

YOU HEARD IT IN THE PRESS ROOM and in the parking lot as people headed to their cars after watching the 49ers beat the Bengals 20–16 in Super Bowl XXIII. You heard it in the bars in downtown Miami and on the streets. "Great game . . . great game . . . hey, that was some game, wasn't it?"

A great game? The final quarter was certainly great—the best in Super Bowl history—but for almost 45 minutes this was not a great game. Then Joe Montana, who saves his best performances for the biggest games, rescued this Super Bowl. So did Jerry Rice and Roger Craig. The cream rose. San Francisco marched 92 yards in the dying moments to pull out the win.

The climax had no play to match the breathtaking touchdown catch Dwight Clark made to cap the great winning drive in the 1982 NFC championship against the Cowboys, but it did have lots of good ones. The first crisis of the drive came on the 10th play. After a penalty, the Niners, trailing 16–13, faced second-and-20 on the Bengals' 45. At this point, Montana admitted, he was "just thinking about getting the field goal that would put the game into overtime."

Montana chose a particularly dangerous play, a square-in to Rice. Bengals cornerback Lewis Billups and safety Ray Horton bracketed the 49ers receiver, and strong safety David Fulcher backed them up. The pass covered 13 yards, but somehow Rice got the ball in the middle of the pack and broke clear for another 14. "It had to be a perfect throw and catch," said Billups. "He had all kinds of hands flashing in front of him."

The ball was on the 18, and Montana found Craig on an eight-yard crossing pattern. "Nothing greedy, I just wanted to get some yards," said Craig. Now the 49ers had second-and-two on the 10, and the Bengals went into a two-deep zone: short and medium coverage on Rice on the right side, the same on split end John Taylor on the left.

The play was 20 Halfback Curl X-Up. Rice went in motion to the left, passing behind Taylor before the ball was snapped, and decoyed into the left flat. Craig, who curled into the middle from the right, was the primary receiver, but he got jammed up in traffic. Taylor put on a little wiggle move and ran straight down the seam. Montana hit him in stride, and the Niners had their third Super Bowl win in eight years.

"That's Joe Montana," said center Randy Cross. "Primary receiver's covered, he goes to the No. 2 man, just like that—reflex."

Montana completed eight of nine passes on the drive for 97 yards. Counting a 10-yard penalty, the 49ers ate up 102 yards on the march.

In the winning locker room, cornerback Eric Wright dumped a bucket of ice water on Niners owner Eddie DeBartolo, and tight end John Frank lifted DeBartolo off the ground in a bear hug and carried him 10 feet, bonking DeBartolo's head on defensive end Larry Roberts's locker. Even NFL commissioner Pete Rozelle was caught up in the euphoria: "Eddie DeBartolo, coach Bill Walsh, you and the great Cincinnati team gave us the finest of our 23 Super Bowls. I don't think there is any question about that."

It did not start out that way. San Francisco's left tackle, Steve Wallace, broke his left ankle on the third play. On the 49ers' next series, Cincinnati's All-Pro noseguard, Tim Krumrie, twisted his left ankle almost 180 degrees as he fell to the turf, shattering two bones in the lower leg. The center of the field at Joe Robbie Stadium, which had been resodded five weeks before the game, was miserable. Big clumps of turf came up. Teams of red-shirted maintenance men ran out during timeouts to try to tamp down the loose sod. The game at halftime was tied 3–3—not since the Steelers led the Vikings 2–0 in Super Bowl IX had so few points been scored in the first half.

The score had progressed to 13–6 Bengals in the third quarter when the game opened up, and the Super

Bowl everyone will remember began. Starting on his 15, Montana hooked up with Rice on a little out pattern that Rice turned into a 30-yard gain. On the next play, Montana connected with Craig on a 40-yard fly. Two plays later Rice caught a pass on the five, wrapped the ball around the goal-line pylon, and the game was tied.

The Bengals then drove methodically for a 40-yard field goal—"Our line was controlling things," said tackle Anthony Muñoz. "I felt we were going to win"—and on the ensuing kickoff a penalty against the Niners moved the ball back to the San Francisco eight. The clock showed 3:10. There was time for one miracle.

"We had them on their eight with three minutes to go," said wideout Cris Collinsworth. "Someone came said to me, 'We got 'em now.' I said, 'Have you [seen] who's quarterbacking the 49ers?' That's what it comes down to. Joe Montana is not human. I don't want to call him a god, but he's somewhere in between." ∎

Walsh, Montana and Steve Young talked things over.

Photograph by Peter Read Miller

THE WAY IT WAS

BY Kevin Fagan

49ers Defensive End

The Bengals had the NFL's most dangerous offense. Boomer Esiason was a straight-up gunslinger, and they had serious threats in Cris Collinsworth, Ickey Woods and James Brooks. Our defensive game plan called for a few different things to try and fluster them. We moved Charles Haley around all over the field, so the Bengals would not know where he was going to be rushing from. And sometimes we deployed a 4–7 scheme—yes, seven defensive backs out there at once. Ronnie Lott was an absolute monster all day at free safety. We also dropped a lot of different guys into coverage, even Pierce Holt, our big, 275-pound end, as a drop-back linebacker in some looks. It was truly a masterly job by our coordinator, George Seifert.

We had an excellent defense and the game felt like a heavyweight battle at times, but this Super Bowl will be remembered for the final drive. It was magic: Joe Montana with a little more than three minutes on the clock, acting as clutch as can be. I can't imagine what exactly I was thinking on the sideline, but I do remember feeling like our offense finding the end zone was inevitable.

Before the season began, when I heard the Super Bowl would be played at Joe Robbie Stadium, I knew how bad I wanted it. I grew up in Lake Worth and went to the University of Miami. I was thinking that playing the biggest game of my life in my own backyard would be surreal. But then winning a championship, especially in that fashion, was a feeling I could have never imagined.

Led by Esiason, the Bengals seemed to take control in the third quarter.

Photograph by Walter Iooss Jr.

XXIII

49ERS | BENGALS

John Taylor put on a little wiggle move and ran straight down the seam. Joe Montana hit him in stride, and the Niners had their third Super Bowl win in eight years.

The game-winning touchdown was Taylor's only catch of the day.

Photograph by John W. McDonough

End Larry Roberts and all the Niners were flat-out delighted with the outcome.

Photograph by John W. McDonough

THE WAY IT WAS

BY Boomer Esiason

Bengals Quarterback

Up to that point, there weren't a lot of great Super Bowls—many were blowouts. This game? Not so much. As you know, it came down to the final drive, and what a drive it was—for the 49ers, at least. The moment, for me, was surreal. We had played a tough, hard-fought game. I didn't have my best performance, but hoped we had done enough to win.

I was so tense on the sideline as the 49ers marched down the field, but there was one distraction. Had we won, I would have likely been named the MVP, meaning I would have been in the famous commercial: "I'm going to Disney World." Well, I remember being on the sideline and a contingent of people from Disney came up to me. They wanted to know if I knew my lines, they wanted to know if I needed any makeup, if I wanted to fix my eye black. And they wanted me to practice saying "I'm going to Disney World! I'm going to Disney World!" They obviously weren't huge football fans, not realizing the significance of the drive or how big of a moment it was for me and my teammates. The game wasn't over yet!

Sure enough, that drive ended with John Taylor's catch with 34 seconds left that proved to be the game winner. As soon as I could say, "I'm not going to Disney World," the cameras disappeared. Those same people who had been bugging me for what seemed like an eternity were gone before I knew it. They ran across the field looking for Joe Montana.

161

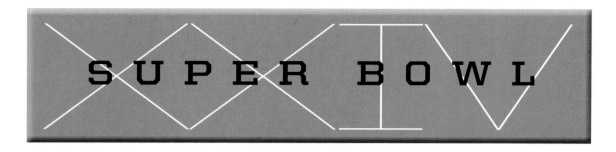

SUPER BOWL XXIV

January 28, 1990
Superdome, New Orleans

HEAD COACHES
GEORGE SEIFERT 49ers | DAN REEVES Broncos

SAN FRANCISCO
49ERS | 55

DENVER
BRONCOS | 10

Pleased to beat you. Rice's prolific day of receptions inspired a tip of his own cap.

Photograph by Richard Mackson

THERE HAS been a fair share of routs in the big game (and a fair share of thrillers too) yet when these Niners were done, and the beaten Broncos had finally caught their breath, the truth was in: This was the biggest Super Bowl blowout of all time.

DOME
70° inside, 61° out

POINT SPREAD
49ers by 13

TIME OF GAME
3:21

TV AUDIENCE
73.9 million

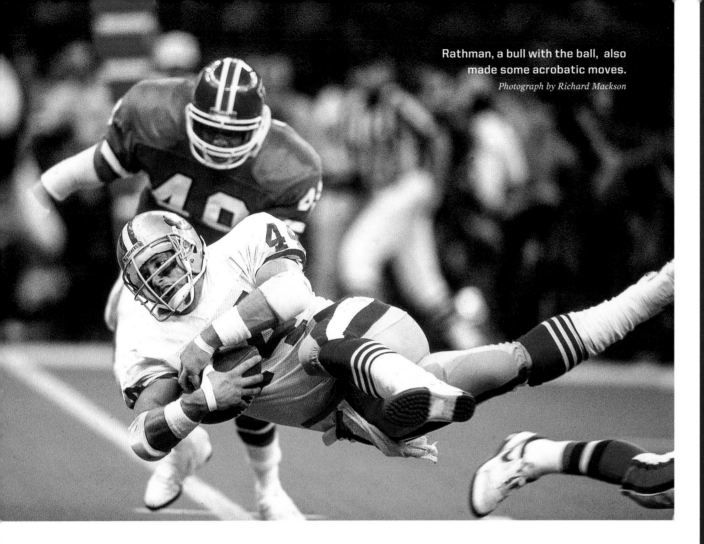

Rathman, a bull with the ball, also made some acrobatic moves.
Photograph by Richard Mackson

Elway, harassed throughout, said after the game, "This is going to live with me."
Photograph by Richard Mackson

JUST THE FACTS

Statistical Leaders

Rushing **ROGER CRAIG** (SF) 20 carries, 69 yds, 1 TD

Passing **JOE MONTANA** (SF) 22 of 29, 297 yds, 5 TDs

Receiving **JERRY RICE** (SF) 7 catches, 148 yds, 3 TDs

MVP JOE MONTANA 49ers Quarterback

The Ring
Inscribed 88 BACK TO BACK 89 with the Golden Gate Bridge

Anthem Performer
Aaron Neville

Halftime Performers
Pete Fountain, Doug Kershaw and Irma Thomas

Attendance 72,919

Ticket Price $125

Behind the Scenes

For three consecutive 49ers touchdowns, quarterback Joe Montana executed virtually the same post pattern route on scoring passes to Jerry Rice (twice) and John Taylor.

They Said It

"Each Super Bowl becomes more precious. The more, the merrier."
—49ers quarterback JOE MONTANA

Not So Fine Fettle

After the AFC championship game, John Elway contracted a virus that caused him to lose 10 pounds. He gained five of those pounds back by Super Bowl Sunday, but had a nasty cough throughout the game.

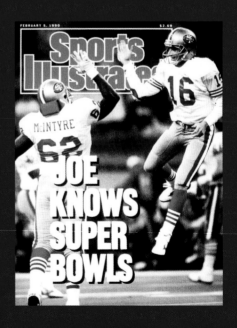

Excerpted from **SPORTS ILLUSTRATED** *February 5, 1990*

AIN'T NO STOPPING 'EM

Denver never had a chance to slow down the machinelike 49ers | BY PAUL ZIMMERMAN

ROOM 5072—JOE MONTANA'S room—Hilton Riverside and Towers, New Orleans, Super Bowl Sunday, 10:15 p.m. Bob Woolf, Montana's agent, puts through a call to another of his clients, Larry Bird. After two rings, Bird picks up the phone and says, "55–10, Joe Montana."

"Wait a minute," says Woolf, laughing. "I'll let you speak to Joe."

Montana, who threw for a Super Bowl–record five touchdowns in the 49ers' shellacking of the Broncos in Super Bowl XXIV, gets on the line. "Hey man, how's the foot doing?" says Montana. "Looks like you're moving a lot better. Yeah, I know, we're homing in on five championships. One more, man. Hey, I'll be watching you. You too. Take care."

Montana hangs up and dials the hotel operator—again. He has been trying to get through to room service. This is his party. Downstairs, the official 49ers affair is in full swing, but that's not his scene: wall-to-wall back-slappers, many of whom wrote him off three years ago, two years ago, last year.

Montana is getting ready for his own people—his uncle and aunt from Monongahela, Pa., friends of relatives—maybe 40, all told. He has put on a white shirt and a tie. On a couch his dad, Joe Sr., is changing his grandson Nathaniel's diaper. Next to him Joe's wife, Jennifer, is pouring '82 Dom Perignon into a water glass and apologizing because room service hasn't brought up champagne glasses yet. Montana finally gets through to room service: eight pizzas, four orders of Cajun wings—wait, better make it six—champagne glasses, like 30 of them.

The TV in the corner is playing a tape of the game. Montana watches his 38-yard scoring pass to wideout Jerry Rice with 40 seconds left in the first half, the play that made the score 27–3 and essentially put the game away. As running back Roger Craig goes in motion, left to right, Broncos nickelback Mark Haynes switches off Rice and picks up Craig. Rice then bends inside on a post pattern and loses strong safety Dennis Smith. Rice is all alone as he crosses the goal line. It's like stealing.

"Haynes was supposed to bump Rice before he switched coverage," says Montana. "He didn't. He gave him a clean release. I faked a slant pattern to John Taylor on the other side, and that froze the free safety, Steve Atwater. They kept following my eyes. Every time I looked somewhere, they overplayed. They showed that on film, and they never changed."

Let's hear it too for the offensive line. At times Montana got as many as three looks to spot his receivers. On the rare occasion when Denver came with an all-out blitz, the Niners' front wall cut the rushers down like a firing squad. "If I didn't get so tired, I could have played three games," says Montana. "I only got touched twice—once when I scrambled out-of-bounds."

With things neatly in place up front, the rest of the offense was merrily efficient. Rice and Taylor flitted through the Denver zone like hummingbirds. Craig bounced off tackles for 103 yards running and receiving. Fullback Tom Rathman, who banged the left side for three short-yardage first downs, pulled off the most remarkable play of the day, corkscrewing his 232-pound body to make a one-handed reach-back catch at the Broncos' 10 to set up the 49ers' third touchdown—a one-yard Rathman plunge. Of course, Montana was the master architect.

"People talk about our great offensive scheme," said inside linebacker Matt Millen. "Yeah, it's brilliant in its conception, but with lesser talent, it's nowhere."

While Montana and the textbook were dismantling Denver's defense, John Elway and the Broncos' offense were unraveling. Elway was subjected to constant pressure, especially by right end Kevin Fagan, who was charging like a maniac. A couple of Elway's passes were batted away by nickelback Tim McKyer, who made the kind of plays Denver's defense didn't. Another Elway pass was deflected by free safety Ronnie Lott. Then Elway started pressing and misfiring, and the interceptions came—two in the second half.

For the Niners the victory completed an unparalleled run of postseason excellence. Greatest team ever? Well, offensively, yes. San Francisco has the perfect scheme and the perfect cast to execute it. And how about Montana, who answered each query regarding his stature among the game's alltime best quarterbacks in the same manner: "I don't want to be judged that way until I retire."

So into the off-season he goes—not to Honolulu and the Pro Bowl ("Elbow's too sore," he says) but to some other sunny isle with Jennifer and the three kids—the Caribbean, maybe. "I hear that in Aruba there's a beach where you can go out 80 yards and the water's only up to your waist," he says. "Perfect for the kids, plus I won't be known there." Don't be too sure. ∎

Guard Harris Barton and linemates shielded Montana.

Photograph by Walter Iooss Jr.

The win completed an unparalleled run of postseason excellence. Greatest team ever? Well, offensively, yes. The 49ers had the perfect scheme and the perfect cast.

Along with his 69 yards rushing, the locked-in Craig caught five passes.

Photograph by Heinz Kluetmeier

BY Jerry Rice

49ers Wide Receiver

We brought back pretty much the same team that we had had the previous season, but now we were a year older and maybe we were a bit better. I remember game-planning for this Super Bowl with our coaches. We had been taught how to handle teams that don't always wrap up their tackles, and that was Denver. The Broncos were known to hit hard, but the fact that they did not always wrap up was a big point of emphasis for our game plan.

Steve Atwater and Dennis Smith were the Broncos safeties, and they were especially fearsome. Atwater was a rookie, but he had had a stellar season, and Smith was just good. We wanted to take them on. The tone was set on our very first drive. I wasn't Joe Montana's first option—he looked for fullback Tom Rathman first, then maybe even tried to find [tight end] Brent Jones. But I was open, so Montana came back to me over the middle, and I caught the ball at the eight. Atwater came over fast, and I took a big hit, but I was able to bounce off and get into the end zone. We all felt really good after that play, and we just started running on all cylinders.

Our defense was great, and sacked John Elway six times, but this was one of the most impressive offensive performances that I have ever been a part of. Being on a team that scores 55 points in the Super Bowl? That's something I will never, ever forget.

BY Dennis Smith

Broncos Safety

The play that did us in came right before the half. We were down 20–3, but we were still in it. There was a timeout and I went to our defensive coordinator, Wade Phillips, and said, "I think we should go three-deep zone. That's what we should do." He nods and goes, "Yeah, O.K.," and puts us in three-deep zone. So many things went wrong on the play. This is how it unfolded: Jerry Rice lined up left, and if no other receiver had gone to that side, I would have taken him like he was my man. But they put Roger Craig in motion past Jerry, so I couldn't go with Jerry because Roger would have gone along the sideline which was my responsibility too. So I kind of watched the play unfold, watched Montana roll out away from me. He pump-faked, and our other safety jumped on it, so there was a huge gap between us. Jerry had the whole side of the field. He broke to the post and I never broke—or didn't break in time. It was too late to get to him.

A running joke in our locker room, especially among the defensive backs, was: Never be in the picture. Of course on this play, I'm in the picture. Every time they show Jerry Rice on this touchdown, you see him looking at me in the end zone.

I can identify with the Buffalo Bills. I played in three Super Bowls, all losses, and this was the third. Each time you get to the big game and lose, the pressure builds to get back and win. Unfortunately, I never got the chance. I just ended up in a lot of pictures.

As far as touchdown catches went, thrice was nice for Rice.

Photograph by Heinz Kluetmeier

HALFTIME

On Super Bowl Sunday some of the most spectacular things happen well away from the football

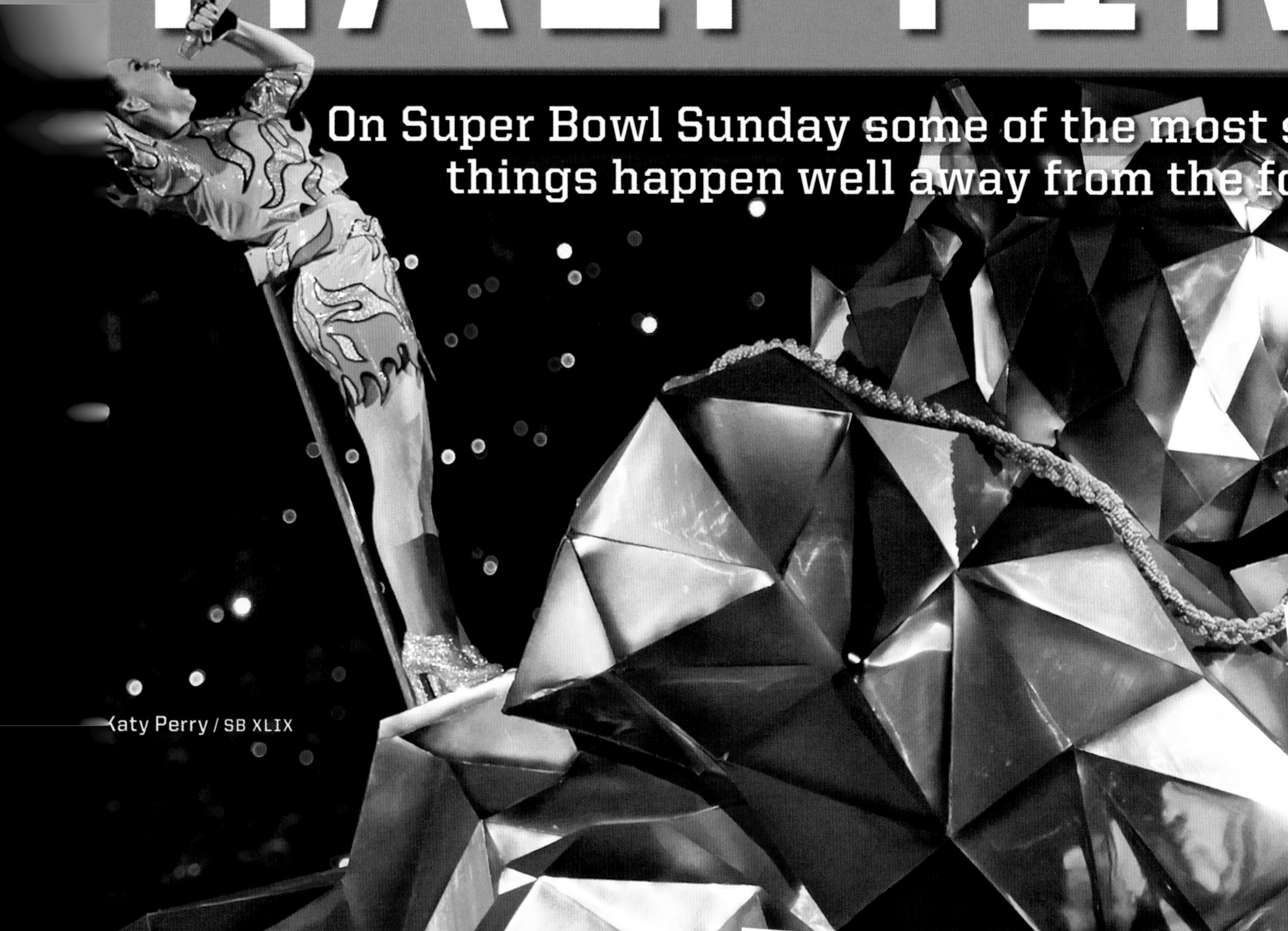

Katy Perry / SB XLIX

Beyoncé / SB XLVII

Riverboat hullabaloo / SB XXIV

DELTA QUEEN

Michael Jackson / SB XXVII

Mardi Gras salute / SB XV

Sartorial flourish / SB XXIII

Helmet gams / SB VII

Rockin' Country Sunday
SB XXVIII

Aerosmith's Steven Tyler with Britney Spears
SB XXXV

DON'T TOUCH THAT DIAL!

Once an afterthought, the mid-game marvel has become must-see | BY AUSTIN MURPHY

IT IS HALFTIME, HEAR IT ROAR. THE 26-FOOT LONG, 16-FOOT HIGH, GOLDEN animatronic lion that carried Katy Perry onto the field for her Super Bowl XLIX halftime medley was designed and built in eight weeks by a team of 30 people in a warehouse in Scappoose, Oregon. Before belting out her hit, "Roar," Perry used a rolling staircase to reach her perch between the creature's shoulder blades. ❡ Now that we know how she got

there, let us ask: How did we get *here*? When did the intermission of a football game become the most culturally significant concert of the year? How did we get to the point where a pop queen borne along by a giant, origami-looking 1,600-pound wildcat was a reasonable entrance for a Super Bowl halftime show?

The answer can be found in Irvine, Calif., in the home of Lucille Walker, and in her collection of scrapbooks. The clippings tell the story of Lucille's husband, who went in for his third open-heart surgery in 1986 and died on the operating table. Tommy Walker was 63. "It's such a shame," lamented Lucille a quarter century later. "Tommy gave his life for entertainment. And nobody knows his name."

Yes, it *is* a shame. And aside from that devotion to entertainment, Tommy Walker just might have a claim to being the most interesting man in the world. In 1934 he performed in Berlin as an 11-year-old trumpet soloist and drum major in his father's American Legion band. Later, while starring in three sports at Black-Foxe Military Institute in Hollywood, Tommy played in the academy's band and also acted in MGM productions. (That's him as the drum major in *Mr. Smith Goes to Washington*.) Tommy joined the Army in '42, scouted behind enemy lines, earned a Bronze Star and a Purple Heart. At USC, after the war, he was the Spirit of Troy drum major—in addition to kicking extra points. Nicknamed Tommy the Toe, he would descend from the stands, shedding his band uniform, trading his shako for a football helmet. The Redskins offered him a tryout.

Instead, Walker became USC's band director. His peppy, whimsical halftime shows, featuring card stunts and pigeon releases, caught the eye of Walt Disney, who hired him to work at the theme park he was building on 160 acres of former orange groves in Anaheim. Walker spent 12 years at Disneyland, and many of its iconic flourishes—fireworks above the castle; Tinker Bell descending along a wire from the Matterhorn—were his creations.

A master of pageantry and a sworn enemy of subtlety, Walker was also a charismatic man whose wide circle of friends included Pete Rozelle. Before the first title game between the AFL and NFL champions, in 1967, Walker urged the young com-

mish to cough up a few bucks for a glitzy halftime show. "Why would we spend all that money?" Rozelle shot back. "That's when everybody goes to the bathroom."

Walker was adamant that he could create a spectacle so engaging that viewers would gladly postpone the call of nature. In the end he produced three such extravaganzas, for Super Bowls I, IV and VII. Although those galas made up a mere fraction of his oeuvre—like the sonnets of Shakespeare or the skateboarding medals won by Shaun White—Walker can still be described, accurately, as the Father of the Super Bowl Halftime Show. Yet considering the overhyped, often incoherent monstrosity into which that event has evolved, he might prefer that you didn't.

IN THE TENSE moments before the armies of Sauron storm the fortress of Helms Deep in *The Lord of the Rings: The Two Towers*, Legolas offers this advice to the bow-wielding battalion around him, "Their armor is weak at the neck!"

"The halftime show is the neck of the Super Bowl," says Bob Thompson, director of the Bleier Center for Television & Popular Culture at Syracuse. "It's where the broadcast is most vulnerable." He is speaking of the show's susceptibility to counterprogramming, such as in 1992, when Fox hijacked 20 million CBS viewers from Super Bowl XXVI's saccharine "Winter Magic" halftime with a riotous episode of *In Living Color.*

Thompson, who calls Super Bowl Sunday the most successful national holiday "since Lincoln gave us Thanksgiving," regards the big broadcast as "three parallel programs." The first is the game. The second is the "film festival put together by the advertising industry." The third is the neck. While the Super Bowl halftime may most years be the most-watched musical performance in the world, Thompson says, "it is certainly not the most beloved."

David Hill, the longtime CEO of Fox Sports, describes the halftime show as "America's multigenerational entertainment for the year." Precisely. For the NFL, the conundrum of annually choosing the performer is similar to a family—grandparents,

Then-NFL commissioner Paul Tagliabue immediately went into a prevent defense. Until Nipplegate the league had given the networks wide latitude in creating their own halftime shows. (CBS had subcontracted this one to MTV, which was informed afterward that it would never work another Super Bowl.) Now, laments Hill, "the NFL chooses the artist, the producer, the director." Which is a shame, he adds, "because a lot of the fun of doing the Super Bowl is the halftime show and the lead-up to it." Minus that, "it's just another huge game."

How would the league cleanse the nation one year after Jackson put "wardrobe malfunction" into the lexicon? Early money was on the aggressively bland ensemble Up With People, which had already performed at four Super Bowls. Concluding, apparently, that Americans had suffered enough, Tagliabue signed off instead on 62-year-old Paul McCartney, whose raciest moment would come during "Get Back," when he sang of the "*lowww*-neck sweater" rocked by the "mommy" of one "Loretta." Subsequent halftimes showcased The Rolling Stones, Prince, Petty, Bruce Springsteen and The Who—a span that might fairly be described as AARP With People.

The NFL has since ventured outside the category of Old Fogies Rock—and been

From far left: Super Bowl I included mapmakers; at V Bunyan and Babe rode smoothly, unlike the boat in the Caribbean (XIII); XVI flaunted Up With People's third appearance; the flag-waving at XXV came during Operation Desert Storm.

parents, kids—trying to agree on one Las Vegas act to see. Entertaining everybody is not just a challenge, says Thompson, it's impossible. "If Tom Petty makes some people deliriously happy, plenty of other people are asking, 'Tom *who?*'"

Petty was one of six consecutive safe and familiar old-fart ensembles booked by a league traumatized by the R-rated finale to its Super Bowl XXXVIII halftime show, in 2004. The camera that captured Janet Jackson's right breast that night after it was exposed by costar Justin Timberlake did so from a football field away. The offending boob—Jackson's, not Timberlake's—was on air for 9/16 of a second. That was long enough for CBS to get hit with a $550,000 fine from the FCC (later voided in court); long enough to stoke the outrage of politicians concerned about America's moral decline. It was long enough to entice 35,000 new subscribers to TiVo, to inspire YouTube and to make "Janet Jackson" the most searched name in Internet history.

rewarded for it. Katy Perry's 13-minute appearance—she was joined by Missy Elliott and Lenny Kravitz—was seen by 118.5 million viewers, making it the most-watched Super Bowl intermission ever. She broke the record set a year earlier, by Bruno Mars, who'd broken the record set by Madonna in 2012. On all three occasions, ratings edged *upward* as the teams broke for halftime. Perry, Mars, Madonna and Beyoncé, who rocked halftime in '13, were chosen in hopes that their appeal might stretch, like one of Keith Richards's neck wattles, across multiple demographics.

Thompson remains underwhelmed. "People pay more than $4 million for 30-second ads [during the broadcast]. This is the most valuable cultural real estate of the year. You've got a captive audience of over 100 million. And this is what they come up with? If I was trying to help an alien understand who we are as a nation, the last thing I would show them is a Super Bowl halftime."

But what if the aliens were already two steps ahead? What if they'd already *infiltrated* the Super Bowl halftime show? How better to explain Up With People?

ON AN IMPOSSIBLY tiny CBS set at Super Bowl X, host Brent Musburger has just handed off to Phyllis George, who is effervescing about the wholesome youths about to take the field, a chipper troupe whose talent level falls between high school variety show and *Waiting for Guffman*. George emphasizes what a privilege it will be to hear "these great kids" produce "some of the greatest sounds in American history!"

That would prove to be a highly generous assessment of the ensuing performance by Up With People, an admirably diverse and deeply earnest act that would later be parodied on *The Simpsons* as the group Hooray For Everything. On this sunny day in Miami, they open with their insipid, eponymous staple, "Up With People"— *Up, up with people! You meet 'em wherever you go!/Up, up with people! They're the best kind of folks we know!* Seriously. That's how it goes.

Up With People was founded in 1965 by J. Blanton Belk, the national director of the Moral Re-Armament movement, in order to provide youth with an alternative

halftime show at Super Bowl XXX. Ross had a killer act, but it ran 13½ minutes. NBC had insisted she trim it to 12, but Steeg pleaded her case and got the extra minute and a half. Accompanied by his son Bryce, then 16, Steeg stopped by Ross's trailer to deliver the news. "She was very happy, obviously," he recalls, "so she gives me a big hug and a kiss." Afterward, Bryce looked at his father and said, "Wow, Dad. You really *are* the man!"

Steeg had worked his way up. The first halftime show he was involved with was "A Salute to the Caribbean," at Super Bowl XIII, in the Orange Bowl. There, a boat "sailed" from isle to isle. "Except we couldn't stop at Haiti," he recalls. The Haitian musicians representing that island had fled, seeking asylum, several days earlier. Halfway through the show, the boat ran out of gas, leaving Steeg to push. ("Not at all," he recalls lying, when asked by a superior whether the boat had malfunctioned.) All that drama unfolded on top of a 120-yard tarp representing the Caribbean Sea. Inevitably, there was trouble rolling it up: One edge needed to be trimmed. Quickly. NFL groundskeeper George Toma shouted, "Anyone got a knife?"

"About eight knives came flying out of the stands," Steeg recalls.

Names of those lost on 9/11 gave gravitas to U2's show at XXXVI. A star-studded wardrobe malfunction at XXXVIII led to safer choices like Springsteen at XLIII, before Madonna (XLVI) and Bruno Mars (XLVIII) helped the NFL get its groove back.

to the antiwar movement. "Its cornerstone," wrote David Allen in the 1967 book *Born to Upturn the World*, "is the burning, almost competitive spirit to live straighter lives than any men have dared to live."

So they did, for three more halftimes—or until minutes after their Super Bowl XX show, when Rozelle turned to another NFL executive and said, "Never f------ again."

The bar was lower in the 1980s; the NFL seemed not to know its own strength. Months before Super Bowl XVI, Jim Steeg, a founder of the NFL's special events department, walked into Rozelle's office and declared, "We've *got* to get Diana Ross to sing the national anthem!"

"Yeah, good luck with that," replied the commissioner.

"They'd never really gone after real star power," recalls Steeg, who succeeded in getting Miss Ross. That made it easier, in 1996, to book her as the headliner for the

He's still a bit defensive, though, about what he insists was the "most unfairly panned" halftime show ever, the unforgettable-for-all-the-wrong-reasons "BeBop Bamboozled" at Super Bowl XXIII in Joe Robbie Stadium. That show featured "the world's largest card trick," performed by the Prince of Prestidigitation, Elvis Presto (in reality, a 33-year-old *Solid Gold* dancer named Alex Cole).

"It was a really good idea," Steeg contends. "The problem was, we had to do it in 3-D because Diet Coke sponsored halftime, and they'd distributed 40 million pairs of 3-D glasses." To revisit the spectacle is to disagree with Steeg: There was nothing unfair about the reviews, which were savage. During his lead-in—"This is the single proudest moment of my life," followed by loud background laughter—and just before he donned 3-D glasses himself, halftime host Bob Costas seemed unable to conceal his mortification at what NBC was about to foist on an unsuspecting planet.

The calculus changed radically in 1992, after Gloria Estefan (supplemented by ice skaters Brian Boitano and Dorothy Hamill) got her head handed to her by *In Living Color* comedians Keenen and Damon Wayans. CBS's Nielsen rating dipped from a 42.1 to a 32.8 that halftime, and the NFL suits had seen enough. The days of jayvee, dinner theater–caliber entertainment were over. The league sent everyone deep. They went after Michael Jackson.

Eleven months before Super Bowl XXVII Steeg sat down with the King of Pop's manager, Sandy Gallin. "I remember pitching them," he says, "and them not really having a clue what we were talking about." At a subsequent meeting, producer Don Mischer pointed out that the Super Bowl would be broadcast in more than 120 countries. Now he had Jackson's full attention.

Steeg recalls Jackson saying, "So you're telling me this show is going live to all those places where I'll never do a concert?" A pause. "I'm in."

"Michael worked harder than anybody [who's done the halftime show], before or since," says Steeg, who remembers seeing Jackson still rehearsing his act at seven the night before the game, in a tent outside the Rose Bowl.

And it showed. Jackson, rocking a bandolier-draped frock coat on loan, apparently, from Muammar Gaddafi, was sensational. The final moments of that show were the most viewed in the history of television at the time.

"All of a sudden," says Hill, the entertainment world saw the value of the Super Bowl halftime show: "That it gave them a worldwide platform to strut their stuff." The NFL has never looked back and now reserves that precious cultural real estate exclusively for blockbuster musical acts. So powerful has the halftime gig become that in the summer of 2014 geniuses in the league office thought: Let's *charge* artists for the privilege of playing the Super Bowl. Roundly mocked for the idea—and told by Katy Perry, among others, to go pound sand—the NFL backed off.

League officials did not want to alienate Perry; finding a commensurate star would not have been easy. The NFL recalled having to re-set in 2002 when Janet Jackson, scheduled to work Super Bowl XXXVI pulled out after the 9/11 terrorist attacks. The task of finding a replacement for Janet Jackson fell to the NFL's top marketing executive, John Collins. Shortly after drawing the gig, Collins saw U2 perform at Madison Square Garden. During one of the band's half-dozen encores that night, the names of the nearly 3,000 people killed six weeks earlier scrolled slowly across the domed roof of the arena. "At first people didn't know what was going on," Collins remembers, "and then you heard, *Oh, my God!*, as they realized. People were reading the names of victims they'd known. It was a heavy moment—an amazing moment."

Collins immediately knew he wanted U2 for halftime. Within two days Bono wasn't just on board with the idea, he was passionate about it. Not surprisingly, this being the cautious, finger-to-the-wind NFL, that enthusiasm was not entirely reciprocated. How would it look, an Irish band commemorating an American tragedy? One TV exec pointed out that a U2 special on NBC had drawn underwhelming ratings.

Not among the handwringers: Roger Goodell, then the league's COO. "He was all for it," says Collins. "Roger gets it." Tagliabue overcame his initial reservations and U2 was a go. The scrolling names would be reprised in New Orleans. The purpose of that solemn roll call, Bono had explained to NFL execs, was to remove the focus from the statistics, the number of deceased, and return it to the individuals.

Stunning in its impact at the Garden, the name-scrolling was exponentially more powerful as Bono belted out "Where the Streets Have No Name" to an international TV audience. The next day Collins got a note from U2 manager Paul McGuinness: "I almost feel sorry for whoever's next."

LUCILLE WALKER HANDS a visitor a yellowing press guide from what's billed as the "Super Bowl Fourth World Championship Game." Tommy's halftime show that day, "Way Down Yonder," blew away anything that had come before. Walker employed 20,000 balloons, 50 American flags, 3,000 pigeons, 37 muskets and three cannons—the weaponry reserved for an on-field reenactment of the Battle of New Orleans. The battle was "complete with exploding cannons and British redcoats being felled by troops under the command of General Andrew Jackson and his unlikely compatriot, the pirate Jean Laffite," according to an appreciation of Walker that appears on the website mardigrasunmasked.com.

Also noteworthy, the appreciation continues, "was the prominence of African-Americans . . . and a jazz funeral procession, with members of local second line clubs strutting across the field. The shebang ended with a mini Mardi Gras parade."

Elaborate as they were, those early productions were bare-bones exercises compared to the megaspectacles of today. Around 900 workers, 400 staff and 450 volunteers—speaking of the armies of Sauron—worked with a frenzied precision, to set up and then strike the stages and sets for Katy Perry's 13-minute show.

Lucille Walker remains . . . underwhelmed. Before bidding her visitor adieu, she offers a confession: For years, she has been unable to watch more than a few moments of any Super Bowl halftime show.

"They don't have anybody who has the showmanship anymore—the pageantry. That's what people want. And that's what we're missing."

Are you listening, NFL? She wants more pageantry. More patriotism. More risk-taking! And, if possible, more pigeons. Get back to where you once belonged. ■

THE MEDIA MONSTER

Just how did the Super Bowl become such an all-platform animal? | BY RICHARD DEITSCH

O N JAN. 16, 1967, THE DAY AFTER THE FIRST-EVER AFL-NFL WORLD Championship Game, now known as Super Bowl I, an article appeared in *The New York Times* describing New Yorkers' reaction to the event. The writer, Bernard Weinraub, put it like this: "New York was gripped by a giddy fever yesterday that began rising at 4 p.m., reached a peak at dusk and began dropping at nightfall. Before the

fever finally broke, a vague madness swept the city: little boys refused to go to the movies, big boys refused to speak, girls—little and big—stormed into kitchens, slammed the door and waited. And waited. "It's impossible," cried Mrs. Lucretia Amari of Brooklyn, while her husband, Dr. S.N. Amari, stared at the Super Bowl football game on television. "He's obsessed with watching all those big lugs on the idiot box." Half a century later, the fever has yet to break. The obsession for the big lugs on the idiot box on Super Sunday is stronger than ever.

That box—and its "smarter" successors—is significant. Year after year, through TV and now through technologies no one imagined in 1967, the game sets viewership and engagement records. Super Bowl XLIX in 2015—a thriller in which the Patriots edged the Seahawks—set a U.S. television record with 114.4 million viewers on NBC. The 13-minute halftime show, featuring a singer (Katy Perry) born 17 years after the first Super Bowl, peaked at 118.5 million viewers, the most for a halftime show. Facebook reported that between kickoff and the final whistle 65 million people mentioned the game, while Twitter logged 28.4 million tweets related to the game and halftime show. That made Super Bowl XLIX (as you might've guessed) the most-tweeted Super Bowl of all time.

Yet even media giants start off small. The first Super Bowl aired on two networks because NFL commissioner Pete Rozelle believed that both CBS (the longtime broadcaster of the NFL) and NBC (the broadcaster of the AFL) had a right to the new championship game. At a cost of $1 million each for the rights CBS drew 26.7 million viewers for Super Bowl I, NBC drew 24.4 million. Of those 51.1 million, none were in Los Angeles, where the game was played. That's because it did not sell out and the NFL mandated a TV blackout within 75 miles of L.A.'s Memorial Coliseum. Today, CBS, NBC and Fox pay the NFL some $3 billion annually for nine-year rights deals that includes three Super Bowls per network. While television has long been the game's dominant medium, the growth of the Super Bowl wouldn't have happened without the writers and photographers covering it. For the inaugural game in L.A., there were 338 credentials given for newspaper, magazine and news service

staffers, 262 for television and radio people and 170 for photographers. That's 770 media credentials. For Super Bowl XLIX the total was 5,500. And that's not even the record. The media list for the 2014 Super Bowl numbered 6,329.

PETE ROZELLE, the NFL's commissioner from 1960 to '89, understood the importance of the media's role in promoting football, and he wanted writers and broadcasters to leave L.A. after Super Bowl I thinking how much better pro football's championship was than the World Series. The writer Mickey Herskowitz, then with the AFL's promotions department, said each room at the Statler Hilton Hotel (the media hotel) received a cheese and fruit basket that included bottles of bourbon and Scotch. Rozelle also began the custom of bussing media to and from the stadium and practice sites. "Pete was sensitive to helping media and TV," said Joe Browne, the NFL's longtime communications head and now a special adviser to the league. "He was always afraid of just one thing—having a lopsided game."

At early Super Bowls reporters enjoyed access they could only dream of today. Jerry Izenberg of *The* (Newark) *Star-Ledger* covered Super Bowl I—as well as 48 other games. He recalls how he and his friend Jack Murphy, the famous sportswriter out of San Diego, drove to Santa Barbara to interview Green Bay players at their hotel. At the front of the hotel stood a man on guard. His name was Vince Lombardi.

"I knew Lombardi was steaming about being in Santa Barbara," Izenberg says. "We pulled up to the hotel, the ocean right on the side, and Lombardi said, 'What are you doing here?' I said, 'We came to talk to your team.' He said, 'We should not even be here.' I knew how to push his buttons so I said, 'This is a beautiful place, isn't it?' He said, 'What do you mean this is a beautiful place? This is hell. Look how pretty it is.' Then he realized that there were 10 players looking down and listening. He said to them. 'And none of you better be in the pool today either.' Then he walked away."

There was no Super Bowl Media Day in those years—at least not as we know it today. During the week before the first game, Izenberg and others wanted to talk with Rozelle about the Coliseum not selling out, so NFL officials put together an impromptu press conference in Rozelle's hotel suite for a dozen print reporters. This was the inaugural State of the League press conference that the NFL commissioner now gives each year in a ballroom in front of thousands of media members.

Detroit News columnist Jerry Green, one of three writers along with Izenberg and *Star-Ledger* beat writer Dave Klein to cover every Super Bowl, says there is no overstating the impact of Super Bowl III—when the upstart AFL Jets defeated the NFL's Colts—on the growth of media around the Super Bowl. Green was at poolside of the Galt Ocean Mile Hotel in Fort Lauderdale when Jets quarterback Joe Namath conducted an impromptu media session for a dozen reporters who wanted to ask him about his having guaranteed a win earlier that week. This media session produced arguably the most iconic photo of Super Bowl Week: a shirtless Namath relaxing on a lounge chair while talking to the overdressed press. (The photograph, which appears on page 34 of this book, was taken by SPORTS ILLUSTRATED's Walter Iooss Jr., one of three photographers to shoot every Super Bowl.) Green, sporting horned-rim glasses and a crew cut, is gazing at Broadway Joe, pen in hand.

By Super Bowl V, the production surrounding the TV broadcast had ballooned to

to address a host of reporters. In 2012, the league started selling tickets to fans to attend Media Day. At Super Bowl XLIX tickets to attend interview sessions of the Patriots and Seahawks cost $28.50. Seven thousand fans coughed it up.

"Media Day is a f------ joke now," Izenberg says. "You are dependent on the personality of the guy much more than before because before you were sitting in his room talking to him. The morning before Super Bowl I, I was in the hotel coffee shop having breakfast with [Chiefs linebacker] E.J. Holub. We were talking about how if they won the game he would get $15,000. If they lost, $7,500. It was an enormous payday. His hands were shaking and he says, 'Feel my palms; they are sweating.' I asked, 'Is that because you have the opportunity to prove yourself against the NFL?' He said, 'No. It's because if we win, we are going to make $15,000.' "

Izenberg says that one of the moments he felt the Super Bowl had crossed the Rubicon into media phenomenon was when MTV veejay Downtown Julie Brown worked Media Day in 1992 and pursued Redskins defensive end Dexter Manley for an interview. "She came bouncing in, jumped into his lap and said, 'Can I talk to you, Dexter?' " Izenberg says. "I said, 'F--- this.' And I walked away."

The two-network deal at Super Bowl I gave NBC's Paul Christman and CBS's Frank Gifford a chance to talk; MTV's Downtown Julie Brown flexed with Washington's Charles Mann at XXVI; at XLIX press and ticket buyers converged en masse at Media Day.

more than a dozen cameras and 100 crew members. Viewership that year was 46 million. Green remembers first being hit in the head by television cameras in the locker room—a standard occupational hazard in recent decades—after Super Bowl VI, and the increased attention soon meant decreased intimacy. Izenberg says the last player he interviewed in his hotel room during Super Bowl week was Cowboys receiver Drew Pearson before Super Bowl X.

The birth of ESPN in 1979 further jacked up coverage during Super Bowl Week and the 2003 creation of the NFL Network ushered in the era of 24/7 weeklong hyperventilations, and between those developments the modern Media Day evolved. Before Super Bowl XX in 1986 the Bears and Patriots, rather than conduct media activities at their hotels or practice facilities, held successive Photo Day sessions at the Superdome on a Tuesday. In '97, the NFL set up individual podiums for players

In 2014 an Austrian TV reporter, Phillip Hajszan, came to Media Day dressed as Mozart (U.S. reporters mistook him for Benjamin Franklin) though by then the standard for Media Day absurdity had been set. In 2008 Ines Gomez Mont, a reporter from Mexico's TV Azteca, had arrived wearing a wedding dress and asked Tom Brady to marry her. "I've never had a proposal," Brady replied. "What is your name, first?"

Okay, so Media Day is not quite a breeding ground for, well, breeding, just yet. But it is a crush like few others in sports, and it seems bound to grow bigger, right along with the Super Bowl's reach. When Media Day began on that Tuesday in 1986, Super Bowl XX was about to be televised to 59 foreign countries. By '93 the number had increased to 101. And in 2015 the game was aired live in more than 25 different languages and in some 170 countries and territories. You know what that means? Only about 87 more lands to conquer. ∎

HALF A MINUTE TO GLORY

For a pretty price, a Super Bowl spot can leave a lasting impression | BY BILL SYKEN

C AREERS CAN BE DEFINED BY A SUPER BOWL PERFORMANCE—NOT JUST for players, or halftime entertainers, but also for the actors in the game's much-anticipated commercials. Consider the case of Jesse Heiman, whose face is more familiar than his name. Nerdy and decidedly plump with a ruddy complexion and curly brown hair, he has appeared in scores of movies and TV shows. He was a pledge in *Old School*;

he pestered Johnny Drama for an autograph in *Entourage*; he watched Peter Parker beat up bully Flash Thompson in *Spider-Man*. A fan made a YouTube compilation of Heiman's extra spots that went viral and earned Heiman a spot on *The Tonight Show*, where he was interviewed by Jay Leno while sitting alongside Jamie Foxx.

But Heiman's fame jumped by an order of magnitude during Super Bowl XLVII, when he was featured in a GoDaddy ad making out with supermodel Bar Refaeli, supporting the company's "where smart meets sexy" campaign. The next day Heiman logged on to Yahoo! and saw himself and Refaeli on the front page. High school acquaintances who had missed his other cameos were friend-requesting him on Facebook. On one plane trip, the pilot left the cockpit to take a picture with the would-be leading man. A documentary crew began following Heiman around to see if the Super Bowl spot could propel him into the showbiz foreground. He even landed the first starring role of his career, as the title character in a short film called *Schmoolie the Deathwatcher*, all because of what was, for him, a Super Sunday. "What people remember from

that game," Heiman says, "are the lights going out [in the Superdome] and me."

Companies spend so much on Super Bowl ads chasing the Heiman experience—that is, they hope that after the game, people will be talking about them. That's why advertisers go all out, pulling stunts to grab viewers' attention. By going for the big score, they increase the sense that the Super Bowl is a special occasion.

In the early years Super Bowl ads weren't much different from others, though some did prove memorable. In 1974 Master Lock ran its classic spot in which a marksman pierces the body of a lock with a bullet. (Master Lock appeared in 21 Super Bowls, investing large percentages of its ad budget on the placement.) Six years later Joe Greene's memorable "Hey kid, catch" ad for Coca-Cola appeared during Super Bowl XIV in which Mean Joe's Steelers beat the Rams 31–19.

But the modern phenomenon of the Super Bowl ad traces to 1984, when Apple aired an ad titled "1984." The 60-second spot, directed by Ridley Scott (*Alien*, *Blade Runner*) was more short movie than traditional ad; instead of overtly promoting the launch of the Macintosh computer or touting its features, the ad re-created the

THE BEST

Bud Bowl SUPER BOWL XXIII

Bottles of Bud and Bud Light competed in a game running parallel to the real action, with scoring continuing throughout. The battle proved so compelling that the Bud Bowl had eight iterations, ending at Super Bowl XXXI.

Hey Kid, Catch SUPER BOWL XIV

The Coca-Cola spot moved slowly and the overblown background music was corny, but the moment when Joe Greene's meanness melted away in the stadium tunnel and he tossed a young fan his jersey remains a pure classic.

When I Grow Up SUPER BOWL XXXIII

A witty, insightful ad for the job-search site Monster.com. Kids talked about hoping to grow up to "be a yes man," or to "be replaced on a whim," or to "file all day." The rare ad that drew laughs and intelligently promoted the product.

Old Milwaukee SUPER BOWL XLVII

In a bizarre spot that aired only in Sherman, Texas, Ardmore, Okla., and Glendive, Mont., a mustachioed, tank-topped Will Ferrell made out with a middle-aged nonsupermodel on a bus for nearly 30 seconds.

Ram Trucks SUPER BOWL XLVII

Chrysler reappropriated "So God Made a Farmer," a talk by radio host Paul Harvey at the 1978 Future Farmers of America convention. Setting the speech to images of the rural U.S. yielded a Super Bowl one-off and an arresting surprise.

atmosphere of George Orwell's book and only mentioned the upcoming product at the end, with the promise "You'll see why 1984 won't be like *1984*." While the spot that made a public splash that year was Wendy's "Where's the Beef?," people in the ad game viewed "1984" as a watershed. "The industry was moving to a very fast, 15-second kind of world," says Peter Daboll, CEO of Ace Metrix, which measures the effectiveness of video advertising. "That ad was the start of the story-telling genre."

The appeal of the long advertisement rose even as those Super Bowl seconds became ever more expensive. In 1967 a 30-second spot cost $42,000 (about $300,000 in today's dollars). For the 2015 Super Bowl a 30-second spot cost $4.5 million. Networks can charge advertisers so much because the Super Bowl provides an extreme version of what sports in general offer—a television program that is watched by a large audience at the same time. The Super Bowl takes the American audience, divided among so many diversions, and brings it together.

That's why, as much as these ads cost, the numbers suggest they can significantly bump a company's bottom line. One study shows that movies which run ads during the Super Bowl do better than ones which don't; another shows that companies' stock prices get at least a short-term boost from a big-game appearance. Super Bowl advertising was key to Career Builder's overtaking Monster.com in the online job search market, says Tim Calkins, a professor of marketing at the Kellogg School of Management at Northwestern. He also points out that Chrysler's 2011 ad featuring Eminem helped spark the brand's resurgence. "The Super Bowl can be a great investment," says Calkins. "If you want to reach a large portion of the U.S. population quickly, there is nothing quite like the Super Bowl."

It is why these ads try so hard—and sometimes too hard—to stand out. "Win the hearts and minds of America. This is what a Super Bowl ad needs to do," says Gretchen Walsh, a senior vice president at advertising giant McKinney who has worked on several Super Bowl ads, including Budweiser's popular talking frogs spot. When she advises clients about advertising in the big game, she urges them to produce a big ad; they shouldn't just take the standard approach of touting a product's functional benefits and hammering its logo. Instead they should try to make the many "Best" lists that appear after the game—and to create a positive impression for their brand that will linger. That last

point is crucial because, as Walsh says, "Will [an ad] increase sales on a Sunday night when people have had 18 chicken wings and six Budweisers? Probably not."

The success of Super Bowl ads can also be measured in the laughs it gets. Typical TV ads deploy humor about 20% of the time. For the Super Bowl it's more than 50%, according to Ace Metrix. But humor can be risky, leading to negative p.r. This happened with bad jokes that backfired for companies such as Groupon *(below)* and Homeaway (in 2011's "Test Baby" a faux infant is launched into a glass pane), and the risk factor explains why those not going for yuks often opt for unassailable earnestness. Take Clint Eastwood's "Halftime in America" pep talk to the nation on behalf of Chrysler in 2012, or a 2014 Chevy ad which honored World Cancer Day.

Walsh says companies have become increasingly conservative in their big-game ads, perhaps, as Calkins says, because "people don't get fired for airing an ineffective piece of advertising on *Modern Family*. They might well be fired for airing an ineffective ad on the Super Bowl." YouTube can be a valuable tool in helping advertisers avoid an expensive mistake. While the Super Bowl ads had traditionally been kept secret so as to surprise viewers at game time, some advertisers now release ads early online, which can increase viewership while serving as a test run. In 2013 Mercedes-Benz teased online an ad featuring curvaceous Kate Upton distracting a team of young football players as they washed her car. "They got a negative response, flipped it and ran an ad with Willem Dafoe as the devil," says Daboll. Upton made only a brief, and more tame, appearance in the Dafoe spot.

So what to make of Heiman's GoDaddy gig? The ad can be found on many Top 10 lists, but on some worst lists too. Every year Calkins's Northwestern students watch the game and grade each ad, and Heiman's spot received a D. In scoring done by Ace Metrix, Heiman's spot ranked 45th out of the 46 that ran during the game, besting only a garish Calvin Klein spot which proved the axiom, "if you're going to show up in your underwear, make sure it's that kind of party." Daboll, the Ace Metrix CEO, offered a key caveat to GoDaddy's low ranking. Keep in mind, he says, that the domain name registrar became known to consumers largely through its Super Bowl advertising. "Their goal is sheer awareness," says Walsh. "The worst thing that happens to an ad is if no one likes it or hates it. Neutral is death." At a Super Bowl party, the last thing you want to be is the guest that no one remembers. ■

THE WORST

Groupon SUPER BOWL XLV
The ad began as if it would be a plea from actor Timothy Hutton on behalf of the people of Tibet, but switched to show Hutton in a Tibetan restaurant, getting a good deal on his meal because of Groupon. Tasteless.

Free to Pee SUPER BOWL XLVI
In "Free to Pee," a young boy ran about searching for a place to relieve himself, and found one in a swimming pool. It didn't cost him anything—just like TaxACT's federal return filing software! People said "Ewwww!" and moved on.

Hulk SUPER BOWL XXXVII
Five months before the Ang Lee movie was released by Universal, in 2003, this ad actually dampened anticipation, because the trailer showed the big green title character with special effects that were not in a finished state.

Nationwide SUPER BOWL XLIX
The ad started with a mop-topped youngster mooning about beautiful moments in life he'd never experience. Then we got the big reveal—the boy was dead. There's a time to talk about preventable fatal accidents, but this wasn't it.

Lemmings SUPER BOWL XIX
One year after its much celebrated 1984 ad, Apple returned with a filmlike spot showing blindfolded businesspeople going over a cliff until one is saved, miraculously, by becoming aware of Macintosh Office software. Obtuse.

Preening Michael Irvin lit up the end zone twice in Dallas's 52–17 Super Bowl XXVII win, the first of two routs over Buffalo.

Photograph by John Biever

Super Bowl XXV to Super Bowl XXXVI

3RD QUARTER

The 'Boys had it (three big game wins). The Bills did not (four big game losses)

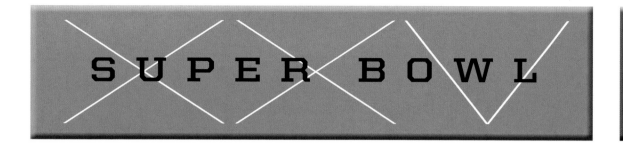
SUPER BOWL XXV

January 27, 1991
Tampa Stadium, Tampa

HEAD COACHES
BILL PARCELLS Giants | MARV LEVY Bills

NEW YORK GIANTS 20

BUFFALO BILLS 19

Lawrence Taylor's fumble recovery in the NFC title game got the Giants to Tampa.

Photograph by John W. McDonough

THE BILLS had a no-huddle offense and the star-stocked makings of a dynasty. The Giants had a defense big and battering enough to make he-men flinch. After 59 minutes this test came down to those two enduring words: wide right.

WEATHER	POINT SPREAD	TIME OF GAME	TV AUDIENCE

71°, mostly cloudy	Bills by 6½	3:19	79.5 million

GIANTS 20 BILLS 19

QTR 4

TIME OUTS 0 0

DOWN 2 TO GO 10 BALL ON 29

Norwood's kick sailed to the right of the goalposts (you can see it below) and never curled in.

Photograph by Ronald C. Modra

Rollicking All-Pro linebacker Pepper Johnson corralled Kelly.

Photograph by John Biever

JUST THE FACTS

Statistical Leaders

Rushing **THURMAN THOMAS** (BUF) 15 carries, 135 yds, 1 TD

Passing **JEFF HOSTETLER** (NY) 20 of 32, 222 yds, 1 TD

Receiving **MARK INGRAM** (NY) 5 catches, 74 yds

MVP OTTIS ANDERSON Giants Running Back

The Ring
10 carat gold inscribed with player's name, number, helmet

Anthem Performer
Whitney Houston

Halftime Performer
New Kids on the Block

Attendance 72,301

Ticket Price $150

Behind the Scenes

Because the U.S. had just commenced Operation Desert Storm in the Persian Gulf, ABC aired a report from news anchor Peter Jennings at halftime, rather than the New Kids on the Block show.

They Said It

"If you want to write a Super Bowl script, this is probably what you have to write. It came down to the last kick."

—Bills quarterback **JIM KELLY**

Museum Piece

The game plan drawn up by Giants defensive coordinator Bill Belichick—in the form of a looseleaf binder and overhead, black-and-white photos—is held at the Pro Football Hall of Fame.

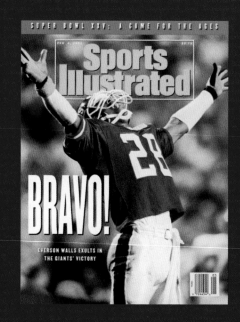

PURE PUNISHMENT

After being pummeled by the Giants, Buffalo lost on a painful play | BY PAUL ZIMMERMAN

WIN ONE SUPER BOWL and you're a Super Bowl–winning coach. Win two and you're a genius, a man with an approach to the game that must be studied and copied. So it is with Bill Parcells, whose Giants beat the Bills 20–19 in a heart-stopper in Super Bowl XXV, four years after New York had beaten Denver in Super Bowl XXI. "Power wins football games," Parcells repeated endlessly amid the postgame locker room turmoil. "Power wins football games."

That philosophy has permeated his approach to the game: Draft big, powerful people to play on both sides of the ball, grind out a rushing game behind a hog-type line, stuff the run on defense and, when the other team passes, make sure the routes are short and the receivers are funneled to the linebackers. Big people attacking little people. It's a rather brutal concept, and it resulted in a whopping advantage in possession time—40:33 to 19:27—that left the Bills' defenders groggy and rubber-legged in the Florida humidity.

New York drives of 11 and 10 plays in the first half and a pair of 14-play possessions in the second, one of which lasted 9:29, sapped the strength of Buffalo's defense. Yet as the game moved to the two-minute warning, the Bills pulled themselves together and forced the Giants to punt from the Buffalo 48. The Bills took over on their own 10 with 2:16 to play, and with eight seconds left they had gotten down to the New York 30. Scott Norwood was lining up a 47-yard field goal try and prayers were being offered on both sidelines.

The kick never had a chance. It started right, but "it wasn't moving, it wasn't being drawn in," said a disconsolate Norwood afterward. The Giants' one-point lead was preserved.

The game highlighted two power runners, New York's Ottis Anderson, who was voted MVP for his 102 yards on 21 carries, and Buffalo's Thurman Thomas, who should have won the award on the strength of his 135 yards on 15 carries, plus five catches for 55 more yards. If there had been an award for courage, it would have gone to the Giants' QB, Jeff Hostetler, who was whacked unmercifully by Buffalo pass rushers in the first half. The worst hit was a straight-up shot by 270-pound end Leon Seals, and on the next series Hostetler was sacked for a safety by All-Pro end Bruce Smith. He bounced back to throw a 14-yard touchdown pass to wideout Stephen Baker in the second quarter.

After Seals leveled Hostetler, the Giants gave the quarterback an ammonia cap to sniff. He later admitted that much of the first half was "kind of a blur." Even in the postgame locker room, Hostetler's older brother, Ron, a former Penn State linebacker, said "He still isn't sure where he is." An ugly purple welt ran almost the length of Jeff Hostetler's left side, and his right temple bore bruise marks. He moved in slow motion, trying to put on his shoes. "How do you feel?" Ron asked.

"Still a little woozy," said Jeff. "Pretty bad headache."

"I knew that if he hung in there, we'd be O.K.," said Ron. "It was like we were back in the yard when we were kids. He'd get knocked down, get up, go into the house crying and then come back out, ready to go."

This time "go" meant helping beat down Buffalo. "I've never been so tired in a football game," said Bills linebacker Shane Conlan. "I was tired in the first quarter. They keep pounding with guys like Anderson. Then they run a play-fake off that, and Hostetler bootlegs and throws that drag pattern to a tight end coming across. You should be on to it, but you're not.

"I broke my face mask on Anderson in the first half. It snapped and turned all the way around to the right side of my helmet. First time I ever broke a face mask."

The Giants defense was equally punishing. "No other team ever hit me this hard," said Bills receiver Andre Reed. "You can't even compare this to anything I've ever been through. They bruised up my whole body."

Thomas, though, kept the Bills in the game. He put Buffalo's final points on the board early in the fourth quarter with a 31-yard run in which he bounced free of safety Myron Guyton's head-on tackle. The TD gave Buffalo a 19–17 lead, and then the Giants went on their game-winning drive—14 plays, 74 yards, 7:32—which ended with Matt Bahr's 21-yard field goal. Hostetler hit four of six passes. Anderson still fought for yards.

"They were sagging," said Bob Mrosko, New York's tight end. "They weren't pursuing as hard. We had told ourselves that no matter what we'd play our style of football. Now it was winning for us."

A game played under the shadow of war in the Middle East, in a stadium with the tightest security of any Super Bowl game, became a classic. It was Parcells's kind of football, Giants football, the fruition of a dream that began eight seasons ago when he became New York's coach. If a legacy is attached to this game, it will be that it was played the way Super Bowls are supposed to be played. ∎

Clouded and bruised by big hits, Hostetler still led.

Photograph by Richard Mackson

183

Anderson's physical running, and this third-quarter score, helped the Giants take a 17-12 lead.

Photograph by Peter Read Miller

BY Carl Banks

Giants Linebacker

We had watched the highlights of the Raiders and Bills matchup in the AFC championship game, and what Buffalo accomplished was one of the most epic offensive performances any of us had ever seen. They ran Oakland off the field. So we all waited patiently to get our game plan from the coaching staff to see what strategy they had in mind. When defensive coordinator Bill Belichick told us his plan, the room kind of fell silent. Some of us were insulted and a few guys cursed at him. Remember, Belichick was a young coordinator back then.

He wanted us to allow Thurman Thomas to run for 100 yards? That didn't fit our bill. A point of pride for our D was not letting any player to run for 100 yards. And now we were encouraged to allow it? A couple guys actually screamed at Belichick. But then he broke it all down for us. He brought it back to the last eight games and explained that the Bills weren't using a traditional run game. Thurman was getting a lot of his yards in the flat, on swing passes. We had to force him to run—let him run, and we could shut them down in other ways.

As we learned, there was a method to Belichick's madness. It was a masterful game plan.

The game was so hard-fought. Both teams played to the point of exhaustion. By the time Scott Norwood lined up for the kick, I remember thinking, "You know, if they win on this kick, I know they earned it." It was a hell of a game.

BY Thurman Thomas

Bills Running Back

Our hurry-up offense, it was fast. I had 20 touches that day, 15 carries and five catches, and felt like I could just go. I think I checked out of the game four times, three times because I needed a breather and one time on the first play of the second quarter when I got hit pretty hard on a tackle by Carl Banks. We felt like we were the best team in the NFL that season, and maybe even the best team that day. I had 135 yards rushing in the game and people say I would have been MVP if we had won, but you don't think about that kind of stuff. It was a devastating loss. It all ended with that field goal. Wide right. I can't tell you how many times I have heard those words, "Wide right. Wide right."

I actually didn't watch the field goal. I was on the bench and I just sat in silence. I waited for the crowd to react. I figured I would know what it sounded like if he made it, and I would know what it sounded like if he didn't. Poor Scott Norwood. The game didn't come down to that missed kick; there were so many missed opportunities before that, so many times we could have clinched it. But, wow, in that moment, it hurt. It was almost disbelief, as if you couldn't realize that something like that actually happened or could happen, that it could end in that fashion. People might say the Bills are losers because we lost four Super Bowls in a row. But you look at us, we accomplished a lot. Four AFC titles, total dominance—we put Buffalo on the map.

"We made them work for everything they got," said Giants linebacker Carl Banks. "The big thing is we played as a team: *t-e-a-m*. I can't emphasize ithat enough."

Thomas, here tangled up in blue, ran splendidly but paid a price.
Photograph by John Biever

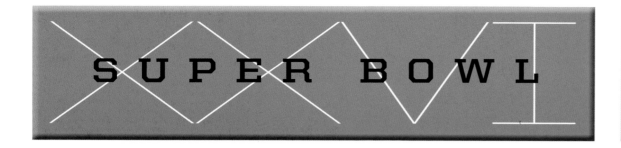

SUPER BOWL XXVI

WASHINGTON
REDSKINS | 37

BUFFALO
BILLS | 24

With free agency awaiting him in the offseason, Rypien came out in fine form.

Photograph by John Iacono

SOME VERY large and very skilled men played for the Redskins, who all season long were the best, most complete team in the NFL. The high-scoring Bills, meanwhile, had their defensive troubles—and that, finally, is what did them in.

DOME

Outside: 26°

POINT SPREAD

Redskins by 7

TIME OF GAME

3:43

TV AUDIENCE

79.6 million

Washington's offensive line—the famed Hogs—protected its quarterback all day, not allowing a sack.
Photograph by John Biever

After Riggs, a goal-line specialist, scored his second touchdown, Washington led 24-0 early in the third quarter.

Photograph by John Biever

JUST THE FACTS

Statistical Leaders

Rushing EARNEST BYNER (WAS) 14 carries, 49 yds

Passing MARK RYPIEN (WAS) 18 of 33, 292 yds, 2 TDs

Receiving GARY CLARK (WAS) 7 catches, 114 yds, 1 TD

MVP MARK RYPIEN Redskins Quarterback

The Ring
Feathers in logo have three diamonds for three titles

Anthem Performer
Harry Connick Jr.

Halftime Performer
Gloria Estefan

Attendance 63,130

Ticket Price $150

Behind the Scenes

On the Redskins' second drive, Mark Rypien hit Art Monk in the end zone for an apparent TD. But in reviewing the play officials saw that the edge of Monk's right foot was on the white end line. The call was overturned, the first time a Super Bowl TD had been nullified by instant replay.

They Said It

"We only hire guys like me ... handsome, elegant, articulate."
— Redskins tackle JOE JACOBY, a hog

Going the Distance at Last

This third title for Joe Gibbs's Redskins was the first after a full slate of games. The 1982 and '87 NFL seasons were shortened by player strikes.

Excerpted from **SPORTS ILLUSTRATED** *February 3, 1992*

ALL-AROUND AWESOME

Behind a gallant QB and a blitzing defense, the Redskins ruled | BY RICK TELANDER

THE WAIT SEEMED INTERMINABLE— maybe it was because of all the time the out-of-towners spent in the Minneapolis Skyway System (15 miles of clean, elevated halls connected to cash machines) searching for Kirby Puckett or Prince or the store where Prince buys his pants— but now, at last, we have the answers to a number of nettlesome questions.

1) If the Redskins played the Bills in the Super Bowl 10 times, with two weeks to prepare, how many times would the Skins win? Answer: nine (10, if Bills defensive line coach Chuck Dickerson were allowed to speak before every game).

2) Does Washington QB Mark Rypien have charisma? Answer: Yes, if completing 18 of 33 passes for 292 yards and two TDs is your idea of excitement.

3) What tool best sculpts ice? Answer: a chainsaw.

4) Whom would you want standing between you and a band of crazed assassins? Answer: the Hogs.

The thrust here is that the Redskins are a good team, a very good team—a damn good team. They won 17 games this season and lost only twice. They whipped their NFC playoff foes, the Falcons and the Lions, by a combined 65–17. They tied the Saints for the best turnover ratio during the regular season with plus-18, and then went plus-13 in the postseason. They have the premier offensive line in the NFL (those Hogs), the best trio of wide receivers (Gary Clark, Art Monk and Ricky Sanders) and the best coach (Joe Gibbs). And for the title they crushed Buffalo 37–24 in a game that wasn't as close as the score suggests.

"If we'd scored before the half," said Bills center Kent Hull, "we could have won." No, they couldn't have. Washington led 17–0 at intermission, but if it had been 17–7 or 17–17, the Redskins still would have won. They are a team of remarkable strength and determination. Boring, perhaps, but disciplined and smart. "If the rest of Washington ran as efficiently as this football team,

Gibbs won his third; Levy lost the second of four.

Photograph by Al Tielemans

there wouldn't be any deficit," said Redskins center Jeff Bostic, while ripping tape off his knees after the game and puffing on a big cigar.

Washington did face one gut-check moment, in the third quarter, after the Bills' Thurman Thomas—who missed the first two plays when he couldn't find his helmet—raced around left end for a one-yard TD to make the score 24–10. Thomas had gained only nine yards in eight carries, but on his TD play he scampered untouched into the end zone. If the Bills had a chance, this was it: Stop the Redskins on their next possession, snatch momentum, and maybe the memory of last year's one-point Super Bowl loss to the Giants would vanish like spring snow.

But up stepped Rypien, the big galoot who in the regular season passed for 3,564 yards and still received almost no respect. Last week Ryp had been taken to task by various analysts for being colorless and

immobile, for never having won the Big One and for having a bad haircut. But he put all that behind him, and working Washington's newly added no-huddle attack he marched the Skins 79 yards to a touchdown. On the drive Rypien completed four of seven passes, the last a 30-yarder that landed softly on the outstretched gloves of Clark as he sailed into the right corner of the end zone. The play was called Scram TD, and it made the Bills want to run and hide.

For Rypien the drive was more sweet vindication. He showed he could produce when it counted, that he wasn't simply a passenger in a big, fast car. Already he had been tested physically. In the second quarter he had been crushed by linebackers Cornelius Bennett and Darryl Talley while throwing an incompletion. Rypien lay on the ground, unable to breathe after the blow to his ribs. Then he got up and staggered to the huddle. "I called the play like this," he said later, making his voice into a weak croak. "I couldn't call the signals, and we almost ran out of time."

He did get the play off, however, throwing a breathless 34-yard strike to Clark. Two plays later, Gerald Riggs scored on a one-yard run, and Washington was ahead 17–0. "We knew we could move the ball," Rypien would say later, and they did, all game. Buffalo's Jim Kelly, meanwhile, was getting hammered by a Washington defense that overwhelmed Buffalo's offensive line, making the Bills' own no-huddle offense look like a panic attack.

Two hours after the game, out on the empty field, Annette Rypien watched proudly as a sportscaster interviewed her husband. With one eye on daughter Ambre, who was eager to jump on Daddy's lap, she smiled and said, "You talk about hitting the jackpot— Super Bowl win, MVP, new contract?" She smiled more. "He deserves it. He deserves the cheers. I don't think 'nice' describes him. 'Nice' is just putting on a face. He's sincere—a real person."

That he is. And a real quarterback, to boot. ■

He's in! No, he's not. Monk's leaping grab for an apparent score made history as the first Super Bowl TD to get overturned by replay.

Photograph by Walter Iooss Jr.

BY Mark Rypien

Redskins Quarterback

At the beginning of the game, the Bills' defense was flying around with reckless abandon. Two of the first three plays we called were short pass plays, three-step drops, and I got hit on both. I went to the sideline when we had to punt and said to our offensive line, "Guys, what the heck's going on?" Here's a group of guys who let me get sacked only seven times all year. I was freaking out a little bit. I was saying, "Hey, this doesn't happen. I don't take seven-step drops or five-step drops and get hit, never mind get buried on three-step drops."

They said, "Relax. These guys are jacked up higher than the Metrodome. Don't worry, we'll wear them down." That reassurance gave me the confidence I needed. If I had had to worry about what the other team was doing and getting beat up every play, I wouldn't have been in the right state of mind. Lo and behold, we did wear them down.

The week before the Super Bowl, Disney had gone to everybody who might have an impact on the game and said, If you win Super Bowl MVP, we have some lines we want you to practice. Really tough lines. [Laughs.] At the end of the game, they came and said, "You're the guy. We're going to do this." I had my three-year-old daughter, Ambre, in my hand. The emotion was sincere. I screamed at the top of my lungs: "I'm going to Disney World!" They said it was one of the better ones they'd seen because it was spontaneous. There was excitement, joy, passion.

BY Jim Kelly

Bills Quarterback

I noticed Thurman [Thomas] wasn't in the game when I got into the huddle. Everyone blows that out so much, that he missed the first two plays because he couldn't find his helmet. The thing is, you always put your helmet in the same place every time. Someone else put on his helmet, no names will be mentioned, realized it wasn't his, and put it down not where he got it. It wasn't Thurman's fault.

I'm very superstitious. Frank Reich, my backup, and I ate lunch every Friday. If we won the week before, we'd go to the same restaurant until we lost. That year, we had been going to the Orchard Park Café and the Friday before the Super Bowl, our table, our chairs, our plates, our silverware, everything was FedExed to Minneapolis so we could sit in the same seats as the Friday before. It was set up where we had pregame meal, off to the side. Unfortunately that didn't work.

After the game I heard the things our assistant Chuck Dickerson had said before the game bad-mouthing Washington's big studs. Going into a game like that you don't need to give a team any more motivation.

I was the quarterback who led our team to four Super Bowls. The more people look back at what we did, the more they're amazed. To have the mental approach we had, when you know you didn't win the year before, and being able to get back year after year after year.

XXVI

REDSKINS | BILLS

Mark Rypien showed that he could produce when it counted, that he wasn't simply a passenger in a big, fast car. "He deserves it," said his wife Annette of the big game glory.

The game helped Rypien land a three-year, $9-million deal to stay with the Redskins.

Photograph by Damian Strohmeyer

SUPER BOWL XXVII

January 31, 1993
Rose Bowl, Pasadena

HEAD COACHES
JIMMY JOHNSON Cowboys | MARV LEVY Bills

DALLAS
COWBOYS | 52

BUFFALO
BILLS | 17

The California sun helped produce a cheerful scene before the Dallas rout.

Photograph by Bill Frakes

WHEN THE Bowl-beleaguered Bills couldn't hold on to the football—nine turnovers!—the young Cowboys knew exactly what to do with it. This win officially put Dallas's late-'80s doldrums in the past. That's right. The Boys were back.

WEATHER
61°, clear

POINT SPREAD
Cowboys by 6½

TIME OF GAME
3:23

TV AUDIENCE
91 million

192

Driving the Cowboys relentlessly, Aikman was dominant—as shown by his 140.7 QB rating.

Photograph by Peter Read Miller

XXVII
COWBOYS | BILLS

HERE TO STAY?

The Cowboys' young talent suggested a Super future | BY PAUL ZIMMERMAN

GET USED TO THE COWBOYS, folks, because they're going to be with us for a long time. Here comes that dread word—dynasty. Oh, my, yes. Everything points to it after the Cowboys ran the Bills out of the Rose Bowl on Sunday by a score of 52–17. Troy Aikman and Emmitt Smith and Michael Irvin and Ken Norton Jr. and Charles Haley—all those implements of destruction that embarrassed and humiliated a proud, battle-tested team are just starting to feel their oats. Coach Jimmy Johnson and his hair spray; Jerry Jones, the owner who hungers for the limelight. You say you're tired of them already? Gee, that's tough, because the whole gang's going to be with us for a while.

Turnovers are at the heart of most NFL blowouts, and the Bills will have to live with a Super Bowl–record nine as they analyze their third straight, and worst, defeat

Postgame glee: Johnson (left) toasted with Jones.

Photograph by Al Tielemans

in the Big One. Two of the turnovers were returned for touchdowns. Three more set up TDs. Another ended a Buffalo drive in the end zone. The other three were window dressing, including a 64-yard fumble return by 292-pound defensive tackle Leon Lett, who went into his hot-dog number a little early and had the ball knocked out of his hand just short of the end zone by Bills receiver Don Beebe. That was at the end, when the game was in its Laurel and Hardy phase and fans were streaming out to beat traffic.

The turnovers were products of a Dallas defense built on speed—of guys firing through tiny gaps before they closed, of backside or blindside pursuit knocking the ball loose. Angles that had looked perfectly fine when Buffalo coaches drew them up on the blackboard suddenly didn't work when those little defensive O's turned into Cowboys players.

Those were the guys who turned the game late in the first quarter. The Bills had taken a 7–0 lead after Steve Tasker blocked a punt, giving Buffalo the ball on the Dallas 16-yard line. Four plays later running back Thurman Thomas was in the end zone. "If you block a punt for a TD, you'll win the game 80 percent of the time," Tasker had said earlier in the week.

The first two Cowboys series, meanwhile, were blanks. "They were taking away my outside reads with that two-deep zone they played," said Aikman. "Emmitt was getting open—one time I heard him hollering at me—but I couldn't see him because their linebackers were getting to me too quickly. I was having a tough time getting into the feel of the ball game."

With five minutes left in the quarter, Buffalo had a first down at midfield, and this is when the game turned. Cowboys nickelback Kenneth Gant, blitzing up the middle, forced Jim Kelly to hurry his throw, and it was picked off by safety James Washington. That set up a 47-yard drive—Aikman to tight end Jay Novacek for the 23-yard scoring pass—that tied the game.

"The touchdown to Novacek [got] Troy his rhythm

and confidence," said offensive coordinator Norv Turner. "It was a helluva throw, down the seam, off a quick drop. . . . After that I felt he was going to be fine."

On Buffalo's next series Haley, a 245-pound speed rusher, raced around 325-pound tackle Howard Ballard and sacked Kelly at the two, forcing a fumble that defensive tackle Jimmie Jones recovered and ran in for a TD. Dallas led 14–7. The Bills had been in their hurry-up mode, going from a no-huddle set, and the Cowboy had answered questions about how they would cope with this offense: They handled it simply. They left one unit in until the series played itself out or there was a break, such as a measurement. "We got the people we wanted in there," said defensive end Jim Jeffcoat. "The Buffalo linemen were tiring before we were."

Haley had his own feelings about the Bills' no-huddle. "I like it," he said, "because it lets me get into Kelly's rhythm. Once I can do that, I can get off on the ball right away and beat the guy blocking me."

On offense, Aikman, Irvin and Smith were also well at work. A long touchdown drive ended with a 19-yard pass to Irvin. On Buffalo's ensuing series, a fumble by Thomas, who was in distress with ankle and shoulder injuries, set up an 18-yard TD pass to Irvin. The Cowboys led 28–10 at the half and 31–17 after three quarters. Two bang-bang touchdowns in the final period—on a 45-yard Aikman pass to Alvin Harper and a 10-yard dash by Smith, the latter set up by Thomas Everett's second interception—put out the lights.

As the clock wound down, Aikman stood to the side, watching his young teammates whooping, hollering and dumping ice water on Johnson. Smith gave Johnson's hair a thorough massage (miraculously, it was back in place for the postgame award ceremony). Haley, who had left San Francisco under a cloud in a preseason trade, put his arm around Johnson and said something. "I thanked him for bringing me here," Haley revealed later, "and giving me a chance to play."

Remember, for Dallas this is only the beginning. ∎

JUST THE FACTS

Statistical Leaders

Rushing EMMITT SMITH (DAL) 22 carries, 108 yds, 1 TD

Passing TROY AIKMAN (DAL) 22 of 30, 273 yds, 4 TDs

Receiving ANDRE REED (BUF) 8 catches, 152 yds

MVP TROY AIKMAN Cowboys Quarterback

The Ring
Included 55 diamonds, the most in a Super Bowl ring to date

Anthem Performer
Garth Brooks

Halftime Performer
Michael Jackson

Attendance 98,374

Ticket Price $175

Behind the Scenes

For the first time since 1985, the Super Bowl did not use instant replay; the owners had voted it out of the game before the season. Replay would have shown that Frank Reich's foot was beyond the line of scrimmage when he connected with Don Beebe on a 40-yard touchdown pass to end the third quarter.

They Said It

"We got ruined. Are we going to be labeled like [multiple Super Bowl losers] Denver and Minnesota have been labeled? That's probably the biggest thing we're disappointed about."

—Bills linebacker SHANE CONLAN

Now That's a Closer

San Diego Padres reliever Trevor Hoffman proposed to his girlfriend Tracy on the scoreboard at the game. She said yes.

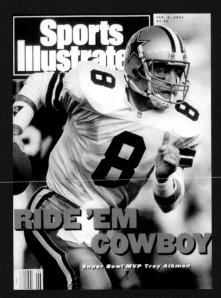

Smith ran for the first of his five career Super Bowl touchdowns.

Photograph by Peter Read Miller

Angles that had looked perfectly fine when Buffalo coaches drew them up on the blackboard suddenly didn't work when those little defensive O's turned into Cowboys players.

Kelly, often under heavy pressure, threw two interceptions.

Photograph by Richard Mackson

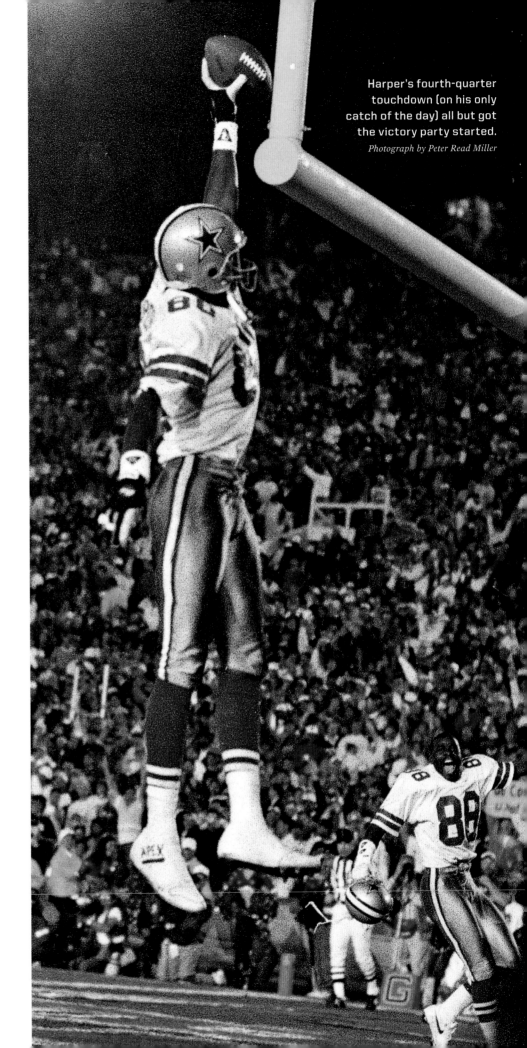

Harper's fourth-quarter touchdown (on his only catch of the day) all but got the victory party started.

Photograph by Peter Read Miller

THE WAY IT WAS

BY Troy Aikman

Cowboys Quarterback

This Super Bowl kind of meant going home. We practiced at UCLA, so not only were the locker room and the practice field comfortable for me—I had just left college four years before—but also some of the equipment guys and the trainers who were at UCLA when I was there were helping out. And of course the game was at the Rose Bowl. It was a perfect situation for me as far as getting ready for the game. We probably had our best week of practice all season. I don't know that a ball hit the ground.

Jimmy Johnson was really good at getting us focused and prepared. Never was he better than the week of that Super Bowl. The speech I remember was on Thursday. He said, "If I laid a 20-foot two-by-four on the ground, how many of you think you could walk across it?" Every guy raised his hand. He said, "I figured as much. Not real hard. Let's picture this: How about if I suspended it, 10 stories in the air?" Guys started visualizing it. Not as many hands. He said, "That's no different from the game we're about to play. It's the same game, played the same way. It's just on a bigger stage. How we're going to go about winning this game is no different than the way we've done it all year." It really hit home with a lot of young guys.

I remember throwing the touchdown pass to Alvin Harper to go up by 21. I knew we had just won the Super Bowl. I raised my finger and gave the number one signal. It's the only time in my career, at any level, that I ever did that.

BY Don Beebe

Bills Wide Receiver

We were bound and determined to finally win a Super Bowl. I remember praying at the 50-yard line before the game. I thought I was going to score the touchdown to win the game. That's how excited I felt.

When it was 31–17 late in the third quarter, we thought it was still a game. Even though things were ugly, we still felt, Somebody just make a play. It turned completely the opposite direction.

With five minutes left, we were getting beat 52–17. We were not coming back; we knew that. I ran a fly pattern down the left side of the field, and as I turned— I was probably 35 to 40 yards down the field—I saw Frank [Reich] moving up in the pocket. At that point, I came to a gradual stop, and I saw the ball hit the ground. Leon [Lett] picked it up. Without even thinking, I took off. As I was running down the sideline right in front of the Dallas bench, I thought, *How am I going to tackle this guy?* As I got close, he slowed down to hold the ball out in front of him, and I knocked it out inside the one-yard line. If Leon had finished running as fast as he could, I would have never caught him. Everyone knows that. But because he didn't finish and I did, we're still talking about that silly play today.

At the time it meant nothing. But the after-effect was more meaningful than if I would have caught that touchdown.

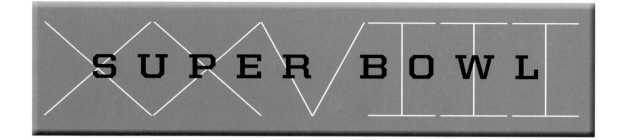

SUPER BOWL XXVIII

DALLAS COWBOYS | 30

BUFFALO BILLS | 13

Smith, the victor, embraced his counterpart, Thomas, the fumbler.

Photograph by John Iacono

FOR THE only time, teams met in consecutive Super Bowls—the Bills in their fourth straight, the brash 'Boys defending the NFL title. For a time it looked as if Buffalo might finally shake the loser's yoke. Instead the team made its own brand of history.

DOME

Outside: 44°

POINT SPREAD

Cowboys by 10½

TIME OF GAME

3:16

TV AUDIENCE

90 million

Dallas's star-laden offense (three Hall of Famers) produced 23 points.

Photograph by Chuck Solomon

Aikman, pursued here by Bills nosetackle Jeff Wright, was sacked twice, but lost a total of just three yards.

Photograph by Jim Gund

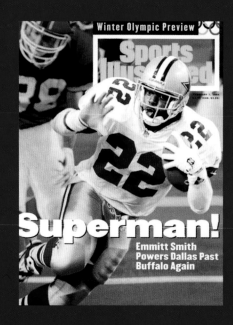

Excerpted from **SPORTS ILLUSTRATED** *February 7, 1994*

TURNOVER, TURNAROUND

Two big plays (for Dallas) and one big blunder (for Buffalo) | BY PAUL ZIMMERMAN

SUPER BOWL XXVIII WILL GO down in history as a blowout because that's what a 30–13 score looks like when you read it in the record book. But the score won't come close to telling the story. The Bills, short-enders for the fourth straight year, had the Cowboys on the ropes and they let them escape.

Buffalo has now lost two Super Bowls they should have won, the first and fourth in this series of consecutive defeats. This defeat was the most disheartening because the Cowboys were ready to be put away. Dallas quarterback Troy Aikman, seven days removed from a severe concussion, was having difficulties. Emmitt Smith's favorite running play, the lead draw, was getting stuffed. Buffalo QB Jim Kelly was picking Dallas apart with short, meticulous passes, and the Dallas defense was on the field far too long against the Bills' no-huddle offense, which literally takes your breath away.

Buffalo had the ball and the lead, 13–6, to open the third quarter. The game had arrived at the point at which someone either steps up to win it or someone does something to lose it. This time both happened.

James Washington, Dallas's 29-year-old reserve safety, turned the game around with two terrific plays. Buffalo's All-Pro running back, Thurman Thomas—and this is the sad part—was the guy who blew it with his second fumble of the game.

Thomas's second fumble, on the third play of the second half, sucked the life out of a team that had taken a lead and an unexpected feeling of confidence into the locker room at intermission. On first-and-10 at the Bills' 43, Thomas took a handoff, slipped through the left side for three yards and was met by defensive tackle Leon Lett, who slapped the ball loose. Washington grabbed the fumble and took it 46 yards to the end zone to tie the score 13–13.

The story of this strange Super Bowl began a week earlier in a dark room at Baylor University Medical

Center in Dallas, where Aikman lay in a semiconscious twilight. He had been knocked unconscious by the right knee of 300-pound 49ers defensive end Dennis Brown in the NFC title game. "It was scary," says Aikman's agent, Leigh Steinberg. "We sat there, he and I, alone in the dark, and his head was kind of in a cloud. He kept asking me the same questions over and over. Finally I wrote the answers out on a piece of paper."

By 4 a.m. Aikman was beginning to function. Seventeen hours later he was at a podium at a press conference in the Cowboys' hotel in Atlanta, answering questions about things he had trouble remembering. Yes, Aikman confirmed, in the hospital he had asked the same questions over and over. And, yes, on the sideline he had turned to injured center Mark Stepnoski, on crutches and in civvies, and asked him why he wasn't playing. No, Aikman said, he didn't have a headache. "I'll be fine," he said.

Fine? Not exactly. After Dallas's Wednesday practice, the first full workout following the 49er game, Aikman was troubled by bad headaches. "Really bad," Steinberg says. "He was having trouble sleeping too."

On Super Sunday, Aikman lined up under center, although the Cowboys did not rely on him alone. On Buffalo's first series after Washington's fumble return, defensive linemen Jimmie Jones and Charles Haley sacked Kelly for a 13-yard loss on third-and-eight at the Bills' 26. After Buffalo punted, Dallas commenced its only sustained drive of the game, 64 yards for a TD. Smith carried the ball on seven of the drive's eight snaps and gained 61 yards, most on a play that bears the simple but descriptive label Power Right.

Washington's interception, on the opening play of the final period, was the crusher for Buffalo. On third-and-six at the Bills' 35, Kelly sent wideout Don Beebe on a crossing pattern. Washington, breaking as soon as Kelly threw, picked off the pass and returned it to the Buffalo 34. Two plays keyed Dallas's ensuing

scoring drive: a checkoff pass to Smith, who shook off linebacker Keith Goganious for a nine-yard gain, and a gutsy 16-yard pass by Aikman to wideout Alvin Harper, with a blitzing safety in his face. Smith put the game away with a one-yard touchdown on the left side. Dallas led 27–13. There was plenty of time left, but Buffalo was finished.

Smith, with 30 carries for 132 yards and two touchdowns, was named MVP. "I wish they could have given co-awards," he said, "so James Washington could have gotten something."

Before these Cowboys are done, most everyone could have some kind of award. This is a young team. Smith is only 24, Michael Irvin and Aikman are 27. Owner Jerry Jones has maneuvered to keep his Cowboys' payroll some $7 million dollars under the new salary cap, which means a good chunk of this team will stay together. Dynasty? Why not? ■

Nothing, but nothing, disturbed the peace of Johnson's hair.

Photograph by Jim Gund

Washington scooped up Thomas's fumble and ran off to the end zone.

Photograph by Peter Read Miller

THE WAY IT WAS

BY Emmitt Smith

Cowboys Running Back

This Super Bowl felt like a regular-season game because we only had a week to prepare. Everything was so compressed. When we played the year before we had two weeks to get our luggage, tickets, everything together. This time we had to get all that done a week ahead of time, during the week of the NFC title game, which made it tough to focus on the people you needed to invite, the rooms you needed to get—and at the same time prepare for the 49ers. Because the Super Bowl was in Atlanta, and I was from Pensacola, Florida, not far away, I ended up needing more than 50 Super Bowl tickets.

Being inside the dome was great because it was extremely cold that week. Having that dome made everything better, even though playing on the Astroturf was not like being in sunny Southern California playing outside on grass as we did the year before. The Rose Bowl could seat close to 100,000 people, and the Georgia Dome sat between 70,000 and 75,000 at that time. The dome was louder, though. When we were trying to come back in the second half, it definitely helped that half of the stadium—if not more—was full of Cowboys fans.

At halftime, the conversation was, We've got to get control of the game. [Offensive coordinator] Norv Turner and Jimmy Johnson made a conscious effort to talk to the offensive line and to me and said, "We're going to run the football, so get ready." Man, did we come out gangbusters. That first drive as an offensive unit in the third quarter—when we ran the ball seven out of eight plays—that drive sent shock waves throughout the entire Bills team.

BY Bruce Smith

Bills Defensive End

We never focused on any prior Super Bowls. We were in the moment. Marv Levy spoke at halftime, and he was very upbeat about our being able to execute and continue that same level of intensity and energy. We knew we needed to sustain that effort and even take it up a notch to have a chance.

Defensively we wanted to fly around the football, and their offensive line was considered one of the best in the NFL—very big, very strong and very physical. That had an effect in the second half, their 300-plus pound offensive linemen playing against our defensive line and our linebackers. Emmitt Smith started running the ball effectively in the second half, and there were some play-action passes they were able to complete. After the game, it was just this overwhelming feeling of, *Not again. We can't believe it.*

There are bigger things to be learned, and Marv talked about it all the time: resilience, overcoming adversity. We have a lot to be extremely proud of. When I look back, I don't see those four straight Super Bowl appearances as an accomplishment that will be repeated. We had one of the most prolific offenses in NFL history. We had talent at roughly every position, one of the greatest quarterbacks to ever put on a uniform, future Hall of Famers all over the place.

We were never happy just to be participating. The comments that we always get from other Hall of Famers is, You guys are the dynasty that never won a Super Bowl. When you look at it in those terms, you're absolutely right. We were a dynasty. We were winners.

"I wish they could have given co-awards," said Emmitt Smith, "so that James Washington could have gotten something."

In his entire eight-year career Washington returned a fumble for a touchdown only once—right here.

Photograph by Chuck Solomon

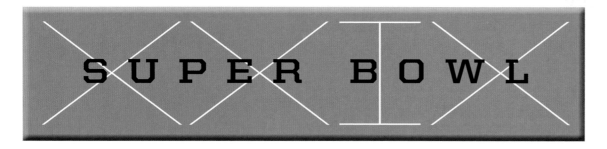

SUPER BOWL XXIX

January 29, 1995
Joe Robbie Stadium, Miami

HEAD COACHES
GEORGE SEIFERT 49ers | BOBBY ROSS Chargers

SAN FRANCISCO
49ERS | 49

SAN DIEGO
CHARGERS | 26

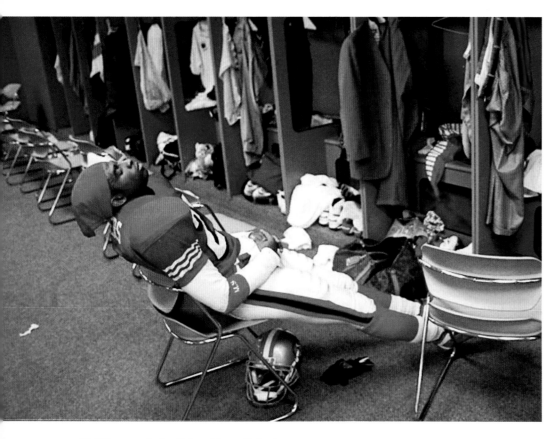

Getting ready for Prime Time: Deion's pregame snooze.

Photograph by Michael Zagaris

THE NFC title game win against Dallas—a 38-28 final—was San Francisco's toughest test. By the time the Super Bowl and surprising San Diego came around, the question was not *if* the Niners would win, but rather by how much.

WEATHER

76°, cloudy, humid

POINT SPREAD

49ers by 19

TIME OF GAME

3:36

TV AUDIENCE

83.4 million

204

Joe who? In his debut as a Super Bowl starter,
Young threw a record six TD passes.

Photograph by John W. McDonough

Excerpted from **SPORTS ILLUSTRATED** *February 6, 1995*

NINERS ALL THE WAY

Its high-powered offense in high gear, San Francisco left no doubt | BY RICK TELANDER

T APPROXIMATELY — NO, check that—at *exactly* one minute and 24 seconds into the first quarter of Super Bowl XXIX at Miami's Joe Robbie Stadium, everybody knew this one was over. Three quarters of a billion people were watching worldwide as 49ers wideout Jerry Rice crossed the Chargers' goal line with a 44-yard touchdown pass from quarterback Steve Young, wearing Chargers safeties Stanley Richard and Darren Carrington like twin tails on his Superman cape. The signal was loud and clear: uh-oh.

That touchdown gave the 49ers the quickest touchdown in Super Bowl history: the opening kick return; a four-yard rush by fullback William Floyd; an 11-yard completion from Young to wideout John Taylor. Then Rice. Boom. Done.

Wouldn't the Chargers have expected Rice, who has scored more touchdowns than anyone else in NFL history, to link up deep with Young, the fellow who has led the league in quarterback rating for four straight years? Well, yes, by golly, they did think of that. Back in December, San Diego, playing its linebackers deeper than normal and using a lot of double coverage on the 49ers wideouts, had been walloped 38–15. San Francisco had nickel-and-dimed the Chargers to death that day. So on Sunday, San Diego moved its linebackers up tighter, played the 49ers wideouts more aggressively on the short stuff and prayed that its safeties could bottle up the middle.

God to Chargers: prayer rejected.

The final score was 49–26 but it probably could have been 63–26, if 49ers coach George Seifert hadn't quit passing and then yanked his offensive stars for much of the fourth quarter. "We're part of history," said Niners guard Jesse Sapolu afterward. "This is probably the best offense people will see in their lifetimes."

The second time San Francisco got the ball, it slowed down just a bit, needing a full 1:53 to march 79 yards for a touchdown. The drive included a 21-yard scramble by Young and was topped off by his 51-yard touchdown pass to running back Ricky Watters, who broke tackles by each of those two snakebit Chargers safeties. That gave the Niners a 14–0 lead with more than 10 minutes remaining in the first quarter.

This was the way everyone feared it would be. The 49ers were favored by 19 points, the largest spread in Super Bowl history, and as the game proceeded, the destruction of the Chargers resembled a train coming off its track, car after car after car. Young threw for a record six touchdowns, and the best way to describe the TDs might be to list the receivers in order: Rice, Watters, Floyd, Watters, Rice, Rice. There was also a nine-yard rushing touchdown, by Watters, but it was nearly lost in the Young passfest.

"This is no streak, man," Young said after the game, referring to the blowout victory march the 49ers had been on. "This is what we do."

Young entered the Super Bowl having thrown for 4,267 yards and 37 touchdowns and by throwing those six touchdown passes and leading all rushers, with 49 yards on five carries, Young effectively exorcised the Joe Montana ghost that had been haunting him for years. Before every game this season tackle Harris Barton would come up to Young and rub his shoulders and say, "I'm taking the monkey off your back."

"Today," Young noted afterward, "Harris said, 'I'm taking it off for the last time.' For a long time I tried to pretend it wasn't there. But I guess it was."

Young cried when the game was over, gushing with pent-up emotion. He hugged the Lombardi Trophy the way a sinking swimmer hugs a life preserver, and then he, not Seifert, gave the postgame speech to the Niners, shouting in a voice hoarse from signal-calling and celebrating: "There were times when this was hard! But this is the greatest feeling in the world!"

Then, with veins bulging in his neck, he almost blew out his vocal cords, screaming, "No one—*no one*—can ever take this away from us! No one, ever! It's ours!"

After his locker-room address Young talked to every TV, radio and newspaper person in the stadium. Then he nearly collapsed. In the limo back to the 49ers' hotel, Young turned shaky, pale and weak. Then he vomited onto the floor of the car. "Well," said his agent Leigh Steinberg beside him, "I'll never wash that shoe again."

Young needed air, so he got out and walked the last quarter mile to the hotel. In his room he was joined by his parents; his four siblings; his girlfriend; some college chums and other buddies—44 people in all. Then he felt sicker. Paramedics arrived. Young was given an intravenous saline solution for dehydration, and he lay on his bed, like an ailing head of state, receiving well-wishers into the wee hours.

"Don't go," he would say whenever anyone tried to leave. "You can stay. Stay! I'm fine. Really, I'm fine."

He really was. ∎

You complete me: Young and Rice embraced.

Photograph by Walter Iooss Jr.

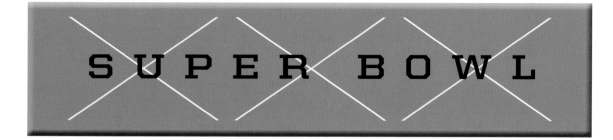

SUPER BOWL XXX

January 28, 1996
Sun Devil Stadium, Tempe, Ariz.

HEAD COACHES
BARRY SWITZER Cowboys | BILL COWHER Steelers

DALLAS COWBOYS | 27

PITTSBURGH STEELERS | 17

THIS IS what a Dallas dynasty looks like: a team stocked with Pro Bowlers and Hall of Famers that very nearly won four straight Super Bowls. Instead, with this triumph over an old rival, the Cowboys made it three of four, a record in itself.

WEATHER	POINT SPREAD	TIME OF GAME	TV AUDIENCE
68°, clear	Cowboys by 13½	3:24	94.1 million

A Super stoked Irvin behaved true to form during pregame introductions.

Photograph by Robert Beck

BY Steve Young

49ers Quarterback

I had been to two Super Bowls, so I knew what I was getting into. I made it a business trip. I did not mess around with anything other than getting ready to play. What you were going to do with your downtime was the key. I basically studied. It wasn't like I was doing it 24 hours a day because you get diminishing returns at some level. We got out and saw Miami and had fun, but there was an eye toward making sure the work got done.

Everyone got his own room at the hotel, but [tight end] Brent Jones and I had been roommates for years. The night before the game, I dragged my mattress into his room so we could be roommates like usual. It was a big mattress. It was a little awkward dragging it down the hall. I slept on the floor, happy as a clam.

Before the game, Mike Shanahan, my offensive coordinator, and I went over the game plan three or four times like we normally do. He said, "We're going to kill these guys." I go, "Well, I hope you're right." He said, "No, really. I want to throw eight touchdowns. Tonight's the night." We came in at halftime, and I had four touchdowns. He said to me, "We gotta get four more." We got two more, and then they pulled me because we were up by so much. He was upset. He wanted eight! I believe if I had stayed in, we would have had eight.

I can imagine what it feels like to be on Everest and to stick a flag in the ground with the wind whipping and you're on top of the world. That sense that there are very few human beings who have been here, and now I've been here kind of thing. That's what it felt like to win that game.

BY Andre Coleman

Chargers Kick Returner

When we first got to Miami, we had a little bit of time before curfew kicked in. We went to this bar, and half of our team and half of the 49ers team were there. We were in there with [Niners cornerback] Deion Sanders and a lot of guys I'd looked up to. You'd think that we wouldn't socialize with those guys, but the reality is we're friends with a lot of guys who play on different teams.

I was a rookie that year, and I was a little naive. I didn't realize how hard it was to make it to a Super Bowl. Walking out on the field for pregame and the warmups, you knew it was a big event. I remember seeing Sylvester Stallone in the stands. He had really good seats. The nerves didn't get to me until right before kickoff, as they're singing the national anthem. The jets fly over and fireworks start going off and then you realize, Wow.

I was in the game to receive the kickoff when we were down 42–10. When I caught the football, I just did what I have been doing on returns ever since I was a kid: Run to daylight. I got loose, got down the sideline and scored. I remember not feeling excitement at the time because I knew we were still down by so much. When you look back on it years later, you realize just how special that moment was. I'll never forget afterward, Deion made it a point to come find me and say how well I did in the return game. For me, that was a highlight because I admired the way he played the game, and I respected his skill set. It meant a lot.

For Young, here about to get a lift from tackle Steve Wallace, everything was looking up.

Photograph by John Biever

49ERS | CHARGERS

As the game proceeded, the destruction of the Chargers resembled a train coming off its track, car after car after car.

A swarm of San Franciscans held Natrone Means to 33 rushing yards.

Photograph by Walter Iooss Jr.

JUST THE FACTS

Statistical Leaders

Rushing RICKY WATTERS (SF) 15 carries, 47 yds, 1 TD

Passing STEVE YOUNG (SF) 24 of 36, 325 yds, 6 TDs

Receiving JERRY RICE (SF) 10 catches, 149 yds, 3 TDs

MVP STEVE YOUNG 49ers Quarterback

The Ring
That's a diamond trophy for each the 49ers have won

Anthem Performer
Kathie Lee Gifford

Halftime Performers
Patti LaBelle, Tony Bennett, Arturo Sandoval and the Miami Sound Machine

Attendance 74,107

Ticket Price $200

Behind the Scenes

Jerry Rice, battling flulike symptoms, was given intravenous fluids on Saturday and again two hours before kickoff. Then, in the second quarter, Rice left the field. He returned three minutes later and played the rest of the game despite a separated shoulder.

They Said It

"When he came out of the room on Friday, he had that Albert Einstein look. I knew we were in pretty good shape."

—49ers quarterback STEVE YOUNG on offensive coordinator Mike Shanahan

The Seven-Figure Spot

The cost to buy a 30-second television commercial during the game hit $1 million for the first time.

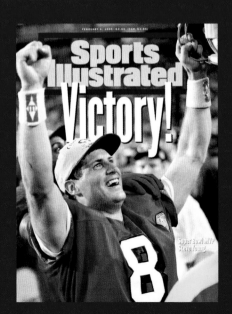

Watters, Watters everywhere:
The running back scored three TDs.
Photograph by Peter Read Miller

Smith took a licking but scored twice, this time in the fourth quarter to put Dallas ahead by 10.

Photograph by Robert Beck

Deion Sanders played brilliantly as a cornerback, and he also beat Willie Williams for this 47-yard catch on Dallas's first TD drive.

Photograph by Richard Mackson

JUST THE FACTS

Statistical Leaders

Rushing **BAM MORRIS** (PIT) 19 carries, 73 yds, 1 TD

Passing **NEIL O'DONNELL** (PIT) 28 of 49, 239 yds, 1 TD

Receiving **ANDRE HASTINGS** (PIT) 10 catches, 98 yds

MVP **LARRY BROWN** Cowboys Cornerback

The Ring
To get the job, the ring designer wooed the Cowboys with a cake that looked like Troy Aikman

Anthem Performer
Vanessa Williams

Halftime Performer
Diana Ross

Attendance 76,347

Ticket Price $200–$350

Behind the Scenes

Pittsburgh players groused that they had only been allowed to purchase 20 Super Bowl tickets, while Cowboys owner Jerry Jones let each of his players buy 30.

They Said It

"He's been second-guessed so much, for a while I thought people had mistaken him for me."

—PRESIDENT BILL CLINTON on Barry Switzer, when the Cowboys visited the White House a week after the game.

Up with Person

Diana Ross left the field in a helicopter as she finished her final song, "Take Me Higher." She was secured to the copter at her waist and had special handgrips on the sides of the open door.

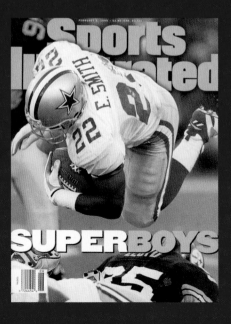

Excerpted from **SPORTS ILLUSTRATED** *February 5, 1996*

COWBOYS | STEELERS

LOVE AND TOUCHDOWNS

Lifting their beleaguered coach, the Cowboys won in style | BY MICHAEL SILVER

THERE WAS ENOUGH LOVE, BOOZE and R-rated language to fill a Texas-sized swimming pool in Barry Switzer's hotel suite Sunday night when the coach of the Super Bowl–champion Cowboys finally got his deliverance. It came in the form of a hug and a speech from a man wearing a checkered suit, black derby hat and superfluous sunglasses. Several hours after the Cowboys had defeated the Steelers 27–17, flamboyant Dallas receiver Michael Irvin burst into Suite 4000 at The Buttes resort and offered a tribute that brought Switzer to tears. "Hey, let me ask you something," Irvin shouted to the assembled revelers. "Is there anyone who deserves this more than Barry Switzer?"

"Hell, no!" answered 50 or 60 of Switzer's closest friends and family members, including football's wackiest pair of suitemates—Switzer's girlfriend, Becky Buwick, and his ex-wife, Kay. After Irvin finished his speech, the gang went back to singing Switzer's praises, reprising a scene that had occurred in the wee hours of last Saturday morning at another party: Greg Switzer, the elder of Barry's sons, was displaying his skill at the piano by improvising riffs on Ray Charles's "What'd I Say," while revelers danced and took turns supplying humorous lyrics. Most of the impromptu verses contained good-natured pokes at Switzer's critics as well as pronouncements of unbridled affection for a man who will probably be remembered as the most maligned coach to win an NFL championship.

Bash him all you like, but give the 58-year-old coach his due. The same goes for owner Jerry Jones and the rest of the Cowboys, who became only the second team to win five Super Bowls (49ers) and the first to win three in a four-year span. "Our guys have taken a lot of shots. Our character has been questioned," Dallas defensive end Tony Tolbert said. "But we came through. Now it's time for us to do the celebrating we deserve."

Before all that, the Cowboys and Steelers staged the best Super Bowl show since the Giants sweated out a one-point victory over the Bills five years ago. Dallas scored on its first three possessions and took a 13–0 lead six minutes before halftime. Pittsburgh then gutted out a 13-play, 54-yard drive that ended with quarterback Neil O'Donnell throwing a six-yard touchdown pass to wideout Yancey Thigpen 13 seconds before the intermission.

A game was on, and had it not been for two interceptions by Cowboys cornerback Larry Brown it might have been the Steelers heading off into the night in search of a victory party. Both interceptions set up Cowboys touchdowns, the latter a four-yard run by Emmitt Smith that clinched the game with 3:43 left.

It wasn't just the interceptions that bedeviled O'Donnell. The Cowboys figured they could rattle the Steelers QB by blitzing and mixing up coverages. They were right. Many of O'Donnell's throws sailed over the heads of his receivers while other passes drifted behind them, forcing them to make difficult catches and leaving them vulnerable to big hits from charging Cowboys defenders.

Dallas's defense deserves credit for sheer endurance. It was on the field for 21:20 of the second half—including a stretch spanning 20 consecutive plays. During the Cowboys' pregame meal, defensive tackle Russell Maryland had addressed his teammates, saying, "We all know the offense is where the money's at," he told them. "But the defense will win this game." His remarks proved prophetic.

After a 46-yard field goal by Norm Johnson cut the deficit to 20–10 with 11:20 left to play, Steelers coach Bill Cowher called for an onside kick. Dallas was caught on its heels, and the kick was recovered by Pittsburgh cornerback Deon Figures. The weary Cowboys defense finally succumbed on that 20th straight Steelers snap, as Bam Morris scored from a yard out to cut the Dallas lead to 20–17 with 6:36 to go.

Afterward Cowboys defensive end Charles Haley, the ex-49er who became the first player to win five Super Bowl rings, said, "They're gutsy. We should have blown them out, but they stayed in there and fought, and pretty soon I thought, Hey, these guys can beat us." Indeed, when the Cowboys were forced to punt on their next possession, it looked as though Pittsburgh might pull off the upset. But with 4:09 left, O'Donnell threw the interception into Brown's arms.

Back in the suite on Sunday night, Switzer took another sip of Jack Daniel's and prepared for what would likely be the sweetest hangover of his life. "This is all you need to know about life," he said. "Compassion and love and caring will take you the furthest. You've got to be around 50 or 60 or 70 years, so you might as well do it that way."

Mark it down: For the 1995 season, and for Super Bowl XXX, Barry's way was the right way. ∎

Switzer was more laid-back than his predecessor.

Photograph by Bill Frakes

213

A bruising blocker for Smith, Daryl Johnston was himself a ball-carrying weapon, here converting a fourth-and-one in the second quarter.

Photograph by Al Tielemans

Aikman became the first quarterback to win three Super Bowls before turning 30.

Photograph by Al Tielemans

BY Larry Brown

Cowboys Cornerback

I understood I had a lot of opportunities coming at me with Deion Sanders on the other side. On my second interception, Deion came and said, "If you get another one, you'll be able to run for governor." I said, "Well, you'll have to be my best man because I couldn't get the interceptions without having a guy like Prime on the other side." The first interception was a gift, the second one I went and got. The first one I think the ball slipped out of Neil O'Donnell's hand, but at the same time, I was where I was supposed to be. You can't just stand on the field as a pro athlete and have things happen to you. For people who said it was easy, it wasn't easy. But I'm smart enough to realize we didn't win the game just because of me.

Emmitt came over at the end of the game and said, "Congratulations!" I said, "For what?" He said, "You won MVP." I said, "I did?" He was so happy for me. Him and Michael Irvin. I remember them grabbing me and hugging me. That was the kind of team that we had. Jerry [Jones] handed me the phone later after the game. Someone says, "This is President Bill Clinton." I'm thinking someone's joking. As he continued to talk I realized it wasn't a joke. You could tell it was the President. That's at the top of my highlight list.

This wasn't just about beating the Steelers. It was about overcoming the letdown of the previous year, losing to the 49ers in the NFC title game. This win encompassed two years of joy. We were ecstatic.

BY Neil O'Donnell

Steelers Quarterback

In 1994 we probably had our best team, and we lost to the Chargers on the last play of the AFC title game. I'll never forget coach Cowher talking to the team the Monday after, when we came in to clean out our lockers. He said, "We knocked on the door, and next year we're going to knock down the door and go to a Super Bowl." I thought the man was absolutely crazy. Sure enough, we came back and beat the Colts on the final drive the next year.

I had a big, nasty beard almost the whole playoffs. We were winning, and the offensive line liked it. There was an opportunity to make some money from Gillette shaving it on national television after the Super Bowl, if we won. I was ready to shave it; it was pretty thick. When I ate, the hair was all in my mouth.

The night before the game they moved us out of our hotel. They said, "Grab your stuff, we're getting out of here." I thought we were going to a movie or something, but sure enough, we went to a whole different hotel. They wanted to move us around so we weren't in the same spot the night before the game.

Few gave us a chance, but we were in the game and felt we could win. I hit Yancey Thigpen with a TD pass and we had momentum going into the half. I recall how long the halftime entertainment was. Crazy. I felt like we were in the locker room for 90 minutes. We came out after halftime and had a couple turnovers. That was it.

The Cowboys figured they could rattle the Steelers quarterback by blitzing and mixing up coverages. They were right.

Brown's picks and long runbacks made him the only cornerback to be named Super Bowl MVP.

Photograph by Al Tielemans

SUPER BOWL XXXI

January 26, 1997
Superdome, New Orleans

HEAD COACHES
MIKE HOLMGREN Packers | BILL PARCELLS Patriots

GREEN BAY
PACKERS | 35

NEW ENGLAND
PATRIOTS | 21

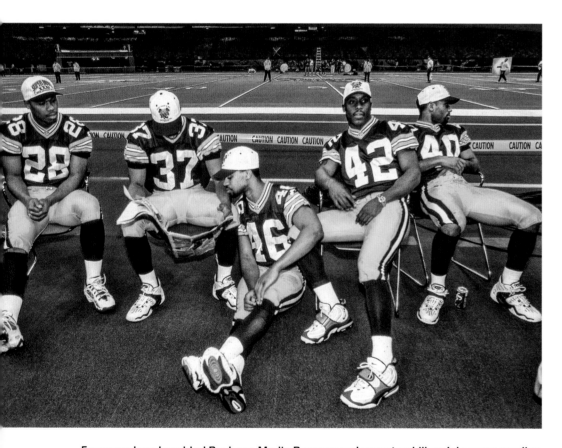

For some less heralded Packers, Media Day was a chance to chill and do some reading.

Photograph by John Iacono

DESPITE BEING heavy favorites, Green Bay found itself trailing the plucky, Bill Parcells-led Patriots. The Packers, though, had a crafty quarterback and a pressuring defense, and then, at just the right time (for them), a return star was born.

DOME
Warmer out (69°) than in (67°)

POINT SPREAD
Packers by 14

TIME OF GAME
3:21

TV AUDIENCE
87.9 million

Ben Coates had six catches and a touchdown, but had Packers like Butler and Robinson (41) keying on him high and low.

Photograph by V.J. Lovero

Statistical Leaders

Rushing DORSEY LEVENS (GB) 14 carries, 61 yds

Passing BRETT FAVRE (GB) 14 of 27, 246 yds, 2 TDs

Receiving ANTONIO FREEMAN (GB) 3 catches, 105 yds, 1 TD

MVP DESMOND HOWARD Packers Kick Returner

The Ring
Yellow gold and 115 diamonds, with a Packers helmet and TRADITION inscribed on the side

Anthem Performer
Luther Vandross

Halftime Performers
The Blues Brothers, James Brown and ZZ Top

Attendance 72,301

Ticket Price $275

Behind the Scenes

After the first quarter the Packers went almost exclusively to nickel and dime packages. The extra DBs let Green Bay blitz a safety or cornerback without sacrificing pass coverage.

They Said It

"He kind of filled me in on helicopters and how to moon them.... He taught me all the things not to do down there."
—Packers QB BRETT FAVRE on New Orleans and pregame advice from Super Bowl XX-winning QB Jim McMahon

Aspiring Expat

Before the game, rumors were rampant that Bill Parcells would leave the Patriots. The coach did not fly home with the team from New Orleans and five days later took a job with the Jets.

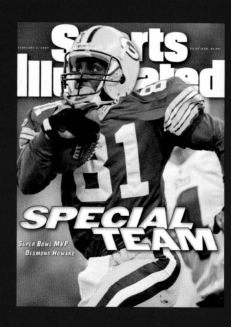

Excerpted from **SPORTS ILLUSTRATED** *February 3, 1997*

PACKERS | PATRIOTS

HOMEWARD BOUND

After 29 years the Lombardi Trophy was headed back to Green Bay | BY MICHAEL SILVER

IN THE HEAT OF A MOMENT THAT WILL forever define Super Bowl XXXI, Desmond Howard couldn't escape the chill of wounded pride. Even as Howard, the Packers' nonpareil return man, raced down the field with the Patriots' kickoff-coverage team in his wake, he carried a Tuna-sized chip on his shoulder. With millions of people worldwide watching him seize the day, Howard thought of one man—Patriots coach Bill Parcells—and said to himself, "I can't believe he's kicking me the ball."

As he reached the midpoint of his Super Bowl–record 99-yard kickoff return, Howard ran right past Parcells, who at that juncture had as good a chance of tackling him as anyone. Howard raced for the score that turned a tense game into an emphatic Green Bay win, a 35–21 final that gave the storied franchise its first NFL title in 29 years. After a week's worth of media coverage dominated by a 55-year-old man (Parcells) who craves attention the way teenage boys crave Beverly Hills Ninja, the game was decided by the men who play it.

"This is a team that plays together," said Packers tight end Keith Jackson. "No one is more important than anyone else, whether you're Reggie White or Brett Favre or a guy blocking on special teams. We don't get down on anyone for making mistakes, and for that reason people don't worry about messing up. That's rare."

Early on, a blowout seemed in the making: Favre and receiver Andre Rison connected on a 54-yard TD catch on Green Bay's second play; New England QB Drew Bledsoe threw an interception on the next possession; and, after a Chris Jacke field goal, the Packers led 10–0.

But by attacking Green Bay's defense with screens, play-action plays and rollouts, the Patriots came back to take a 14–10 lead late in the first quarter on a pair of Bledsoe touchdown passes. "We were completely baffled," said Packers safety LeRoy Butler. "We were missing tackles, they were flying right past us, and they were pushing us around. No one had pushed us around all year, and they were killing us, doing stuff we hadn't seen before. It was a great game plan."

After that second TD, Green Bay defensive coordinator Fritz Shurmur called together the leaders of his unit and delivered a scolding. As Butler recalled it, Shurmur screamed to him, ends White and Sean Jones, nickelback Mike Prior and free safety Eugene Robinson, "Enough is enough! Pull your head out of your a-- and go do what you're supposed to do." Then, to Butler, he added, "Go get Bledsoe. Do whatever it takes. I'll blitz you every play if I have to—just get in his face." Eventually Butler and the Packers did get to Bledsoe, who threw four interceptions and absorbed five sacks while completing 25 of 48 passes for 253 yards.

Favre entered the game after a hard battle with the flu. He spent Thursday night in the hotel, shivering under his covers with a 101° temperature. "I was worried," he admitted late Sunday. "I'd waited my whole life to play in this game, and now I wasn't going to be healthy. But the night before the game I slept great. I fell asleep at 9:30 with the TV clicker in my hand, and I felt pretty good when I woke up. But I was nervous before kickoff, and I kept dry-heaving all game."

Favre was clearheaded enough to burn New England for two TDs after making adjustments at the line. On the first he detected that the Patriots, with both safeties up at the line, were about to come with an all-out blitz. So Favre changed the play from 322 Y Stick, a quick-out to tight end Mark Chmura, to 74 Razor, which called for Rison to run a deep post route. It wasn't the smoothest switch—in the middle of the audible Favre yelled "Oh, s---!" before finally barking out the right signal—but it worked perfectly. Rison turned cornerback Otis Smith around and was open to catch Favre's pass at the 20; then he duckwalked the last yards into the end zone.

After New England had taken its 14–10 lead, Favre put Green Bay up for good with another astute call. He saw the Pats' defensive backs line up in single coverage against a three-wideout set, with strong safety Lawyer

The great White bullied the Pats with three sacks.

Photograph by Walter Iooss Jr.

Milloy on Antonio Freeman, the slot receiver. "A safety on me, playing bump-and-run?" Freeman said incredulously after the game. "I liked my chances." Sensing the Patriots would blitz again, Favre audibled to a blocking scheme designed to give him maximum protection, then found Freeman down the right sideline. Freeman easily outran Milloy for an 81-yard score, the longest from scrimmage in Super Bowl history.

At halftime Green Bay led 27–14 and Howard told Favre, "I'm going to take one of these kicks back; it's only a matter of time." He struck at the perfect moment, after New England had cut the Pack's lead to 27–21. Howard caught the ball at the one, burst up the middle and swept through the coverage for his first kickoff return for a touchdown as a pro. "We were feeling good before that," Patriots safety Willie Clay said, "and then Desmond Howard broke our backs." ∎

BY Desmond Howard

Packers Kick Returner

In the third quarter, the Patriots were marching with a little comeback. They had just scored a touchdown and so they had the momentum. As a team, we needed to take the wind out of their sails. We just needed the opportunity, and luckily I got that with the kick return.

Adam Vinatieri kicked the ball, and right away I knew that I had a chance for a good return. The ball was really high and floated way back. I remember looking down at the field and seeing that I was at about the one-yard line. They hadn't given me much of a ball to return all game, but this one had just the right velocity. So I caught it, and I thought to myself, Here goes nothing.

Don Beebe [yes, the ex-Bill Don Beebe of Super Bowl XXVII lore] made a great block for me in the crease and I just found a seam and started running. The next thing I know, it was just me and a clear path to the end zone—only Vinatieri was there to stop me. And, no offense to Vinatieri, but tackling isn't exactly his specialty. Once I got to the end zone, I was elated. Something came over me and I started to do the robot. Looking back, it looks ridiculous, but at the time, I was like, 'I'm going to do the robot.'

I suppose I made for a pretty good story. I was right on the brink of getting released before the season started. I was a player on my way out, and then there I was, making Super Bowl history by returning a kick 99 yards and then winning the MVP award.

BY Keith Byars

Patriots Fullback

My first year in the NFL, my college roommate at Ohio State, Pepper Johnson, made the Super Bowl with the Giants so I flew to Pasadena to watch him play. The next year, the Redskins played the Broncos, and being that Doug Williams had a chance to be the first black quarterback to win it all, I attended too. I just didn't want to miss that historic moment. After that, I swore to myself, I wouldn't attend a Super Bowl unless I was in it.

It took me 11 years to get there, but thank goodness I did. Before the game, coach Parcells said, "Byars, you're an 11-year vet, 33 years old, are you going to be tired?" I was like, "Coach, are you serious? I have been preparing myself for this game since I was two. If there is ever a game I'm going to be tired, it is definitely not this one. You're going to have to drag me off the field."

Of course there were discussions about Parcells leaving, but that wasn't a distraction for us. It's easy to cop out and use that as an excuse, but it came down to what happened on the field. There were a couple of momentum shifts. My touchdown was big for us. That was a play we ran from time to time and a good one. If you have a running back like Curtis Martin, everyone expects him to run it, so offensive coordinator Charlie Weis changed the pace and called for a screen. Curtis really sold it, I sold it and I was open for a one-yard score. The 99-yard return they got from Desmond Howard was a backbreaker, though. I felt like we did a great job because the Packers didn't have many sustained drives, but the big plays killed us.

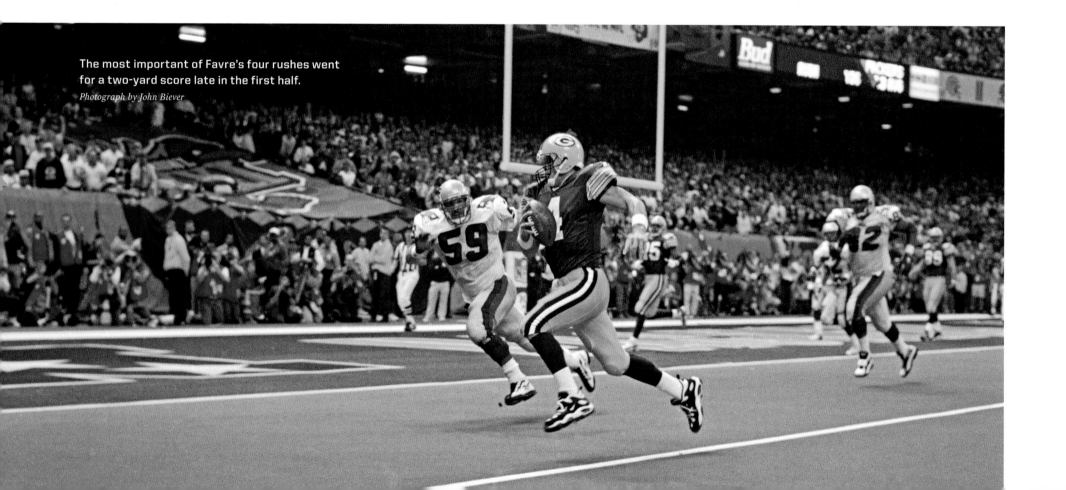

The most important of Favre's four rushes went for a two-yard score late in the first half.

Photograph by John Biever

"This is a team that plays together," said the Packers' Keith Jackson. "No one is more important than anyone else. We don't get down on anyone for making mistakes."

Craig Newsome's fourth-quarter pick essentially finished off the Pats.

Photograph by Walter Iooss Jr.

SUPER BOWL XXXII

January 25, 1998
Qualcomm Stadium, San Diego

HEAD COACHES
MIKE SHANAHAN Broncos | MIKE HOLMGREN Packers

DENVER
BRONCOS | 31

GREEN BAY
PACKERS | 24

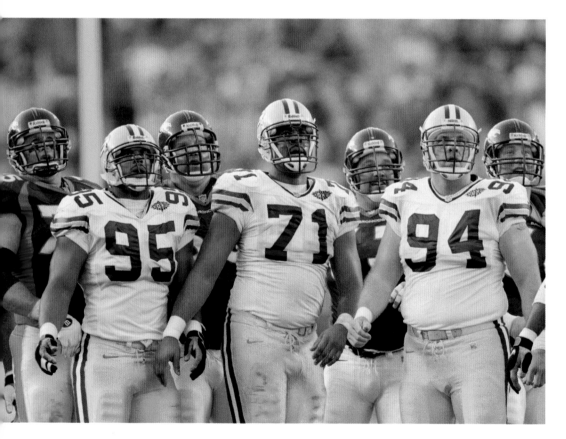

It's up and it's.... Denver's Jason Elam drilled a 51-yard field goal in the second quarter.

Photograph by John Iacono

WOULD JOHN ELWAY ever win a Super Bowl? The great QB was 0 for 3 in the big game and there seemed little hope this year, with his Broncos big underdogs to the reigning champs. Funny, then, how things turn out and how legacies are made.

WEATHER	POINT SPREAD	TIME OF GAME	TV AUDIENCE

67°, sunny	Packers by 11	3:25	90 million

Davis, sprung partly by Shanahan's astute game plan, controlled the play on the ground.

Photograph by Richard Mackson

THE GAME-CHANGER

A bold turn and a dramatic win put a QB, and a franchise, in a new light | BY MICHAEL SILVER

H E SPENT 15 YEARS PUSHING the physical limits of football, making jaws drop and decorating highlight clips with bursts of brilliance. Then, with one fearless thrust of his 37-year-old body late in the third quarter of Super Bowl XXXII, John Elway finally lifted himself and the Broncos to the top. In perhaps the greatest Super Bowl ever, the pivotal moment, fittingly, belonged to one of the NFL's alltime greats.

For all the importance of coach Mike Shanahan's dazzling game plan, of running back Terrell Davis's MVP performance and of the game-ending stand by Denver's defense, it was Elway who elevated himself into immortality and his franchise into the realm of champions with the Broncos' 31–24 upset of Green Bay.

The play said everything about the defiant Broncos and their unlikely march to the title: With the game

Davis (30) and Griffith had a celebratory salutation.

Photograph by Damian Strohmeyer

tied at 17 and Denver facing third-and-six at the Green Bay 12, Elway dropped back to pass, found no open receivers and took off down the middle of the field. He darted right and was met near the first-down marker by Packers strong safety LeRoy Butler, who ducked his head and prepared to unload on the quarterback. Elway took to the air, and Butler's hit spun him around so that he came down feet-forward as he was absorbing another shot from defensive back Mike Prior.

When Elway hit the ground at the four, an adrenaline rush surged through the Broncos. Denver scored two plays later, and though the Packers came back to tie the game, Green Bay was fighting a losing battle against an opponent that had been recharged. The Broncos then launched their game-winning drive from the Packers' 49 with 3:27 to go. "When Elway, instead of running out-of-bounds, turned it up and got spun around like a helicopter, it energized us beyond belief," Denver defensive lineman Mike Lodish said. Added tight end Shannon Sharpe, "When I saw him do that and then get up pumping his fist, I said, 'It's on.' That's when I was sure we were going to win."

Though only an infinitesimal slice of the earth's football-viewing population believed Denver would dethrone Green Bay, the Broncos carried a confidence that belied their station as double-digit underdogs. As early as eight days before the game, Shanahan began telling people he trusted that the Broncos were poised for victory, saying to one reporter, "Just between you and me, we're going to win the game." Shanahan was convinced he could get inside the head of Packers defensive coordinator Fritz Shurmur, who relies on the versatile Butler for frequent blitzing and run support. Shanahan believed that when Denver lined up in a slot formation he could predict Butler's assignment based on the safety's positioning. Denver had spent the season running out of its base alignment and passing from the slot, but on this day all of its runs came from the latter formation. Green Bay

never adjusted. The Broncos gained 179 yards on the ground, even though they ran for no yards in the second quarter while Davis sat out with blurred vision after getting kicked in the helmet during a run.

Sure, Elway's stats were wimpy. He threw for only 123 yards, didn't complete a pass to a wideout until Ed McCaffrey's 36-yard catch-and-run midway through the third quarter and blew a chance to build on a seven-point lead by throwing an end zone interception to safety Eugene Robinson with 11 seconds left in the third quarter. But Elway carried the day with his poise. "That was the ultimate win, there's no question," he said. "There have been a lot of things that go along with losing three Super Bowls and playing for 14 years and being labeled as a guy who has never been on a winning Super Bowl team."

Elway dismissed the Robinson interception from his mind, and when he strutted onto the field with 3:27 left, the score tied at 24 and the ball on the Green Bay 49, he was in control. On his biggest pass of the game, he made a perfect delivery, throwing a quick toss to fullback Howard Griffith that went for 23 yards and gave Denver a first-and-goal at the eight with two minutes left. That set up Davis's winning one-yard touchdown run. "John makes mistakes; he is human after all," Broncos receiver Rod Smith would say later. "But you never see fear in his eyes. He's like a linebacker with a good arm."

It's a measure of how far Denver has come that Elway, who once had to carry his team, didn't have to be spectacular in his finest hour. Shanahan built these Broncos to reflect his own personality— resilient, businesslike and fearless. Strong safety Tyrone Braxton, whose first-quarter interception set up Denver's second touchdown, knew the significance of the victory. "It means everything," Braxton said, "not only for this team but for all the past Broncos. We're not a city of losers anymore. . . . It's been a long, hard road for all of us." ∎

JUST THE FACTS

Statistical Leaders

Rushing TERRELL DAVIS (DEN) 30 carries, 157 yds, 3 TDs

Passing BRETT FAVRE (GB) 25 of 42, 256 yds, 3 TDs

Receiving ANTONIO FREEMAN (GB) 9 catches, 126 yds, 2 TDs

MVP TERRELL DAVIS Broncos Running Back

The Ring
Five diamonds on each side of center is for 55, the total points scored in the game

Anthem Performer
Jewel

Halftime Performers
Boyz II Men, Smokey Robinson, The Four Tops and The Temptations

Attendance 68,912

Ticket Prices $275, $350

Behind the Scenes

Within 30 minutes of the end of the NCAA's Holiday Bowl on Dec. 27, the NFL descended upon Qualcomm Stadium. The goalposts were removed and the sod completely replaced.

They Said It

"There's only so many times you can get hit right in the forehead with a fist, but this time we did the punching."

—Broncos quarterback JOHN ELWAY

Foot Soldiers

Traffic near the stadium was so congested 90 minutes before kickoff that Chargers president Dean Spanos and general manager Bobby Beathard got out of their chartered bus and walked the final stretch into the parking lot.

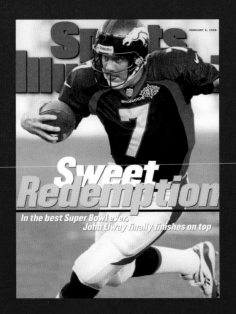

Sweet Redemption
In the best Super Bowl ever, John Elway finally finishes on top

Favre, who lost this second-quarter fumble, was rattled by Denver's blitzes.
Photograph by Heinz Kluetmeier

Diving headlong, and taking a hit in mid-air, Elway made the play of the game.
Photograph by John W. McDonough

Elway didn't put up sterling stats the way he often did, but he led with his confidence and poise.

Photograph by John W. McDonough

BY John Elway

Broncos Quarterback

The funny thing about the famous Helicopter play is that we had practiced it all week and I had told [coach Mike Shanahan] that I didn't really like the play. I explained that if we lined up against a different defense, this play was not going to work. He said, "No, it's been a 100 percent against this formation all year long. It's 100 percent that we get this coverage." Well, sure enough, we get up there and it's not the coverage we expected. Now I don't have a play. I'm standing out there and watching and I knew I didn't have a play and I would have to go outside and scramble outside and try to get something.

I was able to find a seam up on the side, the defense stayed outside, and they kind of stayed back which gave me the opportunity to run for the first down. Then while I was running, I could see three defenders coming right toward me. I figured that they were expecting me to go low and slide. So I said to myself, You know what? I am going to try to use my three-inch vertical leap on them and go right over the top. Yeah, I was putting my whole body out there and I suppose at risk—but it was that important, too. I was almost 38 years old and I knew that I was getting toward the end of my career. This was one of my last opportunities, and that was perhaps the biggest game of my life. We were able to win that thing, and do you know what? That game is my favorite win of all time.

BY Antonio Freeman

Packers Wide Receiver

We had a chance to do something special: win back-to-back championships. All season long, we were the favorites. We really didn't have much turnover from the previous season, and we had weapons on both sides of the ball. We were looking forward to a chance to play in good weather—Green Bay at that time of year was frigid—and we were all pretty confident.

I won't say we underestimated what the Broncos could do, but they came out and just executed everything. As for our offense, our timing was a little off, or we got a little pressured, and we just didn't look like us in the first half. At halftime, Brett Favre was calm. He and I had great chemistry; he could look at me and I would know exactly what he wanted me to do. We both knew we needed to get out there and play our game. And then things kind of slipped away. We were confident that opportunities would come but as the clock ticked down, those opportunities were fewer and fewer. And then it was over, just like that.

The hardest part might have been after we all left the stadium. Every team has a party after the Super Bowl. It's a team function, so you have to go, but that was the last thing any of us wanted to do: party. There were friends and family there, and they were all so proud and appreciative and wanted to celebrate you getting to the peak of your profession. But I remember thinking, I don't want to be here right now. I just want to go home and be alone.

After the game, riding in a limousine with owner Pat Bowlen, Mike Shanahan raised his champagne glass and said, without being brash, "This was just the way we planned it."

Green Bay's Antonio Freeman had a big day, but he felt the crunch of Bill Romanowski (53) and Ray Crockett.

Photograph by John Biever

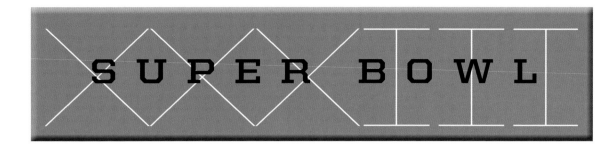

SUPER BOWL XXXIII

January 31, 1999
Pro Player Stadium, Miami

HEAD COACHES
MIKE SHANAHAN Broncos | DAN REEVES Falcons

DENVER
BRONCOS | 34

ATLANTA
FALCONS | 19

JOHN ELWAY and the Broncos were back, and the long-suffering Falcons had finally arrived. The teams knew how to win (both came in at 16-2) but it was Denver's savvy QB and mastermind coach who quickly put Atlanta in its place.

WEATHER
73°, 10 mph wind

POINT SPREAD
Broncos by 7½

TIME OF GAME
3:18

TV AUDIENCE
83.7 million

The sons of receiver Ed McCaffrey, Christian (left) and Max, in the postgame "snow."

Photograph by Robert Beck

228

Elway was in the end zone on a keeper, and the rout was officially on.
Photograph by Heinz Kluetmeier

Tight end Shannon Sharpe brought the ball to the one-yard line, setting up Denver's first TD.

Photograph by Robert Beck

JUST THE FACTS

Statistical Leaders

Rushing **TERRELL DAVIS** (DEN) 25 carries, 102 yds

Passing **JOHN ELWAY** (DEN) 18 of 29, 336 yds, 1 TD

Receiving **ROD SMITH** (DEN) 5 catches, 152 yds, 1 TD

MVP JOHN ELWAY Broncos Quarterback

The Ring
14-karat yellow-gold ring with 120 diamonds and BACK2BACK engraved on one side

Anthem Performer
Cher

Halftime Performers
Gloria Estefan, Stevie Wonder, Big Bad Voodoo Daddy and Savion Glover

Attendance 74,803

Ticket Price $325

Behind the Scenes

Six hours before kickoff, Broncos coach Mike Shanahan was watching *A Night at the Roxbury* with his son, Kyle, in his hotel room. Midway through, Shanahan abruptly left the room and visited John Elway to go over a series of plays one more time.

They Said It

"I don't know if it's John's [Elway's] last game, but if it is, what a way to go out. We've got a lot of guys in there trying to talk him into a threepeat." —Broncos coach MIKE SHANAHAN

Wheel Deal

During Super Bowl week, Broncos wide receiver Willie Green zipped around Miami in a 1999 blue Lamborghini Diablo, which he had rented for the month at $1,900 a day.

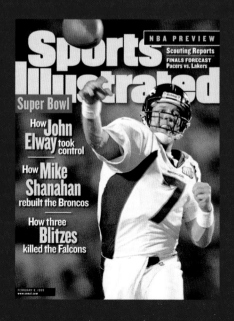

BLAZE OF GLORY

That's how John Elway, with a redemptive day and another title, went out | BY MICHAEL SILVER

THE RAIN POURED DOWN EARLY Monday morning as John Elway stepped onto the balcony of his Fort Lauderdale hotel room and let out a roar that reverberated eight stories below. Elway had just played the game of his life, throwing for 336 yards and a touchdown in the Broncos' 34–19 Super Bowl XXXIII win over the Falcons. With water splashing on his face, a Cuban cigar in his left hand and an American beer in his right, Elway looked and felt like the king of the world. His broad grin reflected a win that went beyond a second straight NFL title. Challenged to a duel by his former boss and tormentor, Atlanta coach Dan Reeves, the 38-year-old QB displayed his grit, slaying not only the Falcons but also his final demons in what was probably the last game of his Hall of Fame career.

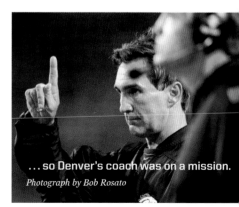

Reeves called out Shanahan . . .
Photograph by Robert Beck

"I never thought it could get any better than last year, but just look at this scene," Elway said, gesturing toward the revelers who had gathered at the entrance to the team's hotel. "You couldn't have planned it more perfectly—no wind during the game, warm weather, a full moon—and now it pours, like a great, big release."

Elway drew on his cigar and flicked some ashes into the rain. The man has always had a flair for the fantastic finish. Had he retired after last season, when he won his first Super Bowl in four tries, Elway's finale would have been heartwarming. Now he can go out in a blaze of glory. "All week long, all the Falcons talked about was stopping our running game," Elway said, his eyes hardening. "I knew they were saying, 'Make Elway beat us.' My thought was, Good, let's go."

Most football fans are versed in the contentious history involving Reeves, Elway and Broncos coach Mike Shanahan, but when Reeves gave the world a refresher course during an emotional press conference 11 days before the game, it set off a war of wills he was unlikely to win. As Denver's coach, Reeves had fired Shanahan, his offensive coordinator, following the '91 season, because he believed Shanahan was trying to undermine his relationship with Elway. (Shanahan has repeatedly denied this.) Despite acts of reconciliation among the three men over the past year, Reeves chose his Jan. 20 meeting with the media to reaffirm his view that Shanahan's work behind the scenes had cost him his job in Denver (after the '92 season). In the wake of Reeves's emotional comeback from quadruple-bypass surgery in December, those old slights were revisited and the Atlanta coach came off looking like the victim again. He had no idea how victimized he was about to be.

"For Mike, this game was personal," Elway said. "I've never seen him more ready for a football game. I knew it meant more to him than any game he has ever coached." Hell hath no fury like a genius scorned.

Atlanta geared its defense to stop running back Terrell Davis, and Shanahan surprised them by having Elway fake handoffs to Davis on several short-yardage plays and instead give the ball to fullback Howard Griffith, who scored twice on one-yard runs. On Denver's other rushing touchdown, Griffith, the lone running back, went in motion to the left, and Elway went in on a three-yard quarterback draw. That gave the Broncos a 31–6 lead with 11:20 to go and sent 74,803 fans into postgame party-planning mode.

Shanahan and offensive coordinator Gary Kubiak made their most significant adjustment on the fly. When they studied a photo of a second-quarter play that resulted in an 18-yard Elway pass to Rod Smith, they noticed the Falcons' safeties had bitten on a fake to Davis, leaving themselves vulnerable in the deep middle of the field. Shanahan suggested Elway run the play again but change Smith's route from a buttonhook to a post pattern. "We hadn't used it in six or seven weeks," Shanahan said. "We hadn't practiced it that way in some time."

Shanahan thought the revised play, Fake 19 Handoff QB Keep Right X Post, could go for a touchdown and with Denver up 10–3 and on its 20 late in the first half, Elway faked a handoff to Davis and hummed one of his sweetest spirals. Smith, a practice squad player in '94 who carries a wrinkled food stamp in his wallet to remind himself of his less fortunate past, blew by Eugene Robinson with an inside-out move, caught the ball in stride at the Falcons' 43 and coasted to the end zone. "There've only been a handful of times this year when we called something in a game that we hadn't practiced that week," said Denver guard Mark Schlereth. "This play was not only a testament to how we prepare but also to how much Mike trusts the players."

Especially Elway, who was so loose the week before the game that he adopted the name of his boyhood hero. Each time he ordered room service or spoke to a hotel operator, he chuckled as he was addressed by his alias: Elway was registered as John Wayne.

Early on Monday, long after victory was his, the old gunslinger hobbled back to room 870 and fielded the only remaining question about his football legacy: Will he ride off into the sunset? For now the answer is yes, but it's not final, and he'll take his sweet time making it official. "Not now," he said as he stepped onto the balcony. There were drinks to down and cigars to puff and loved ones to embrace and nurture. ■

. . . so Denver's coach was on a mission.
Photograph by Bob Rosato

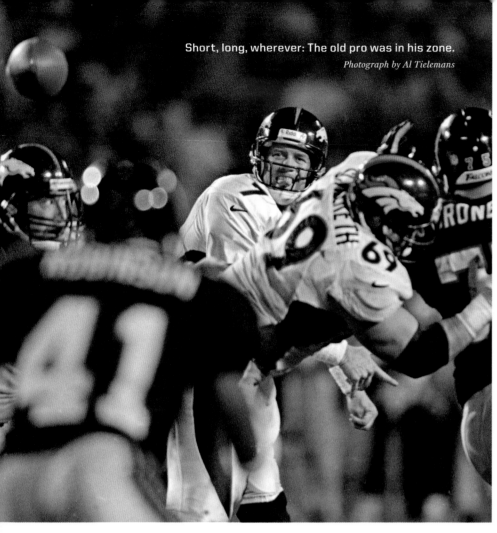

Short, long, wherever: The old pro was in his zone.
Photograph by Al Tielemans

The Atlanta defense had geared to stop Davis, but even then it wasn't so easy.
Photograph by Bob Rosato

THE WAY IT WAS

BY Steve Atwater

Broncos Safety

We were a really confident team. When we stepped on the field, it was like nobody could stop us. When you're the defending Super Bowl champions, every team wants to beat you so badly that it makes you work that much harder and play that much better. That's a battle we fought all season, and as we strung together that 13-game winning streak, we never felt the pressure building for us to be great because we knew we were.

As for me, throughout the year I started to know my tenure with the Broncos was coming to the end. The year before, I had a remarkable season and a fantastic Super Bowl but this year things changed. Our defensive coordinator, Greg Robinson, began taking me out on third downs, which meant they didn't think I could be effective in those situations. It was a sign of the end.

I had no idea this Super Bowl would be my last game as a Bronco, but what a way to go out. The Falcons offense was excellent, led by quarterback Chris Chandler, and to beat him, we knew we needed to bring the pressure. We had a variety of blitzes that we used that day, and what we are most proud of is forcing them into four turnovers in the second half. I will say, the celebration wasn't as great as it was when we won Super Bowl XXXII. We probably celebrated with about 50 percent of the enthusiasm. I'm not quite sure why. We were in a fabulous city and had much to be happy for. Maybe the win just wasn't as big of a surprise.

BY Jessie Tuggle

Falcons Linebacker

For a kid growing up in Georgia—I was born there, I went to college there, I was drafted by the Falcons and spent my entire career there—helping to bring the team to its first Super Bowl was beyond surreal. The moment it hit me, though, was pregame. I stood on the field and looked over to my left and realized that Cher was standing right next to me. (She would be singing the national anthem.) I was thinking, "I can't believe I'm standing next to such a big celebrity!" Then there was the flyover, and the hair on my back was standing up straight.

We were all so excited to be there. We had a fantastic season and were all pumped up for the game. If we had only played like we did in the NFC title game, we would have won. We had upset the best team in the NFC, Minnesota, in Minnesota. But you have to give credit to Elway, he had a great game.

On defense, our game plan was to stop Terrell Davis. I was known for big hits, and I wanted to hit him so hard that I would knock the ball right out of his hands. As for Elway—we hoped that we could limit the big plays. We knew we couldn't let him make game-changing plays. Unfortunately, it didn't go as we planned. We obviously got off to a great start by scoring first but they came back way stronger. We were in it until that 80-yard touchdown by Rod Smith. After that the lead was too big for us to overcome.

XXXII

BRONCOS | FALCONS

John Elway was
so loose the week
before the game
that he adopted the
name of his boyhood
hero. At his hotel he
was registered as
John Wayne.

Smith beat the beleaguered
Robinson, and was gone.
Photograph by Bill Frakes

SUPER BOWL XXXIV

January 30, 2000
Georgia Dome, Atlanta

HEAD COACHES
DICK VERMEIL Rams | JEFF FISHER Titans

ST. LOUIS
RAMS | 23

TENNESSEE
TITANS | 16

NOW THIS was a Super Bowl: a rally from 16 points down, a 73-yard pass for the winning score, the outcome in doubt until the final whistle. Yes, the game was something of a fairy tale, with a Cinderella crowned champion in the end.

DOME
1/2 inch of ice outside

POINT SPREAD
Rams by 7

TIME OF GAME
3:28

TV AUDIENCE
88.5 million

The Rams were bobbing and weaving after the touchdown that made it 16-0.

Photograph by John Biever

Warner's 414 yards passing snapped the Super Bowl record set by Joe Montana 11 years earlier.

Photograph by Bill Frakes

Excerpted from **SPORTS ILLUSTRATED** *February 7, 2000*

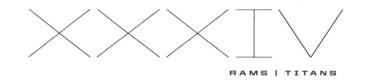

SIMPLY DIVINE

Kurt Warner's story—and this remarkable game—elevated the sport | BY MICHAEL SILVER

H E IS A FAMILY MAN AND A MAN of God, an out-of-nowhere sensation whose story has been called too schmaltzy even for Hollywood. But on the football field Kurt Warner is the quintessential quarterback, a cocksure leader who wants the ball in his hands when everything is hanging in the balance. With Super Bowl XXXIV slipping out of the Rams' grasp, Warner took over. Two minutes and five seconds remained in a tie game with the tireless Titans when Warner, enduring the pain of strained cartilage in his ribs, jogged onto the field, inhaled gingerly and thought, 'It's time for me to win this game.' Cool and slick, Warner dropped five steps in the pocket and, an instant before absorbing a hellacious hit from defensive end Jevon Kearse, launched the 73-yard touchdown pass to wideout Isaac Bruce that gave the Rams a 23–16 win. All across the land spines straightened and eyes moistened, and anyone who has ever been doubted felt a surge of satisfaction.

When the game's wild ending played out a few minutes later, with St. Louis linebacker Mike Jones stopping Tennessee wideout Kevin Dyson at the Rams' one-yard line, confetti flew and fireworks exploded, and the coronation of Kurt Warner, American Sports Hero, was complete. By now we know the 28-year-old's triumphant tale—the family tragedy, the job stocking groceries for minimum wage at an all-night supermarket, the minor league football struggles—and it seems almost clichéd, or somehow beyond belief. Yet the one person who appears unfazed by the improbability of it all is the guy doing the heavy lifting.

"How can you be in awe of something that you expect yourself to do?" Warner asked late Sunday as he rode a team bus from the Georgia Dome to the Rams' hotel. "People think this season is the first time I touched a football; they don't realize I've been doing this for years—just not on this level, because I never got the chance. Sure, I had my tough times, but you don't sit there and say, 'Wow, I was stocking groceries five years ago, and look at me now.' You don't think about it, and when you do achieve something, you know luck has nothing to do with it."

Unlike so many St. Louis opponents, Tennessee refused to sit back and let Warner score at will. Mixing coverages and varying blitzes, the Titans put a major hurt on the quarterback—he injured his ribs while taking a shot as he overthrew wideout Ricky Proehl in the end zone 24 seconds before halftime—and tightened up where it counted most. The red zone was the dead zone for St. Louis, which staked out a mere 9–0 halftime lead despite moving inside the 20 on each of its five first-half possessions.

Then, trailing 16–0 after a Warner-to-Torry Holt scoring pass, the Titans did what they always do: stayed in the fight. Dual-threat QB Steve McNair (214 passing yards; 64 rushing) led a 66-yard drive that ended on Eddie George's one-yard TD run with 14 seconds left in the third quarter. Tennessee missed the two-point conversion, but St. Louis went three and out and George finished the Titans' next drive with a gritty two-yard TD run. Tennessee held again and tied the game on Al Del Greco's 43-yard field goal with 2:12 to go.

Said Mike White, St. Louis's assistant head coach,

Vermeil won the lone Super Bowl of his fine career.

Photograph by John Iacono

"[The Titans have] had so much success in the fourth quarter all year, and they just turned it up. People have been calling them a team of destiny, and it was like they just believed it was their time."

The quarterback of destiny, however, had the decisive say. With the Rams taking over on their own 27, offensive coordinator Mike Martz called 999 H-Balloon, in which Holt lines up wide left and three wideouts start from the right. When Warner saw Bruce would be single-covered by cornerback Denard Walker, he knew where he wanted to go. But Kearse's vicious rush caused the quarterback to release early, and the ball was underthrown. "I was thinking, I hope Ike comes back for it," Warner said later. That's exactly what Bruce did, turning to catch the ball at the Tennessee 43, then freezing several defenders, cutting to the middle and outracing everyone to the end zone.

McNair, though, nearly willed the Titans to a tying TD. With 22 seconds left and the ball on the Rams' 26, he produced one of the most scintillating efforts in Super Bowl history, scrambling more than 10 yards behind the line of scrimmage and bulling free of would-be sacks before releasing a perfect pass to Dyson at the Rams' 10. Tennessee called its final timeout with six seconds remaining. The season came down to one play.

Tennessee sent tight end Frank Wycheck into the end zone, hoping to draw defenders there and hit Dyson underneath. He caught the ball in stride inside the five and had only one man between him and the first Super Bowl overtime game. Jones, however, wrapped up Dyson, whose lunge for the goal line fell short. "It seemed like slow-motion," Jones said. "I couldn't see McNair throw the ball, but I could feel it."

It was the rarest of football events—a Super Bowl that exceeded its colossal buildup, and nice guys finished first and last. ∎

Statistical Leaders

Rushing EDDIE GEORGE (TEN) 28 carries, 95 yds, 2 TDs

Passing KURT WARNER (STL) 24 of 45, 414 yds, 2 TDs

Receiving ISAAC BRUCE (TEN) 6 catches, 162 yds, 1 TD

MVP KURT WARNER Rams Quarterback

The Ring
157 diamonds weighing
approximately 2.75 carats

Anthem Performer
Faith Hill

Halftime Performers
Christina Aguilera, Enrique
Iglesias, Phil Collins and
Toni Braxton

Attendance 72,625

Ticket Price $325

Behind the Scenes

Atlanta was hit with crippling ice storms before the game. Some 300,000 homes and businesses were without power and roads were in such poor condition that neither team could make it to the Georgia Dome on Saturday for its scheduled walk-through.

They Said It

"[A year ago] it wasn't very realistic to think I'd be the starter in the Super Bowl. They were trying to figure out if I was good enough to be the backup."
—Rams QB KURT WARNER

Not in La-La Land Anymore

As Rams owner Georgia Frontiere accepted the Lombardi Trophy she remarked, "It proves that we did the right thing in going to St. Louis."

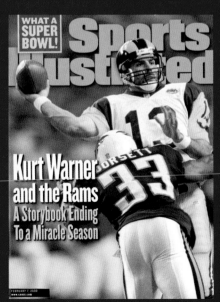

Though Bruce was always a big-play threat, his game-winning Super Bowl catch was his longest reception of the season.

Photograph by Damian Strohmeyer

Warner hit Dyson underneath but Jones dragged him down. So the Titans finished one yard short, despite Dyson's final extension. For St. Louis and a high-jumping Warner (right), the party was on.

Photographs (from top, left to right) by John Biever (4), Bob Rosato and John W. McDonough (right)

BY Isaac Bruce

Rams Wide Receiver

It was the big game, but I remember us being pretty loose beforehand. That was kind of our M.O., we were a really tight-knit team. On the bus going to the game, we were all singing. Our song of choice: the intro to "Showtime at the Apollo." Me and Keith Lyle were snapping, and belting out the line: "It's showtime at the Apollo tonight!"

And we did put on a show—especially in the fourth quarter. The game was exhilarating, and I'll never forget the touchdown that sealed it. The play was called Twins Right Ace Right 999 H-Balloon. What 999 meant was that all the receivers were going deep.

I remember going stride-for-stride with the defender that was on me, but as soon as Kurt Warner threw the ball, I knew it was underthrown. I had always been taught to give the illusion you're running full-speed, then break down at the last minute to catch the ball. So that's what I did, and my defender had no idea the ball was going to be short. *Boom*, *pop*, it felt like slow-motion.

I caught the football and ran toward the end zone. As I got close, I looked up to the JumboTron and I could see the facial expressions of so many of the Rams fans in the stands—pure exhilaration—and also the look of *Oh no!* on the faces of the Titans supporters. I could also see the Tennessee guys chasing me on the field, and I realized they had no chance. Then I saw my teammate, Orlando Pace, stick his big paw in the air celebrating and I knew that something special had just occurred.

BY Kevin Dyson

Titans Wide Receiver

We fell behind 16–0 early, but it could have been worse. The Rams had complete control. Things changed when [Tennessee safety] Blaine Bishop got injured in the third quarter. It was scary to see him get carted off on a stretcher and we were all kind of speechless, dejected. Coach Fisher got us together and said to look over at the Rams' sideline. "Look at them," he said. "They're celebrating like they've already won. Is this how you want to go out?"

After that we were a completely different team. We started to play our physical style: Eddie [George] had his touchdowns and suddenly it was 16–16. Then it came down to the last play. I've thought about that moment a lot over the years. People come up to me about it. It's crazy to think that's what I'll often be remembered for, just one play. The Rams had coverage on my side of the field. They knew it was coming for me. Steve [McNair] threw me the ball, and when I caught it I saw the end zone. I knew Mike Jones was there, but I thought I had better positioning on him and could beat his tackle. Even if he got his hands on me, I still thought I could get to the end zone. But somehow he got his whole body around, and got his left hand on my left knee. I couldn't extend my leg and get that extra few inches we needed. I was down, and that was it. It was over.

I remember sitting there and seeing the confetti fall wondering if I could have done things differently. There were all these cameras in my face, and I knew I just had to get up and stand up. Growing up, I was told to never let your opponent see your disappointment. At that moment, though, it was tough to do.

SUPER BOWL

January 28, 2001
Raymond James Stadium, Tampa

HEAD COACHES
BRIAN BILLICK Ravens | JIM FASSEL Giants

BALTIMORE
RAVENS | 34

NEW YORK
GIANTS | 7

Before the team's big-game debut some Ravens were highly focused.

Photograph by John Iacono

THERE ARE heroes and there are antiheroes, and there are men such as Baltimore's Ray Lewis who are both. The Ravens entered the playoffs as a wild card but their ornery, Lewis-led defense made this the most ferocious team around.

WEATHER	POINT SPREAD	TIME OF GAME	TV AUDIENCE

65°, partly cloudy	Ravens by 3	3:23	84.3 million

The NFL's Defensive Player of the Year, Ray Lewis intimidated offenses even before the ball was snapped.

Photograph by John W. McDonough

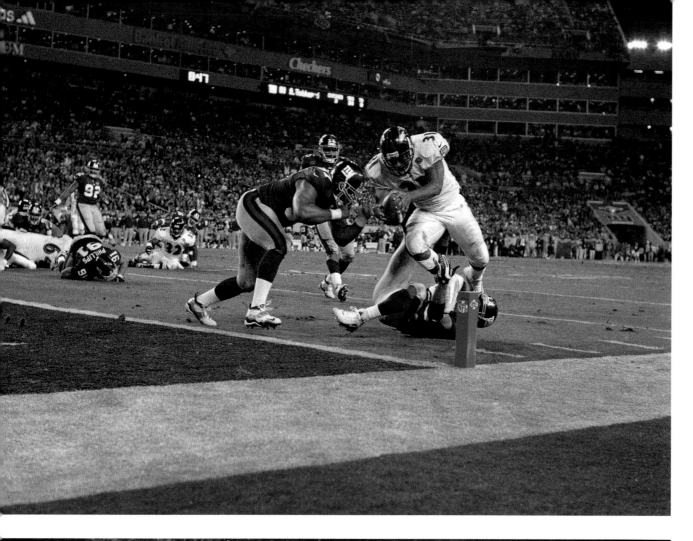

Call it 31 Toss Left? Not exactly. Rookie Jamal Lewis scored on this three-yard fourth quarter run. What happened below might be viewed as a premature spike.

Photographs by Al Tielemans

JUST THE FACTS

Statistical Leaders

Rushing **JAMAL LEWIS** (BAL) 27 carries, 102 yds, 1 TD

Passing **TRENT DILFER** (BAL) 12 of 25, 153 yds, 1 TD

Receiving **BRANDON STOKLEY** (BAL) 3 catches, 52 yds, 1 TD

MVP **RAY LEWIS** Ravens Linebacker

The Ring
A diamond beak, a ruby eye

Anthem Performer
Backstreet Boys

Halftime Performers
Aerosmith, *NSYNC, Britney Spears, Mary J. Blige and Nelly

Attendance 71,921

Ticket Price $325

Behind the Scenes

The Giants went to a no-huddle attack in the second half, an offense they had not run in nearly two months and a strategy that ultimately proved pointless.

They Said It

"If the world wants to see me stumble now, at least I'll stumble with a ring on my finger." — Ravens linebacker **RAY LEWIS**

Take That! And That!

For the only time in Super Bowl history, back-to-back kickoffs were returned for touchdowns—first by New York's Ron Dixon, then by Baltimore's Jermaine Lewis.

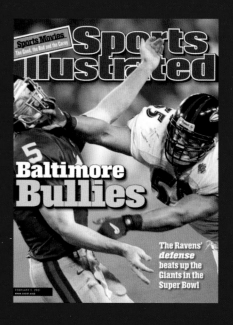

The Ravens' *defense* beats up the Giants in the Super Bowl

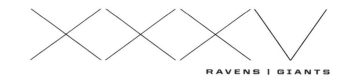

THEY'RE SO RAVENS

Playing a distinct brand of football, Baltimore lived up to its own hype | BY MICHAEL SILVER

FIFTEEN MINUTES BEFORE SUPER Bowl XXXV, Ray Lewis, the Ravens' unrepentant middle linebacker, and Brian Billick, the team's bombastic coach, held a rare, private conversation that underscored a week's worth of public pronouncements. Standing outside the Ravens' locker room, Lewis said to Billick, "They don't understand, do they?" and the coach shook his head no. Naturally, Billick understood all that they couldn't comprehend—they being the Giants, the 3,300 credentialed members of the media and most of the U.S. sporting public. "We'll show 'em," said Billick.

We now know that Billick, Lewis and the rest of the Ravens had a right to be arrogant. In routing the Giants 34–7, Baltimore won the way Lewis and Billick had said it would, with a counterintuitive blend of a statistically challenged offense and a defense whose passion sucks the will out of disbelieving opponents.

Some fans may revile the cocky Ravens, but the Ravens love one another, and it shows in the way their proud defensive players race to the ball. In allowing New York a mere 152 yards and no offensive points, Baltimore was led, as always, by Lewis, who completed one of the most remarkable one-year turnabouts the sports world has known.

Fifty-two weeks earlier, in the wee hours after Super Bowl XXXIV, Lewis was in the midst of a bloody brawl in which two men were knifed to death outside an Atlanta nightclub. Facing murder charges that were dropped when he pleaded guilty to a misdemeanor charge of obstructing justice, Lewis vowed to channel his anger and frustration into a ferocious championship drive. While he alienated outsiders during pre-Super Bowl interviews by bristling at any notion of remorse—at one point going so far as to portray himself as a Christ figure—Lewis spoke loudest with his captivating play.

"To be here after what happened last year," he said from the victory podium, "it's a feeling you can't describe." Later, he added, "I don't mean to disrespect anyone, but we're definitely the best defense of all time."

In any case, it is a dominant enough defense that Trent Dilfer, who started the year as a backup, had the role of a quarterback charged simply with not making mistakes. He wanted more. The day before the game, he talked strategy. "Right now [New York defensive coordinator] John Fox is in his room trying to figure out ways to make me look like an idiot—and I love that. Believe it or not, we think we can gash them with speed.... We love the matchups involving [wideout] Brandon Stokley, so I'm going to get him the ball."

Stokley, a second-year backup from Louisiana-Lafayette, entered the game with a total of 15 catches, while playing in only 10 games this season. "He'll get into the end zone," Dilfer insisted. "Mark my words."

On Sunday, with 6:57 left in the first quarter and the ball at the Giants' 38, Stokley lined up in the right slot for a play called Scat-Left Double-Pump. New York's best cornerback, Jason Sehorn, was covering Stokley in the spread formation. Stokley beat Sehorn off the ball, Dilfer delivered a perfect pass that Stokley caught in stride at the 10, and the 5' 11", 197-pound receiver dragged Sehorn into the end zone. Late in the second quarter Dilfer floated a pass to wideout Qadry Ismail down the left sideline. The 44-yard gain set up a field goal by Matt Stover that gave Baltimore a 10–0 lead.

Baltimore had talked about producing the first shutout in Super Bowl history. (A 97-yard Ron Dixon kickoff return prevented it.) And for all their defensive accomplishments—165 points allowed, a league record for a 16-game schedule; a total of 16 points surrendered to three AFC playoff foes—the Ravens saved their best for last. Baltimore made a mockery of New York quarterback Kerry Collins, intercepting him four times (including Duane Starks's 49-yard TD return), sacking him four times and allowing only 15 completions and 112 passing yards in 39 attempts. New York's

Brad Maynard punted a Super Bowl–record 11 times. "Until you play us, you can't really appreciate the depth of our wrath," said defensive tackle Tony Siragusa.

Emotionally, it all stems from Lewis. Players talk about the day last season when he missed a practice with a knee injury. Recalled Tony Banks, the former starting QB, "The defense was a shell of itself. He came back the next day, and it was great again." In the Super Bowl, Lewis got his hands on five Collins passes, one of which was tipped to linebacker Jamie Sharper for an interception. He had five tackles and was better in space than Captain Kirk.

After the game Lewis stood at his locker, wearing a lavender-paisley-patterned suit and a big grin. He hadn't won over all his critics, but his passionate play made it impossible not to admire him as a football player. For better or worse, Super Bowl XXXV was Ray Lewis's day in the sun. ∎

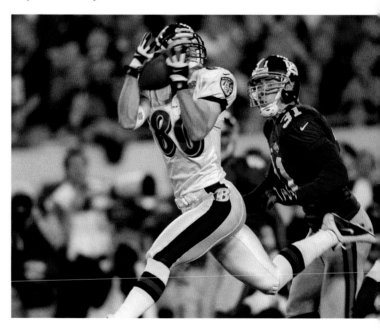

Stokley, beating Sehorn, was Dilfer's premonition man.

Photograph by Al Tielemans

Tackle Sam Adams was among those who rattled Collins off his game.

Photograph by Bill Frakes

BY Jonathan Ogden

Ravens Tackle

We thought that the AFC divisional round matchup between us and the Titans pitted the two best teams in the NFL against each other. Once we got past the Titans, we felt the championship was ours for the taking, that we just had to take care of business against Oakland in the conference final and then, it turned out, against New York in the Super Bowl. All we needed to do was play our game. With all due respect to the Giants, we felt we were physically superior, particularly on defense, and that our offense was not to be overlooked. Behind Trent Dilfer, Jamal Lewis and a great crop of receivers, our offense could put up enough big plays and score enough points to complement our defense and beat any team.

When Jermaine Lewis returned a kickoff for a touchdown in the third quarter, restoring our 17-point lead, I remember watching him run down the sideline thinking, "O.K., I think we may have this thing." When Jamal Lewis grinded out a three-yard run for our next touchdown, in the fourth quarter, that's when I knew it was over.

I had never won a championship at any level—not high school, not college, nothing. So to do it here, on the world's biggest stage, was really remarkable. I have a special relationship with Baltimore; I was the team's first draft pick when it moved here and winning for these fans made me feel even more connected to the city.

BY Amani Toomer

Giants Wide Receiver

I remember walking off the field as the fireworks went off and confetti streamed down and thinking, "Where did it all go wrong?" It went from being the best season ever (at least at that point in my career) to ending, just like that, almost like a car crash. To this day, I am still mad about it—I'm mad about our game plan, I'm mad about the way we played. All year we played our brand of football, then all of the sudden the game plan is to switch it up for one game?

I think the coaches were so intimidated by the Ravens' defense, and they made some decisions I didn't agree with. We tried to play too cute, tried to do too many trick plays and too many things that weren't us. In the big game, you want to at least go down swinging. The way we played felt like an embarrassment. In the second half, we hurried it up and tried to spread it out, and it just didn't work.

So many personnel decisions stemmed because we lost that game. Perhaps our roster would have looked completely different five years down the road if we had won. I look at Kerry Collins—he was a great quarterback for us but his legacy is often defined by the picks he threw in that game. All you want is to find a way to get back to that big stage and get redemption, but it's hard. Only two of us, me and Michael Strahan, made it to the next Giants Super Bowl.

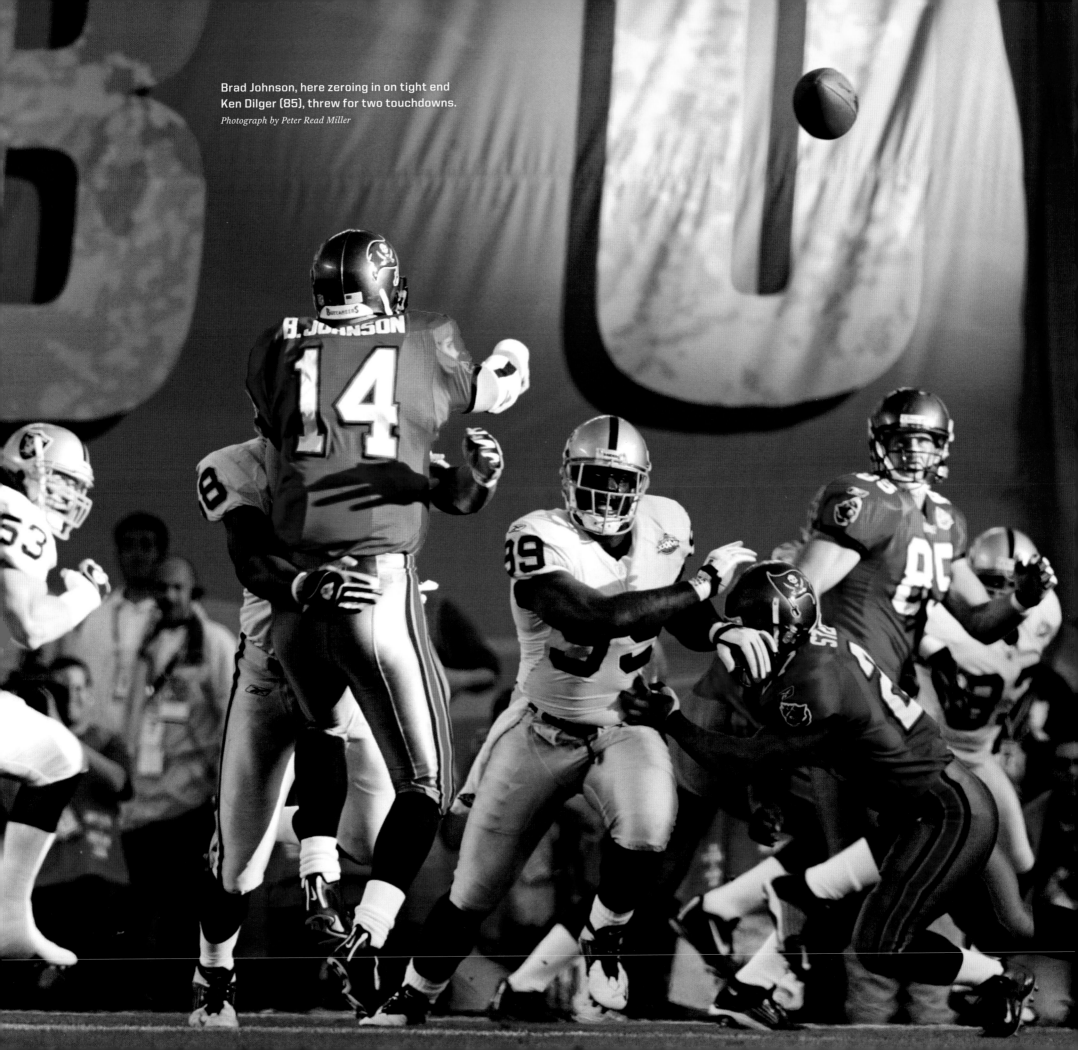

Brad Johnson, here zeroing in on tight end
Ken Dilger (85), threw for two touchdowns.

Photograph by Peter Read Miller

Along with making five catches, fullback Mike Alstott rushed for the first Super Bowl TD in Buccaneers history.

Photograph by Peter Read Miller

JUST THE FACTS

Statistical Leaders

Rushing MICHAEL PITTMAN (TB) 29 carries, 124 yds

Passing RICH GANNON (OAK) 24 of 44, 272 yds, 2 TDs

Receiving KEYSHAWN JOHNSON (TB) 6 catches, 69 yds

MVP DEXTER JACKSON Bucs Safety

The Ring
54 diamonds; Bucs' flag, palm trees, a pirate ship inscribed

Anthem Performer
Dixie Chicks

Halftime Performers
Shania Twain, No Doubt and Sting

Attendance 67,603

Ticket Prices $400, $500

Behind the Scenes

Raiders All-Pro center Barret Robbins disappeared two days before the Super Bowl. He had reportedly stopped taking his depression medication and gone to Mexico. When he returned, on Saturday he was so incoherent that Bill Callahan left him off the game-day roster. Robbins was later found to have bipolar disorder.

They Said It

"We dug the hole and we're pretty good about putting you in and putting the dirt on top of you,"

—Bucs defensive tackle WARREN SAPP

Going Nowhere

Raiders quarterback Rich Gannon, the NFL MVP, had a 10.5 QB rating in the first half, and the team had only one rushing first down in the entire game, tied for fewest in a Super Bowl.

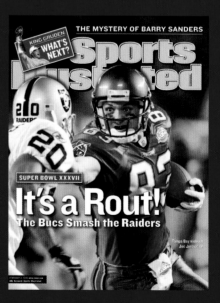

REDEEMING FEATURES

Jon Gruden had his Bucs ready and able to trounce his former team | BY MICHAEL SILVER

MAMA TOLD JON GRUDEN there'd be days like these—days when his dreams would play out with chilling clarity, his incessant intensity would be rewarded and nothing could wipe the blissful smirk from his freckled face. Kathy Gruden couldn't have known that her son's most vivid triumph would come on Super Sunday, but that was always the dream for little Jonny. As a six-year-old in Dayton, he watched the Chiefs upset the Vikings in Super Bowl IV; then, he says, "I went out in the backyard and made diving catches in the mud, pretending I was Otis Taylor."

Thirty-three years later, on a warm, still evening in San Diego, Gruden's dream became reality. The first-year coach of the Buccaneers prodded and cajoled his team to a 48–21 weed-whacking of the favored Raiders, simultaneously showing up his former employer, Oakland boss Al Davis, and validating Tampa Bay owner Malcolm Glazer's desperate pursuit of Gruden's services last winter.

It was a story line only a hokey screenwriter would pitch, with an ending only a mother could love. And so, late on Sunday at the Bucs' team hotel, Kathy entered Room 2086 and started crying as she locked her son in a long embrace and whispered, "I'm so proud of you. You put a lot of things to rest tonight."

First and foremost, Gruden, 39, ended the debate over whether he was worth the ostentatious price (two first-round and two second-round draft picks, plus $8 million) that Glazer paid last February to pry him from the Raiders. We now know that Gruden, as many critics had charged, wasn't worth it—he was worth more. In the words of Bucs vice president Joel Glazer, one of Malcolm's three sons who help him run the team, "He's one in a million. We'd make the deal again without blinking." That was said two days before a Super Bowl in which Gruden, a motivator and a strategist, fielded a team that was as well-prepared for a title game as any that ever strapped on helmets.

"I've never been involved in a game where everything we ran in practice played out so identically," said All-Pro strong safety John Lynch, part of a swift and swarming defense that keyed the victory.

In erasing 26 years of frustration for Tampa Bay and becoming the youngest coach to win a Super Bowl, Gruden proved an old adage: Defense wins championships. In the battle between the Bucs' league No. 1 defense, and the Raiders' top-ranked offense, Tampa Bay intercepted a Super Bowl–record five passes, returning three for TDs; sacked quarterback Rich Gannon, the NFL MVP, five times; and held Gannon to 72 passing yards over the first 40 minutes of the game. At that point the Raiders trailed 34–3. "Their defense was just unbelievable," Oakland fullback Jon Ritchie said. "It was just really, well, perfect."

One of Gruden's prime contributions came during last Thursday's practice, when the former University of

Dayton QB surprised his players by running the scout team during a two-minute drill. Though his passing skills were dubious—"Some of his throws looked like kickoffs," said wideout Reggie Barlow—Gruden simulated Oakland's frenetic tempo. The coach also cracked up his players with a spot-on impression of the irascible Gannon, complete with rapid-fire audibles and profanity-laced admonishments. "It was hilarious, but there was value to it too," Lynch said. "He showed us how Rich despised being limited to one option, how he'd check out of a play two or three times. When it happened in the game, we were ready." According to linebacker Derrick Brooks, "[Gruden] used a lot of their terminology. Gannon used some of the words that Gruden had used during the week."

The defense's heroes included safety Dexter Jackson, with two interceptions; nickelback Dwight Smith, who returned interceptions 44 and 50 yards for TDs; and ends Simeon Rice (two sacks) and Greg Spires, who had a sack, deflected two passes and pressured Gannon into throwing the first interception to Jackson. As cornerback Ronde Barber said. "We're a quick, physical, smart team, and those big [offensive] linemen don't affect us like they do other teams. "

At the hotel after the game Gruden walked from his room toward the lobby for a TV interview, and, just before arriving, he stopped to hug his mother one more time. Then he turned the corner and was seen by hundreds of Bucs fans waiting to enter the team's victory party in a ballroom. Many began pointing at Gruden, snapping photos and yelling, "We love you, Jon!"

The commotion stopped him, and for a moment it looked as if Gruden might get choked up. But, in an instant, the smirk returned, and the most valuable football coach in America strode swiftly onward, a trail of applause in his wake. ∎

Young Gruden chirped and chortled—and delivered.

Photograph by Robert Beck

"Speed kills," said Bucs cornerback Ronde Barber. "We're a quick, physical, smart team. . . . You put anyone on the field today, and we would've done this."

Gannon, here covered by Sapp, got sacked five times and threw five picks.
Photograph by Al Tielemans

BY **Derrick Brooks**

Buccaneers Linebacker

That was the last year there was no bye week before the Super Bowl, and we treated it just like any West Coast trip. We had some personalities on that team, and as far as media day and all the things off the field, we just decided, as a team "everyone be yourself." Guys who like to talk, go talk. But we also made a pledge to each other—the players, no coaches—after each practice, that no one would do something to become a distraction.

Gruden knew the Raiders. We went over everything, not just the tendencies, but their personalities, guys like Charlie Garner and Rich Gannon. Practices were the same as always except for one thing: Gruden played quarterback. The way he tells it, he completed passes all over the field. But really, we let him.

The Raiders had that high-powered offense, and people forget that they made it a game in the second half. On the interception that really put the game away, they were in third-and-long and I knew Gannon would be making a throw in rhythm. I saw early in the play that he didn't see me, and I knew I had him. Once I had the ball, it was just open field in front of me. I got to the 10-yard line and all I could think was "don't fall don't fall don't fall."

Before the season, in March, Jon Gruden told us that if the defense scored nine touchdowns on the season, we'd win the Super Bowl. I have no idea how he came up with that number. Well, my touchdown was the eighth. On the last play of the game, Dwight Smith ran back another interception. That was number 9.

BY **Lincoln Kennedy**

Raiders Tackle

I'm from San Diego, so the moment we got to town for the game I was out, back on the street where I grew up. A lot of media wanted to talk to me, people were calling—it was a lot to juggle, especially when you're trying to enjoy being in the Super Bowl. I went to my high school and got a tremendous welcome. My number was retired, I saw friends I'd lost touch with. To see what they thought of me, I really felt a sense of accomplishment. It was meaningful to be playing in my backyard, to share it with friends and family. But looking back, I regret a lot of it. I didn't realize how much I was overextending myself.

Tim Brown always designated who would give the rah-rah speech before the game and he chose me, "Big Linc, you're up." So I told the team, "We worked our tails off to get here, every man has sacrificed something on some level, you deserve it, for yourself and your teammates, to go out and play the absolute best football you can. There's two teams left, and there can only be one. Today, if you follow me, if you're with me, we'll raise our hands as champions." So I put my helmet up and said, "Who's with me?" And everyone raised their helmets.

Before that game, I was seriously considering retirement. I was mentally and physical burned-out. I was thinking, 'Wow, how amazing would it be to win the Super Bowl in my hometown and then ride off?' But I realized afterward that I didn't play my best and I had let my teammates down. I cried like a baby.

Jackson's MVP award was a symbol of the defense's overall dominance.
Photograph by Bob Rosato

SUPER BOWL XXXVIII

February 1, 2004
Reliant Stadium, Houston

HEAD COACHES
BILL BELICHICK Patriots | JOHN FOX Panthers

NEW ENGLAND
PATRIOTS | 32

CAROLINA
PANTHERS | 29

A pregame moon landing paid tribute to the *Columbia* shuttle crew of a year earlier.

Photograph by Gary Rothstein/Icon Sportswire

YOU DON'T get more gripping Super Bowls: lead swings, six scores in the fourth quarter, a last-second kick that ran the Patriots' win streak to 15. It was all (almost) enough to eclipse that Janet Jackson wardrobe malfunction at the half.

DOME
1st retractable roof

POINT SPREAD
Patriots by 7

TIME OF GAME
4:05

TV AUDIENCE
89.8 million

David Givens's catch at the three-yard line set up the fourth-quarter
touchdown that gave the Patriots their short-lived 29–22 lead.

Photograph by John Iacono

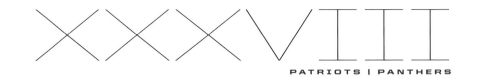
A STIRRING ASCENSION

In the final stages of a thriller, Tom Brady rose to football greatness | BY MICHAEL SILVER

TOM BRADY WAS CAUGHT IN A crowd, yet he felt utterly alone. The Patriots' quarterback was in a ballroom at the InterContinental Hotel in Houston, where a couple of thousand people with some connection to the Pats organization were celebrating the franchise's second Super Bowl win in three years. Besieged by admirers seeking his autograph or a snapshot with him, Brady, clad in a Zegna shirt, a platinum bracelet and dark jeans with a bulky pocket chain, looked beleaguered and bewildered. "I just want to get with my family, O.K.?" Brady kept saying, to no one in particular.

Such is the life of a man suddenly seen as a Super Bowl immortal. The 26-year-old Brady must come to terms with a new level of celebrity. He is more than a football star now. He is the darling of America's sports fans, the successor to Joe Montana and John Elway, the magical passer who can pull out a victory in the final seconds. After picking apart the Panthers' secondary on two dramatic drives in the last seven minutes to lead the Pats to a 32–29 win, Brady was awarded his second Super Bowl MVP. He is the youngest quarterback to win two Super Bowls, and with his movie-star looks, actress girlfriend, tight-knit family and adoring teammates, Brady's life could not be much sweeter.

Also indispensable is New England's hero in a headset, coach Bill Belichick. In addition to being meticulous in his game preparation and the best defensive strategist of his generation, Belichick, 51, has evolved into a stirring speaker—at least behind closed doors with his players. During a team meeting last Saturday, Belichick mesmerized his troops by holding up the Lombardi Trophy that the Patriots had won two years earlier and placing it on a table. The room went silent, and Belichick said, "Look, guys, this is what we're playing for. Let's put this week in perspective: It's not about the parties; it's the trophy. Only 37 teams can say they've owned this. You guys can be the 38th."

For much of the first half, neither team looked worthy of the hardware. The game was scoreless for the first 26:55, the longest drought to open a Super Bowl. Carolina (14–6) had minus-seven yards of total offense, and Jake Delhomme had completed 1 of 9 passes, for a single yard. New England wasn't much better, having squandered scoring opportunities when Adam Vinatieri twice missed field goal attempts.

Then with 5:22 left in the second quarter, Mike Vrabel, the 28-year-old linebacker, steamed around Panthers left tackle Todd Steussie and chopped the ball out of Delhomme's hand. Defensive end Richard Seymour recovered at the Carolina 20. Four plays later Brady threw a five-yard TD pass to wideout Deion Branch, and the bizarre Tale of Two Games had begun: no points in the game's first 26:55 minutes; 61 in the final 33:05 minutes, including 37 in the fourth quarter.

True to their personality under coach John Fox, the Panthers never gave up. "It was a very physical game," said New England linebacker Larry Izzo, "and, like a bad virus, that team wouldn't go away." The most potent Carolina player was Delhomme, who nearly eclipsed Brady as a clutch pocket passer.

Another trophy was all Belichick wanted. He got it.

Photograph by Damian Strohmeyer

Down 21–10 in the fourth quarter, Delhomme put together an 81-yard drive culminating in DeShaun Foster's 33-yard touchdown dash down the left sideline. Soon after that Delhomme lofted a spiral to Muhsin Muhammad who caught the ball in stride at the Pats' 33 and completed an 85-yard touchdown, the longest play from scrimmage in Super Bowl history.

Suddenly New England trailed 22–21 with 6:53 left. "There's no reason to worry," safety Rodney Harrison told cornerback Ty Law. "We've got Tom Brady."

"He was poised," Panthers defensive end Mike Rucker said of Brady. "We hit him a couple of times, but he'd get right back up." On second down from the one with 2:55 left, Patriots offensive coordinator Charlie Weis called 136 X Cross Z Flag, and a certain moonlighting tight end got chills: Vrabel, with two sacks and a forced fumble, had already made a huge impact, but now he was about to catch his first pass since 2002. After a smooth play fake to Antowain Smith, Brady saw Vrabel flash across the middle and flicked the ball to him. Said Vrabel, a father of two boys, "I held it like it was my third child." The two-point conversion gave the Pats a 29–22 lead, but the Panthers weren't done.

Seven plays and 80 yards later, Delhomme zipped a 12-yard TD pass to wideout Ricky Proehl. There was 1:08 left and it was 29–29. "I've been in that situation so many times," said Brady. "So, yeah, I was calm."

With a huge assist from John Kasay, who hooked the ensuing kickoff out-of-bounds to give New England possession at its own 40, Brady and Vinatieri made hearts flutter. On third-and-three from the Carolina 40 with 14 seconds left, Brady found Branch down the sideline for 17 yards. On came Vinatieri, who kicked a 41-yard field goal with four ticks remaining, It was time to ponder the Patriots' potential for a dynasty—and their quarterback's ascent to gridiron icon. ■

JUST THE FACTS

Statistical Leaders

Rushing ANTOWAIN SMITH (NE) 26 carries, 83 yds, 1 TD

Passing TOM BRADY (NE) 32 of 48, 354 yds, 3 TDs

Receiving DEION BRANCH (NE) 10 catches, 143 yds, 1 TD

MVP TOM BRADY Patriots Quarterback

The Ring
32 diamonds, for the 32 NFL teams, around team logo

Anthem Performer
Beyoncé

Halftime Performers
Janet Jackson, P. Diddy, Nelly, Kid Rock and Justin Timberlake

Attendance 71,525

Ticket Price: $400-$600

Behind the Scenes

This halftime show featured the infamous "wardrobe malfunction," which briefly sort of exposed pop star Janet Jackson's breast to a live TV audience. The parties involved said it was an accident.

They Said It

"Was I surprised? Hell no. I play for Bill Belichick. You don't think we watched film on that guy all week? I'd seen everything there was to see." —Pats special teamer MATT CHATHAM on tackling a streaker on the field before the second-half kickoff

Cat Person

New England Patriots coach Bill Belichick owned four season tickets to the Carolina Panthers. He bought them in 1995 to support friends in the expansion team's front office.

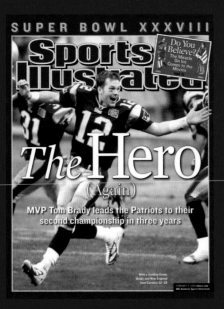

SUPER BOWL XXXVIII

Sports Illustrated

Do You Believe? The Miracle on Ice Comes to the Movies

The Hero
(Again)

MVP Tom Brady leads the Patriots to their second championship in three years

---

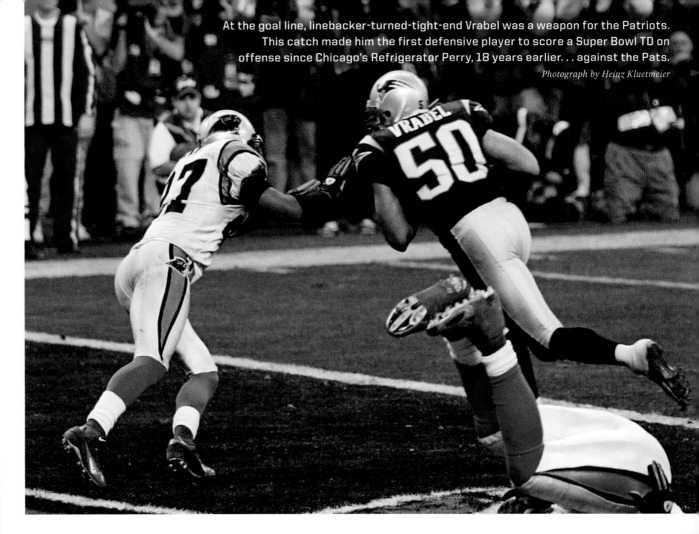

At the goal line, linebacker-turned-tight-end Vrabel was a weapon for the Patriots. This catch made him the first defensive player to score a Super Bowl TD on offense since Chicago's Refrigerator Perry, 18 years earlier. . . against the Pats.

Photograph by Heinz Kluetmeier

Delhomme nearly matched Brady's fourth-quarter heroics, but the Patriots had the ball last.

Photograph by Al Tielemans

"You dream about playing football and you have your fantasies, but you don't ever dream about winning Super Bowls like this," said Tom Brady. "The way it ended is just incredible."

New England had 29 first downs in the game, Carolina only 17.

Photograph by Bob Rosato

THE WAY IT WAS

BY Tedy Bruschi

Patriots Linebacker

Practice that week started at Rice University. At the end of one sideline, where the water coolers were, the field sloped down. Guys were falling and slipping, so the captains went to Bill and said "We've got to get out of here, it's a distraction." Bill Belichick doesn't like distractions. As bad as that was, it was so much fun giving Larry Izzo grief. He was a Rice alumnus, and he got it from all angles, the other linebackers, the rest of the defense, the offense, the coaches. . . . *Real nice Izzo! How about making some donations!*

I've never been part of a game that had that many peaks and valleys. By the end of the first quarter we were thinking, "They're not scoring on us all game." In the fourth quarter, it was one of the few times in my career where I looked to Tom and said, "You guys have to keep scoring because I don't know if we can stop them."

We weren't worried about kicks that game, but we were worried about the snaps. Lonie Paxton had torn his ACL, so we had signed Brian Kinchen as our long snapper. He was a schoolteacher at the time. And he was struggling. He rolled one back. I ate a pregame meal with him. He's buttering his roll with a steak knife, and he nicked his hand! It wasn't bad, but I was like "Dude! You just cut your hand! We're playing the Super Bowl in four-and-a-half hours!" So on that final kick, once the snap was there, once the ball got to holder Kenny Walter's hands, that's when I was relieved.

BY Jake Delhomme

Panthers Quarterback

For pregame introductions, they swing open two big doors. The emotions behind those doors . . . there were literally guys crying because this was the pinnacle, the place you worked so hard to get to.

I put my hand under center for the first snap, and I sent fullback Brad Hoover into motion behind me. I could feel that *thoomp, thoomp, thoomp* of his footsteps, and it was like "All right, it's time to play football."

We couldn't do anything early. But Dan Henning, our offensive coordinator, had drilled into us "these guys are big, they're physical, but we'll wear them down." Sure enough, once the floodgates opened, they opened like crazy.

We had just scored to tie it with a minute left, and I was sitting on the bench. We were developing a plan, thinking we were going to go to overtime. And I heard a moan. But I still thought we would stop them or block the field goal.

I wanted to watch them celebrate, for times when things get difficult during off-season training, I wanted to be able to go back to that moment. But you get roped off, and they move you to the media room and you do interview after interview. By the time I got back to the locker room, it was empty. Almost everybody was gone. I was numb. Assistant coach Mike McCoy walked in with my daughter Lauren, who was two. It didn't take all the pain away, but it put a smile on my face.

Vinatieri (arms raised) was good from 41 yards as time expired, supporting his "Mr. Clutch" nickname and earning him the third of his four Super Bowl rings.

Photograph by Al Tielemans

SUPER BOWL XXXIX

NEW ENGLAND
PATRIOTS | 24

PHILADELPHIA
EAGLES | 21

UNDERDOGS, YES. But the Eagles, a run of three straight NFC title game losses finally snapped, were full of bluster as the game neared. That further stoked the Patriots, who were out for a third title in four years and, who, in classic style, got it.

Bill Clinton and George Bush united to support an appeal for aid to tsunami victims.

Photograph by Bill Frakes

WEATHER

59°, clear

POINT SPREAD

Patriots by 7

TIME OF GAME

3:38

TV AUDIENCE

86.1 million

For the second straight Super Bowl the nimble Branch was a receiving hero.

Photograph by Heinz Kluetmeier

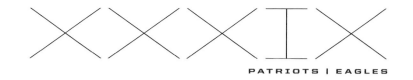

THE MODERN DYNASTY

Calmly and efficiently the Patriots became the team of the century | BY MICHAEL SILVER

BECAUSE THEY DO NOT BEAT you over the head with their excellence or beat their chests in triumph, the Patriots are forever cast as commonplace champions. They are great in the way that a chocolate milk shake is great, as poised and proficient as the Beach Boys' doing background harmonies onstage. What we are learning from the Pats as they forge the first football dynasty of the 21st century is that dominance comes in many forms, and that sometimes doing the little things well can provide the biggest satisfaction of all.

As these Patriots keep escaping with three-point victories and kicking dirt on the Super Bowl's heritage of wretched excess, skipping individual pregame introductions and engaging in low-key locker room celebrations, isn't it time we stop being perplexed by their success? New England's 24–21 victory over the

Brady and Ike Reese executed a two-point play.

Photograph by John W. McDonough

Eagles was another testament to teamwork, tenacity and the strategic acumen of coach Bill Belichick and his staff. And by vanquishing a brasher opponent to claim the NFL's ultimate prize for the second-straight year—and the third time in four seasons—the Pats players also proved they are even more potent than typically perceived.

"Someday I'll have kids and tell them I played on one of the greatest teams of all time, a team with a whole lot of great players," said outside linebacker Willie McGinest, whose deployment at defensive end was the key to New England's surprise scheme change.

Let's get this much straight: The Patriots are more than Belichick's brain and quarterback Tom Brady's golden right arm. Defenders like McGinest, fellow linebackers Tedy Bruschi and Mike Vrabel and strong safety Rodney Harrison, whose second interception of Donovan McNabb iced the game with nine seconds left, showed they're elite players, while unheralded wideout Deion Branch seized footballs out of the cool night sky.

The Pats relied on their patented formula of individual opportunism, selflessness, innovative game-planning and emotion fueled by perceived disrespect. The last of those came after the Patriots received a copy of an e-mail sent from an Eagles official to a member of the Red Sox seeking advice on a prospective victory parade, a missive that Belichick milked for maximum effect during his Sunday morning address to the Pats.

While New England's defense flustered McNabb from the outset, ultimately sacking him four times and intercepting three passes while limiting him to zero rushing yards, its offense began slowly. Down 7–0, the Patriots finally tied the score on Brady's four-yard pass to wideout David Givens 1:16 before halftime. A two-yard scoring toss from Brady to Vrabel in the third quarter gave New England the lead and marked the second straight Super Bowl in which the moonlighting linebacker caught a touchdown pass. Yet when McNabb whipped a 10-yard scoring pass to running

back Brian Westbrook to tie the game with 3:39 left in the third quarter, the raucous Philly fans in attendance asserted themselves like Broad Street Bullies.

If the Philly faithful thought Brady would be fazed, they haven't paid attention the past four years. Following an emotional week in which his grandmother, Margaret, died, Brady exuded calm when the situation was most tense. He was 4 for 4 on the Pats' nine-play, 66-yard drive, with running back Corey Dillon providing the go-ahead points on a two-yard run with 13:44 left. On New England's next drive Brady and Branch hooked up on the play of the night, a pass over the middle on which Branch leaped over the back of Philly cornerback Sheldon Brown for a 19-yard catch. Six plays later Adam Vinatieri's field goal put the Pats up 24–14.

"Outside of that terrible first quarter, we felt we had the game under control," said Branch, the MVP. They kept that control thanks in part to Eagles coach Andy Reid's curious decision to forgo a no-huddle offense while trailing by 10 with 5:40 to go. When the Eagles (15–4) completed a 79-yard scoring drive on McNabb's 30-yard strike to wideout Greg Lewis, only 1:48 remained. After the Pats' Christian Fauria recovered the onside kick, the Eagles' defense held, but New England punter Josh Miller pinned Philly at its own four with 46 seconds left, and Harrison's interception set off a release of red, white and blue confetti.

Belichick, his gray, hooded pullover doused with Gatorade (thanks to Bruschi), celebrated by initiating a hearty group hug with his coordinators, defensive genius Romeo Crennel and offensive whiz Charlie Weis. Both were leaving to become head coaches—Crennel with the Browns, Weis with Notre Dame—but first they wanted to savor a second-straight 17–2 season and the team's historic run. "We said we'd been together a long time," Weis recalled of that hug. "We'd had some good times, some bad, but these are moments we'd always have together.... You can be the richest man in the world and not be able to buy moments like this." ∎

Statistical Leaders

Rushing **COREY DILLON** (NE) 18 carries, 75 yds, 1 TD

Passing **DONOVAN MCNABB** (PHI) 30 of 51, 357 yds, 3 TDs

Receiving **DEION BRANCH** (NE) 11 catches, 133 yds

MVP **DEION BRANCH** Patriots Wide Receiver

The Ring
Team logo is surrounded by 21 diamonds, for the record 21-game win streak completed that season

Anthem Performers
Combined choirs of the Armed Forces branches

Halftime Performer
Paul McCartney

Attendance 78,125

Ticket Prices $500, $600

Behind the Scenes

The Patriots abandoned the 3-4 defense they had played all year for several new looks, including one with two linemen and five linebackers; this allowed them to rush from all areas of the field.

They Said It

"It's hard for me because both of those towns voted for me twice."

—President **BILL CLINTON**, explaining why he declined to predict a Super Bowl XXXIX winner

Lost, in Translation

Pats owner Robert Kraft was in a group of U.S. businessmen who visited Russian president Vladimir Putin in St. Petersburg, Russia, four months after the game. Kraft went in wearing his new Super Bowl ring but left empty-handed; Putin tried it on and pocketed it.

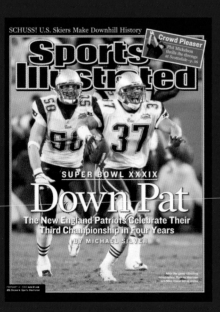

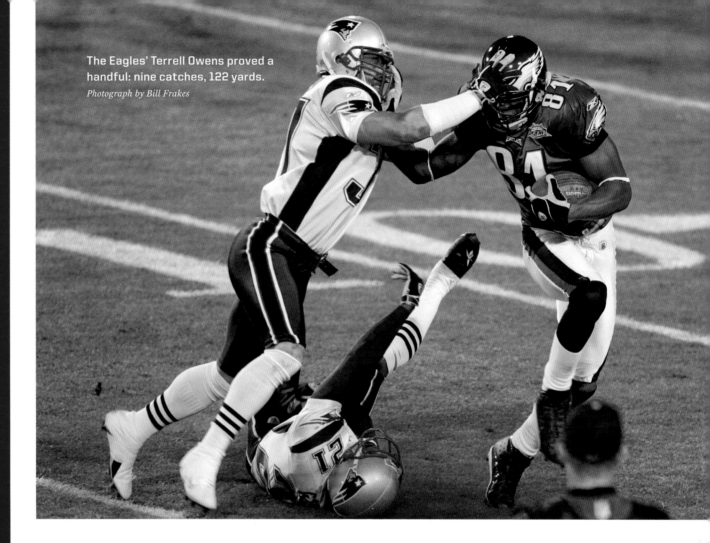

The Eagles' Terrell Owens proved a handful: nine catches, 122 yards.
Photograph by Bill Frakes

Richard Seymour blindsided McNabb on a third-quarter sack.
Photograph by Bob Rosato

XXXIX

PATRIOTS | EAGLES

The Pats relied on their patented formula: individual opportunism, selflessness, innovative game-planning and emotion fueled by perceived disrespect.

Moonlighting linebacker Vrabel made yet another big-game TD catch.

Photograph by John Iacono

BY Deion Branch

Patriots Wide Receiver

On game day I got up early to study and stretch. I made phone calls to people who helped me get to the position I was in. I was on the phone for hours. I had a lot of friends and family already in town, so it was a lot of coaches, going back to Pop Warner. I made about 30 phone calls, and then it was time to get on the bus and go to the stadium.

The play I remember is a catch I made over Sheldon Brown; he was in better position to make a play than I was. I haven't watched the game a lot, but on that play I can see my teammates on the sideline. And the faces . . . it's like, *Where did this guy come from?* I can see Christian Fauria's jaw drop, Tom Ashworth's hands are up over his head. I don't even watch the play, just the reactions.

During their last drive, I was sitting on the bench with David Patten and Troy Brown, and we were talking about how we couldn't let these guys score. The last thing on my mind was how many balls I caught. Then David tapped me on my shoulder, because he saw all these guys with suits gathering behind us. One of the guys said to me, "If you all win, you're going to be MVP." The next thing you know, Rodney Harrison intercepts the ball and we win. But you think about it: The MVP votes come in before the game ends, it was before that last interception. So now Rodney always tells me how I stole his trophy.

I got that trophy, and they gave me a Cadillac XLR. I'm trying to keep it so I can give it to my son. I don't think he's a big fan of the two-seater though; he's always talking about an Escalade. I tell him, "Son, this is the car, this is what you want."

BY Brian Dawkins

Eagles Safety

The game was in my hometown, but it didn't feel like Jacksonville that week. It was freezing. At Media Day, I don't remember the crazy questions or the people dressing up, I remember all the players had to wear sleeves. Media people and cameramen were wearing coats and still shivering.

I may have been back home, but for me, that was a business trip. I practiced, I studied, and I stayed in the hotel. I didn't need to turn my phone off; it never rang. All my friends and family know me well enough that they didn't call to bother me. They knew where my focus was that week.

The waiting was the worst part, especially on game day. We did our meetings and our team meal, and guys went back to the hotel to try to take a nap. But there was no way I could sleep. I sat around feeling anxious until it was time to get on the bus. Same thing at the half. We wrapped up our halftime and then it was like, "O.K., you guys still have another 20 minutes." So we just sat around and waited.

But for me, once I got on the field it really did feel like a regular game. Except for one moment. At kickoff, all these flashbulbs were going off, so many of them. That's something you never see in any other game.

We had played in three NFC title games and lost, but this was the only team that had everything we needed—we had added Jevon Kearse and Terrell Owens. I try not to look back at that game; it doesn't bring up good feelings. After it ended I hung out on the field for about a minute. Then I went to the locker room. I had seen enough.

Dillon's touchdown dive put New England ahead early in the fourth.

Photograph by Al Tielemans

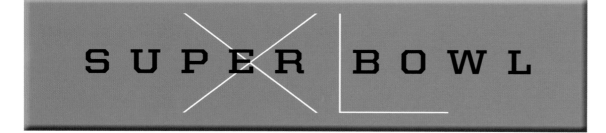

SUPER BOWL XL

PITTSBURGH
STEELERS | 21

SEATTLE
SEAHAWKS | 10

TIME WAS that the injury-racked, barely-above-.500 Steelers seemed less than even postseason material. That was before an eight-game winning streak that ended in confetti, as Pittsburgh became the lowest playoff seed to win it all.

DOME

Outside: 30°

POINT SPREAD

Steelers by 4

TIME OF GAME

3:36

TV AUDIENCE

90.7 million

Shut *up! You're* going to Disney World? *I'm* going to Disney World!

Photograph by John Biever

272

Getting behind the Bus: Roethlisberger
followed Bettis's block into the end zone.
Photograph by David Bergman

Big Casey Hampton (seated) had one of the Steelers' three sacks.

Photograph by David Bergman

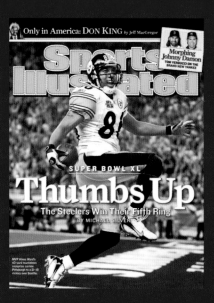

ONE FOR THE THUMB

Depth, trickery and (naturally) a steely D gave Pittsburgh its fifth ring | BY MICHAEL SILVER

ARE YOU READY FOR SOME football, Steelers style? The Seahawks were not, making more mistakes and fewer big plays than a vulnerable Pittsburgh team. Despite a shaky performance from second-year quarterback Ben Roethlisberger and the virtual disappearance of their two marquee defenders, wild-haired strong safety Troy Polamalu and outspoken outside linebacker Joey Porter, the Steelers plodded to their 21–10 win in a game that will be remembered mostly for what its outcome represented: one for the thumb, finally, for 73-year-old owner Dan Rooney, whose club won four Super Bowls in the 1970s; a crowning career achievement for coach Bill Cowher, in his 14th season with the Steelers; and a confirmation that faith in one another and accountability can carry a team past seemingly insurmountable odds.

"Don't ever count us out," Porter said after Pittsburgh had limited the Seattle offense, top-ranked in the NFL, to its lowest point total of the season. "People definitely wrote us off in December, and when you tell somebody they can't do something, proving it wrong is the sweetest joy of all."

Cowher pushed the right buttons on a sloppy Super Sunday, but his most important move came two months earlier, when he walked into the Steelers' training facility the morning after a 38–31 loss to the Bengals. Pittsburgh, at 7–5, was on the brink of playoff elimination. Players shuddered. Would Cowher launch a spit-filled tirade? Would his head explode?

But Cowher turned junior high history teacher instead. Passing out grade sheets, he gave his players an assignment: Watch film of the Cincinnati game and for each play assign yourself a grade (plus or minus) in three categories: technique, effort and how well you followed your assignment. "It was revealing," Cowher said during Super Bowl week, sipping coffee in the team's hotel. "Some guys, like Troy, were overly critical

of themselves; others were a little too lenient. But the most important point I wanted to make was that if each guy did just a little bit more and was accountable for his actions, we could turn this thing around."

The Steelers' self-examination and recommitment spurred an eight-game winning streak that vaulted them from playoff long shots to history-making champions: the first No. 6 seed to win the championship.

Super Sunday belonged to the most unheralded Steelers, such lesser lights as second-year halfback Willie Parker, whose 75-yard burst on the second snap of the second half, helped by left guard Alan Faneca's block on linebacker Leroy Hill, gave Pittsburgh a 14–3 lead. Then there was cornerback Ike Taylor, who atoned for several early lapses in coverage by snagging an interception at the Steelers' five-yard line with 10:46 left and his team clinging to a 14–10 lead.

Four plays after that, the Steelers' biggest pass since Terry Bradshaw hit John Stallworth in Super Bowl XIV was thrown not by Roethlisberger but by wideout Antwaan Randle El, a former standout QB at

Indiana whose 43-yard strike to Hines Ward provided the game's signature moment. Credit another perfectly timed call to offensive coordinator Ken Whisenhunt, who two plays earlier had set up the trick pass by calling a speed screen to Randle El for a seven-yard gain. Then, on first-and-10 from the Seattle 43, Whisenhunt sent in Zero Strong Z Short Fake Toss 39 X Reverse Pass, which was run out of the same formation as the speed screen. "I was so excited," Randle El said, "I had to make sure I didn't give it away."

After Roethlisberger pitched the ball to Parker on the left side, Randle El swung around from his position wide to the left to take a handoff from Parker, then continued rolling to his right as Ward flashed open between three confused defenders. *Throw it to me now!* Ward thought to himself. *Please, please get it to me.* Without breaking stride, Randle El released what he would later call the "prettiest pass" of his life, a tight spiral that Ward caught on the run just inside the Seattle five-yard line, and cruised in for the game's final points with 8:56 to go.

It was a redemptive moment for Ward, whose mishandling of two Roethlisberger passes had symbolized Pittsburgh's offensive futility. The Steelers went nearly four minutes into the second quarter before making a first down, and for much of the evening Roethlisberger (9 of 21, 123 yards, two interceptions) looked discombobulated. His one-word postgame assessment of his overall performance: "Ecch."

Roethlisberger cheered up on the bus to the victory party. "It's not how you picture your Super Bowl moment," he said, "but with this team it had to be that way. Before every game it's, Who's going to step up? ... For the most part it wasn't big-name guys offensively and defensively. That's been the M.O. of this team, why it's such a special team and why we won." ∎

Fancy farewell: Bettis got Zooted up for his last game.

Photograph by John Biever

BY Jerome Bettis

Steelers Running Back

I had announced before the season that this would be my last year and there were so many special moments during Super Bowl week, going home to Detroit. The first was when I got to the team plane. Each of my teammates was wearing a No. 6 Notre Dame jersey, my college jersey. Troy Polamalu is a USC guy. That's almost 100 years of rivalry between those schools. He said, "I'm only doing this for you."

Joey Porter usually brought our team out of the tunnel for games but right before we went out, he called me over and said, "JB, I want you to bring the team out." We did our chant, and then I said "Let's go!" I took off running and thought I had everybody behind me. But Joey held them back. I got to the 50-yard line, turned around and nobody was there! I was like, Where's everybody at? I just kept screaming until they got there. I had no idea that was going to happen. It was an incredible moment that Joey created for me, and I'm forever thankful.

When I got back to the locker room after the game, my first order of business was to talk with Dan Rooney about designing the Super Bowl ring. Everybody else would have a chance to get another one, but this was my only one. I needed to make sure it was done nice. So I went over and said, "Mr. Rooney, I'd love to be on the committee to design the rings." And he said, "O.K., it will be me and you."

After that, I just tried to soak up everything because I knew that was the last time I'd spend with those guys. I was the last one in the locker room that night. And the last thing I did before I left was turn out the lights.

BY Matt Hasselbeck

Seahawks Quarterback

During preseason, they'd always tell us beforehand how much we'd play in that game. For whatever reason, Steve Hutchinson and I would end up at the urinal together before most games. We'd ask each other, "How much do you think you're playing tonight?" So it's before the Super Bowl, it's a little tense in the locker room, and I see him. He has a really serious look on his face and he says to me, "How much do you think you're playing tonight?"

In the moments right before the game, our quarterbacks coach, Jim Zorn, said to us, "We have so much to be thankful for, this is a dream come true, and here we are." Then he said: "Win or lose, that doesn't change how grateful we should be for the year that we've had." In the moments right after the game, when confetti was dropping and the Steelers were celebrating, I remembered what he said, and I think that's what kept me calm.

It really hurt to lose that game though, and I really wanted to hate the Steelers afterward: players, coaches, fans, everyone. But the events that followed were almost divine. We flew to the Pro Bowl. I wanted to hate Troy Polamalu, but we saw him at the beach, playing with his kids, and he could not be a nicer guy. Now I'm friends with him. At the beach, my kids are playing with this other kid and they're the family of Alan Faneca, a Steelers lineman. My wife ended up becoming friends with the wife of Travis Kirschke, a Pittsburgh end, and now he's a good friend of mine. These people I really wanted to dislike ended up becoming my friends. I know there's a life lesson in there for me.

On the double reverse Randle El called on his skills as a college QB to deliver the play of the game.

Photographs by Bob Rosato (left) and Bill Frakes

Photograph by John Biever

XL

S T E E L E R S | S E A H A W K S

"Hines's character symbolizes what kind of team this is: close-knit and physical," said linebacker Clark Haggans. "He's the best receiver in football and one of the toughest people I've ever been around."

Ward's scamper put Pittsburgh up by 11 points with nine minutes left.

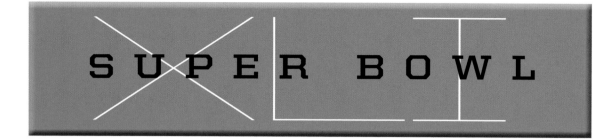

SUPER BOWL XLI

INDIANAPOLIS
COLTS | 29

CHICAGO
BEARS | 17

In the end it was the Bears, and not just these drum skins, who took a beating.

Photograph by Bill Frakes

THE GREATEST regular-season quarterback of all time? Maybe. But Peyton Manning's playoffs had not been great at all. Then on this rainy Sunday in Miami, by rallying the Colts against the rough and ready Bears, Manning added a big credit to his name.

WEATHER	POINT SPREAD	TIME OF GAME	TV AUDIENCE

67°, rain	Colts by 6½	3:31	93.2 million

278

Manning had griped about his line in the past, but he was well-protected on Super Sunday.

Photograph by Bill Frakes

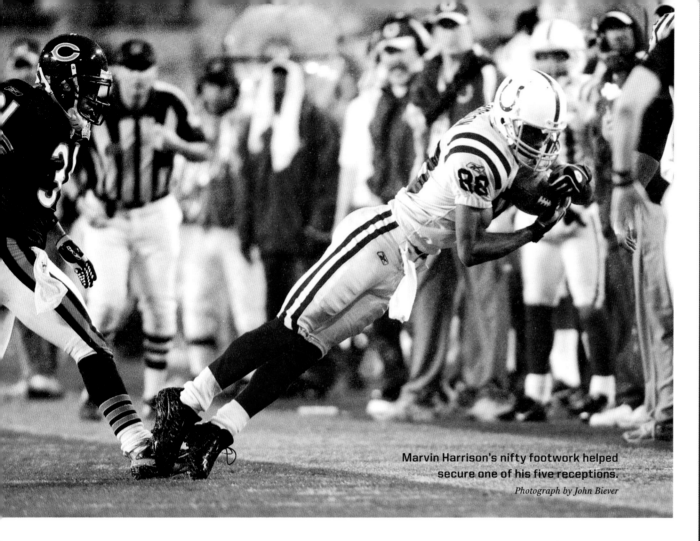

Marvin Harrison's nifty footwork helped secure one of his five receptions.

Photograph by John Biever

Just a rookie, Addai was Manning's go-to guy, with 29 touches from scrimmage.

Photograph by Bob Rosato

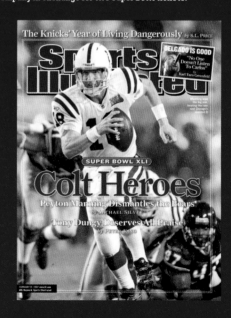

KNOWING HIS WAY

Peyton Manning led his teammates, but also (at last) relied on them | BY MICHAEL SILVER

IN PURSUIT OF A VICTORY THAT would recast his reputation, his heart racing with agitation, Peyton Manning called the boldest and most controversial audible of his career. Twelve days before Super Bowl XLI, Manning stood up in a meeting room at the Colts' training facility and delivered an unpopular decree to his teammates. Colts president Bill Polian had announced that at the team's hotel in Fort Lauderdale during Super Bowl week players would be free to spend time with family members and guests in the confines of their own rooms. Manning disagreed. "I don't think we should let anyone up in the rooms," Manning told the stunned group of players and coaches. "This is a business trip, and I don't want any distractions. I don't want any crying kids next to me while I'm trying to study."

That Manning would get his way was a foregone conclusion—Indy has been Peyton's Place since he was the top pick in the 1998 draft—but sounds of dissent filled the room. "We were heated," recalls cornerback Nick Harper. "People were saying, 'We're grown-ass men. We've got wives and kids, and we'll make those decisions ourselves.' But, you know, it turned out all right."

Hyperfocused, Manning was at his Super Sunday best in leading the Colts to their 29–17 win and shedding his can't-win-the-big-one tag—as did Indy coach Tony Dungy, who defeated his friend and former assistant Lovie Smith in a matchup of the first African-American head coaches in Super Bowl history. Manning overcame a sketchy start and seized control of a sloppy game in a driving rainstorm. Yet the seven-time All-Pro needed lots of help, and relying on teammates to provide it was a sign of his maturation. A year after appearing to criticize his linemen after a painful playoff loss to the Steelers, Manning now understands, as he said late Sunday night in a nearly empty locker room, "that everybody's got to do his part, and you have to trust them all to do that."

On Sunday night fans danced in the Indy streets thanks to players such as halfback Joseph Addai (143 rushing and receiving yards), his backup Dominic Rhodes and cornerback Kelvin Hayden, whose 56-yard pick-six with 11:59 left provided the game's final points. By then Manning had solved Chicago's formidable defense with underneath passes and timely run calls while Indy's far less-heralded D had repelled quarterback Rex Grossman and limited the Bears to just a field goal after the 4:34 mark of the first quarter.

That owner Jimmy Irsay held up the Lombardi Trophy at game's end was a testament to this team's perseverance and togetherness. "Our bonds have been forged through some real-life tragedies," Irsay said. "And those things make you stronger."

The suicide of Dungy's 18-year-old son, James, in December 2005 started the Colts on an emotional, character-testing journey. The shocking home playoff loss in January '06 to the Steelers was followed by, among other events, the free-agent departure of popular running back Edgerrin James; the death of wideout Reggie Wayne's older brother, Rashad, in a car accident in September; and a late-season stretch (after a 9–0 start) in which Indy lost three of four games.

The Super Bowl provided another, immediate test. Chicago rookie Devin Hester took the opening kickoff, danced up the middle, burst to his right and was off. Then Indy's first drive was marked by broken routes, false-start penalties and, finally, a Manning interception. *Gulp.* Said Manning, "We looked like a team that had never played in the Super Bowl."

Manning settled the Colts with 6:58 left in the first quarter. He saw Wayne in the middle of the field and, under heavy pressure, delivered a rainbow that from the receiver's perspective "seemed like it hung in the air forever." Wayne caught it inside the 20 and cruised into the end zone to complete the 53-yard touchdown; Indy trailed 7–6 after a botched extra point.

Though Chicago went up 14–6, Indy responded with an Adam Vinatieri field goal and Rhodes's one-yard scoring run to lead 16–14 at the half. By then the Colts' increasingly energized defenders were confident the game was theirs. "We wanted the ball in Grossman's hands," said Harper. "We'd seen the film. There was no way they would beat us in the passing game." When Grossman got the ball at his own 20 trailing 22–17 with 13:38 left, he underthrew a sideline pass that Hayden intercepted and returned to break the game open.

Much later, rain drenched Manning's dark suit as he left the stadium after midnight, walking briskly ahead of his brother Cooper and their father, Archie, to the last bus bound for the team party. Cooper looked back and, called, "Dad! Come on! We've got to go!" Archie picked up the pace, but it he didn't have to. There, waiting at the bus's front door, was Peyton, smiling like a champion, and there was no way that bus was leaving until the quarterback was good and ready. ∎

After great pain, Dungy (with Manning) made history.

Photograph by Al Tielemans

THE WAY IT WAS

BY Dominic Rhodes

Colts Running Back

I'm a country boy and playing ball is all I ever did. So the day of the game I stayed in my room, got in front of the mirror and practiced my moves. I always did that; it worked, so I always kept doing it. I'd be in front of the mirror, or I'd be visualizing the game in my head, what I was going to do when I'm up against Lance Briggs and Brian Urlacher. On the bed I had laid out the suit I was going to wear. Time went so fast that day. Next thing I knew we were on the bus to the stadium. When we got there, I felt like I was the flyest thing in the place. I was looking clean and ready to roll.

Then when we went out on the field that day, I ran out and honestly, I couldn't see anything at first. The bulbs were flashing, you couldn't see. It was beautiful, even with the rain. Only defensive players get excited about playing in the rain, but the field was immaculate. Making cuts, it felt like playing on Astroturf. And I didn't even wear screw-ins, I was in regular, molded cleats.

When we were halfway through that final drive, I looked around in the huddle, looked into guys' eyes. It was awesome. Jeff Saturday was like, "Let's get you in that end zone again." I was just running. That was the most carries I had in a game that year, but at the end I felt like a rookie again. I gave everything I had in the game. When I got back to my room at night, I was too tired to take off my suit. I put on the TV, made sure what had happened was real. I woke up the next morning, still in my suit.

Bob Sanders rose into the rain for a crucial fourth-quarter pick.
Photograph by Damian Strohmeyer

XLI

COLTS | BEARS

After years of racking up superlative stats, Peyton Manning now understood that "everybody's got to do his part, and you have to trust them all to do that."

Rhodes churned through for a TD.
Photograph by Peter Read Miller

THE WAY IT WAS

BY Devin Hester

Bears Kick Returner

My rookie year, to get to the Super Bowl and to play it so near to my hometown, it doesn't get better than that. I can't tell you how many people asked me for tickets. I tried to tell people: This isn't a regular game. I had my immediate family out, but that was it. We practiced at the University of Miami, and I had just played there the year before, so my college coaches and teammates were at practices. The week was overwhelming. There was Media Day, and I had made All-Pro, so I went to that banquet. And just being back home, it was a dream come true.

Olin Kreutz, our center, told me before the game, "Guys have played 10, 12 years in the NFL and have never had an opportunity to play in this game." I took that to heart, but looking back I didn't appreciate how hard it is to get there. To make it to the Super Bowl as a rookie came too easy. I thought we'd be in the playoffs every year.

I wasn't surprised they kicked to me on the opening kickoff. It's the Super Bowl, and although I did some things as a returner that year you don't want to give up good field position on the opening kickoff. My mentality was, If they kick it to me, nobody is tackling me. I took it into the end zone and they didn't kick to me again.

We had that kickoff return, and on their first possession we got an interception from Chris Harris. We were going crazy on the sideline. It felt like we had the Super Bowl won. But hey, there's four quarters in the game.

SUPER BOWL XLII

NEW YORK
GIANTS | 17

NEW ENGLAND
PATRIOTS | 14

THE PATRIOTS, big favorites in the big game, were going to wind up 19-0. Tom Brady would reign, Bill Belichick would rule. But then the Giants got their rush on and didn't get rattled and, oh yes, completed a pass play that just may live forever.

DOME	POINT SPREAD	TIME OF GAME	TV AUDIENCE
Outside: 61°	Patriots by 12½	3:35	97.5 million

The Giants landed in Arizona six days before the game. After it, they were on Cloud 9.

Photograph by Matt York/AP

Tyree's impossible catch fit right in with the Giants' improbable run.
Photograph by Damian Strohmeyer

Having broken free from several tacklers Manning put the football in the air. Tyree, interlocking with Harrison, came down with it.

Photographs by Bill Frakes (top) and Bob Rosato

JUST THE FACTS

Statistical Leaders

Rushing **AHMAD BRADSHAW** (NY) **9 carries, 45 yds**

Passing **TOM BRADY** (NE) **29 of 48, 266 yds, 1 TD**

Receiving **WES WELKER** (NE) **11 catches, 103 yds**

MVP **ELI MANNING** Giants Quarterback

The Ring
One shank includes phrase
ELEVEN STRAIGHT ON THE ROAD

Anthem Performer
Jordin Sparks

Halftime Performers
Tom Petty and the
Heartbreakers

Attendance 71,101

Ticket Prices $700, $900

Behind the Scenes

Before beating San Diego in the AFC title game, the Pats put in trademark applications for "19-0" and "19-0 THE PERFECT SEASON." T-shirts were available to pre-order online. The *New York Post* retaliated before the Super Bowl by applying to trademark "18-1."

They Said It

"We're only gonna score 17 points?"
— TOM BRADY when told that New York receiver Plaxico Burress had predicted a 23-17 Giants victory

Monky Business

The Our Lady of Guadalupe Benedictine Monastery in Phoenix rented out rooms during Super Bowl week at the rate of $300 per night for double occupancy.

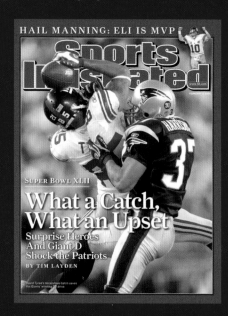

Excerpted from **SPORTS ILLUSTRATED** *February 11, 2008*

A PLACE IN NFL LORE

The Giants ended the Patriots' run at history and did so in stunning style | BY TIM LAYDEN

THIS TIME THE CELEBRATION WAS for the youngest child of a football family, and for the team he helped carry to an unlikely championship. A year ago in Miami, Eli Manning had seen his older brother Peyton transformed by a Super Bowl championship. He had seen Peyton walk into his own victory party so blissfully satisfied that the moment found a place in Eli's soul and changed him as well. "It put a hunger inside me," Eli says. "You always want to win, but after that I felt like I wanted it even more."

A second-floor restaurant at the Giants' team hotel near Phoenix had become a thrumming nightclub early Monday morning, a steady bass beat providing the backdrop to the buzz of victory shared with friends and family at another Manning Super Bowl celebration. It was to have been a historic night for another reason: The Patriots were going to win their 19th straight game and become the second NFL team, along with the 1972 Dolphins, to complete a season unbeaten and untied. They would prove themselves perfect.

Instead, the Giants completed an unexpected and emotional postseason run with a 17–14 win. The performance was built on the underpinnings of a ferocious defensive effort, sustained when quarterback Manning and receiver David Tyree combined on one of the most memorable plays in NFL history, and sealed when Manning threw a 13-yard scoring pass to Plaxico Burress with 35 seconds left. "It's just surreal," Eli said over the noise at the afterparty.

On the Wednesday before the game, at the Giants' Super Bowl headquarters, ends Justin Tuck and Osi Umenyiora sat together reading a newspaper. A headline posed the question, BRADY: THE BEST EVER?

"Is he the best ever?" Umenyiora said of Tom Brady, the Patriots' quarterback, setting up his partner. "We'll see on Sunday," Tuck replied disdainfully.

On Sunday the Giants brought relentless heat to the highest-scoring offense in NFL history. New York had five sacks and knocked Brady down a half-dozen other times. Central to the effort was Tuck's constant movement, making it difficult for Brady to identify where the rush was likely to come from. The Giants manhandled the Patriots' offensive line, which includes three Pro Bowl players, and limited tailback Laurence Maroney to 36 yards on the ground.

The upshot of all this defense—New England's unit also played solidly—was a brutal game in which, after the Patriots took a 7–3 lead on the first play of the second quarter, the teams went 33 minutes, 52 seconds without scoring, a Super Bowl record. Then they played a 15-minute masterpiece, compressing a night's drama into the fourth quarter.

First, Manning threw a TD to Tyree with 11:05 to play. Three series later, Brady completed eight of 11 on an 80-yard drive, capping it with a six-yard TD pass to Randy Moss that put New England on top 14–10 with 2:42 to go. The game rested in Manning's hands.

The Giants needed six plays to move from their 17-yard line to their 44, where, on third-and-five, Manning took a shotgun snap and carved a place in

football lore. Quickly swarmed in a collapsing pocket, he was grabbed by the Patriots' Jarvis Green, a 6' 3", 285-pound defensive end. For an instant Manning disappeared, presumed sacked. Somehow, though, he pulled away from the scrum. Once free, Manning squared himself and lobbed a pass into the middle of the field toward Tyree, who had stopped after running a post pattern. A fifth-year wideout known for his special teams work, Tyree had caught only four passes in the regular season and one in the playoffs.

Now, with the Super Bowl in the balance, he rose high and outfought Patriots safety Rodney Harrison, clutching the ball against his own helmet. "Harrison is a dirty cheap-shot artist and also a heck of a football player," said Tyree. "But once that ball was in the air, it was mine, mine, mine, like a little kid." The 32-yard gain took the ball to the New England 24. Three plays later Manning threw 12 yards to rookie Steve Smith for a first down at the 13 with 39 seconds left.

The Giants' next formation sent Burress alone to the left. The Patriots blitzed, leaving cornerback Ellis Hobbs in single coverage on Burress. Hobbs guessed slant, the play called for a fade, and Hobbs was badly beaten. "End of story," said Eli.

In the weeks and months to come, the Giants will be celebrated and cheered. The Pats will field questions about winning 18 games then ending with a loss. About history denied. But beneath a dome in the desert Sunday evening, time was the province of the winners. Players lingered with family. In the stands scattered groups of Giants fans chanted mockingly, "Eighteen-and-one . . . eighteen-and-one." On the battered grass two of coach Tom Coughlin's grandkids, four-year-olds Emma and Dylan, lay on their backs and swept their arms and legs, making snow angels in the confetti. The only word to describe the scene would be: *Perfect.* ∎

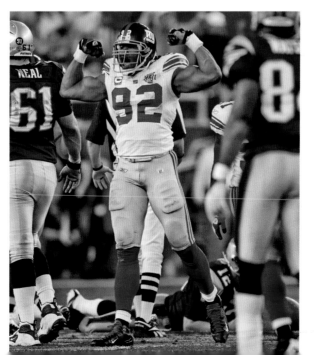

Michael Strahan posed in post-sack splendor.

Photograph by Al Tielemans

"Is Tom Brady the best ever?" Giants end Osi Umenyiora asked, setting up his linemate. "We'll see on Sunday," Justin Tuck replied disdainfully.

Giants, Giants everywhere: Brady got blitzed and banged around.

Photograph by Robert Beck

BY Justin Tuck

Giants Defensive End

I went on the field for pregame, and I looked up at the Jumbotron and it was me, Osi and Strahan. I remember thinking the stadium was brighter than normal, like there was more light. I don't know if there was or not, but it felt that way. Coming into the Super Bowl we were very loose even knowing what was at stake. It was a direct result of how relaxed coach Coughlin was, which is not exactly what he's known for. It was almost like the game wasn't a big deal. We showed up to play football, and here we go.

I remember sacks I had, quarterback hits, tackles for loss. But the plays I didn't make stand out more. One was a quick throw and I had a good rush up the middle. I grabbed Tom Brady's forearm as he threw, but he still made the pass. I found a new respect for Brady considering how many times we hit him. He kept getting up and making plays. I felt we were dominating that game—we could have kept them under 10 points—but it wasn't until that last pass, when Brady threw for Randy Moss on fourth down and he didn't catch it, that we knew we had it.

After that last play, I was walking on the sideline and I saw a Giants fan with an 18–1 sign representing that we'd given New England its only loss. There's a video of me where it looks like my fingers are going crazy. I was trying to make a gesture of 18–1; it's like I was doing the math: I did a 10, then an eight, then a slashing motion, then a one. I couldn't really make it work. But that sign, that's the first thing I remember seeing after we won the Super Bowl.

BY Jarvis Green

Patriots Defensive End

We played well, but we didn't play our best game. With the rush their defense had up the middle, there's nothing Tom Brady could do a lot of the time. But we were focused. We played all the way through, and we had it. Then they made that play, that Eli Manning-to-David Tyree completion.

I feel like it was the longest play I was ever involved in. I was on the center, over front. We got off the ball and got a push inside. I looped around and Richard Seymour crossed my face, Shaun O'Hara choking the crap out of him. I got my hand on Eli's shoulder pad. Later Seymour said, "Man, you pushed me off," and I said, "You pushed me off!" We were both trying to get the cheese, I guess.

We watched a lot of tape on Eli, and normally on a play like this he drops down and takes the sack. But this was the Super Bowl. He got out of all our grasps, backed out of the pocket and threw it. Everyone just stopped, turned and watched the ball. It unfolded so slowly. And then it was just . . . Oh my God, no. I didn't sleep for about two weeks. If I make that play, I'm going to Disney World.

What's funny was I started getting royalty checks in the mail. I didn't know why so I called the NFLPA and they said, "Remember that play in the Super Bowl? There's a Gatorade commercial where Eli gets away from the guy who could have had a sack." They asked if I wanted the checks to stop, I said, "No, no, no." I finally saw the ad later, watched it two or three times. That was enough.

Burress's second catch of the day was the Trophy winner.

Photograph by Bob Rosato

SUPER BOWL XLIII

February 1, 2009
Raymond James Stadium, Tampa

HEAD COACHES
MIKE TOMLIN Steelers | KEN WHISENHUNT Cardinals

PITTSBURGH STEELERS | 27

ARIZONA CARDINALS | 23

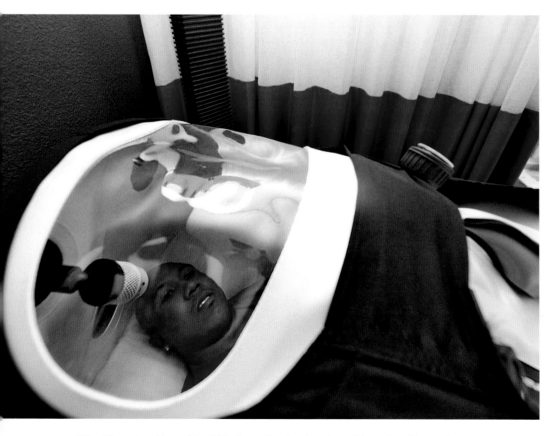

Ward (strained knee) had his hyperbaric chamber shipped to him in Tampa.

Photograph by Michael J. LeBrecht II/1Deuce3 Photography

ON ONE side was a rust-belt team with the richest Super Bowl tradition of all. On the other was a warm-weather upstart that had gone 9-7 in the regular season. Who knew that surprising Arizona would give Pittsburgh all it could handle?

WEATHER
66°, cloudy

POINT SPREAD
Steelers by 6½

TIME OF GAME
3:38

TV AUDIENCE
98.7 million

290

There were 35 seconds left in the game, Holmes had come down inbounds, and the Steelers were about to be champions.

Photograph by Al Tielemans

SUPER BOWL XLIV

NEW ORLEANS
SAINTS | **31**

INDIANAPOLIS
COLTS | **17**

IN ITS first Super Bowl, New Orleans had an offense that could keep up with the powerful, nearly unbeaten Colts. The Saints also had a proud QB, a spirited coach and the heart of a city to lift them. And that made all the difference.

WEATHER	POINT SPREAD	TIME OF GAME	TV AUDIENCE
60°, clear	Colts by 4½	3:14	106.5 million

The Saints' emotional win helped exorcise the spirits of an ignominious past.

Photograph by Bob Rosato

296

As Pierre Thomas dived in for a third-quarter score, the Saints had the Miami crowd on their side.

Photograph by Gary Bogdon

With perhaps the gutsiest Super Bowl call ever, the Saints' onside kick to start the third quarter paid off.

Photograph by Peter Read Miller

Marques Colston led New Orleans with seven catches for 83 yards.

Photograph by Peter Read Miller

Excerpted from **SPORTS ILLUSTRATED** *February 15, 2010*

FOR YOU, NEW ORLEANS

The Saints gave their aching city a win that echoed far beyond the field | BY LEE JENKINS

AT A ROLLICKING HOUSE party in the Ninth Ward, a security guard named Timothy Washington danced a two-step. On the first floor of the Superdome, an electrician named Bruce Bruder sat in silent astonishment in a quiet control room. At an overflowing restaurant on Bourbon Street, a sous chef named Charles Emery raised a glass of champagne with his coworkers. And in the middle of the field at Sun Life Stadium in Miami, quarterback Drew Brees held one-year-old son Baylen, looked up at the night sky and felt confetti falling like raindrops. Brees's wife, Brittany, wiped tears from cheeks stained with her husband's eye black. "My only wish," she said afterward, "is that everybody from New Orleans was here with us."

They would have seen coach Sean Payton lifting the Lombardi Trophy to the stands so fans could touch it, and safety Roman Harper donning black-and-gold Mardi Gras beads as big as grapefruits. They would have heard players shouting names of towns in the Gulf region, from big ones like Baton Rouge to tiny ones like Taylorsville, Miss. The celebration was under way in those places and so many others, punctuating a 31–17 Super Bowl win over the favored Colts and a season that at times felt more like a fairy tale.

At the victory party at their hotel in Miami, the Saints were greeted by a blues band. Several thousand people showed up, the party spilled out onto the breezeway and the lobby. Running back Mike Bell sipped red wine—"This is the first taste," he said—while honorary captain Deuce McAllister, the longtime Saint now retired, stood in disbelief. "Did that really just happen?" he asked.

After 43 years of brown bags at the Superdome and ostrich races at Tulane Stadium, of Archie Manning on his backside, Tom Benson under his parasol and Ricky Williams in his wedding veil, it happened. And if there was a moment at which this beleaguered franchise crossed the threshold, it came with 10:39 left in the game, when Brees jogged onto the field trailing by a point. The first time Brees had ever gathered the Saints in a huddle, when he was a freshly minted free agent with a surgically repaired shoulder, receiver Joe Horn said the QB told his teammates: "I'm here to lead you to a Super Bowl, and anything else is despicable." This time he said only, "Let's be special."

The line was borrowed from New Orleans native and former NBA coach Avery Johnson, who spoke to the Saints on Sunday morning as a video played showing scenes from the 2009 season—nifty catches and big hits—spliced with footage from Hurricane Katrina, homes in ruins, families crowding through the doors of the Superdome to seek shelter. "It gave this game context," said cornerback Greg Fassitt. "The room was dead quiet. You could hear people breathing hard. You could hear sniffling. Those were the only sounds." When the video ended, players started yelling as if they were ready to charge out the tunnel.

With that one sentence—"Let's be special"—Brees brought the Saints back to that meeting room, and then took them to a place they'd never been. He threw seven passes to seven receivers, completing each. For the two-point conversion he threw an eighth pass, to an eighth receiver, Lance Moore, and completed that one too. He will never have Tom Brady's height or Brett Favre's arm or Peyton Manning's pedigree, but in the four years since Brees joined the Saints, he has been more accurate than any of them. After the first quarter on Sunday, he completed 29 of 32 passes. "If Drew Brees has not been in the discussion of the best quarterback in the league," said Saints tackle Jon Stinchcomb, "he is now."

Super Bowl settings can be sterile, but not here. Men came to the stadium in wigs, bras and dresses in homage to the late talk-show host Buddy Diliberto, who had pledged to wear a dress and strut down Bourbon Street if the team made the Bowl. As the Colts lined up with 3:24 left, down 24–17, the energy in the stadium reflected the country's mood: Saints-smitten.

The fairy-tale outcome had Payton riding high.
Photograph by Bob Rosato

New Orleans cornerback Tracy Porter, positioned across from receiver Reggie Wayne, saw Austin Collie go in motion. Porter recognized from his film study what that meant: Manning was throwing to Wayne. "Everything slowed down," Porter said. "The spiral on the ball slowed down. The guys around me slowed down. The crowd noise stopped. It was just me and the football." Wayne ran a turn-in, but Porter got the better break on the ball. Manning's pass hit his hands so hard that the Saints defensive linemen heard the smack. Porter took it 74 yards for the clinching score.

Some say there's no karma in sports, but the Saints were the team of a battered city. Now Joe Lombardi, New Orleans's quarterbacks coach, gets to touch the trophy named for his grandfather. A championship banner will be raised at the Superdome, under the spot where Katrina had torn holes in the roof. Mardi Gras may run all the way to Jazz Fest. Saints be praised. ∎

BY **Tracy Porter**

Saints Cornerback

On Wednesday of Super Bowl week we had the day off. But the defensive back unit was hanging out in one hotel room for three or four hours. We ordered pizzas, guys were sitting on the floor, on blankets, and we watched the entire Colts cut-up. We watched the third-down plays. They ran this one play over and over and over again. And they converted every time. It would be third-and-five, and you'd think, No way they'll run that same play. Then, *boom,* first down. Again, first down. Again, first down. It was unreal. Finally Pierson Prioleau blurts out, "Man, I'm getting tired of watching this play. If they run it during the game and one of us doesn't pick this ball off. . . . " We all started laughing.

So the fourth quarter comes, we're up by seven and they have it at our 31. It's third-and-five. We're in man-to-man, and I see Austin Collie lined up as their No. 1 receiver. He was never aligned at that spot unless they were running that play. As soon as I saw that formation, I knew what was coming. He breaks, I make my break, and when the ball hit my hands all I could think was, *Please don't drop it.* Then it was, *Don't get tripped up.*

I grew up a Saints fan. I remember when they won their first playoff game, after the 2000 season. I remember the "Aints" and fans with paper bags on their heads. Every team has a turnaround, and I knew the Saints would get to the Super Bowl one day. But I never thought I would be part of it. I was more of a basketball player growing up. Then I ended up playing football at Indiana, I got drafted by my hometown team and I won the Super Bowl in my second year. It's unspeakable.

BY **Dwight Freeney**

Colts Defensive End

That week I had a third-degree high ankle sprain I had suffered in the AFC championship game. Normally I would have been out four weeks, so my whole process was just getting the ankle ready for the game. I wasn't around for the normal procedural stuff you do to prepare as a team.

I did a lot of hyperbaric chamber, electro-type therapies, beach walking, beach running, chiropractic adjustments, acupuncture. You name it I was doing it. It became the most famous ankle in Super Bowl history. At media day Deion Sanders lifted the tablecloth at my table to get a camera under there to get a look.

On Friday I had a breakthrough. When I was able to run two or three steps on the beach, I knew I'd be able to do more in another day, go five, six, seven. And then by Sunday I'd be able to hold that speed. In the first half, I felt great. Well, great considering the injury. But halftime killed me. It's such a long break. I tried to ride a bike, stretch it, run on it. But you can't match the adrenaline, you can't match the intensity. All the blood started to cool down, and my ankle stiffened up pretty badly. In the second half, I was a different guy.

On the onside kick I was thinking, *Why are there more Saints out there than Colts?* They had so many guys run on the field during the scuffle, and the refs didn't do a good job. I thought we had the ball. There were obviously other big plays, though, and Drew Brees picked up steam in the second half. If there was any team that I could feel even an ounce of "it's O.K. that we lost," it would be them with what happened with Katrina. But you have no idea how much I try to forget this game.

Brees had a simple message for his troops: "Let's be special." | *Photograph by Al Tielemans*

BOWL · 02.07.10

XLIV

SAINTS | COLTS

Before the game Sean Payton was confident in his cast of weirdos, telling them: "It's a coach's dream to be an underdog when you've got the better team."

Porter read the pass, made the pick and was off for the final score.

Photograph by Peter Read Miller

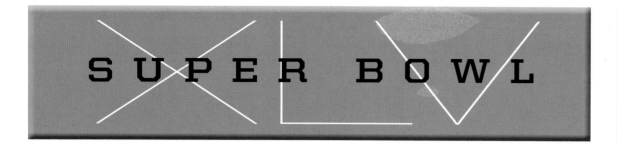

SUPER BOWL XLV

February 6, 2011
Cowboys Stadium, Arlington, Texas

HEAD COACHES
MIKE MCCARTHY Packers | MIKE TOMLIN Steelers

GREEN BAY
PACKERS | 31

PITTSBURGH
STEELERS | 25

An ice storm preceded the marquee matchup which included Rodgers and Harrison.

Photograph by Al Bello/Getty Images

THE MEETING of two flagship franchises promised a worthy big-game battle. And that it was. Green Bay, favored despite entering as a No. 6 seed, led early, then got inspiration from its wounded to hold off Pittsburgh's powerful push.

DOME
Outside: 35°, icy

POINT SPREAD
Packers by 3

TIME OF GAME
3:32

TV AUDIENCE
111 million

Packers free safety Nick Collins returned a first-quarter pick 37 yards for a TD, and a 14–0 lead.

Photograph by Bob Rosato

ARRIVAL OF THE FITTEST

Aaron Rodgers joined the Packers' tradition, leading like a Green Bay great | BY TIM LAYDEN

THE FOOTBALL TRAVELED ONLY 26 yards through the air, beneath the high roof and hulking video screens at Cowboys Stadium. Yet in truth it sailed across years. It left the right hand of Packers quarterback Aaron Rodgers at his own 18-yard line and was caught at the 44 by wide receiver Greg Jennings, who raced across midfield before being tackled. It was a killing completion that would push Green Bay to the brink of victory and the Steelers to the edge of desperation.

Pittsburgh, down early, had rallied to within 28–25, but here on third-and-10, midway through the fourth quarter, Rodgers called out Strong Left, Trips 27 Tampa. When Jennings slashed behind cornerback Ike Taylor and up the middle of the field, Rodgers hit him in dead stride. Six minutes later the Packers had a 31–25 victory and a fourth Super Bowl title.

Long after the game, Rodgers walked across the celebratory locker room warbling a dreadful falsetto version of Usher's "I Don't Know." He fell into a corner cubicle and dressed while quaffing a bottle of grape soda. "That throw was about the last three years of my career," he said. Those would be the three years since he replaced Brett Favre as Green Bay's quarterback. Before that he sat three years behind the Packers legend, and long before that he was a skinny high school quarterback in Chico, Calif., who had to go to the local junior college to earn a shot at a football career.

"The journey has been special," Rodgers said. "You wait, you keep quiet and you take advantage of an opportunity when it comes."

There are two Super Bowls. One is the public spectacle, and the other is the strategic battle that coaching staffs plan but do not discuss. This game was served to the masses as a matchup of storied NFL franchises with nine Super Bowl wins between them, Pittsburgh with six, Green Bay with three, including Super Bowls I and II. A Steelers win would have given image-rehabbing QB Ben Roethlisberger a third ring, and 38-year-old coach Mike Tomlin a second. For the Packers the payoff would be simpler: a return to greatness.

Both coaching staffs knew this: In the regular season, Pittsburgh's defense allowed 62.8 rushing yards per game, the fewest in the NFL by nearly 30 yards. "They're not even going to try to run," Steelers nose-tackle Casey Hampton said before the game. He was right—Rodgers handed off just 11 times. Green Bay coach Mike McCarthy felt the Packers could exploit the Steelers' secondary, given that safety Troy Polamalu, the 2010 Defensive Player of the Year, was limited by an Achilles injury. "We felt we could spread it out four, five wide and use play action to beat them," Green Bay tight end Andrew Quarless said. "We knew their corners were a little suspect when they were singling up."

En route to a 14–0 lead, Rodgers's first completion was to Donald Driver, the tough, veteran possession specialist who was soon out of the game with a high-left-ankle sprain. (Jennings caught two scoring passes, but the memorable receiver was 6' 3", 217-pound Jordy Nelson whose career day included the game's first TD.) Then just before halftime, defensive back Charles Woodson, the Packers' inspirational leader, suffered a broken collarbone. He too, was done.

Woodson's is the voice that the Packers hear. He was the last man to talk to the team before the Super Bowl and he spoke to the team again at halftime, knowing he was finished for the night. Green Bay led 21–10. "Charles said, 'You don't know how bad I want this,'" said linebacker Desmond Bishop. "That was all he got out. Then he got choked up. It was tough."

So were the Steelers after the break—Pittsburgh scored on its first drive of the third quarter, cutting the Packers' lead to 21–17. But on the first play of the final quarter, with Green Bay still clinging to that four-point advantage, defensive tackle Ryan Pickett and linebacker Clay Matthews sandwiched Steelers running back Rashard Mendenhall, forcing a fumble that the Packers recovered. On the ensuing possession Rodgers hit Jennings for an eight-yard touchdown pass. Then, in the final two minutes, with the Packers up 31–25 but Roethlisberger seemingly poised to reprise his Super Bowl–winning drive from two years earlier against Arizona, Green Bay forced three straight incompletions. The victory was sealed.

Now the Packers' locker room is nearly empty. Equipment managers pushing large green carts pick up discarded clothing. Workers rip Super Bowl XLV banners from the walls. Woodson is the last to finish, dressing with one hand—pulling up a sock, contorting himself into an undershirt, grimacing. "I'm a man," he says. "I gotta do this all myself." Actually, if there is a larger lesson here, in a room littered with tape and confetti, smelling of sweat and ringing with the noise of victory, it's this: No one does it alone. ∎

Nelson, in his third season, had a breakout game.

Photograph by Robert Beck

JUST THE FACTS

Statistical Leaders

Rushing RASHARD MENDENHALL (PIT) 14 carries, 63 yds, 1 TD

Passing AARON RODGERS (GB) 24 of 39, 304 yds, 3 TDs

Receiving JORDY NELSON (GB) 9 catches, 140 yds, 1 TD

MVP AARON RODGERS Packers Quarterback

The Ring
The 92 diamonds around the logo represent Green Bay's 92-year history

Anthem Performer
Christina Aguilera

Halftime Performer
The Black Eyed Peas

Attendance 103,219

Ticket Price $600–$1,200

Behind the Scenes

Trying to break the Super Bowl attendance record (103,985), the Cowboys looked to install 13,000 bleacher-style temporary seats for the game. But they fell 766 seats short, as 1,250 spots were deemed unsafe by fire officials and ticket holders were displaced.

They Said It

"[Woodson] tried to speak about what this game meant, and he choked up. There was something about what he said that made me want to play harder." —Packers linebacker DESMOND BISHOP

Counting on the Bling

The night before the game, Packers coach Mike McCarthy had his players and coaches fitted for their championship rings.

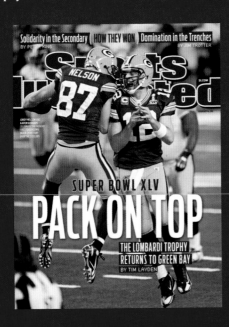

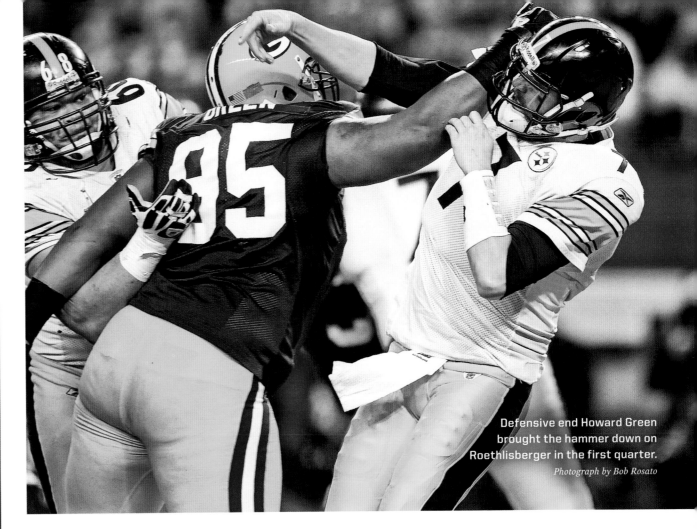

Defensive end Howard Green brought the hammer down on Roethlisberger in the first quarter.
Photograph by Bob Rosato

Woodson broke up this pass before his inspirational halftime performance.
Photograph by John W. McDonough

XLV
PACKERS | STEELERS

"The journey has been special," said Aaron Rodgers of his career path. "You wait, you keep quiet, and you take advantage of an opportunity when it comes."

Jennings's second TD catch put Green Bay ahead 28–17.

Photograph by John W. McDonough

The Packers' plan was to pass first and often.
Photograph by John W. McDonough

THE WAY IT WAS

BY **Clay Matthews**

Packers Linebacker

Two weeks before the game, while we were in Green Bay, we tried to install our game plan, preparing for everything we were going to see. That way there wouldn't be any distractions. We wanted to go down there and be able to enjoy ourselves, because we had put in our work right off the bat.

Still, with two weeks of practice, you see so much of the other team. Certain formations kind of trigger an alert. At the start of the fourth quarter, we had the lead and they were driving. Before this particular snap, there's footage of me saying I didn't feel right about the play, that they were kind of eyeing me down which is usually an indication that the ball is coming my way. When they lined up they showed me exactly what I thought they would. So on the play I came clean over the edge, Rashard Mendenhall was carrying the ball and I was fortunate to put my head on the ball. Desmond Bishop came in and scooped it up. Our offense went down and scored, and the rest is history.

My father played in the NFL for 19 years and he never had a chance to go to the Super Bowl because the Browns lost to the Broncos. My uncle made it to the Super Bowl with the Titans but he lost to the Rams when they get stopped on the one-yard line. And there I was, winning the Super Bowl in just my second year. After the game my family came down to the field. I pulled my father over and said "We did it, Dad!" And he said, "This Super Bowl thing . . . it's actually pretty fun."

BY **Ike Taylor**

Steelers Cornerback

My first Super Bowl was in Detroit, where they had a new dome. My second one was in Tampa and that stadium was really nice. But then you get to Jerry World, and it's like, oh yeah, they say everything's bigger in Texas and they aren't lying. I walked into that stadium, and it was, *Whoa, Mr. Jerry is not playing around here.*

I balled out that game. I was covering Greg Jennings, one of the hottest receivers in the league. When they saw what we were doing, they started lining Jennings up in the slot to get someone else on him. After that game I started calling Aaron Rodgers AR-12. I saw how good that dude was. If you're watching our secondary from a coach's perspective you say, There's nothing more my guys could have done. We played well, but he couldn't miss.

We won the first two Super Bowls I was in so I was used to confetti falling on my head, going to the stands to get my family, carrying my son down to the field. When the game ended, the security guys came out and told us, "We're roping you off, you've got to get off the field, this confetti isn't for y'all." It didn't hit me until I got to the tunnel. And by the time we got to the locker room, I was crying like a baby. I would have rather lost in the AFC championship. Winning a Super Bowl changes your life. It's like a drug. All you can think about is how to get back. We lost that Super Bowl, and I never got back.

SUPER BOWL XLVI

February 5, 2012
Lucas Oil Stadium, Indianapolis

HEAD COACHES
TOM COUGHLIN Giants | BILL BELICHICK Patriots

NEW YORK
GIANTS | 21

NEW ENGLAND
PATRIOTS | 17

THE LEADUP seemed so familiar: the favored Patriots, the upstart Giants, a Brady vs. (Eli) Manning showdown. For New York, on a run after finishing the season at just 9-7, the good news was when the ending felt familiar too.

DOME
First game in Indy

POINT SPREAD
Patriots by 3

TIME OF GAME
3:23

TV AUDIENCE
111.3 million

Lego lord: Brian Alano posed with his 30,000 piece scaled replica of Lucas Oil Stadium.

Photograph by David J. Phillip/AP

Manningham deftly came down with this rainbow from Manning to start the winning drive.

Photograph by John W. McDonough

DOING THEIR THING

With an exquisite final drive the Giants stunned the Patriots—again | BY DAMON HACK

ELI MANNING WAS STILL ON HIS feet early Monday morning, sliding past members of Lady Antebellum and Counting Crows, reveling in a party at the Circle City Bar and Grille in downtown Indianapolis that had momentum to threaten the dawn.

Justin Tuck and Osi Umenyiora, tag-team defensive ends, arrived resplendent in gray suits, ducking behind a black curtain into the mayhem. "We are going to shut New York down!" Umenyiora shouted into his phone. "We are going to shut the whole city down!" Running back Brandon Jacobs came next, carrying a glass in his left hand. "This champagne is just too good," he said. Manning stood in the middle of the bar, the knot of his tie loosened down, top button of his shirt unfastened, a light beer and his older brother Peyton by his side.

"This isn't about me," Eli said above the din, after the Giants' 21–17 win over the Patriots. "It's about the organization and coach [Tom] Coughlin and all our coaches." He paused. "It's about a bunch of young guys," he said, "with something to prove."

Hours earlier at Lucas Oil Stadium, Manning stepped into the huddle with 3:46 left in the game, trailing 17–15. You could almost draw a line to the Arizona desert, where four years earlier he and the Giants had overcome a three-point deficit on a last-minute drive, shocking the football world and short-circuiting New England's perfect season. Several principals were back: Manning and Coughlin, Tom Brady and Bill Belichick, plus enough A-list stars, on the field and off, to give this Super Bowl the feel of a long-awaited sequel.

In the Giants' owner's box, team matriarch Ann Mara reached into her jacket pocket and pulled out her rosary beads. Her right arm in a sling after a fall in church, she said a prayer for Eli. "I asked the Blessed Mother to tell him where to throw the ball," she said.

On first-and-10 from his 12, Manning took the snap and surveyed a defense in Cover Two. He knew the Pats' safeties didn't play wide toward the sideline, and that might allow him a window to find a receiver deep. Manning looked right; Hakeem Nicks and Victor Cruz were covered. On the left Mario Manningham had run a go route up the sideline, sprinting past cornerback Sterling Moore as safety Patrick Chung slid over to help.

Manning let fly a rainbow that dropped into Manningham's fingertips. The receiver stuck both feet inbounds, tumbled over and held on. The completion went for 38 yards, the longest play of the game. "That throw," Giants co-owner John Mara said, "epitomizes why we gave up all those draft picks to get him."

For the eighth time this season, Manning marched the Giants to a winning score in the fourth quarter. When running back Ahmad Bradshaw tumbled backward into the end zone for an excuse-me touchdown, the Pats, down 4, had 57 seconds to work with.

Brady found wideout Deion Branch for 19 yards on fourth-and-16 from his own 14, and five plays later he had the Patriots at midfield, ready for one last, desperate heave. On the game's final play Brady threw a Hail Mary that Tuck said was in the air long enough for him to finish a novel. One member of New York's traveling party fainted in the owner's suite.

When the pass fell incomplete, the Giants' sideline dissolved in celebration, players and coaches dashing everywhere. Manning, Super Bowl MVP for a second time, won a new Corvette, the keys of which ended up in his infant daughter Ava's mouth. Ann Mara scaled nine stairs of a makeshift stage to retrieve the franchise's fourth Lombardi Trophy. A long line of Giants followed her, victorious over New England again.

If accountability and execution characterized New York's undefeated run from 7–7 this season, those qualities were beacons during the Super Bowl. The Giants had two fumbles but recovered both. They trailed 10–9 at halftime and by eight in the third quarter but shut down the Patriots after that. Brady, who at one point completed a Super Bowl–record 16 straight passes, was just 7 of 17 for 75 yards on New England's final three drives, which featured two sacks by Tuck, an interception by linebacker Chris Blackburn and a slightly misthrown pass that slipped through the grasp of the normally reliable Wes Welker.

"We've won so many games like this, at the end, [in] the fourth quarter," Coughlin said. "We talk about finishing all the time and winning the fourth quarter, being the stronger team."

For the second time in five seasons Coughlin outfoxed Belichick, with whom he worked as an assistant on New York's staff from 1988 to '90. The night before the game, Coughlin showed his team highlights of the last six weeks, set to "In the Air Tonight" by Phil Collins. He told them to finish. He told them championships are won by players who love one another, as the Giants do. And he told them he loved them. "Tom Coughlin," Jacobs said simply, "is one hell of a football coach." ∎

Brady started super, before Tuck and Co. got to him.

Photograph by Simon Bruty

Statistical Leaders

Rushing AHMAD BRADSHAW (NY) 17 carries, 72 yds, 1 TD

Passing ELI MANNING (NY) 30 of 40, 296 yds, 1 TD

Receiving HAKEEM NICKS (NY) 10 catches, 109 yds

MVP ELI MANNING Giants Quarterback

The Ring
37 blue sapphires, four marquis diamonds and the words ALL IN and FINISH engraved

Anthem Performer
Kelly Clarkson

Halftime Performer
Madonna

Attendance 68,658

Ticket Price $600–$1,200

Behind the Scenes

With New England at its 44 with 17 seconds left, the Giants were penalized five yards for 12 men on the field; the play ran, burning off eight seconds. The NFL's Competition Committee made the "12 men" infraction a dead-ball penalty in the following off-season.

They Said It

"Good thing I wear size 11. If I wore 11½, I'd have been out-of-bounds." —Giants receiver MARIO MANNINGHAM on his sideline catch that started the winning drive

A Middling Performance

Rapper M.I.A. flipped her middle finger at the camera while on stage with Madonna at halftime. The NFL filed claims with the American Arbitration Association, seeking $16.6 million in damages. The singer reached a settlement with the league in 2014.

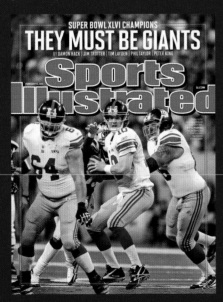

In a bizarre scene, Bradshaw tried to stop himself but plopped down with the go-ahead TD too early, giving the Patriots 57 more seconds of hope.

Photographs by Simon Bruty (3) and Robert Beck

The Patriots' final Hail Mary went unanswered, denied by a crowd of Giants.

Photograph by David Bergman

BY Victor Cruz

Giants Wide Receiver

Practice that week was the same as it had been all season. Coach Coughlin made it exactly like a week that we'd have had back at our facility. But here's the crazy thing: That week, we were perfect. I can't think of a receiver who dropped a ball. No one on defense blew an assignment. We really felt it: Nothing was derailing us from our championship goal.

The day of the game I tried to keep to my routine. I talked to my mom, made sure she was good. I spent a lot of time thinking about the game, visualizing what I would do. I wanted to invest all of my mind and my body into it. I ate light meals all day because I had a lot of butterflies.

In the first quarter it was second-and-goal at the two, and we had a play with two slants going on the outside and a tight end on the back. Eli [Manning] could either hit me on a slant or get me on a diagonal if the defense was playing zone. He saw it was man-to-man, so he kept the play on. I knew he would come to me. I made a move to the inside and the ball was right there. It was the most exhilarating touchdown I ever scored. That ball is on my mantel right now.

As soon as the game ended I was out on the field. We were running around like kids. Then I looked for my family. My fiancée had gotten everyone together, and they'd come down on the field. To get to relish in that moment is something most people never experience. We went out that night, but first I had to take a nap. That was the most physically and mentally exhausting game I've ever been part of.

BY Brandon Spikes

Patriots Linebacker

The craziest part of the week was Media Day. You have the media there and all these celebrities, and they're taking pictures. It showed me the whole world was watching. Getting interviewed by Michael Irvin, a guy I always looked up to? I couldn't believe that. They give you your jersey, with SPIKES on the back and with that Super Bowl patch. That was surreal. That's when it hit me.

Bill Belichick brought me into his office the day of the game. He wanted to know that I was prepared and ready to play my best game, and to let me know he was depending on me to set the tone. That meant a lot. He wanted to make sure I knew how big the game was. But I knew. I had been waiting for it my entire life.

There were plenty of big plays. We forced a couple of fumbles but couldn't recover them. Then when I did recover one, we had too many men on the field. Mario Manningham made that catch on the sideline. On that last Giants touchdown, I was already disappointed that we had given up a big drive. We were letting them score on the last play because we knew we needed to get the ball back. As Ahmad Bradshaw got near the goal line, I took a couple steps toward him. I wasn't going to let him just walk in, I was going to give him a lick as he scored. That's what I do.

I hate thinking about this game. I still get emotional. Having my family experience that game with me was thrilling. But for me, if I'm not going to win, I'd rather not even go.

XLVI

GIANTS | PATRIOTS

"We've won so many games like this, at the end," Tom Coughlin said. "We talk about finishing, and winning the fourth quarter, being the stronger team."

It's not clear where's Waldo in this scene of Giants jubilation, but Tom Brady sure stands out.

Photograph by David Bergman

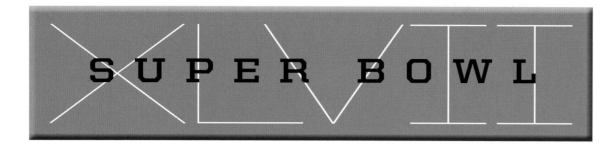

SUPER BOWL XLVII

BALTIMORE RAVENS | 34

SAN FRANCISCO 49ERS | 31

Cornerback Chykie Brown made his mark amid the celebratory postgame debris.

Photograph by John Biever

FAVORED SAN FRANCISCO had a perfect Super Bowl history (5-0), a better season's record and a vaunted D. John Harbaugh's Ravens, though, had the grit to match Jim Harbaugh's 49ers. And on this day, by any lights, Baltimore was the better team.

DOME

Outside: 71°, sun

POINT SPREAD

49ers by 4½

TIME OF GAME

4:14

TV AUDIENCE

108.4 million

314

An eerie third-quarter brownout short-circuited the Ravens' momentum, but they had the power to stand strong at the end.

Photograph by David E. Klutho

Kaepernick led a stirring rally but was stopped by a Ravens defense driven by Lewis, in his final game.

Photograph by David Bergman

Unflappable Flacco finished the day with a Montana-esque 124.2 QB rating.

Photograph by Walter Iooss Jr.

Excerpted from **SPORTS ILLUSTRATED** *February 11, 2013*

ALL THE INGREDIENTS

Winning recipe: a dauntless QB, an electric returner, a goal line stand | BY PETER KING

ON THE RAVENS' PLANE following the AFC title game last month, a voice rose from the back of the charter. "Hey Ray! ... Ray!" quarterback Joe Flacco called to Ray Lewis, who a few hours earlier had wept with joy at the thought of his final NFL game being the Super Bowl. "There's no crying in football!"

The times, in Baltimore, are changing. The quiet 28-year-old quarterback needles the 37-year-old Raven in Winter, one of the greatest (and most complicated) leaders we've seen, on his way out. But change comes to all teams. And now that the Ravens have completed their wild and dusky and fraternal and rollicking 34–31 Super Bowl XLVII win over San Francisco, an orderly succession plan is in place. Baltimore has the organization, the coaching and the quarterback—especially the quarterback—to contend for years. Flacco won't be a hollerer. But as Derek Jeter says, It ain't about what you say. It's how you practice, how you run out ground balls. You lead by example.

Sounds like another Joe.

"Wow," Flacco said of the comparison to the 49ers' Joe Montana. "My idol." They're in history together now, the two Joes, with the most explosive and efficient postseasons. Twenty-three years ago Montana threw 11 touchdowns and no interceptions in a campaign that ended with a Super Bowl XXIV blowout of Denver. Flacco, in Baltimore's four playoff games this season, matched that. And with a 22-of-33, 287-yard, three-TD Super Bowl effort, he earned the game's MVP award, just as Montana did.

There were so many dimensions to this game. The first (non-football-related) delay in a Super Bowl, 34 minutes when a partial power outage in the Superdome darkened the place. The first brother-brother cham-pionship-game coaching matchup in major American sports history. Lewis's farewell game. And the amazing running and throwing talent of Niners QB Colin Kaepernick, who nearly ruined Baltimore's destiny with his second-half comeback.

On the Ravens' first drive, Flacco split 49ers safety Donte Whitner and linebacker NaVorro Bowman, lobbing one perfectly for a 13-yard score to Anquan Boldin and a 7–0 lead. On the third drive, a one-yard toss to tight end Dennis Pitta (Flacco's best friend on the team) made it 14–3. And just before halftime the crisis in the Niners' secondary reached a breaking point. Jacoby Jones is one of the NFL's fastest players, and he badly beat cornerback Chris Culliver for a 56-yard touchdown, making worse a week in which Culliver incurred widespread wrath for saying he wouldn't welcome a gay player on his team. Jones then returned the opening kick of the second half 108 yards to make it 28–6. In the span of two game minutes, Jones had touched the ball twice, gained 164 yards and scored two times.

Soon thereafter a brownout cut most of the building's power, and when electricity finally returned the 49ers' switch went on too. Kaepernick threw and faked and read-optioned and scrambled the 49ers to 23 of the next 26 points. With 10 minutes to play Baltimore led 31–29 as the Niners lined up for a two-point conversion. This will be one of those plays that 49ers fans will re-live for a long time: Ed Reed came on a safety blitz at the snap of the ball (or a 10th of a second early; it was close, though no flag was thrown) and as soon as Kaepernick looked up, he had to heave the ball away.

The next drive showed the essence of Flacco. On third-and-inches from the Baltimore 45, he had four choices: He could sneak; he could run Ray Rice to the left; he could execute an option; or he could throw to Boldin on the right side, about a 12-yard out.

Convert and the Ravens were likely to get at least a field goal. Fail to convert and—well, Kaepernick had been nearly unstoppable. "Their formation took away the run, and it took away the option," Flacco said later. "I don't like to sneak. I always think that's a crapshoot. So I had one choice—throw to Anquan."

Flacco took the snap and looked for Boldin. In the stands his dad, Steve Flacco, was surprised. "Wow," Steve thought. "That's not a high-percentage throw." The pass was right in Boldin's chest—but so was the arm of cornerback Carlos Rogers. Boldin hung on to the ball as he and the D-back fell together. Gain of 15. A field goal made it 34–29 and a Ravens' goal line stand clinched it.

"Hey," John Harbaugh said much later, as he embraced Lewis in the locker room, "remember what I said last night? 'We win tomorrow, we walk together forever.'" Lewis repeated his coach's words, and they parted.

"That's from Fred Shero when he coached the Flyers in the '70s," Harbaugh said. "And that's what we do now. This team won't be the same again, but we're together forever." ∎

Even in victory, John (far left) felt for Jim.

Photographs by Damian Strohmeyer (left) and Robert Beck

Boldin shook off tacklers, showing his pure strength.

Photograph by John Iacono

BY Ed Reed

Ravens Safety

I was more than prepared to play the Super Bowl in my hometown. Everything was lined up, like it was meant to be. I grew up five minutes from the Saints' facility. Not only that, there's a car wash across from the facility where my dad and I used to go all the time—my love of cars comes from my dad. So we're practicing right there, and I had people taking pictures of me, making sure the car wash was in the background. Our team owner, Steve Bisciotti gave me a couple extra tickets and said, "Let me know if you need more." I said, "Man, I could fill the Superdome!" I think I wound up with close to 70 tickets.

That Sunday, I stayed in my room all day. I put on my Miles Davis and Charlie Parker. I was listening to the song "Now's The Time" and thinking, There's no way we can lose. I took a lot of pictures out my window. My room faced the Mississippi River and they had the ferry going across. I'll never forget one of them: The whole boat was solid purple. Nothing but Ravens fans.

That last goal line stand, they were not getting in. Ray Lewis and I were talking about it and everyone was pumped. On fourth down, we were in a zero blitz. And I moved to go where I needed to go, and I saw Colin Kaepernick check Michael Crabtree. So I moved back and there was no way Kaepernick could complete a pass to Crabtree. He tried, and it was incomplete.

On the game's last play they were running it back and Josh Bynes made the tackle. He was my protégé so for him to make the last tackle felt special.

BY Vernon Davis

49ers Tight End

As soon as the NFC championship game ended, there was a focus I'd never seen. All week guys cut themselves off from the rest of the world. I'll never forget the first media session. It was at the hotel, and the room was the size of a warehouse. I walked in and thought, Wow, I have never seen so many cameras and reporters in one room. It was overwhelming, but as the week went on you got used to it. It ended up being cool. The whole week was like that. As soon as you stepped outside the hotel there were all these people, walking, bikes trying to weave through . . . chaotic. That's why I stayed in my room. I'd come out late evening to see my family, but for the most part I stayed in and studied. That's what game day was like too. I listened to music and spent the day getting focused.

We play the game for one reason: to make it to the Super Bowl. When I stepped onto the field the first time, I did a 360 looking around. I will always cherish that moment. The stadium, the decor, the excitement; it was different than any other game. The number of fans and people around the field, and the celebrities there. You know everyone in the world is watching, it's a weird feeling. It feels less like a football game and more like you're going to battle for your country.

The night before, my mentor and I were talking. The words he instilled were "Do not be denied." During the game, that was stuck in my mind. I guess it wasn't our time, but I walked off with my head high. I know we played a great game.

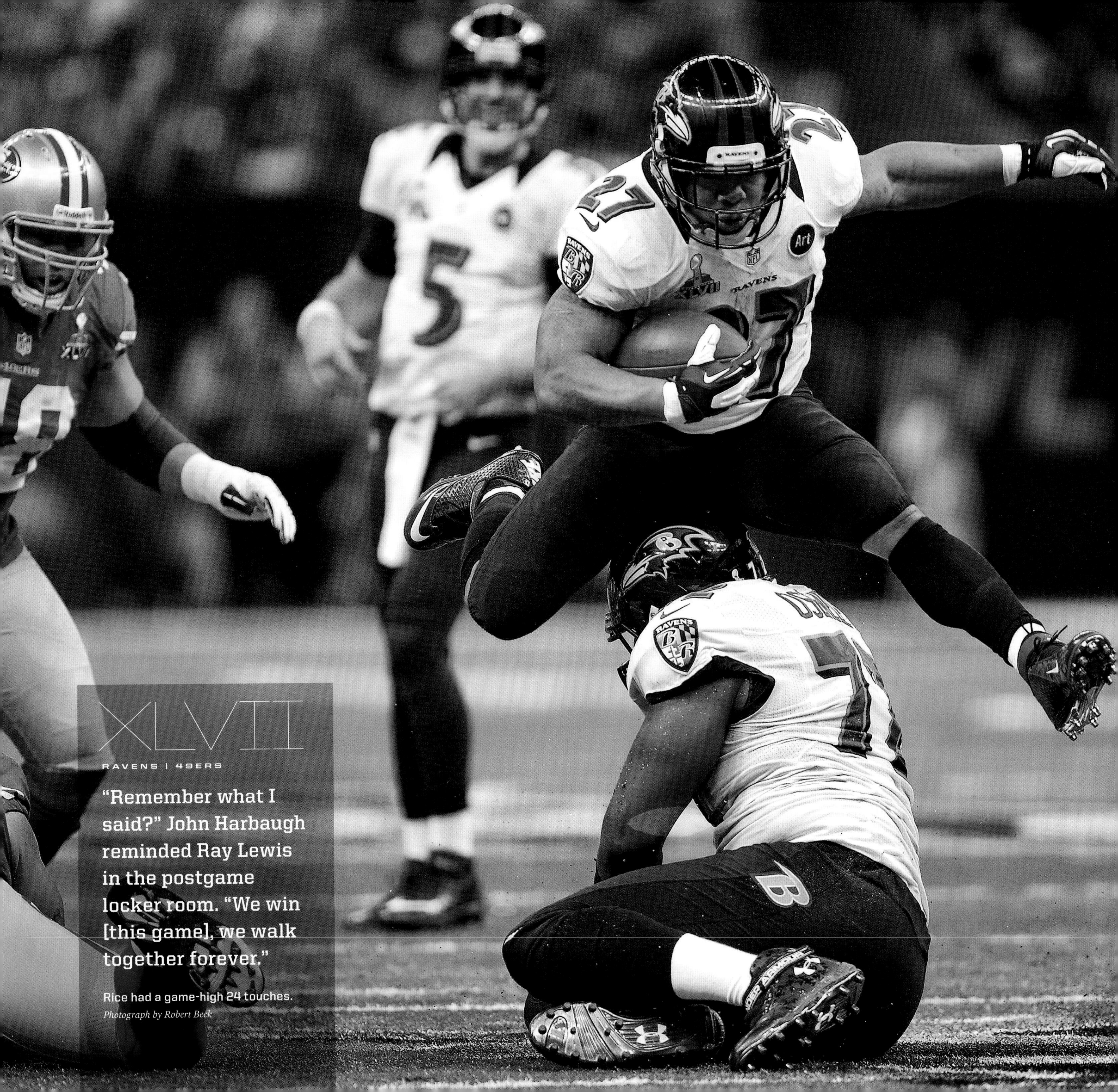

XLVII

RAVENS | 49ERS

"Remember what I said?" John Harbaugh reminded Ray Lewis in the postgame locker room. "We win [this game], we walk together forever."

Rice had a game-high 24 touches.

Photograph by Robert Beck

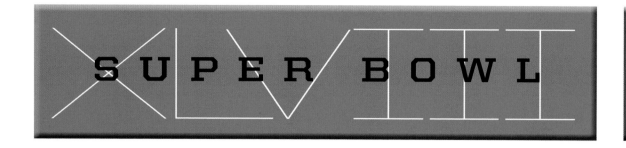

SUPER BOWL XLVIII

February 2, 2014
MetLife Stadium, East Rutherford, N.J.

HEAD COACHES
PETE CARROLL Seahawks | JOHN FOX Broncos

SEATTLE
SEAHAWKS | 43

DENVER
BRONCOS | 8

Chancellor got groomed for the big game by his personal barber at the team hotel.

Photograph by Rod Mar

SEATTLE'S SECONDARY had a name for itself: the Legion of Boom, apt for its brash and hard-hitting ways. But could the unit stop Denver's Peyton Manning from a career-topping win? It wasn't long before the answer was clear: *Boom*.

WEATHER
49°, partly cloudy

POINT SPREAD
Denver by 2½

TIME OF GAME
3:23

TV AUDIENCE
112.2 million

After a post NFC title-game rant raised his profile,
Sherman was a shutdown corner versus Denver.

Photograph by John W. McDonough

Harvin got loose on an 87-yard kickoff return for a touchdown to start the second half.

Photograph by John Iacono

Though he didn't have a typical big game, Lynch was always a threat to move Denver bodies.

Photograph by John Iacono

JUST THE FACTS

Statistical Leaders

Rushing MARSHAWN LYNCH (SEA) 15 carries, 39 yds, 1 TD

Passing PEYTON MANNING (DEN) 34 of 49, 280 yds, 1 TD

Receiving DEMARYIUS THOMAS (DEN) 13 catches, 118 yds

MVP MALCOLM SMITH Seahawks Linebacker

The Ring
Inside engraved with
LEAVE NO DOUBT, SEA 43-8,
WHAT'S NEXT? and 24/7

Anthem Performer
Renee Fleming

Halftime Performer
Bruno Mars

Attendance 82,529

Ticket Price $800-$1,500

Behind the Scenes

During practices Denver coach John Fox lowered the volume on the speakers used to simulate crowd noise because he felt a Super Bowl crowd would be quieter than the usual stadium crowd. Then the Broncos botched the opening snap—leading to a safety—when the center couldn't hear Peyton Manning.

They Said It

"Our receivers were called appetizers, but I think if anybody took a bite out of them, they'd be pretty full."
—Seattle cornerback RICHARD SHERMAN

Rocking the Boat

The week of the game, Broncos media sessions were held onboard a cruise ship, the *Cornucopia Majesty*, docked in the Hudson River.

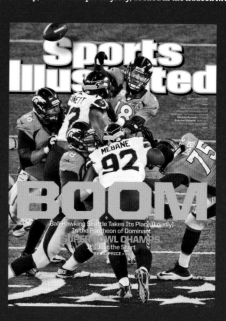

Making them pay: On the Seahawks' bizarre final play Butler stepped in front of Lockette to take the ball, and the game, away.

Photograph by John Iacono

Excerpted from **SPORTS ILLUSTRATED** *February 9, 2015*

FINISHING TOUCHES

A stunning catch, a bizarre play call, an unlikely hero. Yes, that's a wrap | BY GREG BISHOP

DEEP INSIDE THE SHERATON Wild Horse Pass in Chandler, Ariz.—past the hundreds of revelers, the open bars and the buffet stocked with beef taquitos—a smaller, quieter Patriots party carries on. Tom Brady poses for a picture. He chats with old teammates, men he won Super Bowls with a decade earlier, like Tedy Bruschi and Deion Branch. He takes another picture, and another. The QB is wearing designer jeans and a sweater and a white cap with SUPER BOWL XLIX CHAMPIONS on it. His celebration is a series of snapshots, smile after smile. It's 1:43 a.m.

Hours earlier Brady was named MVP of a Super Bowl that was among the most dramatic ever. New England had trailed by 10 at the start of the fourth quarter and then scrapped ahead by four. But as the clock showed 26 seconds left, the Seahawks sat one yard—one Marshawn Lynch dive, one Russell Wilson rollout—from a touchdown and an improbable comeback of their own. Instead an undrafted rookie cornerback from West Alabama named Malcolm Butler ("Scrap" to his teammates) intercepted what Seattle intended to be a game-winning slant pass from Wilson to Ricardo Lockette. The play sealed more than a Super Bowl. It bolstered the argument that Brady, already on the list of history's greatest quarterbacks, may now be alone at the top. In this 28–24 win he set a record for completions in a single Super Bowl (37) and led the Pats on the NFL's largest second-half championship-game comeback. "Tom Brady is the best ever," said cornerback Darrelle Revis. "*Period*. The best. Write that down."

In a ballroom next door, Darius Rucker is performing a hit from when he was with Hootie and the Blowfish called "Time." He sings: *Time, why you punish me.*

Funny thing, time. It can be measured in decades (one since the Patriots' last Super Bowl win), years (three since their last painful loss on that stage), months (four since their season teetered near collapse) and weeks (two since another controversy, Deflategate, in which numerous Patriots footballs were found to have been underinflated during the AFC title game, threatened their collective legacy).

Time can also be measured in seconds, the slim margins between victory and defeat. Brady knows that. All six of his Super Bowls have been decided by four points or fewer. All six could have gone either way. And with 12:10 left in his latest appearance, time was running out. Seattle led 24–14, but Brady methodically drove the Patriots down the field from their own 32. On first-and-goal from the Seahawks' four-yard line he found Danny Amendola in the back of the end zone. Four-yard score. The game clock read 7:55.

The Patriots forced a punt, three-and-out, and got the ball back at their own 36. Brady threw nine times on the ensuing drive, spreading the ball among his targets. On second-and-goal, Julian Edelman got separation at the line on nickelback Tharold Simon and cut left into the end zone. Brady's pass sailed straight and true. The touchdown vaulted the Pats in front, 28–24, with 2:02 remaining.

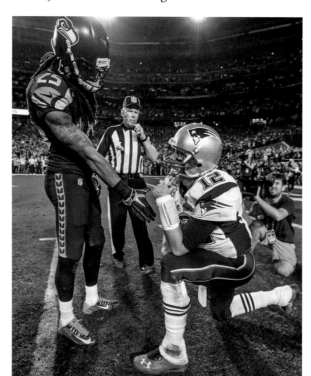

On first down from New England's 38, Wilson lofted a pass deep up the right sideline. Receiver Jermaine Kearse tipped the ball (along with Butler, who made a near-perfect play) as he fell to the ground and, after several bounces, somehow corralled it. The play went for 33 yards and put the Seahawks on the Patriots' five. Brady's legacy, it seemed, would be determined in part by two plays over which he had zero control, two of the most unlikely catches in postseason history: Kearse's grab and David Tyree's head-pinned catch for the Giants on the game-winning drive in Super Bowl XLII.

On the next play Lynch took a handoff and barreled to the one-yard line. With a minute left a Seattle TD seemed imminent. On second down the Patriots packed the line of scrimmage with defenders, forcing the Seahawks, as coach Pete Carroll later tried to explain, into a passing play. The idea, he said, was to throw the ball away if no receiver got open, then run on the next two downs. Instead, Wilson tried to cram a pass to Lockette on a slant route, and Scrap made the pick. "I'm as surprised as everybody else," said Patriots cornerback Brandon Browner, a former Seahawk. "You've got the best running back in the game. . . . Sometimes coaches get too smart."

Afterward, teammates saw tears welling in Butler's eyes as he recalled that he had spotted Wilson glancing toward the Seahawks' receivers, guessed the QB would pass and then jumped the route. It was the play that gave Belichick his fourth Super Bowl win as a head coach, tying the Steelers' Chuck Noll for the most ever. (Brady, meanwhile, joined Joe Montana, his idol when he was growing up, as the only players to win three Super Bowl MVPs.) The Pats though, still had two last, clock-killing plays to run. Then as the final seconds ticked off, Brady knelt on the field, taking a moment to himself before the party began. ∎

Man to man: Richard Sherman congratulated Brady.

Photograph by Al Tielemans

JUST THE FACTS

Statistical Leaders

Passing **TOM BRADY** (NE) 37 of 50, 328 yds, 4 TDs

Rushing **MARSHAWN LYNCH** (SEA) 24 carries, 102 yds, 1 TD

Receiving **JULIAN EDELMAN** (NE) 9 catches, 109 yds, 1 TD

MVP TOM BRADY Patriots Quarterback

The Ring
The biggest bling in Super Bowl history: 10-karat white gold and 205 diamonds with DO YOUR JOB engraved on the shank and WE ARE ALL PATRIOTS on the inside

Anthem Performer
Idina Menzel

Halftime Performer
Katy Perry

Attendance 70,288

Ticket Price $800–$1,900

Behind the Scenes

In the week leading up to the Super Bowl, Tom Brady watched tape of the Seahawks' NFC championship game victory over the Packers. The entire game. Three times.

They Said It

"I'm just here so I won't get fined."
—Seahawks running back **MARSHAWN LYNCH**, repeatedly, during his five-minute mandatory Media Day appearance

Sharing the Wealth

Tom Brady gave rookie cornerback Malcolm Butler the Chevy Colorado truck he won as game MVP. Butler made $585,000 in 2014. Brady has earned more than $150 million in his career.

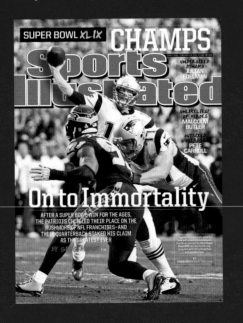

Jeremy Lane's pick killed an early Pats drive (and popped Edelman's helmet) but was costly: The cornerback broke his wrist as he landed and was out for the game.

Photograph by Simon Bruty

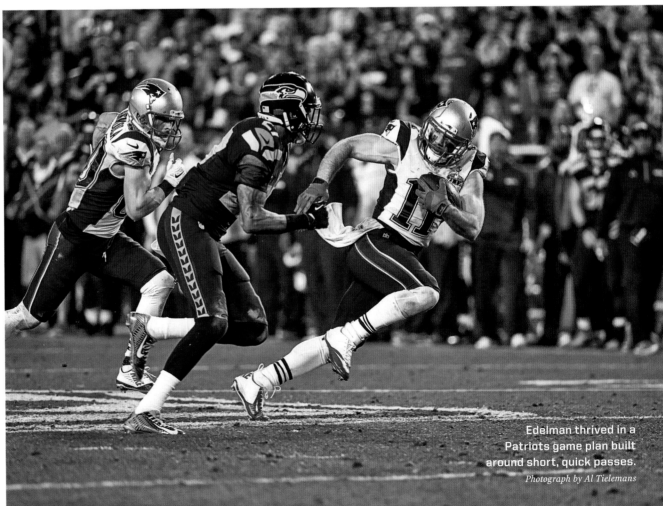

Edelman thrived in a Patriots game plan built around short, quick passes.

Photograph by Al Tielemans

Tight end Rob Gronkowski, his injuries behind him, caught six passes, including this second quarter TD. Yes, Seattle got Gronked.

Photograph by Robert Beck

BY Malcolm Butler

Patriots Cornerback

Of course everyone thought they were going to give the ball to Marshawn Lynch and run it on that last play—even me. The game was on the line, and Seattle was at the one. But our coaches called "Goal line, three corner," which I thought was odd. I still thought Seattle might run, but if they passed, I'd be ready. Earlier in the week, as we prepared for the game, the scout team ran the same exact play in practice: same goal line situation, similar formation. And I got beat. Coach Belichick came up to me and said, "You gotta be on that."

When it came to the game, I knew I had to execute. It was a pick route, and in practice I got picked. This time, my fellow cornerback Brandon Browner did a good job of jamming up his guy to let me get free. Our motto this year was DO YOUR JOB. On that play, I just did my job. It's that simple. When I got the ball, I squeezed it like I had never squeezed anything before. Once I made that play, well, my life changed forever.

I was an undrafted free agent. Before that I was at a Division II program, and before that, a community college. My road to this moment was pretty unlikely, and there were many bumps on the way. Making the NFL was a huge achievement and being in the Super Bowl felt surreal. Everyone says it's crazy, but before the game, I had a vision that I would make a big play. The craziest part is that it came true.

BY Russell Wilson

Seahawks Quarterback

I've watched a lot of games and I've played in a lot of games, and it always hurts to lose. It doesn't matter how you win—you just want to score one more point than they do. The last play we ran in this game was a moment of disappointment. We were right there, we just needed to make that last play, and we would have won. I don't question the play call. Obviously, you have different options. You could hand the ball off to Marshawn Lynch, and that's a great option. It allows us to tick off some time in the clock, and either he scores or maybe we call a timeout. The other option is to throw it, and it's also a great option.

The call we chose—I thought it was a great call. It was a play designed for Ricardo Lockette. He was coming up underneath. There was another read on the other side, but that wasn't the side I was supposed to go to. I trusted my progression on it, and we thought we had them. Everything looked good. When I threw the ball, I thought it was going to be a touchdown. I was like, "Touchdown, second Super Bowl ring, here we go." But Malcolm Butler kind of cut in front of it and made a play. There was a chance for us to catch it, and a chance for Butler to make a play, and Butler came away with it. You have to give him credit, and also Tom Brady and the entire Patriots team. I've watched a lot of Super Bowls, and this was one of the better ones—we just didn't win it.

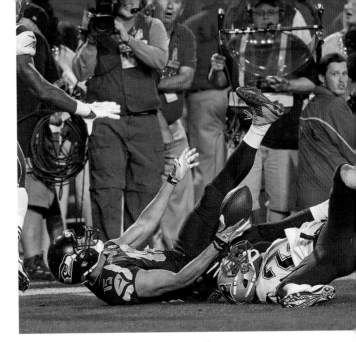

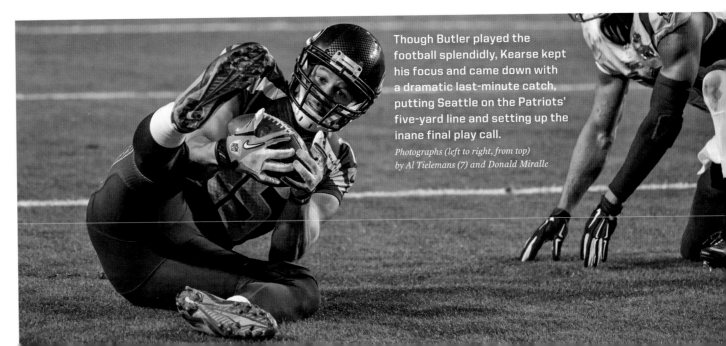

Though Butler played the football splendidly, Kearse kept his focus and came down with a dramatic last-minute catch, putting Seattle on the Patriots' five-yard line and setting up the inane final play call.

Photographs (left to right, from top) by Al Tielemans (7) and Donald Miralle

RANKINGS

THERE HAVE BEEN THRILLERS, and there have been clunkers (the Giants, for one, know from both), and now you can see just where your favorite Super Bowl ranks in history. Using an original and carefully designed formula SI's experts deliver the verdict on each and every big game

THE FORMULA *Games get a point for a lead change or tie in the first three quarters; two for those in the fourth quarter and five in the last two minutes. A point is awarded for each minute of the fourth quarter that the game is within a score. Underdog score is the point spread overcome multiplied by two, and games get five or 10 points for historical significance or a memorable play. Ties are broken by closeness of the final margin. Oh yes, each game gets 10 points, just for being a Super Bowl*

	Lead Changes	Fourth Quarter	Underdog	Historical Significance	Memorable Play	TOTAL
1 Super Bowl XLII | Giants 17, Patriots 14 *An alltime catch by David Tyree and two late lead changes as big underdogs end Pats' quest for perfect season*	10	15	25	10	10	**80**
2 Super Bowl XXXII | Broncos 31, Packers 24 *The "helicopter" dive by John Elway in quest for first title; then Terrell Davis's TD seals upset with 1:45 left*	11	15	22	–	5	**63**
3 Super Bowl XXV | Giants 20, Bills 19 *Before "wide right" drama: a stirring anthem on brink of Gulf War and N.Y.'s late run of third-down conversions*	7	15	13	5	10	**60**
4 Super Bowl XXXVI | Patriots 20, Rams 17 *After Rams tie it with 90 seconds left, Tom Brady's Pats, 14-point underdogs, win on last-second kick*	11	10	28	–	–	**59**
5 Super Bowl III | Jets 16, Colts 7 *Minimal suspense on the field, but result leaves mouths agape as 18-point underdog Jets rise up for the AFL*	–	–	36	10	–	**56**
6 Super Bowl XXIII | 49ers 20, Bengals 16 *Bengals go ahead lead with 4:20 left, then Joe Montana leads winning drive, ending with John Taylor's TD catch*	13	15	–	–	10	**48**
7 Super Bowl XXXVIII | Patriots 32, Panthers 29 *Six scores in fourth quarter, three in last three minutes. Adam Vinatieri's field goal with four ticks left wins it*	16	13	–	–	5	**44**
8 Super Bowl XLIII | Steelers 27, Cardinals 23 *James Harrison's 100-yard pick-six, Santonio Holmes's catch in corner of end zone with 0:35 left stop feisty Arizona*	7	8	–	5	10	**40**
9 Super Bowl XLIV | Saints 31, Colts 17 *Surprise onside kick, Tracy Porter's late pick-six deliver Saints' first title, amid memories of Hurricane Katrina*	4	12	9	–	5	**40**
10 Super Bowl X | Steelers 21, Cowboys 17 *Steelers rally with 14 fourth-quarter points, including 64-yard touchdown catch by Lynn Swann*	4	14	–	–	10	**38**
11 Super Bowl XVII | Redskins 27, Dolphins 17 *Miami's fourth-quarter lead erased by two Redskins TDs; John Riggins's 43-yard run breaks tackles, sets record*	4	13	6	–	5	**38**
12 Super Bowl XLVI | Giants 21, Patriots 17 *Eli Manning's Giants again thwart favored Patriots with last-minute score, Ahmad Bradshaw's six-yard TD run*	6	15	6	–	–	**37**
13 Super Bowl XXXIV | Rams 23, Titans 16 *Three late scores include 73-yard catch by Rams' Isaac Bruce; Titans' Kevin Dyson tackled near goal line on last play*	7	9	–	–	10	**36**
14 Super Bowl XIV | Steelers 31, Rams 19 *Heavy-underdog Rams lead in fourth, but 73-yard Terry Bradshaw-to-John Stallworth pass lifts Steelers*	8	13	–	5	–	**36**

RANKINGS

		Lead Changes	Fourth Quarter	Underdog	Historical Significance	Memorable Play	TOTAL
15	**Super Bowl V | Colts 16, Cowboys 13** *Sloppy (11 total turnovers), but late drama: After Cowboys tie it, Colts win on Jim O'Brien kick with 0:05 to go*	9	15	–	–	–	**34**
16	**Super Bowl XLIX | Patriots 28, Seahawks 24** *Tight fourth quarter: Seattle has ball on one with less than a minute left but Pats' Malcolm Butler makes a pick*	6	8	–	–	10	**34**
17	**Super Bowl IV | Chiefs 23, Vikings 7** *Year after the Jets' historic upset, AFL does it again: Chiefs, 12-point dogs, dominate in last premerger Super Bowl*	–	–	24	–	–	**34**
18	**Super Bowl XLVII | Ravens 34, 49ers 31** *Ravens blowout shifts course after power outage but Niners' big rally stopped by late goal line stand*	–	13	9	–	–	**32**
19	**Super Bowl XIII | Steelers 35, Cowboys 31** *Cowboys tight end Jackie Smith drops TD pass in third quarter and late Dallas rally comes up short*	4	8	–	–	10	**32**
20	**Super Bowl XVI | 49ers 26, Bengals 21** *Niners lead handily much of game until late Bengals TDs tighten score. Plus: epic goal line stand by 49ers*	–	5	–	5	10	**30**
21	**Super Bowl VII | Dolphins 14, Redskins 7** *Undefeated Dolphins, slim favorites in the game, take 14-point lead in first half and hold on*	–	2	–	10	5	**27**
22	**Super Bowl XXXIX | Patriots 24, Eagles 21** *Tied in fourth, Pats go up 10, Eagles close gap late, but strangely kill clock on 13-play TD drive*	6	8	–	–	–	**24**
23	**Super Bowl XXII | Redskins 42, Broncos 10** *Doug Williams, first African-American QB to win a Super Bowl, leads Washington to five second-quarter TDs*	1	–	7	5	–	**23**
24	**Super Bowl XX | Bears 46, Patriots 10** *Bears' blowout serves as a coronation of what many consider the greatest single-season defense ever*	2	–	–	5	5	**22**
25	**Super Bowl XLV | Packers 31, Steelers 25** *Green Bay leads wire-to-wire, but Pittsburgh closes to 28-25 on Mike Wallace TD catch midway through fourth*	–	11	–	–	–	**21**
26	**Super Bowl XXVIII | Cowboys 30, Bills 13** *In rematch Bills lead 13-6 at half and are within a TD in fourth before Cowboys shut door. Bills' fourth straight loss*	5	5	–	–	–	**20**
27	**Super Bowl XXXVII | Buccaneers 48, Raiders 21** *Raiders' juggernaut offense vs. Bucs' stingy D; Tampa prevails by forcing five turnovers (three pick-sixes) in upset*	2	–	7	–	–	**19**
28	**Super Bowl XIX | 49ers 38, Dolphins 16** *Marquee quarterback matchup: Joe Montana vs. Dan Marino. Fins score first, then Montana's 49ers take over*	3	–	–	5	–	**18**
29	**Super Bowl IX | Steelers 16, Vikings 6** *Steel Curtain D allows only 119 yards. Vikes block late punt to score and tighten game; Steelers answer with TD*	–	7	–	–	–	**17**

#1 Giants over Patriots, SB XLII

#19 Steelers over Cowboys, SB XIII

#43 Broncos over Falcons, SB XLIII

#	Super Bowl	Lead Changes	Fourth Quarter	Underdog	Historical Significance	Memorable Play	TOTAL
30	**Super Bowl XL | Steelers 21, Seahawks 10** *Up 14-10 in fourth Steelers extend lead with a gadget play. Seahawks recall many ref calls that went against them*	1	6	–	–	–	17
31	**Super Bowl XXXI | Packers 35, Patriots 21** *Brett Favre's lone title. Big play: Desmond Howard's 99-yard kickoff return after Pats get within six in third*	2	–	–	–	5	17
32	**Super Bowl I | Packers 35, Chiefs 10** *Could AFL champ Chiefs hang with class of the NFL in inaugural Super Bowl? K.C. did keep it close for a half*	2	–	–	5	–	17
33	**Super Bowl XXVII | Cowboys 52, Bills 17** *Cowboys rout on before Michael Jackson at halftime. Bills highlight: Don Beebe knocks ball from strutting Leon Lett*	2	–	–	–	5	17
34	**Super Bowl XV | Raiders 27, Eagles 10** *First wild-card team to win Super Bowl, Raiders are three-point dogs, but their two first-quarter TDs set tone*	–	–	6	–	–	16
35	**Super Bowl II | Packers 33, Raiders 14** *After NFL championship win in Ice Bowl, Vince Lombardi's poignant last game with Pack is rout of AFL champs*	–	–	–	5	–	15
36	**Super Bowl XXIX | 49ers 49, Chargers 26** *Niners take 21-point lead in the second quarter; MVP Steve Young throws for record six TDs, three to Jerry Rice*	–	–	–	5	–	15
37	**Super Bowl XLVIII | Seahawks 43, Broncos 8** *Seahawks come in as 2½-point underdogs, then dominate Broncos—and Peyton Manning*	–	–	5	–	–	15
38	**Super Bowl XXIV | 49ers 55, Broncos 10** *Joe Montana vs. John Elway unfolds without suspense; blowout caps best season for Montana-Bill Walsh Niners*	–	–	–	5	–	15
39	**Super Bowl XLI | Colts 29, Bears 17** *Bears' Devin Hester has TD return on opening kick, but game's a grind. Colts kick field goals. Only one second-half TD*	1	3	–	–	–	14
40	**Super Bowl XVIII | Raiders 38, Redskins 9** *Raiders' Jack Squirek's interception return before half all but seals it. MVP Marcus Allen's 74-yard TD truly does*	–	–	4	–	–	14
41	**Super Bowl XXX | Cowboys 27, Steelers 17** *Lacks magic of teams' 1970s clashes. A Steelers' TD run by Bam Morris makes it close for a few minutes in fourth*	–	3	–	–	–	13
42	**Super Bowl XXI | Giants 39, Broncos 20** *Twenty-four straight points in second half made this least dramatic of Giants' four Super Bowl wins*	3	–	–	–	–	13
43	**Super Bowl XXXIII | Broncos 34, Falcons 19** *Falcons safety Eugene Robinson's arrest for solicitation night before the game more memorable than game*	1	–	–	–	–	11
44	**Super Bowl XXVI | Redskins 37, Bills 24** *Bills never threaten favored, 14-2 Redskins. Two Bills touchdowns in last six minutes provide window dressing*	–	–	–	–	–	10
45	**Super Bowl VIII | Dolphins 24, Vikings 7** *Dolphins score on first two possessions, while Vikes don't reach end zone until the fourth vs. stiff defense*	–	–	–	–	–	10
46	**Super Bowl XII | Cowboys 27, Broncos 10** *After first quarter Broncos never closer than 10. Highlight: Robert Newhouse's halfback TD pass to Golden Richards*	–	–	–	–	–	10
47	**Super Bowl XI | Raiders 32, Vikings 14** *Minnesota's fourth loss is its worst. Raiders lead by 19 points before Minnesota's first TD, in third quarter*	–	–	–	–	–	10
48	**Super Bowl VI | Cowboys 24, Dolphins 3** *Favored Cowboys nearly double Dolphins in time of possession while rushing for 252 yards*	–	–	–	–	–	10
49	**Super Bowl XXXV | Ravens 34, Giants 7** *Early TD pass to Brandon Stokley sets tone for Ravens. Giants' lone score comes on third-quarter kick return*	–	–	–	–	–	10

GO FIGURE

WHAT HEIGHTS they've reached! What lows they've endured! How much we've eaten! Some Super Bowl extremes...

1
Father and son to win a Super Bowl with the same franchise: linebacker/long snapper **Steve** (XXV) and long snapper **Zak** (XLII, XLVI) **DeOssie** for the Giants

25
Times that the loser of the opening coin toss has won the Super Bowl

5
Most wins as player, **Charles Haley** (49ers 2, Cowboys 3)

4½
Most sacks, career, **Charles Haley** (five games)

6
Most appearances as player, **Tom Brady** (Patriots) and **Mike Lodish** (Bills 4, Broncos 2)

4
Most wins as head coach, **Chuck Noll** (Steelers) and **Bill Belichick** (Patriots)

6
Most appearances as head coach, **Don Shula** (Dolphins 5, Colts 1) and **Bill Belichick** (Patriots)

9
Most appearances, **Dan Reeves** (as player 2, head coach 4 and assistant coach 3) and **Bill Belichick** (as head coach 6 and assistant coach 3)

6
Most franchise wins, **Steelers**

8
Most franchise appearances, **Cowboys, Steelers, Patriots**

12
Most seasons between Super Bowl championships as player, **Ray Lewis** (Ravens)

1,605
Most passing yards, career, **Tom Brady**, Patriots (six games)

414
Most passing yards, game, **Kurt Warner**, Rams (vs. Titans, XXXIV)

150.9
Highest QB rating, **Phil Simms**, Giants (vs. Broncos, XXI)

22.6
Lowest QB rating as a starter, **Ben Roethlisberger**, Steelers (vs. Seahawks, XL)

7
Fewest pass attempts as a starting quarterback, **Bob Griese**, Dolphins (vs. Vikings, VIII)

8
Most interceptions thrown, career, **John Elway**, Broncos (five games)

5
Most interceptions thrown, game, **Rich Gannon**, Raiders (vs. Buccaneers, XXXVII)

5
Most fumbles, career, **Roger Staubach**, Cowboys (four games)

354
Most rushing yards, career, **Franco Harris**, Steelers (four games)

204
Most rushing yards, game, **Timmy Smith**, Redskins (vs. Broncos, XXII)

54
Longest field goal, **Steve Christie**, Bills (vs. Cowboys, XXVIII)

64
Most yards gained on one fumble return, **Leon Lett**, Cowboys (vs. Bills, XXVII)

100
Most yards gained on one interception return, **James Harrison**, Steelers (vs. Cardinals, XLIII)

3
Most interceptions, game, **Rod Martin**, Raiders (vs. Eagles, XV)

602
Most total yards gained from scrimmage, one team, **Redskins** (vs. Broncos, XXII)

119
Fewest total yards from scrimmage, one team, **Vikings** (vs. Steelers, IX)

33
Most receptions, career, **Jerry Rice**, 49ers, Raiders (four games)

589
Most yards receiving, career, **Jerry Rice**

8
Most touchdowns, career, **Jerry Rice**

19
Widest pregame point spread, **49ers** over **Chargers**, XXIX

15
Underdogs who have won the Super Bowl outright

3
Fewest points in game, **Dolphins** (vs. Cowboys, VI)

14
Fewest points in game for winning team, **Dolphins** (vs. Redskins, VII)

45
Widest margin of victory in points, **49ers 55, Broncos 10** (XXIV)

1
Narrowest margin of victory, in points **Giants 20, Bills 19** (XXV)

2,500,000
Pizzas ordered in the U.S. on Super Bowl Sunday

1,250,000,000
Chicken wings consumed in the U.S. on Super Bowl Sunday

During Michael Jackson's halftime show at Super Bowl XXVII in Pasadena, fans could see the whole world from the stands.
Photograph by John W. McDonough

MANY PEOPLE had a hand in making this book come into being. First, a big note of appreciation goes out to the SPORTS ILLUSTRATED writers, editors, photographers and reporters who delivered such rich content around each and every Super Bowl over the past five decades. For their invaluable contributions to this project our thanks also go to Stephen Cannella, Chris Hercik, Karen Carpenter, Prem Kalliat, Joe Felice, George Amores, Will Welt, Dwayne Bernard and Adam Lowe. We are grateful for the tireless and exceptional work done by the SI Premedia group, led by Geoff Michaud and Dan Larkin. Lastly, a big thank you to SI Group editor Paul Fichtenbaum and SI managing editor Chris Stone for their support, editorial and otherwise. O.K., we'll say it: They've all been golden.

PHOTO CREDITS
COVER: FRONT: NFL Photos/AP; BACK *(from left)*: Walter Iooss Jr., Heinz Kluetmeier, John Iacono, Neil Leifer, Peter Read Miller. **RINGS:** David N. Berkwitz/Courtesy of the Pro Football Hall of Fame: 24, 30, 37, 42, 48, 54, 60, 67, 72, 78, 85, 90, 99, 104, 110, 117, 122, 128, 135, 140, 146, 153, 158, 164, 182, 188, 195, 200, 207, 212, 218, 225, 230, 237, 242, 248, 256; Courtesy of Herff Jones: 280; Courtesy of Jostens, Inc.: 263, 269, 274, 292, 305, 329; Adam Hunger/Reuters: 311; Schneider Photography: 316; Courtesy of Tiffany and Co.: 298; Kirby Lee/USA Today Sports: 286, 322.
TICKETS: Tim Donnelly/AP: 311; NFL Photos/AP: 24, 30, 37, 42, 48, 54, 60, 67, 72, 78, 85, 90, 99, 104, 110, 117, 122, 128, 135, 140, 146, 153, 158, 164, 182, 188, 195, 200, 207, 212, 218, 225, 230, 237, 248, 269; Evans Caglage/Dallas Morning News/Corbis: 305; Walter Iooss Jr.: 329; Courtesy of the NFL: 280; Erick W. Rasco: 242, 286, 292, 316.
SI COVERS: Robert Beck: 305, 316; David Bergman: 298; John Biever: 153, 195, 237, 256; Simon Bruty: 311, 329; Andy Hayt: 110, 117, 128, 146; Walter Iooss Jr.: 24, 37, 48, 54, 67, 85, 90, 99, 104, 188, 200, 225, 322; Heinz Kluetmeier: 72, 78, 135; Neil Leifer: 30, 42, 60; Richard Mackson: 140; John W. McDonough: 164, 242, 263; Peter Read Miller: 158, 207, 212; Ronald C. Modra: 122; Bob Rosato: 230, 274; Damian Strohmeyer: 248, 286; Al Tielemans: 182, 218, 269, 280, 292. **ADDITIONAL CREDITS:** Page 14: Walter Iooss Jr.; Page 16: Walter Iooss Jr.; Page 17: Michael Zagaris/Getty Images; Page 18: Andy Hayt; Page 19: Walter Iooss Jr.; Page 26: Neil Leifer (2); Page 32 *(from top)*: Vernon Biever/AP, Walter Iooss Jr.; Page 38 *(from top)*: Tony Tomsic/Getty Images, Focus on Sport/Getty Images; Page 45 *(from top)*: Neil Leifer, Dick Raphael; Page 50 *(from left)*: NFL Photos/AP, Walter Iooss Jr.; Page 56: Walter Iooss Jr.; Page 57: Neil Leifer; Page 63: Walter Iooss Jr. (2); Page 68 *(from left)*: NFL Photos/AP, Cliff Welch/AP; Page 74 *(from top)*: Sylvia Allen/Getty Images, Neil Leifer; Page 81: Walter Iooss Jr. (2); Page 86 *(from top)*: NFL Photos/AP, Walter Iooss Jr.; Page 93 *(from top)*: Manny Rubio/USA Today Sports, Al Messerschmidt/AP; Page 101 *(from top)*: Ross Lewis, Heinz Kluetmeier;

Page 107 *(from top)*: Walter Iooss Jr., John Iacono; Page 112: Manny Millan; Page 113: MPS/USA Today Sports; Page 118 *(from left)*: Andy Hayt, Heinz Kluetmeier; Page 125 *(from left)*: John Iacono, Manny Rubio/USA Today Sports; Page 130 *(from top)*: Peter Read Miller, George Gojkovich/Getty Images; Page 136 *(from top)*: Richard Mackson, John Iacono; Page 143 *(from top)*: Tony Tomsic, John Biever; Page 148: John Iacono; Page 149: NFL Photos/AP; Page 155 *(from top)*: Heinz Kluetmeier, Robert Seale; Page 160: Richard Mackson; Page 161: Focus on Sport/Getty Images; Page 167 *(from top)*: John Biever, Rich Pilling/Sporting News/Getty Images; Page 168 *(clockwise from left)*: Robert Beck (2), Heinz Kluetmeier; Page 169 *(clockwise from top left)*: Damian Strohmeyer, NFL Photos/AP, Doug Pensinger/Getty Images, Al Messerschmidt, Robin Parker/International Sports Fotos, Heinz Kluetmeier; Pages 170–171 *(from left)*: Vic Stein, Herbert Weitman, Manny Rubio/USA Today Sports, Manny Millan, John Biever; Pages 172-173 *(from left)*: Bill Frakes, Pierre Ducharme/Reuters, Jeff Haynes/Reuters, Simon Bruty, Donald Miralle; Page 175: NFL Photos/AP, David Longstreath/AP, Erick W. Rasco; Page 184 *(from top)*: Al Messerschmidt, Peter Read Miller; Page 190 *(from top)*: Richard Mackson, Al Tielemans; Page 197 *(from top)*: Damian Strohmeyer, NFL Photos/AP; Page 202 *(from left)*: Jim Gund, Manny Rubio/USA Today Sports; Page 209 *(from left)*: Peter Read Miller, Al Tielemans; Page 214: Peter Read Miller (2); Page 220 *(from left)*: Al Tielemans, Doug Pensinger/Getty Images; Page 226 *(from top)*: V.J. Lovero, John Biever; Page 232 *(from top)*: David Durochik/AP, Al Pereira/Getty Images; Page 239 *(from left)*: Walter Iooss Jr., Allen Kee/Getty Images; Page 235 *(from top)*: Paul Spinelli/AP, Allen Kee/Getty Images; Page 250 *(from left)*: Kathy Willens/AP, David E. Klutho; Page 259 *(from top)*: Bob Rosato, Tom Pidgeon/Getty Images; Page 265 *(from top)*: Damian Strohmeyer, Al Tielemans; Page 271 *(from left)*: Al Tielemans, Ezra Shaw/Getty Images; Page 276 *(from left)*: Bob Rosato, Al Tielemans; Page 282: John Biever; Page 283: Bob Rosato; Page 289 *(from top)*: John Biever, Bob Rosato; Page 295: Bob Rosato (2); Page 300 *(from left)*: John W. McDonough, John Biever; Page 307 *(from top)*: Bob Rosato, John Biever; Page 312 *(from top)*: Al Tielemans, G. Newman Lowrance/AP; Page 318 *(from top)*: John Biever, Simon Bruty; Page 325 *(from top)*: Bill Frakes, Matt Slocum/AP; Page 330 *(from top)*: John W. McDonough, John Biever; Page 333 *(from left)*: Bill Frakes, AP, John W. McDonough; Page 335 *(clockwise from top left)*: Walter Iooss Jr., John Biever, Sandro Sciacca/Getty Images, Lauri Patterson/Getty Images; Endpapers: David Bergman.

TIME INC. BOOKS: PUBLISHER Margot Schupf ASSOCIATE PUBLISHER Allison Devlin VICE PRESIDENT, FINANCE Terri Lombardi EXECUTIVE DIRECTOR, MARKETING SERVICES Carol Pittard EXECUTIVE DIRECTOR, BUSINESS DEVELOPMENT Suzanne Albert EXECUTIVE PUBLISHING DIRECTOR Megan Pearlman ASSOCIATE DIRECTOR OF PUBLICITY Courtney Greenhalgh ASSISTANT GENERAL COUNSEL Andrew Goldberg ASSISTANT DIRECTOR, SPECIAL SALES Ilene Schreider ASSISTANT DIRECTOR, FINANCE Christine Font ASSISTANT PRODUCTION DIRECTOR Susan Chodakiewicz SENIOR MANAGER, SALES MARKETING Danielle Costa SENIOR MANAGER, CATEGORY MARKETING Bryan Christian MANAGER, BUSINESS DEVELOPMENT AND PARTNERSHIPS Stephanie Braga ASSOCIATE PREPRESS MANAGER Alex Voznesenskiy ASSISTANT PROJECT MANAGER Hillary Leary EDITORIAL DIRECTOR Stephen Koepp ART DIRECTOR Gary Stewart ASSISTANT MANAGING EDITOR Gina Scauzillo